ANDREA PALLADIO

W S Hamer

Coll Pemb
Oxon
2000

ANDREA PALLADIO

THE ARCHITECT IN HIS TIME

BRUCE BOUCHER

PRINCIPAL PHOTOGRAPHY BY PAOLO MARTON

Abbeville Press Publishers   New York London Paris

For Venetia and Miranda

Front cover: Villa Malcontenta, Gambarare di Mira (Venice).
Back cover: Nave of San Giorgio Maggiore, Venice.
Frontispiece: Villa Rotonda, Vicenza.

EDITORS: CONSTANCE HERNDON, ABIGAIL ASHER
PICTURE EDITORS: CHRISTA KELLY, KIM SULLIVAN
DESIGNER: JOEL AVIROM
DESIGN ASSISTANTS: JASON SNYDER, LAURA LINDGREN
PRODUCTION MANAGER: LOU BILKA

First edition
2 4 6 8 10 9 7 5 3 1

Library of Congress Cataloging-in-Publication Data

Boucher, Bruce.
Andrea Palladio : the architect in his time / Bruce Boucher ;
principal photography by Paolo Marton. — Rev. and updated ed.
p.   cm.
Includes bibliographical references and index.
ISBN 0-7892-0300-6 (paperback)
ISBN 0-7892-0416-9 (hardcover)
1. Palladio, Andrea, 1508–1580—Criticism and interpretation.
2. Architecture, Renaissance—Italy. I. Palladio, Andrea,
1508–1580. II. Title.
NA1123.P2B68   1998
720'.92—dc21   97-15294

Contents

PREFACE
6

I

PALLADIO'S FORMATION AS AN ARCHITECT
9

II

VICENZA AND PALLADIO'S FIRST PALACES
31

III

EARLY VILLAS AND VILLEGGIATURA
59

IV

THE BASILICA
93

V

MATURE VILLAS
111

VI

RELIGIOUS ARCHITECTURE
151

VII

BRIDGES
181

VIII

THE *QUATTRO LIBRI*
205

IX

PALLADIO'S LATE STYLE
235

MAPS	CHRONOLOGY	GLOSSARY	NOTES	BIBLIOGRAPHY	INDEX
268	270	272	275	300	310

PREFACE

Andrea Palladio is arguably the most influential architect the western world has ever produced. That statement can be made more confidently now than at any time in the past fifty years, for the decline of the modern movement in architecture has led to a renewed interest in the classical style and the works of Palladio. Although he lived a life of relative obscurity Palladio never lacked for admirers and followers, nor have his buildings been neglected by scholars. From the eighteenth century, books and articles have been written about him, and in our time the stream of publications has turned into a flood. Moreover, the "Palladio industry" has created a formidable bibliography, which can seem inaccessible to all but the initiated. There are, of course, any number of books dealing with Palladio's architecture, but they tend to focus on his villas and individual buildings or treat his oeuvre in catalog form. The only recent book conceived as an accessible survey of Palladio's achievement is James Ackerman's 1966 study, which remains unrivaled as a concise introduction to Palladio. But strangely there has been no other book offering a more detailed account of the subject or taking into account the developments in scholarship of the last quarter century.

This book was conceived to fill that gap. My own experience of lecturing on Palladio in London and at the Palladio Center in Vicenza has shown that there is a great general interest in Palladio's architecture not addressed by the specialist literature of recent years. My intention has been to provide a synthesis of Palladio's career—his achievements as architect and theoretician seen against the backdrop of his times, his patrons, and the architectural practice of the Renaissance. An important aim of the book was to give a more rounded picture of Palladio's buildings, and a generous complement of illustrations was essential to this purpose. Abbeville Press gave me the possibility of commissioning more than one hundred new images, and the gifted photographer Paolo Marton ably translated this intention into fact. Together we have traversed the Veneto and Venice, studying buildings and establishing the best photographs to convey specific points in the text. Marton has given of his time and energies beyond the call of duty, and I am grateful to him for advice and support in the planning of this book. The result, I think, is a more integrated work on Palladio than would otherwise have been the case.

In scholarly terms my debts are nearly as long as the Palladian bibliography. In the first place I must acknowledge the advice and encouragement of the three men who are the leaders in this field: James S. Ackerman, Howard Burns, and Renato Cevese. My interest in Palladio was first stimulated by Ackerman's *Palladio,* and my admiration for his book grew during the preparation of my own. My attraction to Italian Renaissance architecture was subsequently confirmed by study under Howard Burns at the Courtauld Institute of Art and later by collaborating with him and Linda Fairbairn on the Palladio exhibition held at the Hayward Gallery in London in 1975. Many of the ideas and the general approach to him in this book stem from that fruitful period of research in 1974 and 1975, and it would be difficult to acknowledge the extent of my debt to Burns. As for Renato Cevese, I first came to know him during the Palladio Summer School in Vicenza in 1973 and had the privilege of teaching with him at the Summer Schools in 1987 and 1988. His encyclopedic knowledge of Vicenza and the Vicentino are recorded in his magisterial catalog of the Vicentine villas and his guide to Vicenza.

Work on this book was begun during my time in Vicenza in 1987 and 1988. The actual writing began during a period as a Humboldt Fellow at the Kunsthistorisches Institut of the University of Bonn in 1989, where I had the advantage of discussing my work with Gunter Schweikhart and Andreas Beyer. A subsequent stay in Berlin enabled me to discuss Palladio's architecture with Wolfgang Wolters. In London my friends Paul Davies and David Hemsoll shared their knowledge of Michele Sanmicheli and Veneto architecture, and they were always willing to listen to my ideas and criticize them. Roland Mainstone kindly read the chapter on Palladio's bridges and made invaluable comments on its content. In Italy and elsewhere the number of people who helped me in the preparation of this book is legion, but I should like especially to thank: M. Elisa Avagnina, Alessandro Bettagno, Ursel Berger, Donatella Calabi, Tancredi Carunchio, Giorgio Ferrari, Linda Fairbairn, Antonio Foscari, Caterina Furlan, Filippa M. Aliberti Gaudioso, Amanda Lillie, Franca Lugato, Paola Marini, Paolo Morachiello, Stefania Mason Rinaldi, Maria Vittoria Pellizzari, John Pinto, and Elwin Robison. A special acknowledgment must go to Abigail Asher, for seeing the manuscript through the press, and to Joel Avirom, for the flair he brought to its design.

The positive reception of the first edition of this book has led to frequent requests for a paperback version, more compact and available at a price within a student's budget. Fortunately, it has proved possible to create a new edition, and I am grateful to Abbeville Press for allowing me to introduce here some corrections and amendments to the original text and notes, in light of recent publications. The bibliography of this edition has also been expanded to include new articles, particularly from the *Annali di Architettura*, the yearbook of the Palladio Center in Vicenza, and from the volumes published by the Center for Renaissance Studies of the University of Tours under the editorship of Jean Guillaume. The chronological table and glossary of the first edition are now complemented by maps showing the location of Palladio's main buildings in Vicenza, the Veneto, and Venice.

I often think of Inigo Jones's journey through Italy in 1613–14 when he travelled with a score of weighty, architectual tomes. Few of us today would contemplate that, but at least this new, more user-friendly version of *Andrea Palladio: The Architect in His Time* should fit comfortably into a suitcase or a backpack for a trip to Vicenza.

Bruce Boucher
5 June 1997

ANDREAS PALLADIVS
ex eleganti antiqua tabella
apud March.^s Capra Patricios Vicetinos

I
PALLADIO'S FORMATION AS AN ARCHITECT

T HEY WERE CREATED IN A SHORT TIME FOR ALL TIME. EACH ONE OF THEM IN ITS BEAUTY was even then and at once antique, but in the freshness of its vigor it is, even to the present day, recent and newly wrought." Plutarch's description of the buildings of the Acropolis provides a concise definition of classical architecture, and if any buildings since antiquity fulfill these criteria, the architecture of Andrea Palladio does.[1] The crisp lines, elegant proportions, and classicizing porticos of his houses and churches are immediately identifiable and combine functionality with beauty in a way that is both modern and timeless. Palladio's career spanned most of the sixteenth century, the period of the High Renaissance in his native Veneto, but his career was unusual compared to that of other great Renaissance architects like Bramante and Michelangelo. For one thing, Palladio never trained as an artist but rather as a stonemason, gradually working his way up from the workshop to become the unofficial first architect of Venice by his death in 1580. For another, his style, widely appreciated and imitated by his contemporaries, also gave rise to one of the most influential and enduring of architectural movements: Palladianism became an article of faith in the eighteenth century and spread Palladio's gospel from Potsdam to Providence.[2]

For an architect of such influence, Palladio the man remains in obscurity. The bare facts of his life are meager, and there is not even a wholly reliable portrait (plate I).[3] In a sense this is irrelevant, for Palladio left his fullest biography in his drawings and buildings. Nevertheless the details of his life are a crucial starting point.

I. Francesco Zucchi (1692–1764). *Palladio.* Ashmolean Museum, Oxford. Engraving, 15.8 x 10.1 cm.

Though long associated with Vicenza, Palladio was born in Padua, the major city of the land empire of the Venetian Republic. His family lived in the parish of San Michele, where the future architect was born as Andrea di Pietro dalla Gondola on November 30, 1508.[4] His grandfather Francesco was a gardener and his father, Pietro, earned a living as a mill worker, grinding grain and transporting it by boat. From his occupation and earlier family connections with the Paduan waterways, Pietro acquired the nickname "dalla gondola." Andrea's mother, Marta, is simply defined in the documents as *zoppa*, or lame, and seemingly died when Andrea was a minor. His father had friends in other crafts, and it is significant that Andrea's godfather was a sculptor and stonemason named Vincenzo Grandi.[5] Perhaps through Grandi, Andrea was introduced to the world of architecture and came to be apprenticed to a local stonemason, Bartolomeo Cavazza, in 1521.

It was hardly an auspicious moment for an architectural career. The War of the League of Cambrai (1509–16) had seen Venice pitted against the major European powers and in danger of losing her *terraferma* possessions.[6] Padua was taken and retaken the year after Palladio's birth, and the marauding actions of Imperial and Venetian forces disrupted the economy of the Veneto well into the 1520s. Andrea's early years must have been precarious, and survival against a backdrop of plague and famine was no small achievement. For a boy interested in architecture, however, Padua offered a showcase, chiefly through the agency of one man, Alvise Cornaro.[7] Cornaro was one of those figures, often found in the Renaissance, in whom charlatanism and genius were liberally mixed. Of modest origins, he aspired to the Venetian aristocracy and grew wealthy through land reclamation, some shady financial dealing, and the administration of the bishop of Padua's estates. Cornaro also shared the taste of many wealthy contemporaries for architecture and translated a portion of his money into buildings from the 1520s onward. Then as now, persons of standing were expected to display magnificence, and architecture offered a durable and visible way of proclaiming status, whether by creating a new palace or remodeling an old one, by endowing a chapel or underwriting the cost of a church. Once the preserve of the higher aristocracy, such gestures filtered down to the bourgeoisie during the Renaissance, and few would have disagreed with the statement of Giovanni Rucellai, Alberti's patron and one of the great builders of fifteenth-century Florence. "I think I have given myself more honor, and my soul more satisfaction, by having spent money than by having earned it, above all with regard to the building I have done."[8]

2. Giovanni Maria Falconetto(?) and Gualtiero dall'Arzere(?). Frescoes in the entrance hall of the Odeo Cornaro.

Architecture became Cornaro's avocation from the 1520s. Having studied the classical treatise by the Roman architect Marcus Vitruvius Pollio and the mid-fifteenth-century one by Leon Battista Alberti, he began to formulate his own ideas and projects. Cornaro also found the ideal assistant in Giovanni Maria Falconetto, a Veronese painter of antiquarian tastes. Giorgio Vasari said that Cornaro turned Falconetto from a mediocre painter into a good architect, and there is some truth to this.[9] Anticipating the relationship of Giangiorgio Trissino and Palladio, the two men studied the antiquities of Rome and collaborated on Cornaro's major projects, chief among them the Loggia and Odeo Cornaro, both additions to Cornaro's Paduan dwellings (plate 2). Finished in 1524, the Loggia was a manifesto of the new Central Italian style of architecture created by Bramante and his circle earlier in the century at Rome (plates 9, 13). The Loggia was more ornamental than functional, but its correct use of the Doric and Ionic orders served as an example that was imitated by Palladio in his earliest buildings (plate 24). Falconetto's signature here and on his two city gates for Padua (plate 3) self-consciously imitated the inscription by the Roman architect on the Arco dei Gavi in Verona[10] and reflected his enhanced status as well.

3. Giovanni Maria Falconetto (1468–1535). Porta Savonarola, Padua, 1530.

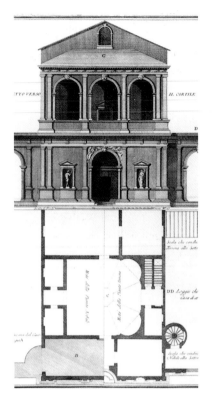

4. G. A. Battisti (eighteenth century). *Elevation and Plan of the Odeo Cornaro,* from *Rilievi della Loggia e dell'Odeo Cornaro.* Biblioteca of the Museo Civico Correr, Venice. Engraving.

The Odeo Cornaro was a later and more substantial creation. In plan (plate 4) it was modeled upon a Roman structure, wrongly believed to have been the country house of Marcus Terentius Varro, the author of a famous treatise on agriculture, but copied by architects from the late fifteenth century.[11] The Odeo has a central vaulted octagon with corner niches, and its lateral rooms are symmetrically disposed. The Bolognese architect Sebastiano Serlio praised its design because the octagon was indirectly lit from adjacent rooms, which made it cool in summer (it could be heated in winter by ducts beneath the floor, in the manner of a Roman bath).[12] The antique form of the Odeo Cornaro was completed by frescoed and stuccoed decoration, which reflected recent trends in Central Italian architecture. Its villalike qualities found their way into projects by Serlio and early designs by Palladio (plate 35).

Falconetto also built a theater in the antique style for Cornaro at Este and furnished a new facade for the parish church of Codevigo near Cornaro's major estate, works that demonstrated an interest in the antiquities of Verona as well as Rome. Falconetto had an eye for telling details in moldings and decorative elements, which he blended in his works. With the facade at Codevigo (plate 131), he interpolated tabernacles from a now-destroyed Roman gate at Ravenna between Doric columns on high bases, possibly inspired by the Arco dei Gavi; it was an unorthodox but effective combination that Palladio would later recall in his facade for San Giorgio Maggiore (plate 128).[13]

Palladio had ample time to study the Odeo and Loggia almost twenty years later, during the late 1530s, when his mentor Giangiorgio Trissino took him to Padua for an extended stay. His first acquaintance with this rarified sphere would have come fleetingly in the 1520s during his Paduan apprenticeship with the stonemason Bartolomeo Cavazza. His first master belonged more to the world of artisans than architects, and his known work imitated developments in Venetian architecture around the turn of the century competently though without flair.[14] Cavazza's contract with Andrea followed the normal conventions: he promised to feed and clothe his charge—except for his shirts—and to instruct him in the craft of masonry, paying him one ducat per annum over five years with a final settlement of six ducats at the end of the apprenticeship. The later receipt of a stipend indicates that Andrea already had an acquaintance with the craft, which he may have acquired through his godfather, Vincenzo Grandi, then at work rebuilding houses in Padua. Under Cavazza, Andrea would have learned the trade of carving stone and of building houses from the ground up. Much of his time was probably spent in carving window and door frames, fireplaces, and cornices; through this, he developed a feeling for architectural details that remained with him throughout his career and was not the least element in his success. But relations between master and pupil grew strained, and Andrea broke his apprenticeship in April 1523. Cavazza traced him to Vicenza, where the boy had recently settled with his father. There was a reconciliation of sorts, but Andrea broke away again and formally enrolled in the Vicentine guild of stonemasons one year later. Thus began the long and fruitful connection with his adopted city.[15]

Andrea was doubly fortunate in establishing himself in Vicenza. The workshop that he joined was more congenial than Cavazza's and it also gave scope for developing his talents in design. Its patrons, Giovanni di Giacomo da Porlezza and Girolamo Pittoni, were well regarded and involved in public and private projects. Pittoni specialized in the sculptural side of the practice while Giovanni dealt exclusively with architectural commissions.[16] The workshop, which was known as the Pedemuro bottega from its location on an eponymous street in town, paid for Andrea's matriculation fee in the guild, a recognition of the young man's talent. He lived and worked on the premises, and Giovanni became his chief mentor; indeed so closely did the two work that even after Palladio left the firm they collaborated on the temporary decorations for the entry of Cardinal Ridolfi in 1543 and submitted jointly the initial design for the city's Basilica arcades in 1546.[17] Giovanni da Porlezza was also on good terms with Michele Sanmicheli, and this connection enabled Andrea to encounter the great Veronese architect, whose work had a strong impact on him in the 1540s. Beyond that, Vicenza was a wealthy city—as Palladio would later describe it, "not very large in circumference but full of the noblest intellects."[18] It was a city under Venetian rule but distant enough from Venice to be fairly autonomous. Vicenza enjoyed a tremendous building tradition in the fifteenth century and was now on the verge of a second expansion in domestic architecture. Its well-educated nobility came to regard architecture as a means of putting their city on the cultural map. Palladio listed several of his patrons in the introduction to his great treatise, *I Quattro Libri dell'Architettura*, and his publication of their palace designs was as much a celebration of Vicenza as it was of his own genius.[19]

We can catch glimpses of Andrea and the Pedemuro bottega during the 1530s. For Francesco Godi, they created a new portal for the church of Santa Maria dei Servi, just off the main piazza of Vicenza, in 1531.[20] The design features a small but imposing arch and pediment, with fluted Corinthian columns and moldings that reveal an awareness of the new Central Italian style just being introduced into the Veneto by Sanmicheli and Sansovino. It was unlikely that Andrea would have produced such an accomplished design at that early date, but the Servi portal indicates that the Pedemuro workshop knew how to obtain the latest models for their clients. Another branch of the wealthy Godi family gave Andrea his first opportunity to display his talent with their villa of around 1537 (plate 49), and they returned to the Pedemuro bottega for a burial chapel around 1546.[21] During the 1530s, Andrea consolidated his position within

the workshop and may have played an active role in the design of the high altar of Vicenza's Cathedral, executed between 1534 and 1536 (plate 5).[22] A handsome and lavishly inlaid work, the high altar is classical at one remove, being distantly related to Roman triumphal arches but more closely patterned upon the contemporary architecture of Tullio Lombardo and his circle. Fluted Composite columns are its chief feature, probably based upon studies of Roman orders preserved among Palladio's earliest drawings (plate 6). The commission was an important one for the workshop, not only because of its site but because of the patron, Aurelio Dall'Acqua, a learned and well-connected aristocrat representative of the social class that helped make Palladio's career.

By 1534, at the age of twenty-six, Andrea felt secure enough in his job to marry Allegradonna, the daughter of a carpenter named Marc'antonio. She had been in service with Angela Poiana, a Vicentine noblewoman who provided a dowry, and over the course of the years she bore him five children: Leonida, who became an architect and worked with his father; Marc'antonio, who gravitated towards sculpture and worked with Alessandro Vittoria in Venice; Orazio, who studied law in Padua; Zenobia, who married a Vicentine goldsmith; and Silla, who was secretary of the Accademia Olimpica during the erection of his father's theater. Of his children, Zenobia, Silla, and Marc'antonio survived their father.[23]

Two years after Andrea's marriage the Pedemuro workshop was probably entrusted with a small public commission, a new double portal for the Domus Comestabilis (plate 7), which led from the Basilica to the house of the Venetian governor or *podestà*.[24] It is an accomplished work, close to a design later published by Sebastiano Serlio, and it displays a sensitivity for classical models demonstrated in early Palladian works like the Villa Gazzotti at Bertesina (plate 57). The portal of the Domus Comestabilis has been plausibly ascribed to Andrea, and it presents us with many of the figures recognizable in his later works. On the whole, the architecture of the

5. *(opposite)* High altar of the Cathedral, Vicenza, 1534–36.

6. *(right)* Entablature from the Arch of Titus, late 1530s. Museo Civico, Vicenza (Vic. D 10v). Pen and ink, 41.2 x 28.5 cm.

7. Palladio(?). Portal of the Domus Comestabilis, Basilica, Vicenza, 1536.

Pedemuro workshop in these years anticipated Palladio's later orientation towards classical models, although the references have the effect of quotations embedded in vernacular architecture. Andrea could have continued like this for several decades turning out minor works of distinctive if uninsistent quality, but he had the luck to attract the attention of his first great benefactor, Giangiorgio Trissino.[25]

Trissino stands out as the catalyst in the architect's career. He opened his house and the intellectual circles of the day to the younger man, trained him in architectural theory, took him to Rome three times, and, not least of all, bestowed upon him the grandiloquent name by which he was ever after known: Palladio.[26] Like most of Palladio's Vicentine patrons, Trissino was a member of the feudal aristocracy deprived of power by Venetian rule; like many of them, he also rebelled against Venice during the War of the League of Cambrai, entering the city with the army of the Emperor Maximilian I in 1509 and leaving when the Venetians recovered the city. A period of forced exile ensued, spent at the court of Pope Leo X in Rome and as his ambassador elsewhere; only in 1516 with the intervention of the Medici pope was Trissino allowed to recover his estates and enter Vicenza again. A talented polymath, Trissino played an active part in the intellectual debates of the early sixteenth century, advocating the reform of the Italian language, the introduction of a standard currency, and a new system of weights and measures. He wrote a classical tragedy, *Sofonisba,* which was much admired, and an epic poem, *Italia liberata dai goti,* which was not.[27] Trissino's interest in architecture stemmed from his humanist training and his passion for order and systems; it was sharpened by his experience of Rome, where he knew and admired Raphael, and indeed the palaces and villas produced in the reign of Leo X remained his touchstone for good architecture twenty years later.

After a semiwithdrawal from public life, Trissino devoted much of his energy and wealth toward the creation of a suburban villa at the large estate of Cricoli, near Vicenza (plates 8, 10).[28] Embellished by formal gardens, a fountain, and a grove, the new villa replaced an earlier house between 1532 and 1537, and it became a showpiece of contemporary architecture, much like Cornaro's buildings in Padua. Like the Loggia and Odeo, Cricoli is textbook architecture, but of a high order. Trissino lavished much attention on the principal facade, which is all that remains of his ambitious building. With its double order of Ionic and Corinthian pilasters, the facade is reminiscent of a discarded idea for the garden loggia of Raphael's Villa Madama as later published by Serlio (plate 9).[29] Since Serlio's design was published after Cricoli's completion, Trissino must have had access to the architect's drawings, probably consulting him on the plans for the villa. He made his own adjustments to the proportions, however, following Vitruvius's precepts for the moldings of the Ionic bases and the dimensions of the Corinthian capitals; the introduction of figures of Minerva and Peace in the niches above also invites comparison with the architecture of Falconetto and Sansovino (plate 157). The plan is equally noteworthy for its tripartite division into a central core with loggia, *salone*, and lateral wings composed of small, medium, and large rooms. The symmetrical disposition and simple proportions of the spaces anticipate Palladio's architectural language to such an extent that Cricoli has occasionally been cited as one of the architect's first buildings, although this could not have been the case: the building reflects the idiosyncratic though well-informed taste of its patron, and if Trissino employed the Pedemuro workshop to execute his design, then Andrea would have participated as a junior member of the firm.[30] Probably in this way he first had access to Trissino's knowledge of architecture and caught the older man's attention.

Paolo Gualdo, the first biographer of Palladio, tells us that Trissino appreciated Andrea's gifts while he was still a member of the Pedemuro workshop.[31] Thereafter, as Gualdo has it, Trissino established a close relationship with his charge, explaining to him Vitruvius's text and taking him to Rome where Palladio measured and drew the theaters, arches, and temples. This account corresponds to the facts as we know them, for Palladio dropped out of his old workshop after 1537 and was mentioned in correspondence as being with Trissino in Rome at various times in the 1540s.[32] Before this Palladio may have spent some time at Cricoli, which was not only a villa but also the seat of an academy by which Trissino set great store—down to his death in 1550, Trissino himself conducted a cross between a Platonic academy and boarding school at his suburban villa, where lectures and discussions on literary and philosophical topics took place as well as physical exercise and music-making.[33] Undue attention to rank was avoided, and persons of no social standing could gain admission by virtue of their talents. Such academies were a familiar feature of Italian life from the middle of the fifteenth century, and virtually no town of any significance was without one. Trissino hoped his academy would outlive him and even stipulated in his will that it should be put under the protection of the doge of Venice if his own family died out. This did not happen, but the informal gatherings between aristocrats and clever individuals of humbler birth were reborn in the Accademia Olimpica, which numbered Palladio among its early members and commissioned its theater from him (plate 201).[34]

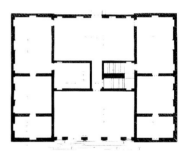

8. *(top) Plan of the Villa Trissino at Cricoli*, from Ottavio Bertotti Scamozzi, *Le fabbriche e i disegni di Andrea Palladio*, 1796.

9. *(above)* Sebastiano Serlio (1475–1554). Woodcut of alternative design for garden facade of the Villa Madama, probably by Raphael, first published in Book III of *Le Regoli generali dell'architettura*, 1540.

The academy must have been a movable feast because it went with Trissino on extended sojourns to Padua, Ferrara, and Venice from 1538 to 1541 and subsequently to Rome. It was during the months in Padua that Palladio had the opportunity to meet Cornaro and study Falconetto's works more closely. He may have had occasion then to look at drawings of antiquities made by Falconetto before his death in 1535, for several of his early drawings are of monuments that the Veronese architect must have drawn.[35] Palladio enjoyed enough contact with Cornaro to give him a glowing tribute in the *Quattro Libri*, and he absorbed something of Cornaro's approach to writing about architecture, especially his straightforward treatment of the elements of house-building and his concern with addressing a lay audience.[36] In Padua Palladio also made the acquaintance of two other members of Cornaro's entourage, the stuccoist Tiziano Minio and the painter Gualtiero dall'Arzere; with Minio, also a member of Sansovino's circle, Palladio made his first documented appearance in Venice in 1548 while dall'Arzere, later Minio's brother-in-law, was one of the artists involved in decorating the Villa Godi in the 1540s.[37] In the circle of Cornaro and his son-in-law Giovanni Cornaro, Palladio would also have met intellectuals like Daniele Barbaro (plate 167), with whom he subsequently collaborated on an illustrated translation of Vitruvius.[38] Such contacts gave Andrea the possibility of discussing architecture and the

10. Giangiorgio Trissino (1478–1550). Facade of the Villa Trissino at Cricoli (Vicenza), 1532–1538.

ancient world with educated amateurs who had the benefit of Latin and a knowledge of the ancient world. Some of this antiquarian "table talk" rubbed off on him and found its way into his checklist of famous Roman monuments, published in 1554 as *L'Antichità di Roma*.[39]

In addition to Palladio, a painter with a flair for rustic poetry named Giambattista Maganza participated in these activities.[40] Trissino's cultivation of artists, which paralleled Cornaro's promotion of Falconetto and the dialect playwright Ruzzante, prompted his taking both protégés to Rome, clearly with the intention of exposing them to the new style of architecture and painting. The great transformation in Palladio's life came with the impact of his successive Roman trips in the 1540s as well as a final one in 1554, prior to the publication of Barbaro's *Vitruvius*. Obviously, he knew something of ancient architecture from the drawings he had copied and from books, but he candidly recorded in his own treatise, the *Quattro Libri*, "finding the remains of ancient structures worthy of much greater study than I originally thought, I began to measure in the minutest detail every part of them."[41] In those days this was easier said than done, as drawings by Marten van Heemskerck (plate 11) and other contemporaries show. Many of the most famous buildings were submerged in debris or disfigured by subsequent additions; often there was no agreement on what the ruins were, and excavating was a costly, time-consuming business. Serlio spoke of being able to make detailed drawings of the Theater of Marcellus thanks to the scaffolding erected when his master Peruzzi was turning it into a palace, and when the French architect Philibert de l'Orme recalled late in life his study in Rome he emphasized the "great labor, expense, and outlay . . . for ladders and ropes and to excavate the foundations. . . . All this I could not do without a certain number of men who followed me, some to earn . . . and others to learn."[42] Palladio surveyed and made drawings of the temples and baths on site, returning to his study to make fair copies. To save time and money, he had recourse to other architects' drawings, which he repro-

11. Marten van Heemskerck (1498–1574). *View of Roman Forum in 1535*, 1535. Kupferstichkabinett, Staatliche Museen, Berlin. Pen, ink, and wash, 21.6 x 55.5 cm.

duced and subsequently revised in the light of his developing architectural theory.[43] A number of these drawings must have circulated in the Pedemuro workshop, and Palladio may have had access to those that Serlio brought with him to Venice as well as others left by Falconetto at his death. His earliest attributable drawings tend to be perspective studies of Roman architecture, based upon other sources (plates 5, 12). In the case of two studies after Roman triumphal arches, Palladio replaced the capital copied from a second-hand source with a subsequent version, pasted over the earlier one (plate 5). It was a characteristic example of his critical approach to his sources, demonstrating his need to revise work in light of direct study from the antique. Perspectival elevations were, in any case, a superannuated convention for architectural draftsmen by 1540; Alberti and Raphael had previously described a new way of rendering buildings whereby elevations and sections were shown in strictly orthogonal or geometric projection. Alberti associated perspective views of architecture with painting, noting that such drawings introduced distortions in the illustration of a building's component parts; Raphael endorsed Alberti's distinction between artists' drawings and those of architects, and it was during his period as architect of St. Peter's that the convention of elevations and sections in orthogonal projection—the forerunner of the modern architectural draftsmanship—became established.[44] This new style of architectural drawing had the advantage of reproducing component lines on a grid of right angles without distortion. Palladio applied this new technique to his own projects, as opposed to

12. *Portico of Octavia*, late 1530s–early 1540s. Museo Civico, Vicenza (Vic. D 26). Pen and ink, 44.6 x 29.4 cm.

making copies after other architects, and used it exclusively in his later career. He also redrew all his early perspective studies of ancient buildings as orthogonal elevations with a view to publication (plate 12), and the compression of space created by such drawings yielded an important impact on Palladio's own concept of design: the spatial ambiguity inherent in orthogonal elevations gradually became a dynamic ingredient in his own architecture from the 1550s onward, both in drawings (plates 188 and 189) and in executed works (plates 118, 187).[45]

Palladio's contact with classical architecture in the 1540s left him dissatisfied with hand-me-down copies, and even with his first publication, *L'Antichità di Roma*, he explained his wish to "see with my own eyes and measure everything with my own hands."[46] Raphael once lamented, "Vitruvius gives me much light but not enough," and Palladio would have endorsed that opinion.[47] Early evidence of this critical stance can be seen in three drawings of capitals and entablatures from Roman triumphal arches (plate 5). All three were copied from earlier sources and show the capital with its entablature moldings rendered in perspective. Obviously the capitals did not please Palladio because in each case he covered the received version with a second piece of paper on which a more accurate capital has been drawn. In other cases, like a beautiful study of three antique bases, the original ink drawing is supplemented by further measurements and sketches made by the architect some years later.[48] Like Raphael and Peruzzi, Palladio scoured classical architecture for beautiful and unusual motifs that he could apply to his own buildings. Unusual capitals and bases for columns (plate 180) or examples of Roman brickwork were drawn and filed away for later use. A distinctive structure like the Portico of Octavia (plate 12), closed at either end by a relieving arch, would become a standard solution for palace and villa loggias precisely because it was the only one of its kind known to Palladio.[49] He adapted the distinctive Ionic capital of the Temple of Fortuna Virilis in Rome and the portico of the Temple of Minerva at Assisi (plates 180, 182) for much the same reason since they solved specific problems with flair and individuality.[50]

Palladio's interest in ancient architecture was not confined to Rome alone but included those structures available in nearby towns as well as Vicenza, Verona, and even as far afield as Nîmes.[51] A letter by Marco Thiene, a cousin of Palladio's early patron Marc'antonio Thiene and a member of Trissino's Roman circle, mentions Palladio's visits to Albano, Tivoli, and Palestrina in 1547; his encounter with the great Roman hillside complex at Palestrina in particular had a profound impact on the architect's own imagination, drawing forth overpowering reconstructions of the site (plate 206) and leading ultimately to his most famous tribute to the antique, the Villa Rotonda (plate 208).[52] But it was the Roman baths that made the greatest impression upon Palladio, just as they did upon most visitors to Rome, above all introducing a sense of space and scale as dynamic components in his own buildings. Relatively well preserved thermal complexes like those of Diocletian and Caracalla became the touchstone for Palladio's reconstructions of other, less well-preserved baths like those of Agrippa (plates 184, 185). Inevitably his reconstructions suffer from an exaggerated sense of the symmetry of classical architecture, but his thoroughness in measuring and projecting whole structures from the often meager evidence stands in sharp contrast to Serlio, who never attempted an elevation of the baths because of the difficulties of such an undertaking and the "poor quality" of the architecture itself.[53] Palladio did not agree and studied the baths for ways of combining large and small spaces, for the variety of their vaulting, and for their unusual spatial configurations. Even from his earliest villa and palace designs (plates 59, 60) he strove to incorporate columnar screens, cross vaulting, and rooms with apses. When he came to design convents and churches, Palladio imposed the language of the baths onto whole projects like Santa Maria della Carità and San Giorgio Maggiore (plates 113, 114), and his belief that the baths and temples preserved elements of Roman private as well as public architecture remained influential until the time of Robert Adam.[54]

Palladio's initial response to the antique was inevitably random and not informed by a grand design. That only came during later visits and was given focus by his decision to publish his own treatise on ancient and modern architecture as well as by his collaboration with Daniele Barbaro on the latter's annotated translation of Vitruvius. Exposure to Barbaro was as beneficial to Palladio as his initial experience of reading Vitruvius with Trissino, for it enabled the architect to clarify his ideas about the theory and practice of Roman architecture, the nature of temples and their precincts, and the planning of houses, villas, and even cities. Palladio's and Barbaro's inspection of monuments strengthened the critical approach to Vitruvius that distinguishes Barbaro's commentary and Palladio's *Quattro Libri.* Barbaro's method of verifying the Roman architect's treatise against the evidence of Roman buildings and other classical texts became the basis for Palladio's approach to reconstructing classical temples in Book IV of the *Quattro Libri.*[55] The drawings that Palladio prepared for Barbaro's publication also proclaimed the architect's extraordinary knowledge of classical architecture more than a decade before the appearance of the *Quattro Libri* (plates 168, 200).

At first, Palladio's attention was probably divided equally between ancient and modern Rome. In their trips together, Trissino would have shown him the buildings that had been built during his own time in Rome, namely the architecture of Bramante, Raphael, and their followers. This would have included the small palace built by Bramante for a family named Caprini and now better known as the House of Raphael (plate 13). So often copied, the palace had a novelty for contemporaries that is difficult to recapture, but Bramante's genius lay, as Vasari put it, in "imitating the ancients with new inventions."[56] The bold rustication around the ground-floor doorways and mezzanine windows blended elements from antique tombs and Trajan's Market in the Roman Forum; this level served as a podium for the coupled Doric columns scanning the *piano nobile,* itself a refinement of a motif that went back to Alberti's Palazzo Rucellai. Both rustication and the orders had already entered the vocabulary of Renaissance architects, but here Bramante endowed them with a classical rigor that later architects found compelling. Bramante's approach not only allowed the functional elements of a Renaissance palace to be slotted into a classicizing system, it also had the advantage of economizing on cost—instead of using all stone, the basic material was brick rendered with a mixture of plaster and crushed marble that could be modeled to resemble stone.[57] This technique derived from Roman architecture and it had the merit that the actual stone component in the facade was confined to moldings, columns bases, and capitals. The House of Raphael owed its influence in part to this feature, for it was widely imitated in areas like Mantua, Verona, and Vicenza where brick was the common building material and stone only available at a price.

Trissino would also have taken Palladio to look at variations on Bramante's theme, such as Raphael's Palazzo Branconio dell'Aquila (plate 30), a brilliant tour de force of stuccowork in an alternative antique mode; likewise they would have studied the inventive use of rustication in Giulio Romano's Roman works, among them Palazzo Adimari Salviati.[58] Palladio may first have entered

into the spirit of antique architecture through the work of Bramante and his followers, especially those projects rivaling the magnitude of ancient Rome: new Saint Peter's, the Cortile del Belvedere, and the Villa Madama (plate 16). With Saint Peter's, Bramante recast Christian architecture on a scale resembling the great Roman monuments, the Pantheon and the Basilica of Maxentius, and no architect could ignore the challenge posed by the dimensions and vocabulary of his design.[59] For Palladio, Saint Peter's became a point of departure for his own church architecture (plate 129), albeit modified by his study of Bramante's models. The Cortile del Belvedere initiated Palladio into that integration of architecture and landscape which bore fruit in several of his more ambitious villa designs; it also directed him to Bramante's models, the imperial villas at Albano and Tivoli as well as the Temple of Fortune at Palestrina.[60] The potency of the Villa Madama was all the greater for the young architect because, though unfinished, it offered him the most comprehensive modern re-construction of a classical villa in terms of decoration, variety of room types, and gardens. Raphael also showed Palladio that it was possible to combine elements from various classical sources to create novel effects. To take one example, the garden facade of the villa employs a distinctive colossal order of Ionic pilasters, itself unprecedented, combined with convex base and frieze taken from the Composite order of the now destroyed Arco di Portogallo in Rome.[61] The license used by Raphael in culling classical motifs and putting them together in new forms struck a chord with Palladio, and his own creative treatment of the antique owes much to Raphael's example here.

13. Donato Bramante (1444–1514). *House of Raphael*, engraving by Antonio Lafrery, 1549. The Metropolitan Museum of Art.

Palladio established his own version of the new Roman architecture in Vicenza, but he was not without precursors in surrounding areas. Falconetto has already been mentioned, whom Vasari saw as the first of the new wave of architects to bring the "good architecture" to the Veneto.[62] Jacopo Sansovino, who enjoyed fame as a sculptor and architect in Florence and Rome, established himself as the reigning architect in Venice after the Sack of Rome in 1527. During the 1530s he designed a series of impressive public buildings for the Piazza San Marco, and Palladio later called his Marciana Library (plate 81) "the most magnificent and ornate structure built since ancient times."[63] But Palladio rarely had occasion to imitate the scale and sumptuousness of Sansovino's buildings in his early career, and when he replaced Sansovino as the driving force in Venetian architecture his style had evolved in quite another direction. Two other figures, Michele Sanmicheli and Giulio Romano, played a more prominent role in the formation of Palladio's architectural language and deserve more attention here. Like Sansovino, both trained in the circles of Bramante and Raphael before moving away from Rome in the 1520s, Sanmicheli to his native Verona and Giulio Romano to Mantua. There the similarity between their careers ends, for Sanmicheli became a military engineer for the Venetian Republic and was employed privately by Veronese patricians while Giulio basked in the status of court artist to Federico Gonzaga.

14. Michele Sanmicheli (1484–1559). Palazzo Canossa, Verona, begun c. 1530.

Sanmicheli's career offers the closest parallel to Palladio's through the nature of his work in Verona. After the Sack of Rome he was taken up by a number of local patrons and created for them his own version of the new Roman palace style.[64] Chief among his new patrons was Ludovico Canossa, who resembled Trissino in coming from an old aristocratic family and having known life in the Rome of the Medici popes. The Palazzo Canossa was commissioned around 1530 and fully exhibits Sanmicheli's power as an architect (plate 14), manipulating the language and techniques of Bramante's House of Raphael but on a more palatial scale. It displays a fine sense of dramatic contrast between the rusticated ground floor and a flatter scansion of the *piano nobile;* moreover, Sanmicheli's feeling for details—the linking of horizontal moldings across the facade and the juxtaposition of smooth and rough textures—was not lost on Palladio, who incorporated these features in his earliest designs (plate 25). The example of Palazzo Canossa led to further commissions in a sequence that would be repeated a decade later by Palladio in Vicenza. Sanmicheli's Palazzo Bevilacqua, for instance, was begun shortly after Palazzo Canossa by another aristocratic family related by marriage to the Canossa. The evident family rivalry sparked another variation on the House of Raphael, this time a richly embellished Corinthian *piano nobile* surmounting a rusticated Doric ground floor. Both floors convey an almost sculptural delight in ornament, and the facade as a whole illustrates Sanmicheli's introduction of motifs taken from Veronese antiquities. The alternating vertical and spiral fluting of the Corinthian columns and the shifts in scale of the arches is based upon the Roman Porta Borsari, which stands a little way from Palazzo Bevilacqua on the same street as Palazzo Canossa.

The complexities of the Palazzo Bevilacqua facade are unmatched by Sanmicheli's other Veronese works, but his city gates continued his attempt to create a modern architecture to equal Verona's antiquities. In his own day, these were Sanmicheli's most famous works, and Vasari believed they rivaled their Roman prototypes.[65] The first of them, the Porta Nuova (plate 15),

15. Michele Sanmicheli (1484–1559). Porta Nuova, Verona, 1533–40.

16. Raphael (1483–1520). Loggia of the Villa Madama, Rome, begun 1518. The decoration of the garden loggia, originally unglazed, was by Giulio Romano and Giovanni da Udine.

displays a starker handling of its theme than Falconetto's gates at Padua. The mixture of boldly cut masonry blocks punctuated by an engaged Doric order and a Vitruvian scroll frieze conveys the intended impression of strength; it also makes a classical model like the Porta Maggiore in Rome seem tame by comparison. It is not surprising that Palladio had a study for the Porta Nuova among his own drawings, and his close observation of this aspect of Sanmicheli's work is apparent in early facades like that of the Villa Pisani at Bagnolo (plate 43).[66]

The influence of Sanmicheli on Palladio's early career cannot be overemphasized, as the subsequent chapters will show. Sanmicheli was the only architect of major standing with whom Palladio had extensive contact, through the Pedemuro workshop and through the proximity of Verona and Vicenza. Like Palladio, Sanmicheli came from the mason's yard and understood the effectiveness of details in overall architectural design. He also had a well-developed appreciation for antique architecture, which he could share with the younger architect. Much of Palladio's work in the 1540s can be seen as an intellectual apprenticeship to Sanmicheli, and his early projects for the Basilica arcades were clearly drawn with an eye to Sanmicheli's contemporary works (plate 79).[67] Equally important for Palladio was Sanmicheli's attention to the decoration of his palaces and villas, for he established a group of young Veronese artists—among them Paolo Veronese and Bartolomeo Ridolfi—capable of working in a style similar to that

17. Giulio Romano (c. 1499–1546). Detail of facade of the Palazzo del Te, Mantua, begun 1525.

current in Rome. Many of these artists began to appear as collaborators on Palladio's palace and villa decorations as early as the late 1540s.[68]

Palladio's relationship with Sanmicheli was obviously close; with Giulio Pippi, called Romano, the ties were less direct but equally determinant. Born in 1499, Giulio was only a few years older than Palladio, but he had the good fortune to train in Raphael's workshop, becoming a trusted lieutenant before his master's death in 1520. His exposure to the range of Raphael's activities, from fresco and panel painting to architecture, provided the ideal background for his summons to Mantua in 1524.[69] There he performed a variety of tasks for his youthful master, the marquis (later duke) of Mantua, becoming so indispensable that, as Vasari put it, nothing could be built in Mantua without his approval.[70] For our purposes, his most important work was the Palazzo del Te, a *villa suburbana* that he designed and decorated for Federico Gonzaga (plates 17, 18). The villa began as a stud farm and hideaway for Federico's mistress, Isabella Boschetti, but from 1527 onward it was cleverly redeveloped by Giulio as "an example of architecture and painting for our times," to use Serlio's words.[71] Giulio applied the techniques that he learned under Raphael at the Villa Farnesina and the Villa Madama to transform the external

18. Giulio Romano (c. 1499–1546). Atrium of the Palazzo del Te, Mantua.

and internal appearance, masking the irregularities and dazzling the beholder with his ingenuity and erudition. The brick facades were rendered to look like stone, with engaged Doric columns over vigorous rustication in a manner recalling Bramante's upper court of the Belvedere. The interiors, too, were invested with a monumentality that belies their scale through a relatively inexpensive decor.

The Palazzo del Te was extremely important in transmitting the new Roman style to Northern Italy, Mantua being located on the edge of the Veneto as well as near Milan and Bologna. Palladio would have been able to visit Mantua relatively easily from Vicenza and probably passed through on some of his journeys south in the 1540s. His attention would have been drawn to Giulio's work when Giulio visited Vicenza for a consultation on the Basilica arcades in 1542, shortly after the Thiene family began their new and ambitious palace in Vicenza (plate 31) (probably after a design by Giulio).[72] The debate over Giulio's role in Palazzo Thiene goes on, but the intensity of Palladio's response to his work in the early 1540s is unquestionable. Several projects testify to Palladio's experiments with variegated rustication, aedicules, projecting voussoirs, and ground plans reminiscent of the Palazzo del Te (plates 55, 67). The construction of Palazzo Thiene in the mid-1540s also taught Palladio valuable lessons in managing a large-scale project, and he gradually imposed his own ideas on the palace after Giulio's death in 1546. This phase in Palladio's career overlapped with his interest in Sanmicheli, and he extracted as much as he could from the personal styles of the older men by imitation.

Palladio's early years were remarkable by the standard of his times. His talent was recognized and developed by Trissino and further stimulated by his encounters with Rome and with Barbaro's systematic approach to the antique. In Vicenza, he was groomed by influential backers to assume the position that Sansovino, Sanmicheli, and Giulio Romano held in their own cities. Palladio had the genius to rise to the challenge; within a decade, he would take his place among the great architects of the previous generation.

II

VICENZA AND PALLADIO'S FIRST PALACES

IN 1482 THE VENETIAN DIARIST MARIN SANUDO TRAVELED THROUGH THE VENETO AND KEPT a record of his observations. He gave a detailed account of Vicenza, noting its three miles of walls, its five gates, and the two rivers, Bacchiglione and Retrone, that gird it; of its buildings, he mentioned the palace of justice and the cathedral, both still under construction, the seats of the Venetian magistrates, several churches, but only one private palace, the Casa Pigafetta completed only the previous year.[1] One hundred years later the French essayist Michel de Montaigne jotted down his first impressions of Vicenza as "une grande ville, un peu moins que Verone, où y a tout plein de palais de noblesse."[2] Montaigne arrived just months after Palladio's death, and, significantly, it was the secular stamp of the city, its multitude of palaces, that caught his attention. The famous bird's-eye view of Vicenza in 1581 shows many of Palladio's palaces were then half-finished or only just begun (plate 20), and the cumulative effect must have been remarkable, especially for a traveler from across the Alps. A generation later, Montaigne's response was followed by those of Thomas Coryat and Inigo Jones, and by a steady stream of eighteenth- and nineteenth-century pilgrims coming to worship at the shrine of Palladio: his revolutionary impact on Vicentine architecture ensured the city's fame as well as his own.

The alacrity with which the Vicentines turned what was a small town into a building site can hardly be exaggerated. Palladio's contemporaries were mad for building in a way that

19. Portico of the Palazzo Chiericati, Vicenza.

courtiers in Elizabethan England or German barons along the Weser River would have understood.[3] What makes Vicenza so extraordinary is the scale and quality of building that took place in one architect's lifetime and within a town of less than twenty thousand inhabitants.

To understand the Palladian phenomenon in Vicenza, we must step back and look briefly at Vicenza in the period prior to Palladio's arrival in 1524. The city is situated at the eastern end of a long valley running between the Veneto and Lombardy and bounded by the Monti Lessini to the north and the Monti Berici to the south. Its land has always been fertile, and notwithstanding the growth of a cloth and silk trade,[4] agriculture was the principal source of wealth in the fifteenth and sixteenth centuries. In Palladio's day, the city center still bore the recognizable traces of its Roman origins: the *decumanus* or principal street, running east to west, and the *cardo*, running north to south, divided the center into

quarters. Vicenza's nucleus lay within its medieval walls, and here stood the chief manifestations of religious and civic power, crystallized in the cathedral and the buildings around the Piazza dei Signori, respectively.[5] Circling the public palace were subordinate squares for the sale of grain and produce while an open area called the *isola* served as a port at the end of the old *decumanus,* the present-day corso Palladio, in the east; tanners and millers, among them Palladio's own father, set up shop along the rivers. The main families of Vicenza, who constituted the core of the ruling class, had their palaces along the corso and on adjacent streets. As was often the case in medieval communities, these families staked out different sectors as their power bases. Thus the Godi, one of the wealthiest families, held a number of houses just below the main piazza and around the Servite monastery while the Thiene, who may have been the richest family in Vicenza, owned most of a large, oblong block north of the corso. A principal street like the contrà Porti ran north from the old *cardo* and contained a preponderance of palaces owned by the Porto family, as the name suggests.[6] Beyond the inner walls lay newer settlements, corresponding to the city's gates and

20. *(top)* Battista Pittoni (c. 1520–1583). Detail of *Bird's-eye view of Vicenza,* c. 1581. Pen and ink with blue wash, 130 x 140 cm.

21. *(above)* View of contrà Porti with the Palazzo Colleoni Porto and Palazzo da Porto Festa, Vicenza.

the main roads leading to the other centers of the *terraferma*, as the Venetian land empire was called. Here building was less dense with a number of monastic foundations and suburban dwellings with large gardens.

During the Middle Ages, Vicenza had been fought over by its larger neighbors, Padua and Verona, but the city voluntarily placed itself under Venetian protection in 1404, thus becoming the first born of its Veneto possessions.[7] This gesture not only recognized the *Realpolitik* of Venetian power over its hinterland, it also brought Vicenza peace and prosperity on a scale unknown since the thirteenth century. Since Vicenza was no longer a pawn in *terraferma* politics, the nobility turned to building, as is evident from the large and varied Gothic palaces that cluster about streets like the contrà Porti (plate 21), contrà Zanella, and also along the corso Palladio.[8] Few documents survive concerning these buildings, but they seem to have been part of a burst of private construction between the 1440s and about 1480, which prefigured the activities of Palladio's day. One wealthy Vicentine named Gaspare de Cadamonza listed three palaces worth 1,700 ducats in his will of 1491, holdings not atypical of the upper strata of local society.[9] Some of these monuments, like the imposing Cà d'Oro palace on the corso, the Palazzo Sesso Zen Fontana in contrà Zanella, or the Colleoni Porto palace on contrà Porti, rank among the most important examples of Gothic architecture in the Veneto, and the number and variety of houses surviving from this period testify to the extensive construction in hand during the third quarter of the fifteenth century. Not surprisingly, Vicentine Gothic is Venetian in origin, and the loggias with ogival arches, the quatrefoils, leafy capitals, marble incrustations, and open-work balconies all mirror the appearance of slightly earlier Venetian palaces. In a way, Vicentine Gothic can be understood as a reflection of cultural imperialism, the attempt by a subject state to assimilate the style of its nearby rulers; courtyards with Venetian wellheads, external staircases, and the rare interior space also bring this point home. Of course, Venetian palaces evolved to meet the peculiar requirements of building on sandy subsoil and in a dense urban context. This led to a tripartite division of houses around a central spine with a grouping of windows and generally balanced distribution of smaller rooms in the wings.[10] In Vicenza there was no reason to adopt such plans, and the result is that the sites of palaces, many of them modernized older dwellings, were extremely varied. Thus, the entrance halls are often wider than in Venice, the ground floor did not usually include a mezzanine, and the *salone* did not run at right angles to the facade but rather parallel to it. This was the case with the Cà d'Oro, the Sesso Zen Fontana, and Colleoni Porto, among others, although a palace like the Porto Breganze, described by Alvise da Porto as "recently built" in his will of 1483, shows a roughly symmetrical grouping of rooms about a central courtyard (plate 22), anticipating Palladio's ambitious design for Palazzo Thiene.

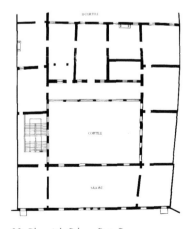

22. *Plan of the Palazzo Porto Breganze.*

The beginnings of a new Renaissance style appeared as early as the 1470s, the date of the handsome portal on the Gothic facade of the Palazzo Porto Breganze. Even more striking is the facade of the Palazzo Braschi Brunello on the corso Palladio, where the ground-floor arcade tends toward roundheaded arches while on the loggia of the *piano nobile* reliefs of classical putti and Roman emperors are set in spandrels (plate 23).[11] The most remarkable shift in taste came with the Casa Pigafetta, singled out for praise by Sanudo during his visit of 1482. Begun in 1444, the house was extensively rebuilt around the same time as Palazzo Braschi Brunello was going up. It has a small facade, one entirely of stone, which makes it a rarity in Vicenza. The stone employed was the reddish *marmo di Chiampo*, also used for the facade of the cathedral, and no element of its surface was left unadorned, from the ground floor with reliefs of entwined roses and the motto *Il n'est rose sans éspine* to the upper floors where Gothic and Renaissance motifs vie for attention. Whimsical and not without French chivalric overtones, the Casa Pigafetta represents the extreme of elaborately wrought facades found in a more Gothic idiom on the Palazzo

23. Architect unknown. Loggia of the Palazzo Braschi Brunello on corso Palladio, Vicenza, late fifteenth century.

Garzadori Fattore.[12] Both palaces preserve the rich effect prized by fifteenth-century Vicentine patrons, an effect that the poetaster Giovan Battista Dragoncino evoked as "proud palaces with facades and foundations of adamantine rustication."[13] Gilded and painted, the late fifteenth-century palaces of Vicenza underscored the wealth and aspirations of its citizens.

The earliest signs of the Renaissance style were derivative and often seem little more than an overlay of new elements on older ones. Sometimes, as with the Palazzo Sangiovanni on contrà Santissimi Apostoli, a Gothic loggia has been "modernized" by the introduction of Corinthian columns, swags, and putti. The result looks incongruous, wedged as it is between a pointed arch below and a Gothic loggia above. Such attempts at bringing older buildings into line with more contemporary tastes were not uncommon even though they betrayed a lack of understanding of the principles behind Renaissance design. The mongrel nature of such architecture was probably what Palladio had in mind when he condemned "the old style, which had no merit in it" in the introduction to the second book of the *Quattro Libri.*[14]

The improvements made to the loggia of the Palazzo Sangiovanni must date from the early sixteenth century, shortly before Palladio joined the workshop that has been credited with this conversion.[15] No doubt Palladio had occasion to participate in similar work as well as larger projects during his years with the Pedemuro workshop and through his experience of Trissino's villa at Cricoli.[16] What is probably his first and, in terms of surviving drawings, best documented palace is not mentioned in the *Quattro Libri* but nonetheless shows his grasp of the new style from Central Italy. The work in question is the Casa Civena, which stands on the edge of

24. Facade of the Casa Civena, Vicenza.

town facing the Retrone River (plate 24). The house was altered around 1750, expanded in the nineteenth century, and suffered serious damage during World War II.[17] Construction probably began in 1540, the date on a foundation medal mentioned in an eighteenth-century account; this was also the year in which Andrea di Pietro dalla Gondola was first recorded by his nickname of Palladio.[18] Casa Civena was built on the site of a house previously owned by the humanist Aurelio Dall'Acqua, who had commissioned the new high altar of the cathedral from Palladio's old workshop between 1534 and 1536 (plate 6). Dall'Acqua died in March 1539, and his heirs disposed of the property to the four Civena brothers. It is tempting to see the project as having been initiated by Dall'Acqua and then taken over by the Civena where they acquired the property. There are grounds for assuming this to have been the case: Dall'Acqua is known to have had dealings with the Pedemuro bottega and belonged to the same intellectual circles as Trissino and Palladio's other early patrons while little is known of the Civena family; by the same token, his death came so close to the beginning of construction as to strengthen the plausibility of seeing Dall'Acqua as the original instigator. In any case, the house was well advanced by April 1542, although the last payment to the builders only came in 1546.[19]

Since Casa Civena has undergone so many changes, Palladio's intentions can best be appreciated by the series of preliminary drawings and in the plan first published by Bertotti Scamozzi.[20] The drawings share a U-shaped plan, a similar distribution of rooms in the wings, an entrance hall, twin staircases, and a facade consisting of a covered arcade on the ground floor.

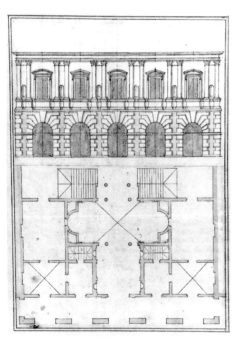

25. *Project for the Casa Civena,* c. 1541–42. (RIBA XVII/14.) Pen, ink, and wash over incised lines and chalk underdrawing, 32.3 x 23.1 cm.

Palladio evidently put his greatest efforts into one of them (plate 25), the most elaborate of the suite of drawings. It consists of a plan and elevation, not drawn to the same scale but pasted together for presentation. The plan here pays homage to Bramante's Roman architecture: the square entrance hall is articulated by niches flanked by pilasters and opens onto a crossing with apses in a manner reminiscent of Bramante's church of San Biagio della Pagnotta, which Palladio may have sketched on his first trip to Rome; the combination of cross-vaulting and columnar screens further points to Bramantesque works inspired by the antique, such as the nymphaeum at Genazzano.[21] Whatever its source, the significance invested in the entrance hall and stairs is remarkable for such a small palace. In part this can be explained through the nature of the patronage, which was a *fraterna* or group of brothers planning to occupy the house jointly. Hence, the emphasis on two large staircases in the preliminary studies must reflect a division of the house down the middle with parity maintained by identical sets of rooms.[22] Hence, too, the upgrading of the vestibule as a common area that would have functioned as an additional room in warmer months; its enhancement by vaulting and Serlian arches would have made it more than a typical entrance passageway.

The facade of Casa Civena complements the Central Italian resonances of the plan. The drawn elevation displays handsome rusticated arches on the ground floor and paired Corinthian pilasters framing pedimented windows above. This is more elaborate than the facade as exe-

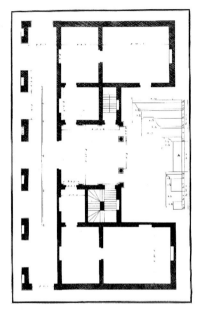

cuted. As has often been said, Bramante's Palazzo Caprini or House of Raphael (plate 13), was the ultimate source for this basic formula.[23] Palladio would have initially been acquainted with Bramante's design through Sanmicheli's variations on it in his Veronese palaces. The distinctive pattern of the ground floor rustication in plate 25 is similar to that on the town side of Sanmicheli's Porta Nuova, which was finished by 1540, and on the Raphaelesque Palazzo Caffarelli Vidoni in Rome.[24] Such conspicuous borrowings are what one would expect from a fledgling architect learning through imitation—Palladio had not yet mastered the sources of the new Roman style, and it was only during the 1540s that he began to speak with his own distinctive voice.

The scaling down of the Casa Civena project may have been dictated by one brother's pulling out of the *fraterna* in April 1542, at a moment when designs may still have been fluid as far as the entrance hall and stairs were concerned.[25] As built, the house preserved the U-shape of the earliest project with more modest staircases and the "Palladian" sequence of small, medium, and large rooms to either side of the vestibule (plate 26). Though amplified in the eighteenth century, the vestibule still retains vestiges of its original form: a segmental vault and Serlian arch anticipate the more ambitious atrium of Palazzo da Porto Festa or the Villa Pisani at Montagnana (plates 27, 88). We know little of what the inner rooms looked like because extensive changes have destroyed their original appearance; externally, the facade remains (plate 24), but its impact has been diluted by the nineteenth-century blocks that flank it. The portal beneath the arcade contains rusticated Tuscan pilasters supporting a broken pediment—a copy of a Roman doorway

26. *(top) Plan of the Casa Civena*, from Ottavio Bertotti Scamozzi, *Le fabbriche e i disegni di Andrea Palladio*, 1796.

27. *(above)* Vestibule of the Casa Civena.

that Serlio dubbed "licentious" and the type of mannerism Palladio would later condemn in the *Quattro Libri*.[26] The main facade consists of five bays; a rusticated ground-floor arcade with sunken panels suggests a modified Serlian arch with oculi, a type of solution favored by the architect in early villa drawings and in his projects for the Basilica (plates 55, 79).[27] Paired Corinthian pilasters flank windows with alternating triangular and segmental pediments; here, too, in its flat, two-dimensional quality, the appearance comes close to facades by Sanmicheli and Falconetto, but it also reflects the basic *piano nobile* solution later adopted in Palazzo Thiene (plate 31). As with virtually all of Palladio's domestic facades, that of Casa Civena is brick rendered to look like stone, with true stone dressings for important elements like imposts, string courses, window frames, and bases and capitals of the orders. In addition, the Casa Civena demonstrated Palladio's eye for detail through such motifs as the connecting molding between the bases and capitals of the pilasters and through his feeling for the effect of rustication (although this latter has been compromised by the restoration after the war).

Palladio's interest in Roman palace facades of the previous generation is also recorded in a series of drawings, all probably for the same unknown project (plates 28, 29).[28] They appear to date from the period of the Casa Civena and show the architect experimenting not only with variations on the House of Raphael but also with designs by Raphael himself. The drawings exhibit a tripartite division of the facade with a mixture of large and small orders, aedicules, and rustication. As a group, they share the timidity and two-dimensional quality of the Casa Civena's facade and of some of the early villa studies. The most Raphaelesque is plate 29, which also seems the earliest and least developed. On both floors it employs a solution like that of the *piano nobile* of Palazzo Branconio dell'Aquila (plate 30); equally Raphaelesque is the rusticated ground floor of plate 28, copied from the distinctive Roman palace designed for Jacopo de Brescia.[29] Most notable, perhaps, is the inclusion of a motif that would later gain Palladio fame, the temple pediment. Here, the pediment has been integrated with the roof of the house, much as was the case in a contemporary villa like that for the Pisani at Bagnolo (plate 43). But the full exploitation of the pediment in Palladio's palace and villa facades remained almost a decade away.

Such early drawings reveal the architect's slow mastery of the new style, but if any one project served as a catalyst in accelerating Palladio's development, it would have been Palazzo Thiene. Work was well advanced on the Casa Civena when he first became involved with this most ambitious of his domestic projects. As published in the *Quattro Libri*, the palace would have occupied an oblong block in the heart of the city, bounded by the contrà Porti to the west, the

28. *(opposite, top) Facade project for unidentified palace,* early 1540s. (RIBA XVII/19.) Pen, ink, and wash over incised lines, 21.9 x 26.5 cm.

29. *(opposite, bottom) Facade project for unidentified palace,* early 1540s. (RIBA XVII/26.) Pen, ink, and wash over incised lines, 14.2 x 22 cm.

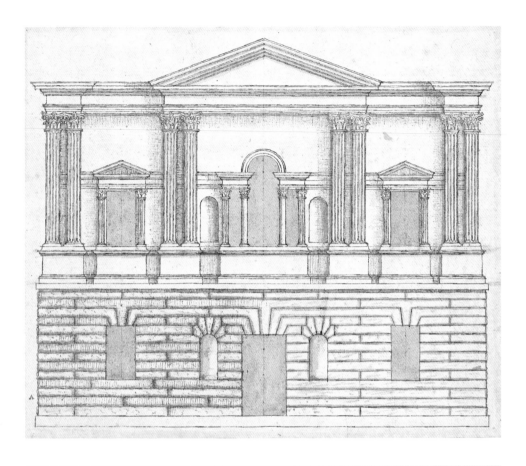

FACCIATA DEL PALAZZO ET HABBITATIONE DI RAFAELE SANTIO DA VRBINO SV LA VIA DI BORGHONOVO FABRICATO
CON SVO DISENGNO L'ANNO MD·XIII·IN
CIRCA E SEGVITO DA BRAMANTE DA VRBINO

small stradella di San Gaetano to the east, an even smaller alleyway called the stradella della Banca Popolare to the north, and the corso to the south (plate 31). Conceived for Marc'antonio and Adriano Thiene, the palace, with its four wings ranged around a monumental courtyard (plates 32, 176), would easily have outdistanced any other Vicentine project by Palladio, in terms of both scale and adherence to a Roman style. But only a fraction of the design was ever realized, and its dating and even Palladio's authorship have been called into question.[30]

The Thiene were one of the wealthiest, if not *the* wealthiest, family in Vicenza, holding extensive estates in the countryside as well as substantial property in town.[31] Already in the fifteenth century they had built two adjacent palaces on the contrà Porti, one a Gothic house of the first half of the century, the other a larger early Renaissance structure dating from the 1490s.[32] The latter palace was ordered by Ludovico Thiene, the grandfather of Palladio's patrons, and designed by Lorenzo da Bologna, who also built the choirs of the Cathedral and the church of Santa Corona. Ludovico's palace has an imposing, two-story facade with diamondlike rustication on the contrà Porti and a second wing extending almost the whole length of the stradella della Banca Popolare. It was thus L-shaped in plan and probably had a loggia on two sides of the courtyard; the concept of a palace occupying all or part of the large block may

30. Raphael (1483–1520). *Facade of the Palazzo Branconio dell'Aquila, Rome.* Engraved by P. Ferrerio and published 1655. Building executed between 1518 and 1520.

have originated with Ludovico Thiene and was then fostered by Ludovico's son Giangaleazzo, who had an unspecified building project in hand in 1524–25.[33]

The next stage in the development of the site came with Giangaleazzo's sons, who concluded a contract with two stonemasons for the construction of a house on the space now occupied by the Palladian building in 1542. Here, too, information is scanty; no sum of money is mentioned, nor is the scale of the house indicated even though mention is made of dressed stone and pilasters to be furnished. *"Magistrum Andream quondam Petri,"* (that is, Palladio) appears in the contract as a witness, something taken as a sign of his involvement; the document's date has occasionally been interpreted as the origin of the project, later published in his treatise.[34] Indeed Palladio's involvement would seem remarkably unproblematic were it not for the fact that the British architect Inigo Jones jotted down the following comment on the Palazzo Thiene in his copy of the *Quattro Libri:* "Scamozzi . . . saith that thes designs wear of Julio Romano and executid by Palladio & so yt seems."[35] Jones visited Vicenza in 1614 and studied Palladio's architecture extensively; he also had the advantage of drawing firsthand upon the knowledge of Vincenzo Scamozzi, the most gifted architect of the generation after Palladio. Born in 1552, Scamozzi grew up in Vicenza and had a thorough familiarity with Palladio's career, although his opinions were colored by an antipathy verging on the pathological. So while Scamozzi's pronouncements must be taken cautiously, the question remains: What role did Palladio play in designing the Palazzo Thiene?

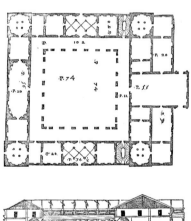

31. *(left)* Exterior of the Palazzo Thiene, Vicenza.

32. *(above) Plan and section of the Palazzo Thiene* from the *Quattro Libri.*

Standing today in the stradella di San Gaetano, one sees a two-story fabric of seven bays with a further three bays merging into an older building around the corner. The external facades constitute an essay in rustication, the ground floor consisting of large, rough-hewn blocks of local sandstone from the Monti Berici as well a bands of bricks hammered to achieve a rocklike texture. The ground floor is punctuated by windows and courses, the windows surmounted by lunettes of which the keystone abuts the string course above. On the *piano nobile*, the rustication is toned down to give the effect of smooth chamfered blocks overlaid by Composite pilasters and broken by sandstone aedicules with Ionic columns and banded rustication. Textures are further enriched by the Ionic entablature moldings that run between the aedicules as well as the smooth bands linking the Composite capitals. The effect is similar to early facade studies like plate 28 but richer, the elements not so much contrasting with each other as being brought into equilibrium through the medium of rustication. The format is altered on the interior facades, where the ground floor becomes a succession of arches constructed of uneven, cyclopean blocks of sandstone with corresponding arches framed by Composite pilasters on the *piano nobile*.[36]

Even in its unfinished state, the concept of Palazzo Thiene distinguishes itself from any other Palladian palace in the extent to which it is steeped in the language of Giulio Romano. Indeed, the facades and some interior features are so much in Giulio's mode as to give added weight to Scamozzi's pronouncement. This is especially true of the street facade, which reads like an enlarged copy of Giulio's Roman house with its varied rustication, projecting voussoirs, and, above all, its distinctive window tabernacles. The unusually tall proportions of the *piano nobile* and the placement of the pilaster bases directly upon the string course finds a specific parallel in Giulio's Palazzo Stati Maccarani in Rome while the introduction of an attic above the *piano nobile* of the courtyard is reminiscent of the original appearance of the facades of Giulio's Palazzo del Te.[37] An equally striking mark of Giulio's style can be seen in the Tuscan columns of the vestibule; there the column shafts have been left unpolished, a metaphoric extension of the rusticated facades found previously only in the atrium of the Palazzo del Te (plates 18, 33).

The Palazzo Thiene distances itself so conspicuously from Palladio's early palace and villa designs that it is difficult not to concur with Scamozzi. It does seem plausible, as has been suggested recently, that Marc'antonio and Adriano Thiene solicited a design from Giulio, then the most distinguished architect available.[38] The Thiene had long-standing connections with Mantua, where Giulio was based, and may well have engineered the invitation to Giulio at the end of 1542 to consult on the arcading of the Basilica. Certainly at that time he could have elaborated upon his initial proposals, though he was known to send designs for projects at a long distance without being personally involved.[39] From the *Quattro Libri* we know, too, that the Thiene brothers were keen amateurs of architecture, and in this context the strongly Giulian nature of both their palace and their villa at the nearby village of Quinto gains in significance. In both one finds the same reworking of Giulio's vocabulary and a similarly Roman ground plan, elements that are quite removed from Palladio's general practice at this date. The excep-

tional character of both designs must reflect the brothers' taste and ambitions more than Palladio's, not unlike the later case of the Barbaro villa at Maser.[40]

For Giulio, the oblong Vicentine site would have conjured up major Roman buildings like the Cancelleria, Palazzo Farnese, or even his own Palazzo del Te in Mantua, and one can imagine him proposing something along similar lines to the Thiene. Indeed the audacity of the project bears a resemblance to the architect's utopian recommendation to the Vicentine town council for isolating the Basilica in the center of a large square surrounded by arcading.[41] Such a concept would have struck an alien note in Vicenza at that time, but it is just the sort of grandiloquent gesture one would expect from an architect trained at the court of Leo X and accustomed to planning on a large scale. In contrast, Palladio was only beginning his career in 1542, still a relatively unproven commodity and, if his early drawings are anything to judge by, not yet capable of producing such a bold and unconventional design. Consequently, it is very easy to imagine that the proposal that eventually found its way into the *Quattro Libri* sprang from the fertile brain of Giulio Romano. But whatever Giulio proposed in his short visit to Vicenza

33. Atrium of the Palazzo Thiene.

cannot have been comprehensive nor could he have supervised the construction. This worked to Palladio's advantage, for he would have been the only local architect capable of understanding and directing such an undertaking.

Nevertheless, the project must have undergone a slow gestation and evidence suggests that it may only have gotten underway by the mid-1540s. In 1546 Marc'antonio Thiene was recon-firmed in his knighthood and about that time his brother-in-law Iseppo da Porto may have begun plans for his new palace in the contrà Porti, making it a propitious moment for serious building to begin on a new Thiene palace.[42] Over the next decade the basic Giulian design was subjected to alteration so that it became less like Giulio's own work and more like Palladio's, especially as it moved from the ground to the first floor. Thus the articulation of the *piano nobile* finds parallels in earlier facade designs like plates 28 and 58, and details such as the Composite pilasters, balustrades, and the cornice are typically Palladian. Even the famous tetrastyle atrium has been subtly reworked, both in proportions and in its vaulting; as executed, it resembles the kind of cross-vaulted atria found in the Palazzo da Porto Festa or the Villa Pisani at Montag-nana (plate 88) rather than Giulio Romano's barrel-vaulted atrium at the Te.[43] Palladio clearly used the experience of building Palazzo Thiene as a way of getting inside Giulio's architectural personality, much as he mastered the conventions of Central Italian palaces.

It may well be that the Thiene brothers intended to embark upon the new palace as the first stage in a larger project that eventually crystallized in the plan of the *Quattro Libri*, whose pages display the magnitude of the brothers' ambition (plate 32). The palace would not only have occupied a sizable chunk of the city center, it would also have been the largest structure on the corso, complete with portico and an entrance 55 Vicentine feet deep. Its dimensions would have exceeded those of Palazzo Strozzi in Florence and rivalled Palazzo Farnese in Rome: extending some 130 Vicentine feet, the main facade would have dominated the corso; the prin-cipal entrance would have been flanked by workshops with mezzanines above while on the *piano nobile* identical suites, each two rooms deep, were projected.[44] The other three wings would have been only one room deep, those on the east and west wing mirroring one another while the northern wing would have had a central ovoid *salone* similar to the vestibule in the later Palazzo Chiericati (plate 42). Each corner would have had an octagonal room, inspired by those found in the Baths of Caracalla or more directly by the Odeo Cornaro (plate 2). Their deployment here had a practical as well as an aesthetic rationale: the shape gave Palladio a way to mask the irregularities at the corner of the palace where walls were thicker and the two wings were not in perfect alignment.

Examining the plan in the *Quattro Libri*, one can also see that it was simply devised through the replication of the east and west wings and the closing of the block by what would become for Palladio a fairly typical domestic ground plan on the corso wing. Sketches by Palladio con-firm that the grandiose project was already being planned by the mid-1540s and remained viable into the next decade.[45]

By the end of 1551 construction had evolved to the extent that the interior decoration was being planned. This aspect of the palace is often cited in discussions of chronology, but it is of equal importance in understanding how thoroughly the architect and his patrons were adapting the new Central Italian style. The sculptor Alessandro Vittoria, who proved himself to be the most gifted stuccoist of his generation at Palazzo Thiene, is documented as being in residence there by the end of 1551 and remained into the first months of 1553; rooms like the palazzo's *sala dei principi* are justly celebrated as among the high points of Veneto plaster-work (plate 34).[46] The stuccoist Bartolomeo Ridolfi may have worked alongside Vittoria initially but eventually replaced him upstairs in the *sala dei miti*. The frescoing by Anselmo Canera and Bernardino India, with grotesques by Eliodoro Forbicini, must have taken place about the same time as Vittoria's work.

The overall effect is of a richness unparalleled in Vicentine palaces. Palladio had previously demonstrated a sensitivity to novel interior effects in his early palace and villa designs, as can be seen in the *salone* of the Villa Pisani at Bagnolo (plate 66), but the sophistication and variety found in Palazzo Thiene is of a higher order. From an architectural standpoint, the most notable aspect of the palace is the range of ceilings introduced by Palladio, including a domical vault on the ground floor with a proper cupola above, as well as pavilion and barrel vaults. Both the shapes of the vaults and their decorative programs inevitably reflect the examples of the Odeo Cornaro in Padua, Giulio Romano's work in Mantua, and, notably, Sanmicheli's Palazzo Canossa in Verona. The interiors of Palazzo Canossa preceded those of Palazzo Thiene only by a few years at the most and contained vaulted ceilings with frescoes and plasterwork by artists who subsequently entered Palladio's circle.[47] This could hardly be coincidental, given the ties between Palladio and Sanmicheli and the proximity of Verona to Vicenza.

It was a peculiar feature of Verona that several families produced generations of artists and architects during the Renaissance—Sanmicheli himself came from this milieu, as did Paolo Veronese, Battista Zelotti, Bernardino India, Anselmo Canera, and Battista dal Moro, to name but a few. Often related by marriage and forming a cohesive social set, they also responded in similar ways to the new style fostered by Sanmicheli and by Giulio Romano in nearby Mantua. Some, like Francesco Torbido and Battista dal Moro, had experience working after designs by Giulio Romano, and the Veronese artists around Sanmicheli formed an informal team ready to follow suggestions and to amplify basic decorative schemes.

Palladio was drawn to these artists by virtue of common interests and shared links with Sanmicheli. Their assimilation into his projects around 1550 can also be seen as part of the wholesale adoption of Central Italian models by Palladio's patrons, just as Marc'antonio Thiene's marriage to a member of the Veronese aristocracy must have encouraged the use of Veronese artists in Palazzo Thiene. Palladio's exact role in this process has been frequently debated and will concern us again later. Obviously, his recourse to the same artists in a succession of projects stemmed from the architect's personal preference, but it was also related to the

34. Alessandro Vittoria (1525–1608). Ceiling of the *sala dei principi* of the Palazzo Thiene.

effects he introduced into domestic architecture, namely, varying the heights and designs of ceilings to suit their other dimensions. This approach went back to Alberti, who advocated a pleasing variety in the shapes and decoration of rooms, and it had been practiced by Raphael and Giulio Romano.[48] Up to a point, Palladio would certainly have had a hand in determining the role of his decorators, if not in assigning, for instance, subject matter. The themes of the surviving frescoes in Palazzo Thiene are exclusively classical, ranging from the stories of Proserpina and Psyche to the *Aeneid* and Ovid's *Metamorphoses,* and draw upon models like Villa Madama and Palazzo del Te. Here, Palladio probably had little to offer his collaborators, but he would have had more to say when considering the general layout of vaults. Thus Palladio may have suggested to Vittoria that he adapt the frescoed scheme of the octagon of the Odeo Cornaro for the ceiling of the *sala dei principi,* although the amplification of detail would have been left to the sculptor. The bust of Henry II of France among the worthies of ancient Rome must reflect the wishes of the patrons to celebrate the family's strong links with the French court.[49] The sumptuousness of the surviving interiors, especially in a small room like the *sala dei miti,* conveys an idea of the grandeur in which the Thiene lived.

The great project for a quadrangular palace did not survive the 1550s, the death of Adriano Thiene in 1550 and of his brother ten years later effectively putting an end to the idea. Construction ground to a halt between 1556 and 1558, the dates inscribed on the external and internal string courses of the palace. On the eastern facade, only seven of the projected twelve bays were carried out, and only three bays on the northern facade. Marc'antonio's son Ottavio established himself as a *condottiere,* spending little time in Vicenza, and with the death of his son Giulio in 1633 Marc'antonio's line was extinguished. Though the palace remained in Thiene hands until 1871, no more was done to it.[50] Palladio's publication of the whole plan in the *Quattro Libri* left the patrons' intentions as a matter of public record, though he must have realized that it was a dead letter. Obviously there are inaccuracies in the published design (plate 32). For one thing the irregularities of the site have been tidied up and basic problems such as the difference in height between the corso and the courtyard have not been addressed. In addition, the plan shifts inexplicably from ground to first floor on the main block, and there is precious little evidence of how the facade would have looked.[51] The four pages devoted to the palace in the *Quattro Libri* do, however, constitute the strongest proof that Palladio felt the project to be his own. His modifications to its Giulian origins and his supervision of it earned him that right.

Despite its contradictory elements the project for Palazzo Thiene was not as implausible as is sometimes suggested, given that the Thiene owned over two-thirds of the land on the proposed block and obviously wished to build on a significantly larger scale than any other Vicentine family. The external facade shows signs of having been broken off unexpectedly, but judging by the placement of the portal the intention was to extend the eastern wing to the present-day corso, the point that the three non-Thiene properties began. Marc'antonio and his brother may have hoped that the family would realize the project by stages in successive generations, much as occurred with the Palazzo Chiericati.[52] Instead, it remains a splendid fragment, one considered by some of Palladio's contemporaries, even in its incomplete state, as "the most beautiful and embellished palace that exists in the magnificent city of Vicenza."[53]

Palazzo Thiene may have marked the beginning of Palladio's ascendancy in Vicenza, but the palace of Iseppo da Porto was the earliest example of what became a standard Palladian solution. The Porto were among the most prominent of Vicentine families and enjoyed a close political alliance with the Thiene, a connection cemented by the engagement of Iseppo to Livia Thiene, the sister of Palladio's patrons, in 1542.[54] Iseppo's marriage and the close proximity of his palace to that of the Thiene have often been regarded as the prime elements leading to Palladio's commission. While this is undoubtedly true, there would have been an element of competition as well. The contrà Porti, the street on which Iseppo built, was the visible power base of his family and boasted several Gothic palaces, including the splendid Colleoni Porto and Porto Breganze (plate 21). Iseppo's uncle Francesco had greatly enriched himself as paymaster of the Venetian army and held court in the Palazzo Colleoni Porto as well as in the family's large Gothic villa at Thiene.[55] (It was for the courtyard of Palazzo Colleoni Porto that Serlio designed a classical wooden theater in 1539, a structure, like Trissino's villa at Cricoli, that presaged the new style in Vicenza.) Little is known of Iseppo's personality, but he clearly saw the commission of a new and extensive palace as a means of enhancing his own reputation vis-à-vis his uncle and the Thiene.

Family tradition had it that an older Gothic palace on the site had burned down, and as early as 1543 Iseppo was contemplating a building project on adjacent property.[56] His ideas soon took shape, for the new house was already habitable by December 9, 1549, the date da Porto drew up a contract with a stonemason named Giacomo di Merlino for the completion of the palace's facade. The contract specifies that the stonemason should complete the remaining part of the facade "in the manner and form of the facade now finished," over the course of three years: the first for the ground floor, the second for the *piano nobile*, and the last for the attic.[57] The contract must have been faithfully executed, for the date of 1552 could once be seen on the facade and inscribed on a fireplace within.

The most important information to be gleaned from the contract is that both the palace and part of its facade were already standing by the end of 1549, which would place the genesis of the palace in the mid-1540s. Such a dating would make sense in terms of Iseppo da Porto's marriage and of the initial stages of the Palazzo Thiene. The two enterprises can be seen as much closer in conception than was previously believed, which lends color to the suggestion of competition between the two families. At the same time it throws an unusual light on domestic building practices, for the facade may have been left in a state of some uncertainty until a late stage, when only a portion was completed. This may seem strange, but the practice has analogies with religious architecture, where the facade was invariably the last component to be built.[58] Why such a practice was adopted here cannot be explained, although it may reflect a change of workshop. In any case, the first stages of Palazzo da Porto Festa must have been underway by 1546 at the latest. If the palace was being built by that date then the preliminary studies have to be placed around 1545, thus indicating that Palladio's thoughts on domestic architecture matured rapidly in the first half of the decade. The surviving drawings are noteworthy because they show the architect pulling together various strands from earlier villa and palace projects. The drawings include ground plans and studies for the facade, the former proving that Palladio and his patron thought in terms of two residential blocks from the start.[59] In both drawings, the

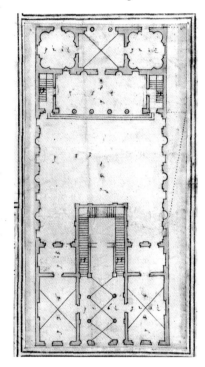

main block on contrà Porti is conceived as a simple sequence of five internal spaces, two lateral rooms flanking the vestibule on either side. The more ambitious (plate 35) contains an unusually deep entrance with cross vaulting reminiscent of the vestibules of the Theater of Marcellus, terminating in twin staircases that project into the courtyard. The courtyard itself, articulated by pilasters that flank niches on the side walls, ends in a small structure reminiscent of one of Palladio's early villas. Like the main block, this *villino* has two stories and a central loggia, probably of the same (Doric?) order as the pilasters in the courtyard. The suite of rooms behind its loggia demonstrates the variety found in the early villa drawings, even down to the central motif of cross vaulting and a Serlian arch. These drawings give us, in essence, the concept of main block and satellite that eventually found its way into the later, even more ambitious project for the *Quattro Libri* (plate 190). The inspiration for this solution stemmed from a similar grouping of buildings in Alvise Cornaro's Odeo and Loggia (plate 4), and the overlapping of these drawings with the early villa designs indicates that Palladio did not yet think of palaces and villas as essentially distinct types. The second block was never realized at Palazzo Porto, possibly because of difficulties over the property, and the project eventually published in the *Quattro Libri* belongs to a later chapter in the architect's career.[60]

The remaining drawings deal with the facade and chronicle the movement toward its definitive solution.[61] Their initial concern appears to be with rustication, manifest through the various mixtures of brick and ashlar, of rougher versus more polished effects. Palladio's evident dissatisfaction with all alternatives is reflected in the totally different effect found in the facade as built (plate 38). Of these sheets, plate 37 is the most interesting in

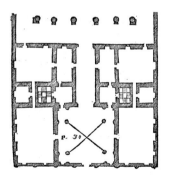

35. (*top*) *Alternative plan for the Palazzo Porto.* Pen, ink, and wash over incised lines, 19 x 18.3 cm. (RIBA XVI/8c.)

36. (*above*) *Detail of plan for the Palazzo Porto* from the *Quattro Libri.*

terms of the alternative solutions proposed for the facade. Among other things, the drawings prove that by the mid-1540s Palladio had evolved the proportions of the orders that were to remain a constant feature of his later architecture. Their employment in plate 37 is tied to different solutions proposed for the upper part of the facade. On the right, the facade is conceived as one floor, articulated by Corinthian pilasters on a high socle and framing windows with alternating triangular and segmental pediments, as well as mezzanine windows ultimately derived from Raphael's Palazzo Branconio dell'Aquila (plate 30). The more slender proportions of the Corinthian pilasters (here slightly more than I:10) convey a sense of lightness to the *piano nobile* and were later adapted for the upper floor of Palazzo Chiericati. For the alternative on the left, the same basic features have been rearranged to produce a different effect. Here for the first time Palladio employed an engaged order on a facade and began to explore more plastic effects. The shorter Ionic semicolumns rest directly on the string course and support a tall attic, while the entablature is enriched by another echo of Raphael, a convex frieze similar to that found on the garden facade of the Villa Madama.

As executed, the facade corresponds very closely to the left-hand alternative in plate 37, the most notable divergence coming on the ground floor where simple ashlar blocks rest upon a sandstone basement. The treatment of the rustication is shallower, less in the mode of Palazzo Thiene, and is enlivened only by blind arches and mascarons. Above, the first floor and attic cor-

37. *Alternative facade solutions for the Palazzo Porto.* (RIBA XVII/9r.) Pen, ink, and wash over incised lines, 28.3 x 40.6 cm.

respond to the elevation drawing without the convex frieze but with a complement of plastic decoration. To compensate for the absence of the distinctive frieze, Palladio did introduce a learned feature here in the form of columns that have a Vitruvian base as opposed to the standard attic one[62]—the device is typical of Palladio's eye for detail, and also served to advertise his familiarity with antique architecture. The attic conjures up reminiscences of the Arch of Constantine and its captives, but here the central figures are not prisoners but rather Iseppo da Porto and his second son, Leonida, in antique dress.[63]

38. Facade of the Palazzo da Porto Festa, Vicenza.

Palladio's facade is more compact than its Gothic neighbors but imposes its presence on the street through its height and dominant position (plate 38). The oblique line of the frontage probably follows the foundations of an earlier building, but this is used to advantage since it creates the effect of a small square and renders the facade more conspicuous. The ground floor has been given monumental proportions with respect to the upper floor, doubtless to emulate the nearby Palazzo Thiene, but the *piano nobile*, which lacks comparable height, appears pressed between the lower floor and attic.[64] In its proportions, the Palazzo Porto differs from, say, the House of Raphael, for the ground floor in Vicentine palaces was normally inhabited by the owner and contained reception rooms. It is taller, and its verticality is emphasized by the proportions of the windows and by the projection of the entablature, continued by the pilaster strips and statues of the attic. The final impression is of a closed but powerfully defined surface.

The ground floor of the palace is dominated by the large atrium that leads through a narrow passageway to the courtyard. Articulated by four Doric columns and supporting a handsome cross vault (plate 36), the atrium is the first sign of Palladio's mature style in interior design. Eight semicolumns correspond to the columns and flank niches or the doorways on the main axis. As a type, Palladio's atrium developed naturally from the Serlian arches of the Casa Civena and the atrium of Palazzo Thiene; it was also informed by Vitruvius's account of tetrastyle atria in Roman houses.[65] In general, Palladio favored a regular cube as the shape of this room because the distance between the columns would be equal to their height and because they "support a vault and render the area above secure," as the architect put it. The solution was handsome, robust, and practical (since it reduced fire hazard) while embodying the intersection of the functional and aesthetic that recurred continually in Palladio's architecture. In his later villas and palaces, this kind of atrium metamorphosed into a *salone,* capable of being placed anywhere along the central core of the house (plate 88).

Only two rooms on the left-hand side of Palazzo Porto's ground floor now retain some semblance of their original appearance, the rest, including an oval staircase installed by Scamozzi, having been swept away by wholesale redecoration in the early nineteenth century.[66] Paintings by Veronese and Domenico Brusasorzi and stuccowork by Ridolfi had been created here about the same time as the Palazzo Thiene was being decorated by some of the same artists. The presence of the overlapping "mafia" of Veronese artists can be explained by competition between the Thiene and da Porto families for their services, but another reason may have been the aggregation of Iseppo da Porto and several other members of his family into Veronese citizenship and, hence, the Veronese aristocracy, in 1546. This would have opened direct contact between da Porto and Verona, thus rendering him better disposed toward Veronese artists than may otherwise have been the case. Da Porto was obviously a discerning patron since he commissioned two handsome and early full-length portraits of himself and his wife from Veronese.[67] Iseppo da Porto maintained an interest in architecture and connections with Palladio down to his death in 1580. He served as an overseer of the Basilica arcades between 1561 and 1562 and, as an executive member of the town council, authorized construction of the Loggia del Capitaniato in 1571–72. Around the same time he embarked on a villa at Molina, near his uncle's holdings at Thiene, for which Palladio furnished the design. Though both the palace and villas remained in the da Porto family, neither were altered after Iseppo's lifetime.[68]

Palazzo Chiericati, the last of Palladio's early palaces, followed close upon the projects for the Thiene and da Porto (plate 39). When the architect received four gold scudi for his drawings in November 1550, Girolamo Chiericati noted that the designs were ready "many months before." Certainly the palace has many features that recall earlier projects like the Casa Civena as well as the great villa projects of the decade to come.[69] Palazzo Chiericati proved more pivotal in the long run, however, and marked a quantitative leap in Palladio's development as an architect.

Any discussion of Palazzo Chiericati must take into account its site, a long but narrow parcel of land at the eastern edge of the town. There the corso debouched into an irregular piazza called the *isola*, which served as a river port as well as a cattle and wood market. The family palace of the Chiericati bordered on the *Isola*, although it faced the corso. Adjacent to the palace, however, there were three smaller houses that faced the square, and these were inherited by Girolamo in a division of family property with his brothers in 1546. At that time Girolamo reserved the right to build on his property, intentions that must have quickened when he was appointed one of the overseers of the Basilica arcades in 1548.[70] The experience also brought him into close contact with Palladio, whose architecture impressed him very much. Chiericati advocated Palladio's project for the Basilica arcades at the decisive council meeting in April 1549, so it was no coincidence that Chiericati opened the account book for his own palace the same month that he became overseer of the Basilica arcades in November 1550.[71] By then, Palladio had prepared the drawings that were presented to the town council a few months later.

The confines in which Palladio had to build presented him with an unusual challenge not entirely dissimilar to the Casa Civena. There, too, the site dictated a long narrow building with wings and a central block only one room deep (plate 26). In both cases the setting was on the periphery of town and faced a river, and in both cases living space was maximized by building the upper floor over an arcade. Such solutions were commonplace in Northern Italian cities, and a loggia here must have been in the architect's mind from an early stage. On March 19, 1551, Chiericati petitioned the town council for permission to erect a portico thirteen feet wide along the length of the facade of his proposed new palace. He explained that this would be "for his greater convenience and for the convenience and ornament of the city," and as an inducement he offered the city a slice of his property on the corner of the corso.[72] In the petition, Chiericati mentions that his intentions had been encouraged by "experienced architects and many distinguished citizens," which suggests that Palladio's designs had already been circulated among influential council members like Marc'antonio Thiene and perhaps his colleagues on the Basilica project, Gabriele Capra and Giovanni Alvise Valmarana. Permission was granted and construction began immediately.

Several drawings allow us to reconstruct aspects of the evolving design. Two features emerge as paramount: a loggia is present in some form in all the drawings, and the temple pediment makes its first appearance in the scale and form familiar from Palladio's later works. In plate 41, a separate study for the *piano nobile*, the center of the facade is brought forward to accommodate a five-bay portico while the wings are simply articulated by an engaged order, Composite in the one, Doric and Ionic in the other.[73] This solution, with its full-scale temple pediment, marks a distinctive step toward classic two-story villas like the Villa Cornaro at Piombino Dese and the Villa Pisani at Montagnana (plates 85, 86), and it again shows how fluid were Palladio's distinctions between town and country houses. These drawings probably represented a halfway house between building without a portico—not a serious alternative in view of the narrowness of the site—and the alternative of including a loggia running the length of the facade, as described in the proposal of March 1551. The remaining drawing, actually dating much later and made for the woodcut of the *Quattro Libri,* shows the second solution, which, though it was more expensive, would have been easier to justify to the council than a portico projecting abruptly into the square.

This change to a continuous loggia prompted the dropping of the central pediment, which lost its raison d'être in the new horizontal emphasis of the facade. The new facade design also echoed the tradition of superimposed loggias often found in Veneto houses, albeit by inverting the normal expectations of solids and voids by closing it in the center and opening it at the sides. With elegance and economy, Palladio solved the problem of providing a public right-of-

39. Palazzo Chiericati, Vicenza, 1551.

40. Paintings by Giambattista Zelotti, stuccoing by Bartolomeo Ridolfi. Ceiling of square room in the Palazzo Chiericati.

way while substantially increasing the owner's living space. His solution also demonstrated his sensitivity to the potential of the *Isola*, for the loggias were designed to create a substantial facade at a commanding point in the piazza. The construction of Palazzo Chiericati marked the beginning of the upgrading of this area, further enhanced by Palladio's designs for Palazzo Piovene all'Isola and the Teatro Olimpico.[74]

The importance of the facade to the design as a whole is confirmed by a glance at the ground plan (plate 42). Because the site is so narrow, the palace is only one room deep at the entrance, a situation Palladio disguises by turning the entrance into a handsome, biapsidal vestibule running parallel to the facade. Around the vestibule are grouped symmetrical suites of rooms that move toward a pocket-sized courtyard. They interlock proportionally as their dimensions develop from 12 x 12 to 12 x 18 to 18 x 30, and 16 x 54 for the vestibule, the latter of which, as Ackerman noted, must surely have been meant to be 18 x 54, thus making all proportions multiples of six.[75] The lateral suites terminate in compact spiral staircases for servants while two more monumental staircases for the *signori*, the owner and his family, lie behind the vestibule facing onto the rear loggias. This last feature is of particular interest because it represents the first appearance of a formula that only slightly later finds expression, complete with temple pediment, in the garden facades of the Villa Pisani at Montagnana and the Villa Cornaro at Piombino Dese (plates 87, 85); in plan, it also bears a family resemblance to the portico of the villa that Palladio designed a few years later for Girolamo Chiericati's brother, Giovanni.[76]

Palladio's mastery of design is present not only in the general concept but also in its balance of practical and aesthetic considerations. Like many of his villas, the palace has a semi-basement for the stores and kitchen. This was prudent since the piazza was subject to flooding, and it also meant that the ground and upper floors were free for more ceremonial aspects of civic life. On a symbolic plane the basement created a pedestal for the house, distancing it from the mercantile nature of the piazza below, while the central steps flanked by stylobates preserved something of the original temple-front concept of the earliest designs (plate 41). The ground-floor arcading is unequivocally functional, but the architect's

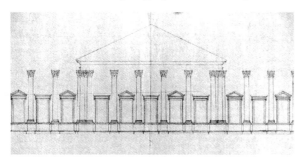

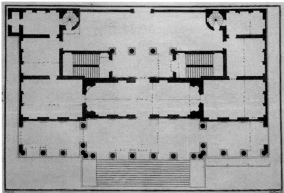

41. *(top) Project for* piano nobile *of the Palazzo Chiericati.* Pen and ink over incised lines, 44.6 x 59 cm. Worcester College Library, Oxford, England, H.T. 93.

42. *(above) Plan of the Palazzo Chiericati,* from Ottavio Bertotti Scamozzi, *Le fabbriche e i disegni di Andrea Palladio,* 1796.

imagination has transformed it into a classical stoa, casting even the soffit in terms of coffering borrowed from Roman triumphal arches (plate 19). The solution for the end bays is also inspired by the antique, in this case by the Portico of Octavia in Rome. It was a work admired and drawn by Palladio, one consisting of a double file of Corinthian columns closed at either end by a relieving arch (plate 12). This motif commended itself to Palladio for the reinforcement of the floor above even as it provided a natural caesura for the building at either end of the arcade. The open nature of the facade lends itself to comparison with villas, a connection that was reinforced by its location on the periphery of Vicenza—again, not unlike the Villa Rotonda.[77] Reminiscent of Bramante's and Raphael's facade for the Vatican Palace or Ferrante Gonzaga's suburban Villa Simonetta near Milan[78] the facade was as resolutely Central Italian in its own way as was that of Palazzo da Porto Festa or the Basilica. By 1551 the Palladian revolution was well launched in Vicenza.

Unfortunately, Palazzo Chiericati was destined to remain a fragmentary signpost of that revolution. Work stopped around 1557 with only four bays realized, a little more than a third of the building. The palace was described as incomplete in Girolamo Chiericati's will of that year, and although his son Valerio moved into the new structure in 1570, construction was effectively abandoned until the facade was brought to conclusion a century later.[79] Enough was built in Palladio's time, however, to create an elegant suite of rooms in the left-hand wing. The rooms have vaults calculated to enhance their other dimensions, a phenomenon also found in the nearly contemporary villas at Poiana, Montagnana, and Piombino Dese. Stucco cornices by Ridolfi accompany frescoes by Brusasorzi, Zelotti, and grotesque work by Forbicini. Once more, echoes of Palazzo del Te and of Sanmicheli's Palazzo Canossa are apparent, and the collaboration of Zelotti and Ridolfi in the pavilion vault of the second stanza (plate 40) is of a quality rarely achieved in contemporary Veneto interiors.[80]

When the neo-Palladian architect Bertotti Scamozzi published a guide to Vicenza in 1761, he described the facade of Palazzo Chiericati as worthy of a prince.[81] It was a perceptive comment, for it laid bare the strategy embraced by Palladio and his patrons in most of his Vicentine projects. Indeed Palazzo Chiericati can be seen as a microcosm of the Palladian phenomenon that, through the quality of design and the unswerving adherence to a new and distinctive style, invested these palaces with a status beyond their actual scale and the relatively humble nature of their materials. The readiness with which the Vicentine aristocracy adopted Palladio and his architecture transformed the face of their city in ways already apparent when Montaigne visited it in 1580. The overlapping of public and private patronage in Palladio's Vicentine career implies, moreover, a deliberate intent on the part of men like Girolamo Chiericati, Iseppo da Porto, and Marc'antonio Thiene, who saw the creation of their own palaces in much the same terms as the building of new arcades for the palace of justice: both gestures reflected honor on their city and on themselves. Palladio's patrons shared a common outlook and a commitment to building based on the assumption that family tastes and economic circumstances would remain constant and that the identity of their *casata* or lineage would be embodied by their *casa* for centuries to come.

EARLY VILLAS AND VILLEGGIATURA

VENICE FACED ONE OF THE MOST SEVERE TESTS OF ITS EXISTENCE AT THE BEGINNING OF THE sixteenth century. The War of the League of Cambrai (1509–16) saw the Republic under interdict from the pope and pitted against the major powers of Europe, its land empire overrun. As the war began, the Venetian nobleman Girolamo Priuli tried to make sense of the collapse of Venetian fortunes by drawing up a list of the principal sins of the city. These included pride, maladministration, debauchery, and homosexuality though, as a banker, Priuli understandably forgot to mention usury in his lament.[1] Convinced that God was punishing Venice for its moral corruption and for straying from its mercantile origins, Priuli cited the acquisition of land in the *terraferma* as one of the most deplorable traits of contemporary Venetians. Noble and commoner alike built palaces and houses within a day's ride of the city and were corrupted by soft living and the delights of the countryside—"instead of merchants they have become peasants without any knowledge of the world."[2] Leaving aside his criticisms, Priuli's remarks are noteworthy because they indicate how commonplace land investment was in the Veneto by the date of Palladio's birth.

Land investment was not an innovation of Priuli's day—many Venetian and Veneto nobles held large estates going back several generations, in some cases centuries—but agriculture did not begin to offer high yields for investment until the turn of the sixteenth century.[3] Venice's acquisition of a large land empire had been prompted in the early fifteenth century by a concern for secure borders, and during the course of the century the substantial land holdings of the

43. The Villa Pisani at Bagnolo (Vicenza).

monastic orders were reorganized in a fashion that sharply increased agricultural profit. Having been allowed to decay, monastic estates were gradually set to rights, often through investments by Venetian nobles: land was drained, canals created, profitable crops like rice planted, and handsome profits were the result. When Venice almost lost its Veneto possessions during the early 1500s, attention was drawn to the mainland, both over concern for steady supplies of food and because of the trend toward higher prices for agricultural produce. The introduction of maize from America created a new market for a grain ideally suited to the plains of the Veneto, and agriculture came to be seen as a safe and potentially lucrative alternative to trade. As Alvise Cornaro put it, agriculture was the true alchemy because it made many monasteries and some private citizens wealthy.[4] The Venetian state established an office to supervise uncultivated land by two decrees of 1545 and 1556, and Venetians were encouraged to invest in the *terraferma* at advantageous prices. By 1564 ecclesiastical holdings in the Veneto were reckoned to produce over one million ducats per annum, more than the income of the Venetian Republic itself from the *terraferma*; in general terms, Venetian income from capital investment in land by clergy and private individuals rose fourfold during the sixteenth century.[5]

It would be wrong to interpret this shift toward land as simply a question of finance or a peculiarly Venetian phenomenon. Italy was never a feudalistic society in the manner of France or England, but the possession of land did carry a social cachet there as well. The fourteenth-century chronicler Giovanni Villani complained of the mania for estates around Florence in terms that anticipate Girolamo Priuli's, and the Venetian ambassador to Florence remarked in 1527 that Florentines "have this weakness, that they go about the world to make a fortune of twenty thousand ducats and then spend ten thousand on a palace outside the city."[6] Throughout Italy, agriculture was seen to be a safer investment than trade but also a dignified occupation, "the fairest and more appropriate for a gentleman," as Roberto di Spilimbergo wrote. Since the activities open to gentlemen were increasingly limited to bearing arms and holding public office, agriculture became an important source of income.[7]

Down to the sixteenth century virtually all villas served some agricultural function. Vespasiano da Bisticci remarked on Cosimo de' Medici's pronounced interest in husbandry and described him at his villa of Careggi, pruning vines and reading the *Moralia* of Saint Gregory. Cosimo's grandson Lorenzo was likewise noted for his keen interest in agriculture, and by the end of his life the greater part of his income derived from his estates. He created a model dairy farm at Poggio a Caiano before building the great showpiece of his villa there.[8] Even the spectacularly situated villa of Lorenzo's uncle Giovanni de' Medici at Fiesole was not built simply to enjoy the views onto Florence below. It, too, had an agricultural dimension, although this seems to have taken second place to its situation, carved out of the rock and solidly built, as Vasari reported. The variety of terraces and gardens at the Villa Medici anticipated the later Medici showpiece, the Villa Madama in Rome (plate 16), and it, too, became something of a tourist attraction as early as 1475, when the Venetian nobleman Paolo

Morosini asked Lorenzo de' Medici's permission to see it.[9] The villas at Poggio a Caiano and Fiesole mark the beginning of a shift in the balance between the agricultural and aesthetic aspects of *villeggiatura*.

Practical activity and recreation combined in the growing fashion for *villeggiatura* or villa life, but also drew stimulus from antiquity. Initially this was more a literary than an architectural phenomenon. The revival of interest in classical literature led to printed editions of those Roman writers who extolled the virtues of country life—Cato, Varro, and Palladius, among others.[10] Their ranks were joined by the fourteenth-century writer Pier de' Crescenzi, whose treatise on country life became a veritable best-seller, while the sixteenth century witnessed the birth of a new genre of books on the social aspect of villas. When the Florentine humanist Marsilio Ficino praised the conjunction of the arts and agriculture at Careggi or when the Vicentine nobleman Bernardino Pagello wrote of living in the country and tending his fields, both men were not rejecting the city in favor of a rural existence; instead, they were following the tradition that brought urban culture to the farm, a tradition established by the writings of Boccaccio and Petrarch.[11] Villas were intended to encompass both aspects of life, as Machiavelli's famous remark about his days at San Casciano confirms: "When evening comes, I return home and go in to my study. On the threshold I strip off my muddy, sweaty, workday clothes, and put on the robes of court and palace, and in this graver dress I enter the antique courts of the ancients and am welcomed by them."[12]

Girolamo Priuli's lament for the old order constituted a minority opinion, but he was right to see the connection between investment in land and construction on it: it has been calculated that twenty-two of the Veneto villas date from the eleventh to the fourteenth centuries, and eighty-four from the fifteenth century, but two hundred fifty-seven date from the sixteenth century,[13] a veritable building boom in rural housing of which Palladio was only the most conspicuous beneficiary.

Fifteenth-century villas derived from regional prototypes and traditional agricultural buildings, and the Veneto was no exception to this rule. A once-popular theory held that Veneto villas were descended from Romano-Byzantine portico villas via Venetian palaces, but this has met with considerable skepticism; indeed, it would seem hard to maintain such a theory in the face of the wide variety of building types employed in the fifteenth century, nor is there any evidence that classical ruins were studied by architects and patrons before the time of Bramante and Raphael.[14] There was no distinctive tradition of rural domestic architecture in the Veneto prior to Palladio's day, and surviving structures vary from a string of loosely connected buildings around a court, to a tower with adjoining loggia (plate 45), to the monumental, pseudo-castellar types that were little more than transposed palaces (plate 46).[15] While individual elements in the Veneto villas did change in the quattrocento, the types as a whole did not. Even where Venetian Gothic loggias were adopted, they were not always accompanied by ground plans typical of a Venetian palace, since such plans were not eminently suitable for rural

housing. In this way, the dissemination of Venetian architectural elements in villas parallels that of the adaptation of such features in urban dwellings in Vicenza and elsewhere and were rarely cases of straightforward adaptation. Nor did the owner's house really begin to emerge as an entity distinct from the surrounding villa complex until the turn of the sixteenth century. The first examples of these are the almost mythical seat of Caterina Cornaro near Asolo, the Villa Porto Colleoni at Thiene, and the Villa Giustinian at Roncade (plate 44).[16] But none of these could be described as typical farmhouses. Their functions were more palatial—in the full sense of that word—than the majority of rural dwellings, typified by buildings like the Villa Piovene (plate 45) at Brendola or the Villa Capra at Carrè.

44. Tullio Lombardo(?) (c. 1455–1532). Portico of the Villa Giustinian, Roncade, Treviso.

This lack of a definite type continued well into the sixteenth century, a situation reflected by the ambiguity of the word *villa* and by the way in which country houses were otherwise described. The Romans applied the term to a variety of country or suburban dwellings, often built on one floor and constructed around a central atrium. They ranged from the simple compounds of the late Republican period to the more elaborate complexes found at Pompeii and Tivoli or described in the letters of Pliny the Younger.[17] Long before Palladio's day the word *villa* was used in Italian to describe a country estate but was rarely delimited to the principal house that stood there. Palladio invariably refers to these as *casa di villa*, roughly equivalent to the English phrase "country house," and it seems clear that he did not regard it as typologically distinct from the town house. When discussing decorum in domestic architecture, he even went so far as to state that "the house of the patron should be built with due regard to his family and status . . . as in the city."[18] Indeed most of his remarks on villas are prosaic, cast in the pragmatic and functional terms of terrain, running water, and other aspects of the working farm that were established concerns long before Palladio's day.

It is important to emphasize Palladio's roots in the Veneto tradition of rural architecture even though he quickly began to challenge its limitations, eventually creating a new and distinct type of country house in his own villas. His first experiences of such agricultural complexes came with his work in the Pedemuro bottega, in particular with the villa built for Girolamo Godi at Lonedo di Lugo in the northern reaches of the Vicentino. Girolamo was one of three sons of Enrico Antonio Godi, a noted doctor of laws whose branch of the family was called *Godoni* or the "big Godi" because of their great wealth.[19] In Vicenza, the family owned a large palace as well as other

45. Architect unknown. Villa Piovene, Brendola (Vicenza), second half of the fifteenth century.

houses just below the Piazza dei Signori. Their holdings at Lugo were of recent origin—Enrico Antonio mentions the acquisition of "land and laborers' houses" in his will of 1536 but no *casa domenicale* or owner's house, which probably means that none yet existed. The Godi owned 190 *campi* divided into several parcels, of which the largest included a hill with commanding views over the Astico valley below (plate 49). It was on this hill that the family's house was begun in the late 1530s. The stable block to the north of the villa bears the year 1533, perhaps a first stage in the site's development, which was carried out by Girolamo and his brother Pietro shortly after their father's death. The inscription over the entrance attests that the main house was effectively finished by 1542, though work continued well into the 1550s. Girolamo Godi's name stands as patron in the inscription, and this is confirmed by Palladio in the *Quattro Libri*. As Girolamo never married, the intention was clearly to build a house for his brothers and nephews to share with him. In any event, his nephews inherited the house at his death. In 1542 the house was valued at the large sum of thirteen hundred ducats, while the neighboring house of the Piovene, to which Palladio later gave a portico, was only valued at three hundred ducats thirty years later.[20] Needless to say, relations between the two aristocratic families were strained by the arrival of the Godi in Lugo, and

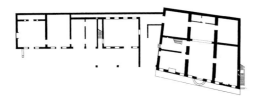

46. *(above)* Architect unknown. Villa Trissino at Paninsacco (Vicenza).

47. *(left)* Plan of Villa Trissino, Paninsacco.

this sometimes erupted into violence—at one point Orazio Godi burst into the Villa Piovene with some of his retainers and shot Fabio Piovene, who was hiding in a wardrobe.

The house built by the Godi at Lugo represented a major investment, and it is not surprising that they turned to the Pedemuro workshop for its execution. The workshop had executed the portal of the Servite church in Vicenza for a collateral branch of the family in 1531, and Giovanni da Porlezza appeared in notarial acts of Enrico Antonio Godi and his family during 1536–37, just when the villa would have been begun. By that date the workshop had furnished the handsome portal of the Domus Comestabilis in the old town hall, a work probably by the young Andrea Palladio (plate 7).[21] Already in the late 1530s, Palladio had acquired a reputation as an architectural specialist within the workshop, and this may explain how he emerged as the dominant figure at the Villa Godi within a few years. Certainly he was established as such by 1540 when he is recorded as receiving the first of several small payments there as "maestro Andrea architetto."[22]

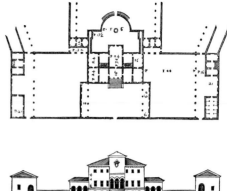

48. *Plan and elevation of the Villa Godi* from the *Quattro Libri.*

The Vicentine historian Giuseppe Marzari described the Godi house as a *"palazzo superbissimo,"* a most splendid palace—indeed it was clearly conceived on a palatial scale, much like the earlier Villa Trissino at Paninsacco (plates 46, 47) or Sanmicheli's contemporaneous Villa Soranza, which the Villa Godi resembles. In the *Quattro Libri,* Palladio praises the site as "a hilltop with splendid views," and the visitor approaching from below cannot fail to be impressed by the massive stone walls that define the parterre on which the villa sits. Although the earlier stable block to the north may mark the first stage in exploiting the site, it can hardly have been planned by Palladio, for it gave him difficulties when he had to reconcile it with the rest of his project in his woodcut of 1570 (plate 48).[23] To build on the scale the Godi wanted, an enormous amount of effort went into extending the space available by shoring up the hilltop. The purpose of such conspicuous expenditure was probably twofold: on the one hand the house would dominate the surrounding countryside, thus expressing the owner's status; on the other, the effort allowed the remarkable vistas offered by the site to be exploited. Otherwise the house would have been more compact and not so extended on its east and west facades.

Large and gaunt, the main house shares some features with earlier rural architecture, notably its scale, the absence of an architectural order, and its tripartite division. The awkward spacing of the windows on the front, which allowed the chimney flues to be inserted between them, is

49. *(overleaf)* Villa Godi, Lonedo di Lugo (Vicenza).

typical of vernacular architecture. The main house is divided into three blocks with the central one recessed on the main facade but projecting on the garden. This may have been inspired by Sanmicheli's La Soranza, but the emphasis given to the *piano nobile* invites comparison not only with La Soranza but also with Sansovino's monumental Villa Garzoni near Padua (plate 50).

The plan of the Villa Godi is much more schematic than one finds in Palladio's later villas. It continues the symmetrical bias of earlier works like Trissino's villa at Cricoli, and it has a similar division between loggia and *salone* on the central axis. In the Villa Godi, the projecting wings have similar sets of four rooms on the main floor, three of equal dimensions and the fourth subdivided to provide space for a stairwell. As an ensemble the rooms, which have a traditional beamed ceiling in the manner of fifteenth-century villas and palaces, lack the spatial coherence of Palladio's mature domestic architecture, and their relationship to the loggia and *salone* is decidedly awkward. In typical fashion, the mezzanine above was given over to the storage of grain while the ground floor was occupied by the kitchen and other services. The handling of the ground-floor vaulting with its inset lighting is impressive, foreshadowing solutions found in Palladio's later villas (plate 51). But while the severity of the main facade is unusual by the standards of the architect's later works, its significance may be exaggerated: it could reflect Alvise Cornaro's dictum that a house could be attractive without columns or decoration, but the bareness here might originally have been mitigated by frescoing or by a fictive rustication of the kind surviving elsewhere in Palladio's early villas (plate 69). As it stands, the facade is not devoid of classical touches, chiefly in the profile of the cornice, which was adapted from that of the Coliseum and known to Palladio from Sebastiano Serlio's third book on architecture, published in 1540.[24]

The unadorned exterior of the main block of the Villa Godi does not prepare one for its sumptuously frescoed interior. The whole of the *piano nobile* has been given over to one of the ear-

50. Jacopo Sansovino (1486–1570). Villa Garzoni, Pontecasale (Padua), late 1530s–1540s.

liest surviving cycles of the sixteenth century,[25] created by the artists Gualtiero dall'Arzere, Battista dal Moro, and Giambattista Zelotti. The last two were part of the Veronese *équipe* that formed around Michele Sanmicheli, but Gualtiero came from the Paduan circle of Alvise Cornaro. Cornaro recommended frescoes as a cheap alternative to tapestries for interior decoration and preferred landscapes and grotesques to figural compositions since it was difficult to find artists capable of the latter.[26] A similar policy seems to have been adapted here with Gualtiero's frescoes, which were probably the first and were generally confined to classical landscapes, grotesques, and fictive reliefs (plate 52). Though not of the highest caliber, they are extremely interesting since they echo elements in the decoration of the Odeo Cornaro, where Gualtiero's brother-in-law Tiziano Minio had been employed as the stuccoist (plate 2). Gualtiero died around 1552–53, and his place was taken by Zelotti and Battista dal Moro. A marked elevation in quality resulted in the northern wing and in the *salone*, which bear the stamp of Zelotti's handiwork and demonstrate a more ambitious commitment to narrative scenes, chiefly from ancient history (plate 53).

It was with the *salone*, probably in preparation for frescoing, that Palladio's later interventions around 1550 were concerned. At that date he was paid for the *"disegno della sala,"* which must refer to the substitution of the original thermal window with the present Serlian one.[27] By then, Palladio had more than a decade of experience behind him and was thoroughly saturated in contemporary Roman architecture. The garden hemicycle and wellhead of 1555 were probably the last touches the architect put to the villa and were calculated to emphasize its central axis. The hemicycle

51. View of kitchen at the Villa Godi.

exploited the difference in level between the house and its surrounding fields in a manner reminiscent of Bramante's Cortile del Belvedere while the well-head recalled the profile of Michelangelo's benches before the Palazzo del Senatore on the Capitoline Hill.[28] These late additions, together with the imposing scale of the house, were probably in Bertotti Scamozzi's mind when he wrote that, even if it lacked elegance, the Villa Godi possessed a robustness and elements of grandeur.[29]

If Palladio's first villa has a staccato effect, it is largely because of a confluence of architectural ideas not quite in balance. This is especially understandable if one accepts the Villa Godi as a project in which Palladio's role only became decisive as building proceeded, much as was the case of the slightly later Palazzo Thiene in Vicenza. The great cleft between the Villa Godi and Palladio's later villas can be explained by his first experience of Rome and its architecture in 1541, when the former was almost completed. After this overwhelming encounter, Palladio sought to introduce a host of motifs and concepts into his domestic architecture, and villas were the obvious means of doing so. In this, Palladio followed the lead of Giuliano da Sangallo and Raphael, whose villas had a great impact on him. These elements began to coalesce in a Palladian style in a host of early villa studies and projects, of which the Villa Valmarana at Vigardolo was one of the first. Situated a few kilometers north of Vicenza, the villa (plate 54) stands on the site of what may have been a Roman camp that had existed as a feudal domain at least from the thirteenth century. The property was inherited by two cousins, Giuseppe and Antonio Valmarana, around 1540; Antonio's father, Pietro, had been a jurist and friend of Palladio's future patron Girolamo Chiericati, and Antonio eventually obtained feudal investiture of Vigardolo from the bishop of Vicenza. In a land valuation of 1541, Giuseppe Valmarana listed the holdings at Vigardolo as 170 *campi*, together with a house for laborers, a stable, and "the beginnings of another house."[30] The new house at Vigardolo still exists and closely corresponds to an important early drawing by Palladio (plate 55). The drawing must be

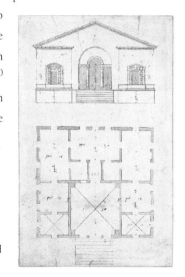

52. (*opposite, top*) Gualtiero dall'Arzere (fl. 1529–1552). Landscape frescoes in the *sala dei cesari* of the Villa Godi, late 1540s.

53. (*opposite, bottom*) View of the *salone* of the Villa Godi.

54. (*above*) Villa Valmarana at Vigardolo (Monticello Conte Otto, Vicenza).

55. (*right*) *Study for the Villa Valmarana.* (RIBA XVII/2r.) Pen, ink, and wash over incised lines, 40.7 x 26.3 cm.

one of the first made by the architect after his earliest Roman trip and reads like a manifesto of his later style: the compact, slightly rectangular block is divided down the middle by a large loggia and smaller *salone* separated by a hallway. The documents indicate that the villa was intended for occupancy by both branches of the family, which may explain why the entrance to the lateral suites is from the *salone* rather than the loggia. The suites contain a typical sequence of small, middling, and large rooms in a simple numerical relationship of 2:3:5 (12, 18, 30 Vicentine feet), and between *salone* and loggia are small spaces for internal stairs. As has often been observed, the plan goes back to Trissino's Cricoli (plate 8), though enriched by new elements derived from the antique; in particular, the motif of the columnar screen and cross vault of the loggia as well as the broken pediment of the facade derive from the Roman baths, which were among the most well preserved of Roman ruins and became a touchstone for much of Palladio's architecture. In addition to the broken pediment, the facade bears other evidence of Palladio's study of classical and contemporary architecture: the main floor is raised on a high socle with a handsome flight of steps flanked by stylobates in the manner of a Roman temple; the window aedicules with their prominent rustication were adapted from Giulio Romano; and the central Serlian arch was a motif associated with Bramante and his circle.[31] These details compensate for the essentially simple design of the building as a whole.

As built, the villa is considerably more modest than Palladio's drawing, but this may be the result of its protracted building history. Dalla Pozza observed that only half the villa dates from the early 1540s, the rear portion having been constructed after 1560.[32] The facade did not receive the elaborate tabernacles on the drawing nor a broken pediment, and the loggia and *salone* were given a simple beam roof—probably because of its substantial dimensions (ten by ten meters). The facade does, however, boast one sophisticated feature in terms of the Serlian arch with a Doric order: its frieze has been suppressed, leaving only the architrave and cornice. This was a legitimate classical motif, found on the Crypta Balbi in Rome and given general currency in Palladio's day by Raphael's use of it on the facade of Palazzo Branconio dell'Aquila and by Giulio Romano in the atrium of the Palazzo del Te (plates 30, 18).[33] On the front of the house the lateral rooms were given pavilion vaults more elaborate than those indicated in the drawing. The villa was once extensively frescoed but only a few fragments now survive. Despite its incomplete execution, the Villa Valmarana remains an important testimonial to Palladio's rapid development as an architect in the early 1540s, and many of the features essayed here would reappear in subsequent villas like that at Poiana (plates 71–75).

Another of Palladio's early villas that did not find its way into the *Quattro Libri* is that designed for Tadeo Gazzotti at Bertesina (plates 56, 57). Like Vigardolo, the villa is of modest dimensions, located on the outskirts of Vicenza and now engulfed by its suburbs. Its origins were not feudal but were part of the kind of land speculation deplored by Girolamo Priuli.[34] In fact the original patron, a tax collector of humble origins, lost money on the investment and went bankrupt in 1549, a useful reminder that purchasing land, particularly on a small scale, was not a foolproof means of getting rich (although the estate was purchased by a Venetian nobleman soon after Gazzotti's forced sale). Gazzotti acquired the land as early as 1533–34, with a house and laborers' dwellings already in place. Palladio's contribution has been generally dated to the years 1542–43 when its patron's fortunes were at their height, and the sophistication of the overall design and its details would confirm the early 1540s as the plausible date of construction.[35] Like Palladio's first town palace, the Casa Civena (plate 24), the Villa Gazzotti bears the stamp of Bramante's influential Palazzo Caprini (plate 13), the facade similarly composed of

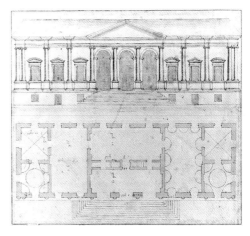

56. *Preliminary study for the Villa Gazzotti.* (RIBA XVII/27.) Pen, ink, and wash over lead underdrawing and incised lines, 32.6 x 37.6 cm.

stuccoed brick with membering in sandstone from the Monti Berici. Single Composite pilasters frame the seven bays of the facade, the outer ones containing windows with triangular pediments while the central three bays have large, roundheaded arches. Coherence is given to the facade by the presence of a triangular gable above the central arches, the first appearance of the temple motif in Palladio's architecture. This motif provides the focal point for the facade and would soon evolve into the portico of the mature villas. The overall effect is further enhanced by the quality of detail in the architectural profiles and by the way in which moldings link together—again a hallmark of Palladio's works, this one inspired by the example of Michele Sanmicheli (plate 14). Behind the loggia is a handsome vaulted porch and portals whose pediments and consoles match those on the windows.

A preliminary drawing (plate 56) shows that Palladio's first ideas called for a more ambitious solution, as had been the case with Vigardolo.[36] In plan, the sheet reads like an imploded version of Vigardolo, with loggia and *salone* occupying the same area as the flanking suites of three rooms. Stairs have been squeezed into the narrowest possible space and the sequence of the minor rooms is not particularly adroit, although various vaultings are proposed. The exterior is even more imposing, with Ionic semicolumns and Pantheonic tabernacles for the windows, this last reminiscent of Raphael's courtyard facade at the Villa Madama. Palladio considered semicolumns for the rear facade, too, but this was dropped, probably to make economies. As built, the front is literally a facade, one that ends abruptly at the corners, which have been shortened by one bay from the drawing. The grand staircase proposed for the entrance was replaced by a haphazard affair at a later date. The final sequence of rooms was also rethought and rendered more compact, with the *salone* becoming T-shaped and cross-vaulted. This is the most notable of the interior features and marks the beginning of the vaulted central rooms that became such a feature in later villas.

Even at this early stage in his career, villas drew the best from Palladio, and a group of drawings illustrate how intensively the problems of villa design engaged him during the early 1540s. Sharing stylistic affinities, these drawings explore themes common to Palladio's first independent works even though their purpose has been a matter of conjecture (plates 58, 59). The most remarkable of these early studies is plate 59.[37] It takes as its point of departure the Odeo Cornaro and related projects by Serlio for villas with a central *salone,* but the scale of Palladio's project is far larger than these. In plan and elevation it is dominated by the cruciform *salone,* cross-vaulted and rising one and a half stories. The position and height of the *salone* requires it to be lit by large thermal windows, and the customary suites have been expanded in L-shaped patterns on either side. The main facade bears Palladio's favorite motif of this period, the *Serliana* and a biapsidal loggia. The living quarters surmount a service floor whose large, arched portal originally had a rusticated surround; the portal is framed by twin flights of stairs reminiscent of the terrace steps of the Cortile del Belvedere. The drawing demonstrates a boldness and scale unusual in contemporary villas even as it contains the germ of later projects. Above all, the focus upon a central *salone* of palatial proportions lit from above would eventually lead to the achievement of the Villa Malcontenta (plate 112) and the Villa Rotonda (plate 205).

57. Villa Gazzotti Marcello Curti at Bertesina, Vicenza.

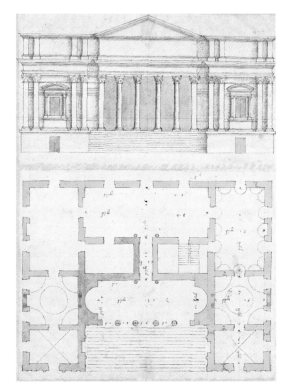
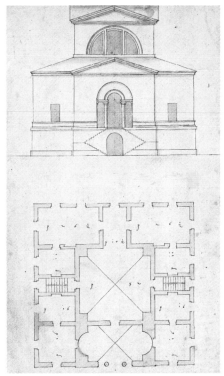

These projects remained on paper, but Palladio soon saw an opportunity to bring similar ideas to life with the second major villa commission of his early practice, that for the noble Venetian family of Pisani at Bagnolo (plates 43, 64, 66). Placed first among the villas in the *Quattro Libri*, it held a crucial importance in his career, for it gave him his earliest opportunity to build in a thoroughly modern mode and on a substantial scale. The villa at Bagnolo is also unusual for the number of preliminary studies—four in all—that survive. They allow us to trace the evolution of Palladio's ideas from his earliest villas to something more mature.[38] Probably the first of these display lateral suites of rooms and a biapsidal, cross-vaulted *salone* rather than corresponding features in the Casa Civena studies and some early villa drawings. But they differ from these projects through the introduction of two new motifs: a portico in the shape of a hemicycle and concave-convex stairs, both inspired by Bramante's famous exedra of the upper court of the Belvedere. Even before going to Rome, Palladio would have known Bramante's work through Serlio, but the villalike associations of the Belvedere would have impressed the young architect when he could actually study it in 1541. The studies for the Villa Pisani mark a stage in which Palladio was liberating himself from his former, more static approach to villa design; the later phases in the villa's evolution assume a different form and

58. *(above, left) Study of villa with pediment.* (RIBA XVII/16.) Pen, ink, and wash over incised lines, 37 x 27.3 cm.

59. *(above, right) Study of villa.* (RIBA XVII/1r.) Pen, ink, and wash over incised lines, 38.2 x 23.4 cm.

introduce a cruciform *salone* in various guises around L-shaped suites of rooms. The central loggia has been developed ambitiously with a combination of piers and columnar screens, apparently suggested by Raphael's projected ambulatories for the new Saint Peter's.

The one elevation that survives (plate 60) represents an ambitious essay in combining a

variety of classical motifs. Quoins define the semibasement's sections and contrast with the smooth treatment of the upper floors. Small towers frame the building, a feudal touch reminiscent of the pre-Palladian villa on the site.[39] The center is dominated by an elaborate loggia whose concave movement is answered by the concave-convex staircase. A large thermal window surmounts the loggia, providing light for the *salone* behind; the corner rooms are lit in turn by distinctive windows adapted from those of the Temple of the Sibyl at Tivoli.[40] In plan, the space between the *salone* and the flanking rooms is divided into compact stairs and service units. The corner rooms of the towers are now conceived as octagons in the manner of the central room of the Odeo Cornaro (plate 4). The final design does not survive and was probably composed of elements drawn from the various preliminary sheets. This would explain why the plan of the villa (plate 61) is closest to plate 60 but with the elaborate loggia jettisoned in favor of a simpler form. Evidently questions of expense led at a fairly late stage to this scaling down, the effects of which can be seen in the flanks and roofline of the building (plates 43, 62).

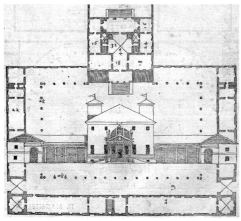

60. *(top) Penultimate plan and elevation of the Villa Pisani.* (RIBA XVII/17.) Pen, ink, and wash over incised lines, 41.5 x 27.6 cm.

61. *(above) Woodcut of the Villa Pisani from the Quattro Libri.*

The pains taken by the architect over this project are understandable if one considers the history of Bagnolo.[41] The estate had originally been granted to the old Vicentine family of Nogarola by the della Scala, then rulers of the Vicentino, in the fourteenth century. The Nogarola enjoyed feudal rights over the sur-

rounding countryside, but the property was confiscated by Venice in 1412 when the family led attempts to withdraw Vicenza from Venetian rule. They only regained their estates, together with the title of counts of Bagnolo, in 1505, but Girolamo Nogarola lost the estate and title definitively when he became one of the leading rebels against Venice during the War of the League of Cambrai. The vast estate—around 1200 *campi* or approximately 463 acres—and its feudal title were auctioned by the Venetian government, and the land was purchased by Giovanni Pisani at half the market price. The Pisani were one of the four wealthiest patrician families in Venice and may have obtained the estate at such favorable terms because they could buy it *en bloc.* Giovanni Pisani immediately launched into opening up roads, creating canals, and cultivating rice in the swampy plains of Bagnolo. The act that transferred ownership of the Pisani conveys an idea of what the estate was like before Palladio's intervention: "around 1200 fields in various neighboring parcels with a granary and sixty fields enclosed by a wall, planted with vineyards, mulberry and fruit trees, a courtyard with house, barn, and dovecote . . . two mills placed on the river, one above the bridge, the other below it . . . and the burnt palace of the owner."[42] The house was damaged during the War of the League of Cambrai, but some idea of its appearance is preserved in a sketch on the sixteenth-century map of the site. This shows a horizontal block with a balcony toward the river and a dovecote-tower over the entrance, which, unlike the present house, faced away from the river.

62. Aerial view of Villa Pisani Ferri, Bagnolo (Vicenza).

Palladio's summons would have come around 1542 when the eldest of Giovanni Pisani's sons, Vettor, married Paola Foscari. Construction must have been in full swing by 1543, for a land valuation of 1545 refers to the palace as newly built. The Pisani were aided by their right as lords of Bagnolo to draw upon the free labor of the local inhabitants one day a week, and no doubt feudal labor contributed to the rapid completion of the house.[43] Retaining the feudalistic tower motif, Palladio's building is approximately the same mass as its predecessor. The house was reoriented toward the river, with semicircular stairs, reminiscent of Palladio's preliminary drawings, leading up to the *piano nobile.* The patrons ultimately decided upon a closed facade (plate 43) with a rusticated frontispiece of three roundheaded bays framed by Doric pilasters supporting a pediment. The pediment also bears the family coat of arms, a feature often employed in Palladio's later villas. The use of rusticated pilasters invites comparison with Palladio's early designs for the Basilica arcades (plate 79) and also points to a common source in the architecture of Michele Sanmicheli. In particular, the central motif with pediment resembles the outer facade of Sanmicheli's Porta Nuova (plate 15), then recently completed and a drawing of which by Palladio's nephew Marc'antonio Palladio survives.[44] At this stage in his career, Palladio was strongly influenced by the Veronese architect and experimented with simi-

63. Rear facade of the Villa Pisani.

larly dramatic effects in rustication; the use here of Veronese limestone for the stonework also underscores the stylistic affinities.

As executed, the house displays the vertical distribution of functions habitually found in Palladio's later villas. Palladio tells us that the semibasement was reserved for the kitchen and services, and, in keeping with its lowly functions, the floor is lit by rectangular windows with heavy rusticated surrounds. In contrast, the main floor is privileged by more elegant window moldings, the presence of an order, and a pediment. As there is only one living floor, the stairs are essentially for service from the kitchens or access to the granary above. The architect did not, however, enjoy complete control over the external design: the main facade and towers do not marry well with the rear block of the house, as can be seen from aerial and lateral views (plates 62, 43). This is especially clear in the clash of cornices between the towers and flank of the building, which lends credence to the possibility of an abrupt change of plan during construction.

Palladio's control over design and his eye for detail are best experienced on the interior, especially after the sympathetic restoration of the building in the 1970s. Its quality is evident from the loggia itself, where the biapsidal chamber has been invested with Doric pilasters and moldings echoing those of the facade (plate 64). This spare but eloquent language continues in

64. Interior of the loggia of the Villa Pisani.

the splendid T-shaped *salone*, which can be entered from either of the principal fronts or from the largest rooms of the apartments (plate 66). The most public of the interior spaces, the *salone* rises to a height equal to that of the lateral rooms and the mezzanines above. Here the architect realized the first of those one-and-a-half-story rooms considered in early drawings like plate 59 and culminating in the Villa Malcontenta (plate 112). The *salone* is articulated by Doric pilasters with bases and capitals in limestone, which stand out against the white *marmorino* surfaces. The walls support a vault divided into barrel and groined sections terminating in thermal windows, and the ceiling is frescoed in an *all'antica* style, part grotesques and part classical scenes. The density of this painted decoration contrasts with the austerity of the walls but was meant to recreate an interior like the garden loggia of the Villa Madama (plate 16) or the Roman baths as Palladio must have imagined they once appeared. Here for the first time one can appreciate Palladio's unswerving commitment to antiquity.

The apartments are less self-consciously designed and more intimate in scale, as befits their purpose. These rooms would have been reserved for the Pisani and their closest associates and are entered from the loggia or the *salone*. They constitute the now customary sequence of small, medium, and large rooms of simple proportions—1:1, 1:1½, 1:1¾, following Palladio's instructions in the first book of the *Quattro Libri*.[45] The enfilade of their doorways invites the visitor to explore them; spacious and well lit, they show their creator's attention even in details like the window embrasures and moldings.

The Villa Pisani remains one of Palladio's most successful works, despite its incompleteness. Neither the rear stairs nor the *cortile* as a whole was finished although it is the elevation that is given pride of palace in the *Quattro Libri* woodcut (plate 61). The portico shown in the woodcut must be a reworking of the original project for publication, as it is alien to Palladio's style in the 1540s; it could date from the early 1560s when Palladio created the colossal Doric arcade in a nearby field on the Pisani estate.[46] What *was* built at Bagnolo shows a maturity of conception not found in Palladio's other early villas and is arguably the greatest achievement of his first decade as an independent architect.

Had the Villa Thiene at Quinto ever been finished, it might have outshone even the Villa Pisani (plate 65). The patrons of the villa were the brothers Marc'antonio and Adriano Thiene, for whom Palladio had built the magnificent Palazzo Thiene in Vicenza. Following the death

65. *(above)* Villa Thiene at Quinto (Vicenza).

66. *(opposite)* The *salone*, the principal reception room of the Villa Pisani.

of Giulio Romano in 1546, Palladio became sole architect of the new palace, and it was around this date that he began planning the villa on the Thiene estate at Quinto, a short distance to the east of Vicenza.[47] As early as 1473 Marco Thiene, the grandfather of Palladio's patrons, had been created count of Quinto by the Emperor Frederick III and built a house on his property. The estate suffered plundering in 1514 and would have been overdue for reconstruction by the 1540s, but just what Palladio began to build around the middle of that decade has been a subject of controversy. It is generally agreed that the original project could not have been the elaborate plan published in 1570 showing two houses facing a central courtyard and linked to other courts by arcades and farm buildings. This was an embellishment of what already existed on the site, an expansion of the original nucleus for the *Quattro Libri*. A drawing in Oxford represents an earlier stage of the project and is probably closer to the architect's first proposal (plate 67).[48] This shows a main block with entrance sala and loggia flanked by lateral apartments facing the Tesina River on one side and an inner court on the other. The principal courts have columnar arcades, and further arcaded courts are shown to either side. Of this complex, only the suite of rooms to the north still survives, a fragment of interest if only for the perceptible imitation of Giulio Romano in its articulation by Doric pilasters and niches (plate 17). The similarities with the Palazzo del Te and Palazzo Thiene hardly need emphasis, suggesting that the choice of style here must owe as much to the patrons' taste as to the architect's. But the Giulian element has been purged of some of its stronger overtones, and, as was the case with the *piano nobile* of the family's palace, Palladio's more restrained hand is evident.

Reading together the Oxford drawing and the section of the building illustrated in the *Quattro Libri*, we can interpret some of the features found in the initial project. Several aspects are reminiscent of the drawings for the Villa Pisani at Bagnolo, which suggests that the Thiene knew and wished to emulate those plans. For one thing, the orientation of the villa towards the river in

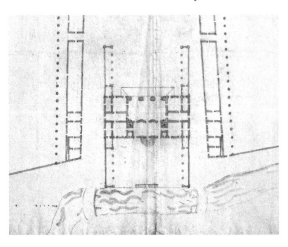

67. *Project for the Villa Thiene.* Worcester College Library, Oxford, England (H.T. 89). Pen, ink, and wash, 44.4 x 58.7 cm.

the Oxford sheet, with the elaborate mooring and semicircular steps to the main house, finds a parallel in the Bagnolo studies, while the alignment of a *salone* with a loggia points more towards an interpolation from the Palazzo del Te. Both the woodcut in the *Quattro Libri* and notes by Inigo Jones, however, show that this entrance chamber actually resembled the *salone* of the Villa Pisani, for it stood one and a half stories high and was lit by thermal windows. Presumably the building recorded in the Oxford drawing was planned for the Thiene brothers, who would have occupied the suites to the north and south of the main axis. The depar-

ture of Adriano to France in 1547 under suspicion of heresy slowed the initial momentum, and only the northern suite and the entrance were in fact built. Later, in the eighteenth century, the loggia and entrance were razed and the exteriors remodeled. After many interventions and changes in the fabric, now only a few vaulted ceilings and the frescoed decoration by Giovanni de Mio still conjure up some of the grandeur of the villa as intended by Palladio and his patrons.

Two other villas round out the picture of Palladio's activity in this sphere toward the end of the 1540s—the Villa Saraceno at Finale di Agugliaro and the Villa Poiana at Poiana Maggiore. Both were under construction at approximately the same time, though the Saraceno may have been the first to be started. Like many other Vicentine families, the Saraceno had owned the property on which Palladio built their villa for several generations.[49] In 1519 Pietro Saraceno had left the property at Finale jointly to his sons Biagio and Giacomo; the land was divided in 1525, with Giacomo commissioning a new house, the opaquely named "Palazzo delle Trombe," at some point before 1546, when the house was mentioned in a family document (plate 68). The same document indicates that Biagio Saraceno occupied a *casa domenicale* with a value of five hundred ducats. This has sometimes been interpreted as the villa designed by Palladio, but it is more likely to have been an older family house since a recently discovered document of 1556

68. Architect unknown. Palazzo delle Trombe, Finale (Vicenza).

mentions Biagio Saraceno as the owner of "a new house, not yet finished," with a value of eleven hundred ducats: this must be Palladio's villa. The two documents point to a genesis of the villa in the late 1540s, most probably during the period from 1548, when Biagio Saraceno was a deputy of the Vicentine city council and involved in the decisions that led to commissioning the Basilica arcades from Palladio.

It is instructive to study the brothers' villas since they were conceived about a decade apart and pinpoint shifts in villa design. Both houses occupy similar positions vis-à-vis their surrounding farm buildings and perimeter walls, just as both are symmetrical in plan, have semibasements, and were given facades with classicizing motifs. Despite these features, the Palazzo delle Trombe conveys a cramped impression through its artless treatment of the facade and the irregular placement of windows. Though the Villa Saraceno is similarly compact, it does not sacrifice lucidity and proportion: the windows are fewer, making the facade seem more spacious, and the presence of a central pediment draws together the individual elements in a hierarchical order (plate 69). The Palazzo delle Trombe could have been built by the Pedemuro workshop with Palladio's participation during the 1530s. The gulf between it and the Villa Saraceno can best be explained by Palladio's experience of Rome during the 1540s and by almost a decade of independent practice that lay behind him when he came to the latter project. Both in plan and elevation, it is a classic statement of Palladio's approach to domestic architecture, one that shared the conviction expressed in Alvise Cornaro's

69. Facade of the Villa Saraceno at Finale (Vicenza).

writings that a house could be attractive without columns provided it was well designed. The villa's facade can be seen as a reprise of earlier designs like the Villa Valmarana at Vigardolo, and Palladio was capable of returning to this simple, pared-down style even later in his career when he furnished similar "frontispieces" for the Villas Caldogno, Zeno, and Forni.[50] Palladio realized that his solution for the Villa Saraceno was attractive and "classical" while being eminently suited for a patron who did not wish to spend vast sums on a villa facade.

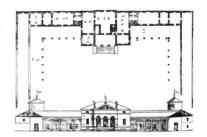

70. *Plan of the Villa Saraceno* from the *Quattro Libri.*

The villa remained a fragment at Biagio Saraceno's death in 1562. The villa itself corresponds to the grandiloquent plan published in the *Quattro Libri,* with the loggia and T-shaped *salone* filling the center of the block and bound by pairs of rooms to either side; a small *barchessa* or shed to the right of the farm was added, and that only in the seventeenth century. The lateral rooms are the same height as the *salone* but have beamed as opposed to vaulted ceilings. As with the Villa Pisani at Bagnolo, stairways were planned for the narrow areas between the loggia and *salone* although only one was carried out. The plan is spatially economical and anticipates the more sophisticated manipulation of rooms found in the Villa Badoer a few years later (plates 70, 94). Evidence of the building suggests that economies were also made during construction: while the semibasement was realized on the right side, the other contains only rubble. Though austere, the facade preserves traces of lightly incised lines of rustication where its *intonaco* or rendered surface is still intact.[51] Local sandstone has been employed sparingly for moldings on the corners of the building, moldings that run across the facade establishing visual links in the manner of the facade of the Villa Pisani. The interior has fared less well than the exterior and virtually none of the original features survive. Since Palladio's service wing was never built, the main floor space was cannibalized to accommodate basic functions; only proportions of the attic granary, which fills the entire dimensions of the house, and fragments of frescoes in the loggia and *salone* testify to ambitious plans never fully realized. Fortunately, the villa has been purchased by the British Landmark Trust and was the subject of an enlightened restoration, which may encourage similar projects with other Veneto villas.

The Villa Poiana at Poiana Maggiore brings us to the end of Palladio's first decade as a designer of villas (plate 73). With virtually no documentation surviving, the villa is generally dated to the late 1540s and was recorded as still unfinished in 1555. The patron, Bonifazio Poiana, was active in Vicentine life during the 1550s and lived in the same district of Vicenza as Palladio. Moreover, the architect's wife was once in the service of Poiana's wife, Angela, who gave Allegradonna a dowry upon her marriage to Palladio. In addition to these personal ties with the architect, the Poiana were an old Vicentine family whose connections with the village of Poiana Maggiore in the southern Vicentino extended back to the early fifteenth century. A substantial fifteenth-century villa with turret stands across the road from the Palladian complex and probably served as an earlier family residence.[52]

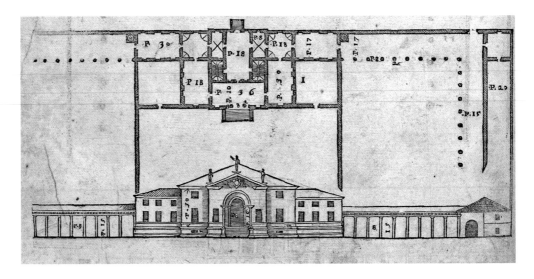

The Villa Poiana has a pivotal quality among Palladio's first villas, with some features reminiscent of Palladio's projects from the early 1540s and others anticipating the more mature
villas of the next decade. This transitional character is clear from the one surviving sheet of
drawings for the project, showing a blocklike house with a loggia to the left and a closed court
to the right.[53] In the drawing the house has a square atrium leading onto a T-shaped *salone* with
cross vaulting not unlike the preliminary studies for the Villa Pisani at Bagnolo. To either side of
this central axis, the apartments describe the letter *L*. Palladio mooted the final solution to the
villa by suggesting either a rectangular atrium with a reduced *salone* or two loggias back to back;
he also considered a two-story *salone*, which would have been lit from a clerestory above, something that harkened back to earlier projects like plate 59.[54] As built, the villa's atrium was
brought to the front and reduced to a rectangular cross-vaulted space that leads into a similarly
proportioned, barrel-vaulted *salone.* Around these elements are grouped familiar suites of small,
medium, and large rooms, and beyond this nucleus two substantial wings, each containing two
rooms, were proposed (plate 71). The published plan bears close resemblance to the Villa
Badoer, and the presence of wings also points to those houses that followed closely upon the
Villa Poiana: the Villa Pisani at nearby Montagnana, the Villa Cornaro at Piombino, and the
Palazzo Antonini at Udine (plate 173).

Only the central block of the villa was built in Palladio's lifetime, with a single wing added
to the left at the end of the sixteenth century, but what was constructed is notable for the faith-
fulness with which it follows the plan in the *Quattro Libri.* The facade shares many features with
the Villa Saraceno and like it is deceptively simple in appearance. Here, too, there are traces of
incised lines in the *intonaco,* suggesting the original use of rustication to mitigate the facade's
severity. The central motif is once again a Serlian arch pierced by oculi, recalling the Braman-

71. *Plan of the Villa Poiana* from the *Quattro Libri.*

tesque villa at Genazzano, and the broken pediment is another favored ingredient from the architect's early years. Although the curiously simple moldings of the main windows are strange and probably date from after Palladio's time, by contrast the mezzanine windows and cornice are more typically Palladian.

What makes the villa so impressive, though, is not so much the exterior of the building as its interior, from the handsome vaults of the semibasement to the large attic granary (plates 72, 74). In particular, the orchestration of space on the *piano nobile*, with its shifts of axes and variation in the vaulting of rooms, gives us the first fruits of Palladio's mature villa style and stands as one of his most impressive achievements in domestic architecture. The motif of the Serlian arch is integrated into the cross vaulting of the atrium and then reappears, establishing the curve of the barrel vault of the *salone* behind; a second Serlian arch is used on the rear

72. The central *salone* of the Villa Poiana. The frescoes have been attributed to Eliodoro Forbicini.

73. The Villa Poiana
at Poiana Maggiore.

facade, its oculi open to provide additional light for the interior (plate 75). The agreeable resonance of the two core rooms spreads out to the surrounding apartments with their sequence of
coved ceilings, pavilion vaults, and cross vaulting for the smallest rooms. Although not in the
best state of preservation, the frescoes are among the most attractive in any Palladian villa. The
architect himself records the presence here of the Veronese artists Bernardino India and
Anselmo Canera as well as the stuccoist Bartolomeo Ridolfi—probably not coincidentally, the
same artists who worked on the Palazzo Thiene during that decade. The atrium, however,
appears to have been painted by another and better Veronese artist, Giambattista Zelotti or
someone of his circle.[55] The themes are those typical of villas: the gods and demi-gods of
antiquity, classical landscapes, and scenes of battle and triumph. The most remarkable room is
the large *sala* to the right of the entrance, the *sala degli imperatori*, where India and Canera frescoed fictive statues of Roman emperors flanked by Ionic columns beneath further *all'antica* decorations in the coved ceiling (plate 172). The resemblance between this room and Palladio's
reconstructions of the Roman Corinthian hall (plate 171) has often been remarked, and it

74. Attic of the Villa Poiana.

clearly represents a moment when the architect played a role in the interior decoration; additionally, it anticipates the kind of effect he achieved with real columns and statuary at Montagnana and Piombino (plates 88, 89).[56]

The loss of gardens, orchard, and fish pond in the late nineteenth century is more noticeable at Poiana than in many other villas because of the excessively barren impression now given by the house and its fields.[57] Defined by hedges and beds of flowers, the immediate surroundings would have served as a foil to the building; the transition from gardens to orchard and fields would have resembled that found in paintings by Pozzoserrato and other artists. The austerity of Palladio's design would have been mitigated by a calculated contrast between nature and artifice.

During the building of the Villa Poiana, Palladio had been taken up by prominent Venetian patrons like Francesco Pisani, who held a large estate at nearby Montagnana, and Girolamo Cornaro at Piombino. By the end of the 1540s, he had become the most important domestic architect in the Veneto, and the stages in his progress to this position can be charted through the Villa Valmarana at Vigardolo, the Villa Pisani at Bagnolo, the Villa Saraceno at Finale, and others. A few years later, his distinctive style of villa architecture was well enough recognized that a suburban Vicentine villa could be described as constructed *alla palladia* even though Palladio was not its author.[58] The author of Palladian architecture had now emerged.

75. Rear facade of the Villa Poiana.

IV
THE BASILICA

IN MARCH 5, 1546, THE DEPUTATI AD UTILIA, THE EXECUTIVE OF THE VICENTINE GOVERNING
council, recommended to the Council of One Hundred a project by "master Giovanni and
Andrea Palladio" for completing the arcades of the city's public palace. In addition, they
advised that a trial bay of the loggias proposed by the architects should be erected in situ, before
a final decision was reached. This proposal was approved by a large majority, and a full-scale
wooden model was executed by the following January. Further deliberations followed, and Palladio was asked to submit additional designs before the Council of One Hundred formally
approved the project, now simply identified as his. This occurred on April 11, 1549. With its
vote, the council made a radical break with the past and set in motion the transformation of the
city center under the hands of its chosen architect.[1]

The vote of the council broke a deadlock that had lasted half a century and became a significant gesture in the rehabilitation of Vicenza after the convulsions of the previous decades.
To appreciate the significance of this commission and why Palladio designed the arcades as he
did, the history of the building must first be considered and its importance for the city of
Vicenza.

In point of fact, *buildings* rather than the singular *building* would be a more accurate term, for
Palladio's stone loggias throw a cloak over a medieval congeries of structures that had grown
together since the thirteenth century. The first mention of the communal palaces on the site
dates from 1262, at which time there was a palace already termed old (*palatium vetus*) on the
western side with a newer communal palace facing it. Further to the east lay a private palace, the
Palazzo Bissari, which, together with its tower, was acquired by the city for its leading magis-
trate or *podestà* in 1211.[2] These buildings were flanked to the north by the main square of

76. Aerial view of the Basilica and the Piazza dei Signori, Vicenza.

Vicenza, then called Piazza Peronio, by the fishmarket to the west, and, on a lower level to the south, the vegetable market, or Piazza delle Erbe. At that time, the Piazza Peronio was less than half its present length and was crossed on the north by the second main road of Roman Vicenza, the *cardo maximus*, running south toward the Piazza Erbe and the Retrone River. The *cardo* separated the old and communal palaces at the ground-floor level, though the two were attached by a connecting passageway on the upper floor. No record exists of what the old palace looked like, but it contained administrative offices and a chapel. More is known about the communal palace, which was supported by large arches on the ground floor and occupied an area corresponding to the easternmost five bays of Palladio's loggias. The structure was built in two phases and contained on its upper floor a large chamber for the meetings of the Vicentine Great Council. On the ground floor the building was divided into two unequal blocks by a passageway running parallel to the *cardo*. The appearance of the building must have been reminiscent of other medieval town halls such as those of Como or Milan, or the later Palazzo dei Trecento in Treviso—namely an oblong block supported by arcades with a main floor given over to an assembly hall.

Though disparate in size and age, the Vicentine palaces were referred to as one entity, "palatium civitatis," from the thirteenth century. Their location and scale reflected the emancipation of Vicenza from its earlier vassalage under its bishop and its transformation into the autonomous state of a *comune*, a process repeated across Northern Italy during this period.[3] But emancipation proved short-lived, receiving its first setback in 1236 when the Emperor Frederick II and Ezzelino da Romano sacked Vicenza. At that time the public palaces were burned and remained derelict until the end of Ezzelino's domination, in 1259. Some attempt at rehabilitation was undertaken then, and shops were ordered to be cleared from the Piazza in 1264.[4] But Vicenza soon drifted under Paduan control, remaining a satellite of Padua and subsequently of Verona until 1404 when the Vicentines gave themselves up to Venetian rule in order to avoid falling under Padua again. The instability and exploitation suffered by Vicenza during this period was reflected in the decline of self-government and a concomitant neglect of public buildings, something only gradually put to right in the period of relative peace and prosperity ushered in by Venetian rule.

Some attempts to patch up the old palaces had been made before the fifteenth century, and the large council chamber in the communal palace was given a new brick vault in 1393. Still, only a disastrous fire in 1444 rendered the state of the city buildings so precarious as to make a radical intervention necessary. Even then, however, work proceeded slowly, for the congestion of the area made any intervention problematic. Finally, following the collapse of part of the old palace, work began in earnest in 1451. Money for the rebuilding came from the Venetian government, and the new structure was designed by the city's architect, Domenico da Venezia.[5] It was symptomatic of Vicenza's cultural dependence on its new masters that both funding and expertise for the building should have come from Venice; indeed in its mid-fifteenth-century state the palace would have evoked comparisons with the Venetian Palazzo Pubblico, which today we call the Doge's Palace, and with Padua's Palazzo della Ragione, itself only recently restored.

The original appearance of Domenico's building can only be approximately reconstructed. Standing on the remains of the earlier public palaces, at ground level it preserved a division in three parts, reflecting the passageways traversing the previous buildings and describing an irregular trapezoid in plan. These elements were welded together into one vast brick *salone*, measuring 53 x 22 x 22.5 meters on the upper level. Covered by a beamed keel vault, the *salone* is one of the great monuments of northern Italian Gothic architecture. An idea of its appearance can be seen in Giovanni Bellini's *Pietà* in the Accademia, Venice, where the city in the background has some of the characteristics of Vicenza; it can also be seen in Marcello Fogolino's additions to the *Madonna delle Stelle,* where the city is spread out at the Virgin's feet. These paintings show that the palace was reminiscent of the Paduan Palazzo della Ragione in profile while its marble cladding derived ultimately from that of the Doge's Palace.[6] The new public palace marked the first example of Vicenza recognizing the symbolic importance of public buildings, and, together with the many Gothic palaces appearing in the latter part of the century, the communal palace also reflected the economic revival of the city.

Domenico da Venezia's palace was finished by 1460. The following years witnessed its gradual physical isolation on the main piazza, now called "dei Signori" after the Venetian governors who lived on the square.[7] Extraneous surrounding structures were removed, and the palace was further embellished by the addition of loggias between 1481 and 1494. Apparently not part of Domenico da Venezia's design, they were nevertheless present on his models in Padua and Venice—some form of arcading would have seemed de rigueur for a Northern Italian palace of the late fifteenth century as was the case with the Palazzo Pubblico in Brescia (plate 77). The creator of the Vicentine loggias was Tommaso Formenton, who became architect to the city in 1467. As with the Palazzo della Ragione in Padua, Formenton's double order of arcades were designed to gird the building, masking its lack of uniformity at ground level. The loggias had the appearance of a series of large roundheaded arches on the ground floor with a pair of smaller pointed arches for each bay on the *piano nobile.* The stone employed on them came from quarries in the mountains to the east and north of Vicenza. There were no arcades to the east where the building faced the Palazzo del Podestà, but it had nine bays on the northern facade facing the Piazza dei Signori, eight on the south facing Piazza delle Erbe, and five on what is now the Piazzetta Palladio. The configuration of the old bays is significant because these are precisely the same number of bays adopted by Palladio for his arcades over half a century later. In both cases, the reason was the same: both Formenton and Palladio faced the problem of marrying a uniform style of arcades to an irregular building (plate 78). The ground-floor arches had to observe the divisions of the old palaces and their passageways, although these were significantly wider across the center of the main facade where the two passageways crossed through the building; likewise the corner bays, determined by the adjacent structures, were considerably narrower.

77. Architect unknown. Palazzo Pubblico, Brescia, begun 1492.

The whole building was finished with the construction of a new staircase in 1496 under the northwest corner of the arcading, on which Pietro Lombardo of Venice was consulted.[8] But the Vicentines had little time to enjoy the completed state of their palazzo since the loggias on the smaller western side of the building collapsed that same year. Formenton, who had departed for Brescia to plan a new public palace there, was by now dead. Consequently, the Vicentines began a long series of consultations, which carried over into the 1540s. The first professional opinion came from Antonio Rizzo, then *proto,* or chief architect, of the Doge's Palace in Venice.[9] Rizzo's advice was relatively straightforward. He proposed rebuilding the loggias with bays of the same size on both floors, much as he had done with the eastern wing of the Doge's Palace; as a simpler alternative, he recommended reinforcing the structure by substituting piers for columns, especially on the corners of the building. Rizzo's advice was not immediately accepted, and further opinions were canvassed. In the end, however, his more ambitious proposal prevailed, and work began on dismantling the western arcades in 1496. Two years later contracts for the new stonework were given out. Meanwhile Rizzo unexpectedly fled Venice after being charged with embezzlement in 1498. His successor there, Giorgio Spavento, was approached by the Vicentine council for an opinion. He effectively proposed a return to Rizzo's more modest proposal of reinforcements on the corner piers, leaving the rhythm of larger ground-floor bays versus smaller upper ones as it existed. Work began in 1499, and the loggias of the western side were restored by 1500.

This hybrid project might have survived had it not been for the political upheavals that disrupted Northern Italy after Pope Julius II proclaimed a holy war against Venice in 1509. For the next two decades Vicenza repeatedly changed allegiance and only the most urgent repairs on the palace and its loggias could be undertaken. After the upper order of loggias on the Piazza dei Signori threatened to fall in 1525, they were invested with scaffolding between 1527 and 1532. The sight of their dilapidated public palace cannot have been pleasing to the Vicentines, and finally toward the end of the 1530s, money and the will to do something about the building prevailed. Consultations were once again invited, but this time the Vicentines began casting a wider net. Jacopo Sansovino, the architect of the procurators of San Marco, in Venice, came in 1538; Sebastiano Serlio, also living in Venice, came the following year; Michele Sanmicheli, the leading architect of Verona, stayed for two weeks at the end of 1541; and Giulio Romano, court

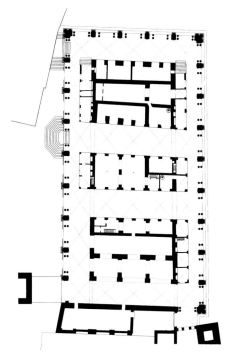

78. *Plan of the Basilica.*

79. *Preliminary design for the Basilica.* (RIBA XVII/22.) Pen, ink, and wash over incised lines, 15.7 x 28.5 cm.

architect of the duke of Mantua, appeared later in 1542.[10] Little evidence is preserved from any visit except for Giulio Romano's. His arrival in Vicenza was evidently something of an event, and the Great Council minutes refer to him as "no common architect but rather celebrated and famous." He was paid handsomely for his visit and left behind a design and a report, the latter actually being entered in the register of the council.[11]

Essentially, Giulio warned against trying to alter the Gothic nature of the building and advocated a continuation of the arcades in the pattern begun in 1499. First, he believed the piers on the corner bays should be strengthened. As for the other columns on the ground floor, they could also be reinforced by turning them into piers, much as he himself had done in the church of San Benedetto Po near Mantua.[12] Giulio felt strongly that any attempt to graft a new style onto the old palace would prove discordant or would entail wholesale rebuilding, and so he proposed a return to the appearance of the palace as left by Formenton in the 1490s.

Giulio's final, longer-term remarks concerned the urban context of the building. Here the prescription was curious, not to say utopian, for he suggested raising the level of the Piazza delle Erbe and lowering that of the Piazza dei Signori in order to fashion one large square. This new piazza would leave the civic buildings isolated in the middle and could, he argued, be enclosed by loggias. Undoubtedly Giulio had in mind something like the contemporary piazza in Loreto, with its uniform arcading, or the Piazza Santissima Annunziata in Florence.[13] His proposal reflected "progressive" architectural thinking of the day, but if carried out the result would have looked like something out of a painting by De Chirico. In any event, Giulio did not sway the Vicentines.

By this time, however, Palladio was being groomed for the role of city architect by his patron Giangiorgio Trissino. Their trips to Rome during the 1540s can be seen in this light, and clearly his intensive study of the antique left a mark on all aspects of his work.[14] In addition, his familiarity with the work of Sanmicheli and Sansovino bore fruit when the young architect submitted his design for what had effectively become a competition.

Palladio did not arrive at a solution in one step. Two drawings give evidence of his preliminary thoughts.[15] One in particular (plate 79) illustrates some of the difficulties he had to confront. As mentioned earlier, any solution for the loggias of the public palace had to respect the irregularities of the ground plan, with its narrow corner and wider central bays, dictated by the passageways crossing through the building (plate 80). Both of the surviving drawings reflect a common approach to the problem. In order to convey a sense of uniformity and regularity to the facade, Palladio endowed his loggias with thick piers, rusticated on the ground floor and smooth above. In the context of the period, the drawings are unexceptional and invite comparison with earlier projects such as Sangallo's courtyard of the Palazzo Farnese in Rome or Sansovino's Library of San Marco in Venice (plate 81), where a Roman solution of an engaged order and arch were employed. Moreover it has been plausibly suggested that Palladio's projects may derive from ideas submitted by Sanmicheli during his consultation on the loggias a few years earlier.[16] Certainly the rustication is typical of Sanmicheli and of Palladio's earlier Sanmichelian facade for the Villa Pisani at Bagnolo. The specific solution in plate 79, in fact, can be compared with a slightly later palace design by Sanmicheli for Rovigo, a similarity that strengthens the plausibility of a common source. Plate 79 also introduces a Serlian arch or *Serliana* in the upper floor. Here, too, precedents existed in the form of a woodcut elevation for a Venetian palace, which Serlio had published a decade earlier.[17] Serlio's design may have been adapted from a proposal for the

80. Interior view of ground-floor arcade, Basilica.

Vicentine loggias. But by reducing the piers to a single engaged order, flanked by smaller columns that form the Serlian arch, it contains the germ of Palladio's winning solution. By comparison, Palladio's adaptation seems ungainly and had to be discarded. The reasons behind this are not hard to fathom. In striving for a uniform solution to the loggias, Palladio opted for small, identical arches. These had to be restricted in size owing to the height of the building's floors, which were, of course, predetermined. Yet the size of Palladio's openings would have seriously restricted access and light, and the result would have proved practically cumbersome and awkward.

Several intervening stages in the design of the loggias have been lost, but Palladio's winning design of 1546, which is now lost, must have been closer to what was subsequently built than to the drawings just considered. Ultimately he adopted a solution with a *Serliana* for both floors, reminiscent of Serlio's woodcut as well as Sansovino's Library, a similar building that had been under construction since 1537. There Sansovino employed an engaged order and Serlian arch on the *piano nobile* similar to Serlio's woodcut; this would have been introduced by Sansovino in order to strengthen the walls against the lateral thrust of the vault planned for the Library.[18] Palladio faced a similar structural problem with the vaults of his arcades, and the double *Serliana* provided additional insurance against collapse. In Palladio's final solution, this motif has an authority lacking in his earlier drawing, for here the Serlian arch is not simply detached from the bay structure but rather knitted into it through the continuous moldings of the imposts running behind the larger engaged columns. The ingenuity of the solution lay in the flexible nature of the *Serliana*: while the central bay remained constant in its proportions, the lateral ones could be expanded or contracted to suit the width of a given opening. Thus on the narrower corner bays of the building the lateral openings of the *Serliana* virtually do not exist; as one moves toward the center of the facade, the bays widen correspondingly, and so do the lateral openings of the *Serliana* (plate 82). Palladio's solution solved two problems at once: it gave a gloss of uniformity to an irregular building and allowed a maximum of flexibility in dealing with the requirements of each bay.

The adoption of the double *Serliana* also caused Palladio to reconsider the corners of the building. Originally he seems to have thought in terms of Sansovino's Library where a column and pilaster were superimposed on a square pier, but in the end he settled for three engaged columns to turn the corner. Palladio was always sensitive to the problem of corners, and his choice in this case had the merit of buttressing the corner piers—again, with a view toward potential weakness—while also having the sanction of antiquity. His inspiration for this kind of pier came from Roman triumphal arches such as the Arch of Titus or that of the Gavi in Verona, where the piers had engaged columns on the corners. The closest parallel to Palladio's Basilica piers is a Roman arch that Palladio probably studied first hand in the years prior to 1546, the Arch of the Sergii in Pula, on the Istrian coast and then a possession of Venice.[19] This arch had been a leitmotif in Venetian Renaissance architecture, employed as the model for the land portal of the Arsenal and for the lower portion of Rizzo's monument to Doge Antonio Tron in the Frari, among other things. In this context, its appeal to Palladio lay in the clustering of columns around the corner, which gave a more plastic effect while providing a smooth transition between the facades. More importantly, their trapezoidal shape disguised the fact that the corners were either obtuse or acute but *not* at right angles. Any other solution, such as the ones envisaged in Palladio's preliminary designs, would have emphasized the irregularities of the buildings' lines.

Palladio was obviously conscious of the classical associations of the Piazza dei Signori and the communal palace; the former stood on the site of Roman Vicenza's forum, and the latter was, as he would later term it, a modern-day Basilica or court of justice.[20] In his winning model, he conveyed an appropriately antique image to bring Domenico da Venezia's building up to date. Unlike Giulio Romano, Palladio and his backers had correctly gauged the mood of the city, and he presented the council with a design rivaling the recent public palace of Brescia (plate 77) and Sansovino's Library.

Who were his backers on the council? Trissino has already been mentioned, and his role was certainly crucial in explaining Vitruvius to the young architect and in taking him to Rome, especially during 1545–46 just prior to the submission of Palladio's design. But Trissino does not seem to have taken an active part in the council meetings between 1546 and 1549. During the latter part of this period the overseers in charge of the preliminary trials for Palladio's model were Gabriele Capra, Girolamo Chiericati, and Giovanni Alvise Valmarana.[21] Charged with reporting to the council on the three principal proposals for the completion of the palace, in the decisive meeting of April 11, 1549, Valmarana and Chiericati were recorded as having spoken "eloquently" and "aptly" in favor of Palladio's design. These men must be credited with swaying the council toward adopting the project of the young local architect. Once Palladio's design was adopted, these same overseers set his monthly salary at five scudi, and during the two years of their stewardship, they spent the conspicuous sum of 2,245 ducats on materials and construction.[22] Palladio's close working relationship with these men and their successors also led to private commissions. Thus, it is not surprising to find that his first private commission after the Basilica was for Chiericati's palace on the edge of the city center, and some years later Valmarana's widow would entrust Palladio with the design of the new family palace.[23] These examples were multiplied over the next decades as members of the Trissino, Piovene, Caldogno, Garzadori, and Angaran families sat as overseers of the Basilica project and turned to Palladio to design palaces and villas that gradually transformed the appearance of Vicenza and its territory.

But that is to anticipate. On the Basilica project, Alvise Sbari, some twenty years Palladio's senior and a former member of the Pedemuro bottega, became the architect's second-in-command and exercised a monopoly over commissioning work on the new arcades, which were to begin in May 1549.[24] But first Sbari was dispatched to the quarries of Piovene to order the blocks of chalky-white limestone for the new structure. Vicenza had rights over these quarries, which were only a few kilometers from town and produced a compact, durable, white stone not unlike the Istrian stone commonly used in Venetian buildings. Before any work could be done in Vicenza, however, the roads between Piovene and Vicenza had to be improved, bridges strengthened, and special carts called "mad cars" constructed in order to carry the weight of stone. The blocks were some five meters long, and transport proved as expensive as the quarrying. In the early months, much of Palladio's time was spent measuring and checking supplies of stone.[25] By August 1549 there were twenty-two thousand bricks in the Piazza, and excavation for the foundations of the corner pier on the northwest side of the building began. Construction proceeded slowly at first because of the late arrival of stone and the necessity of demolishing the old loggias on the western side. Those built by Formenton on the north and south facades were allowed to stand for the time being.

The actual work of constructing the new arcades preceded according to a time-honored formula: each bay was subcontracted to two masons responsible for carving the stone blocks and their architectural membering as well as for putting them in place. Their recompense was 220 ducats, or 240 for the corner piers, which were more demanding. The figural elements—key-

stones and the bucrania of the frieze—were carved separately by other masons, including Palladio's nephew Marc'antonio. By March 1550 parts of the arches facing west on what is known as the Piazzetta Palladio were already in place although they were almost immediately disassembled; subsequently the pier on the northwest corner also had to be rebuilt.[26] No reason is given for this, but it may have stemmed from miscalculations in scale or stress. The great caution shown here may perhaps be indicative of the care taken by Palladio and his patrons to avoid a disaster like the one that had occurred in 1496. By January 1552 the corner pier had been rebuilt. Three successive arches of the Doric order on the Piazza dei Signori were standing in June 1553, and work progressed, bay by bay, across the main facade. Down to 1552 more than four thousand ducats had been disbursed for the new loggias, at which point the city council decided to curb expenditure the following year by placing an annual ceiling of one thousand

81. *(above)* Jacopo Sansovino (1486–1570). Detail of corner solution for the Library of San Marco, Venice.

82. *(opposite)* The northwestern corner of the Basilica as seen from the Piazza dei Signori.

ducats on the project. Nevertheless the fifth and middle bay of the facade on the Piazza dei Signori was in place by September 1554, and the next two bays quickly followed. Palladio then shifted attention to the northeast corner pier, the one adjacent to the Palazzo del Podestà. Previously the old arcading had been attached to the *podestà*'s residence, but Palladio had the connection demolished, thus establishing a precise visual break between the two structures. The northeast corner bays were finished by the end of September 1556, and their construction defined, so to speak, the framework of the main facade. Work continued on the western facade in 1558, and a motion by the council that year reflected the growing public perception of the new structure's importance to Vicenza: "There is no doubt that our palace yields to no other public building in Italy in architecture or beauty, and every day it is being brought to a perfect form."[27] Only one bay was missing from the Doric order on the main piazza in November 1559 while four of the five bays were finished on the western facade. By July 1561 the whole of the Doric order on these two sides was complete save the cornice and steps.

Behind this seemingly straightforward account the one great crisis of Palladio's career is concealed. Beginning in October 1559 the council, faced with famine and the need to borrow money to buy grain for its people, cut the annual expenditure on the loggias by half.[28] Then on May 20, 1560, the Deputati ad utilia, the council's executive committee, ordered the suspension of new building. In view of the straitened finances of the city, it was further deemed "incorrect" to pay Palladio's stipend. Although the sum involved was only five scudi per month, it provided the architect with a basic wage, and Palladio's finances in those early years were far from flush; often he or his wife had to ask for advances in order to make ends meet. For the next two months Palladio went without pay, but this decision provoked enough discontent for the Venetian *podestà* to convene the Great Council on July 22. Ninety-five members turned out, an unusually large number for the time of year and an indication of how seriously the Vicentines took the matter. Girolamo Feramosca, a doctor of laws and legal advisor to the council, proposed a compromise whereby Palladio would be reinstated but with his stipend reduced to two-and-a-half ducats, corresponding to the halving of expenditure on the loggias. By this date, however, the executive committee of the council had changed, and among its new members was Marc'antonio Thiene, patron of one of the most conspicuous palaces built by Palladio (plate 31). The deputies led a counterattack, arguing that "considering the very great importance of the palace, which could not be built without the presence of Messer Andrea Palladio," the architect should be reinstated with his customary salary, although the council would reserve the right to reduce or deprive Palladio of his money.[29] This proposal carried the day.

Though the two months of uncertainty must have caused Palladio great anxiety, he was luckier than some. In another case that also illustrates the often problematic nature of the master-servant relationship between patron and architect, his older contemporary Sansovino was thrown in prison, stripped of his salary for two years, and fined by his employers when part of the Library of San Marco's vault collapsed in 1545.[30] As long as things went well, architects would be given latitude, but mishaps could bring crushing reversals. The solution adopted in Sansovino's case typifies those sanctions kept in reserve by patrons. Fortunately, they were not used here, although Palladio's stipend remained pegged at five scudi for the rest of his life. The sum was just enough to live on, and probably calculated to keep Palladio dependent on the good will of his masters. Even so, Girolamo Feramosca launched a second attack on Palladio in 1563.[31] He tried to have the commission for designing new benches in the chamber of deputies given to his own protégé, Gian Domenico Scamozzi, who later built Feramosca's villa near Vicenza. The motion was defeated by a large majority, but Feramosca must have represented a current of opinion within Vicenza, people who felt that too many commissions were going Palladio's way. This may also have marked the beginning of the enmity that Scamozzi's more gifted son Vincenzo felt toward Palladio. In part the problem may have stemmed from the relative flexibility of Palladio's position after the first demanding phase of work on the loggias was over. By 1550, he was able to obtain leave to go to Brescia for a consultation on the public palace there; he made a similar trip to Verona in 1551, competed for an important job in Venice in 1554, and was again given leave "to attend to business with some Venetian gentlemen" the following year.[32] Palladio's comings and goings and his evident ambition were not well received in some quarters of Vicenza.

Money remained in short supply between 1561 and 1564, and the small sums available were chiefly spent on finishing the two principal ground floor facades. More stone was ordered from Piovene, but there was an attempt to suspend work entirely in 1563. Fabio Monza, a nobleman and friend of the architect, describes in his diary how he went to the council meeting "to help Palladio," and the proposal was decisively defeated.[33] Palladio could count upon a large measure of confidence within the ruling circle of Vicenza, and, what is equally noteworthy, the Vicentines themselves clearly saw the conclusion of the new arcading as central to civic pride. The particular significance of the loggias can be seen in the unusual decision to begin work upon their upper floor in 1564 rather than embarking upon the third ground-floor facade facing the Piazza delle Erbe. Such a decision must have been taken deliberately since construction had already begun on the first bay of the third main facade.[34] Evidently the council or the overseers of the project felt work would be less likely to stop if the upper floor were already begun, and in this way the two principal facades would be finished first. As it turned out, they were right to adopt this strategy.

Palladio delivered a design and model for the Ionic order in March 1564. His ideas are preserved on a sheet (plate 83), which shows the bay of the northwest corner where construction subsequently began.[35] A far cry from his preliminary studies, the drawing in question shows the architect's mature style as a draftsman. The meticulous crosshatching and crude approximations of classical orders have disappeared in favor of a clear, crisp orthogonal elevation of the kind invariably used by Palladio after his first years. Even here, though, significant differences from the actual building emerge: the plinth lacks the additional fascia, or base molding, and a parapet instead of a balustrade is used as well as a flat frieze rather than a convex one. Each of these changes had a telling effect upon the design of the upper order and was indicative of Palladio's eye for detail. The convex frieze, which actually marks a reversion to an idea sketched in one of Palladio's earlier drawings, endowed the building with a richer, more plastic profile; the balustrade gave a more open appearance to the arches and, incidentally, corresponded to the balustrades on Formenton's upper loggia. But the most interesting of these adjustments was the extra fascia for the plinth (plate 84). This also seems to have been a last minute change, perhaps prompted by the delay in starting the upper floor. Alvise Sbari, who contracted to execute the first arches of the Ionic order, had died before work began, and his partner had disappeared. A second contract was drawn up with another mason, Pasqualino da Venezia, in 1566, and there the cost of executing each bay was raised from 242 to 255 ducats because of the extra base molding "added by Messer Andrea Palladio."[36]

Four Ionic bays—two on the Piazza dei Signori and two on the Piazzetta—were finished by April 1570. This meant that from two principal viewpoints, the present contrà Cavour and the contrà Muschiera (leading to the cathedral), the building would have appeared virtually complete. But again fate intervened, and major work was abandoned for several years. Vicenza donated the conspicuous sum of twelve thousand ducats to the war against the Turks, and public attention was focused on rebuilding the Loggia del Capitaniato (plate 195), facing the

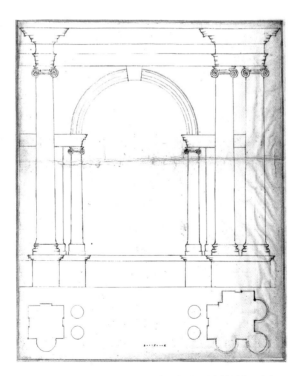

83. *Elevation of the upper story of the Basilica.* (RIBA XIII/8.) Pen, ink, and chalk over incised lines, 46 x 37.2 cm.

84. Detail of Ionic order on upper floor of the Basilica.

public palace on the opposite side of the square.[37] Meanwhile, brick vaults were constructed to connect the new Ionic arches to the palace, but little else was done. This state of affairs did not sit well with the city council, which passed a resolution in May 1572 emphasizing "that it was necessary to continue in the best way possible such a beautiful and renowned enterprise."[38] The result was a grant of three hundred ducats per annum and a recommendation that the overseers of the building should draw up contracts with masons for the construction of further bays. The following month witnessed just such a contract for six more bays with Battista Marchesi, who had collaborated with Palladio on the bridge over the Brenta River at Bassano del Grappa; this time the costs were counted in advance and came to 825 ducats per bay, of which 25 covered labor.[39] Still, only two bays were built by 1584 when a new contract was drawn up with Giovanni Antonio Grazioli, this time at a price of 900 ducats per bay. Grazioli's work evidently satisfied the overseers, for he received a second contract for the remaining arches in November 1585.[40] By 1597 Grazioli had produced twelve bays or almost one a year.

The facades on the northern and western sides were now complete as well as the re-entrant bay toward the Palazzo del Podestà. At the same time, the classicizing statues that crown the arcades were ready for installation. Such figures were expected on public buildings and were ordered cheaply from local sculptors at five ducats each.[41] Grazioli then signed a new contract for the remaining arcades facing the Piazza delle Erbe at a cost of one thousand ducats per bay, the steep rise reflecting inflationary pressures on material and transport.[42] When Grazioli died in 1599, his brother Giovanni assumed responsibility for completing the work.

On the Piazza delle Erbe, a special problem arose that Palladio may never have seriously addressed. This concerned the 2.5-meter drop in level between the piazza and the ground floor of the public palace. As built, the lower ground floor consists of rusticated blocks of stone, punctuated by doorways for shops and the handsome, faceted staircase. Both must have been interpolations by the Grazioli brothers and were probably dictated as much by considerations of economy as by aesthetics. Once this problem was solved work proceeded swiftly on the final facade: by 1605 five bays were done, followed by another three by 1610. The last arches were executed by 1614, although they were only paid for in 1617 when the accounts for the project were finally closed.[43]

Palladio never lived to see his handiwork completed, and after his departure for Venice in 1570 he had little contact with the project. But he laid down a pattern for the later stages, which allowed the building to run itself. The passage on the Basilica in the *Quattro Libri* was written with feeling and justifiable pride. "I have no doubt," Palladio states, "that this structure could be compared with ancient buildings and numbered among the greatest and most beautiful that have been created since classical times, both for scale and decoration as well as for material. Being entirely of very durable stone, the blocks have been dressed and fitted together with the greatest skill."[44] Palladio called the new building a basilica in recollection of those palaces of justice that stood on public forums in Greece and Rome, and the name stayed with it. His poetic license was justified for his remarkable Basilica, which brings the classical vocabulary to the service of modern architecture. No contemporary building, not even Sansovino's Library, uses Roman forms with the authority of Palladio's work here. The brilliance and elegance of his solution for the loggias would be hard to exaggerate, but the willing cooperation of the city of Vicenza in this enterprise also deserves credit. For a city of some twenty thousand inhabitants to spend over sixty thousand ducats on such a project becomes all the more impressive if one recalls that Venice, a city with a population some eight times larger, spent a similar amount on one of the few major civic projects of the period, Sansovino's Library.[45] The commitment to building manifested by Vicenza in this period was remarkable and cannot simply be ascribed to its wealth. After all, no similar phenomenon can be found in Padua or Verona or Brescia, which were larger and equally wealthy. Instead, it is a reflection of a fairly conscious desire on the part of the Vicentines to enhance the appearance and, with it, the status of their city. Their alliance with Palladio produced the Basilica, the most conspicuous element in the transformation of Vicenza.

V

MATURE VILLAS

THE 1550S SAW PALLADIO AT THE HEIGHT OF HIS POWERS AND OCCUPIED WITH DOMESTIC architecture as he never would be again. After a complex gestation the Basilica was underway, and its steady rhythm of work gave Palladio financial security as well as the flexibility to travel for study and commissions. His collaboration with Daniele Barbaro on the latter's translation of Vitruvius gathered pace prior to publication in 1556, and the first steps toward the *Quattro Libri* had occurred, as Barbaro and the Florentine writer Doni both noted.[1] Palladio also began to cast his eyes in the direction of Venice with his application in 1554 for the post of *proto al Sal*, or architect of the Salt Magistracy.[2] Greater experience and a deepening knowledge of the antique also led to a qualitative leap in Palladio's architecture, and nowhere is this more evident than in his villas.

What makes the villas of this period so arresting is that they document a change in attitude away from the concept of an agricultural holding with a house and toward a type of country house with specific artistic and cultural associations. Certainly villas of distinction were built before this decade, but works like the Villa Madama, the Palazzo del Te, or the Villa Imperiale near Pesaro remained splendid in their isolation while the generality of villas continued to be more modest and functional in design. Even a building like the Villa Pisani at Bagnolo, for all its antique and modern resonances, occupies a different sphere from the Villa Malcontenta or even the Villa Cornaro at Piombino.

During the middle of the sixteenth century the development of the villa as an architectural form became chiefly a northern Italian, especially a Veneto, phenomenon.[3] A quickening of interest can be seen not only in the creation of the Magistrato sopra i Beni Inculti, founded in 1545 to encourage land reclamation and investment in the Venetian provinces, but also in the

85. Garden facade of the Villa Cornaro, Piombino Dese.

number of books on agriculture and villa life that came off the printing presses in the same period. These included classical treatises on agriculture and de Crescenzi's *Opus ruralium commodorum,* which appeared in Italian translation and went through innumerable editions; in addition, a new type of book came into being, one that celebrated the more literary and humanistic aspects of villa life.[4] Written and published chiefly during the 1550s, they reflect new expectations of what could be loosely termed a villa life-style. A particularly vivid example is Anton Francesco Doni's short and somewhat fantastical account of different kinds of villas, *Le Ville.*[5] Here he lists five types, ranging from the *villa civile* of a ruler to the *podere di spasso* for gentlemen, the *possessione di recreatione* of the bourgeoisie, the *casa di risparmio* for the artisan, and the *capanna dell'utile* or simple farmstead of the peasant. The distinctions between the villas of rulers and those of noblemen and merchants seem more of degree than kind. Indeed what is noteworthy in Doni's essay is not so much the social hierarchy of buildings—that, after all, could be found in Serlio's account of private housing—but rather the almost exclusive preoccupation with the urbane aspects of villa life. Imposing staircases, loggias, polished floors, tapestries, frescoes, gardens with pergolas and labyrinths: these fire Doni's imagination. While his approach is more elaborate than other writers', he does share with them an approach to villas as mainly social and aesthetic creations. The primary purpose of the villa as a house rooted in an agricultural community is all but forgotten, to the point that the differences between villa and palace decoration are minimal.[6] Palladio's comments on villas in the *Quattro Libri* never go this far—his treatise is essentially practical and keeps the functional aspects of the villa firmly in balance against its social and cultural side.[7] But his mature villas created an artistic pattern that more than any other distilled the new requisites of villas into a model that proved to be one of his most influential creations.

The first step in this shift in Palladio's approach to villa architecture can be traced to one work in particular—not, as it happens, a villa but rather a palace. The work in question is Palazzo Chiericati (plate 39). We have already seen how pivotal this palace was in Palladio's early career. Coming just after the success of the Basilica competition, it demonstrated a boldness of concept and presented new features that anticipated Palladio's later domestic architecture.[8] Its two-story solution with a semibasement and a double order of arcades, as well as a central pediment in its preliminary designs, finds immediate correspondence in Palladio's subsequent villas. This is not surprising since the palace was sited on the edge of Vicenza and could almost be construed as a *villa suburbana.* By 1552 the central motif of the Chiericati's courtyard facade, the double loggia, had been used again, crowned by a pediment, in the Villa Pisani at Montagnana and the Villa Cornaro at Piombino, which were built for patrons from two of the most distinguished patrician families of Venice.

The Villa Pisani resembles Palazzo Chiericati, lying as it does just outside the brick walls of Montagnana in an area that was and still remains a suburb called San Zeno.[9] Like a palace, the villa consists of a rectangular block fronting onto the street and with a garden at the rear (plates

86, 87). There are no agricultural buildings on the estate, for the villa owes its origins to another form of economic power, water. One wing straddles a small stream called the Fiumicello on which the Pisani family owned mills.

The family was a powerful one in the area, but Francesco Pisani was obviously interested in consolidating his presence in Montagnana. Not only did he begin building his house there around 1552, he also intervened to secure for Paolo Veronese the significant commission of the high altar of the collegiate church of Montagnana in 1555 and was instrumental in involving Palladio in designs for a new choir for the church in 1564.[10] Pisani may have become aware of Palladio through his cousin Daniele Barbaro, who held a canonry at Montagnana, but the architect could as easily have been drawn to Pisani's attention by the recent construction of the Villa Poiana (plates 71–75), only a short distance away from Montagnana.[11]

Pisani must have been impressed by the Villa Poiana's aggressively modern design, but he evidently required something more palatial. In plan and appearance, the house can be explained by reference to its setting, one facade facing town and the other the family estate. Both facades are dominated by the central motif of a double loggia of Doric and Ionic columns surmounted by a pediment; on the town facade, a "closed," applied order is employed while an "open" loggia faces onto the more private area of the garden, just as with Palazzo Chiericati. On the main facade, the frieze of the "nobler" Ionic order gives the patron's name while in the tympanum above winged victories support his coat of arms. Photographs leave a gaunter impres-

86. Facade of the Villa Pisani, Montagnana.

sion of the facade than is the case, for the surface is rendered and lightly incised to seem like rusticated stone. This effect, called *bugnato graffito,* is more evident on the main facade than on the garden entrance, where an insensitive resurfacing has left a drab yellow plaster coating of the kind often found on historic monuments in Northern Italy.[12] With a whiter, *marmorino*-like surface, the contrast between the rendering and the window surrounds would have mitigated the bleakly neoclassical appearance of the villa.

In plan, too, the Villa Pisani is closely linked to Palladio's palace designs, especially the Palazzo Iseppo da Porto in Vicenza and the Palazzo Antonini in Udine (plates 36, 173).[13] In all three cases, the architect employed a familiar tripartite division with a central atrium or *salone* flanked by a suite of small, medium, and large rooms. With the later Villa Pisani and Palazzo Antonini, the atrium of Palazzo Porto becomes an interior room, the columns making no small contribution to their beauty (plate 88). The Villa Pisani further develops the facade's motif of the applied Doric order, which becomes in the *salone* a series of four freestanding and eight applied columns supporting a handsome cross-vaulted ceiling. This room received the greatest attention from the architect because it combined the functions of entrance hall and reception room, and beyond this point many visitors would not have penetrated. Here Palladio created a form of counterpoint between columns, vaulting, and the niches occupying the corners of the room. These are filled with stucco figures of the four seasons by Alessandro Vittoria, who shortly before had made a brilliant debut with Palladio in Palazzo Thiene.[14] At the Villa Pisani,

87. *(above)* Garden facade of the Villa Pisani.

88. *(opposite) Salone* of the Villa Pisani. The stucco figures are by Alessandro Vittoria.

however, architecture and sculpture combine to create a more restrained effect reminiscent of Palladio's recreation of the interior of ancient houses in the *Quattro Libri*.[15] The Doric order is itself compressed with only an architrave and cornice, a feature that could be called mannerist though sanctioned by antiquity.[16]

How far the tone established by the entrance hall continued in the adjoining rooms cannot now be determined. The lateral stanze still have coved ceilings while the square rooms directly behind them are cross-vaulted and the small serving rooms are barrel-vaulted, all in keeping with Palladio's treatment of such rooms elsewhere and with his advice in the *Quattro Libri*.[17] Beyond this, the original decoration was overlaid in the nineteenth century. The same can be said for the upper level, which conforms in plan to the ground floor though the ceilings are all flat. As a refinement upon Palazzo Porto, the stairs here assume a more important role and occupy what would have been additional rooms on the garden facade. This becomes common in later two-story villa and palace projects, and can be explained by the fact that the stairs were not simply for service but formed part of the route through which the Pisani and their guests would move.[18] Keeping this purpose in mind, Palladio created a winding staircase that describes an oval pattern as it goes to the first floor and attic above. The stairs take their light from the loggia as well as the garden and lateral facades and can be seen as a development on the double staircase solution for Palazzo Chiericati.

Although the villa corresponds to the plan in the *Quattro Libri* rather closely, there is one significant and much discussed difference.[19] Palladio's woodcut treats the house as a nucleus for a much grander project comprising triumphal arches and corner towers. In this way the plate in the *Quattro Libri* can be compared with that for the Villa Pisani at Bagnolo or the Villa Thiene at Quinto as being a later revision of the original project.[20] The accompanying text explains that streets flanked the building on either side, a situation that Palladio turned to the benefit of the design by creating bridges over the roads to the wings that housed services and the kitchen. In abstract it seems a clever idea, but it would have come into conflict with the true circumstances of its site. The villa was built too close to the moat running around the town walls to allow space for such a wing, nor is there evidence that such work was contemplated. Both the fenestration and the continuation of the Doric frieze around the lateral facades argue against this. In all likelihood, the Villa Pisani was conceived as a self-contained block.

The Villa Cornaro at Piombino was under construction at virtually the same time as the Villa Pisani and can be read as a variation on the same theme.[21] Indeed their juxtaposition on facing pages of the *Quattro Libri* could hardly have been coincidental. In both buildings we find a two-story solution with double loggias, a similarly squarish hall framed by Palladio's standard sequence of rooms, and oval staircases flanking the garden portico. Both are recognizable as a reworking of basic motifs, although at the Villa Cornaro the *salone* has four columns but a more traditional, beamed ceiling (plate 89). The corridor has been brought forward to the front of

89. *(opposite) Salone* of the Villa Cornaro.

the house, necessitating an adjustment of the lateral rooms. The porticos, too, are conceived in a different fashion: that on the garden facade is *in antis,* flush with the facade, as was the case with the Villa Pisani, while the portico of the principal facade has been brought forward like that of Palazzo Chiericati. This was not entirely a new solution for Veneto villas ever since the architect of the Villa Giustinian at Roncade (plate 44) had applied a similar two-story loggia with pediment to its main facade.[22] But while the loggia of the Villa Giustinian simply abuts the villa block, Palladio's portico is integrated, proportionally and aesthetically, with the building. Palladio carries his pursuit for coherence further by aligning the columns of the *salone* with those of the porticos, a touch characteristic of his working methods and also found in his churches. He also records in the *Quattro Libri* that the columns of the Corinthian loggia are one-fifth thinner than those of the Ionic order below, something that gave a greater sense of verticality to the building as a whole.[23]

The Villa Cornaro owed its origins to the division of the large estate of Girolamo Cornaro, son of Zorzi Cornaro, one of the wealthiest men of his day in Venice, and nephew of the last queen of Cyprus, Caterina Cornaro.[24] The division happened in 1551 when the bulk of the estate and the existing house passed to the eldest son, Andrea, whose younger brother Giorgio then needed a house from which he could supervise his own land. Why Giorgio turned to Palladio for the task is not easily explained, but by this date the architect had more than a decade's experience in villa design and was beginning to be patronized by the Venetian aristocracy. The surviving accounts for the Villa Cornaro are comparatively full and throw much light on contemporary architectural practice. As was often the case, Palladio provided only the designs and is recorded as having occasionally been present, for the actual supervision of construction was done by two *fattori* or foremen. Work began in 1552, and the villa was habitable by September 1553. Palladio came twice to supervise work on the upper floor in April and May 1554, receiving his last payment in October of that year. Giorgio Cornaro married in March 1554 and could have moved directly into his new house, although the villa was still referred to as unfinished in 1573 and the wings that appear in the *Quattro Libri* plate were only added in 1590. As was the case with the Villa Poiana, the wings of the Cornaro follow the basic design recorded in the woodcut, although they do not step back from the line of the facade and the first floor has two windows instead of three.

Among the archival references, a payment to a sculptor named Agostino Zoppo deserves comment. Zoppo was a talented sculptor and bronze-caster in Padua, perhaps best known for the monument to Livy inside the Palazzo della Ragione there.[25] At the Villa Cornaro he created the Ionic capitals on the ground floor. The fact that these were ordered from a Paduan sculptor reflects more than perfectionism on the part of patron and architect; such capitals were difficult to carve and required skill perhaps not available locally. In this context, it is worth observing that the Corinthian capitals of the upper story are not stone but terracotta (plate 90), like those of the Tempietto at the Villa Maser.[26] Here the only explanation that

comes to mind is lack of expertise and the need for economy, and it remains an unusual case in Palladio's domestic architecture.

Serlio remarked upon the Venetian fondness for the Corinthian order, and its appearance on the Villa Cornaro is one of many elements that can be construed as a concession to Venetian taste.[27] The double loggia is also a familiar feature of Venetian palaces, as are the roundheaded windows and columnar hall with beamed ceiling. What distinguishes these features from Venetian vernacular architecture is the rigorous way in which they are merged with Palladio's

90. Detail of the upper loggia on the garden facade of the Villa Cornaro.

91. View of vaulted lateral room at the Villa Cornaro. The frescoes date from around 1716 and are by Mattia Bortoloni.

architectural system. Thus the columns of the loggia not only follow Palladio's recommended proportions, but the Ionic order is given a eustyle formula for its intercolumniation.[28] Palladio's mastery of the ancient orders gave a stamp of authority to his buildings that few of his immediate competitors could rival. But he was also blessed with an intuitive sense of the ways in which the orders could be adapted to the requirements of modern architecture. One such example can be seen in the Ionic order of the Villa Cornaro's *salone*. Here, four columns support the wooden ceiling and each has a canted volute, one turned at a forty-five-degree angle to the main face of the capital. This is reminiscent of the so-called Temple of Fortuna Virilis in Rome where the canted volute gave a graceful turn to the capitals of the corner columns (plate 180). As Palladio mentioned in his account of the temple in the *Quattro Libri*, it was an unusual solution but an attractive one.[29] When faced with creating freestanding Ionic columns for the *salone* of the villa, he adapted this motif much as did the architect of the Roman temple. He would later return to it for the *salone* of the Palazzo Antonini in Udine and the solution for the corner of the upper order of the Basilica, among others. Above the capitals, the beams are treated as if they were an architrave, thus enhancing the logic of the order as was done with the Doric entablature of the Villa Pisani. This idea is continued around the walls by the beams that support the coffering of the ceiling.[30]

Although the stucco decoration of the *salone* was carried out after Palladio's day, the niches were designed by him perhaps to receive statues of famous members of the Cornaro family.[31] Ancestor worship was a notable feature of Venetian life, and few patrician families were as fond of celebrating themselves in public as were the Cornaro. So it is not surprising that the decorative program concentrated on historical figures rather than mythological ones, as was the case with the Villa Pisani. The lateral suites, with frescoes by Mattia Bortoloni and stuccowork by Bartolomeo Cabianca, bear an early eighteenth-century appearance, but their vaults (plate 91) and marble fireplaces were executed after Palladio's designs and invite comparison with the Villa Pisani as well as later works like the Villa Malcontenta. Here as elsewhere, Palladio's sensitivity to room dimensions and to details such as fireplace moldings give a particular richness to his domestic architecture.

Palladio's attention to staircases also developed in these years. The interior oval staircases of the Villa Pisani already demonstrate this, but at the Villa Cornaro the external stairs are also noteworthy. Once again one can see a relationship with the Palazzo Chiericati, for the presence of a semi-basement in the Villa Cornaro determined the need for a more conspicuous approach, both front and back. More like ramps than proper staircases, they deflect attention from the semi-basement and provide a graceful bridge between the house and its surroundings.

Like all of the villas, the materials used for the Villa Cornaro are simple—brick, wood, and plaster—although the architect's inventiveness transmutes them into something nobler. Nowhere is this seen more clearly than in the external facing. The basement has been left as exposed brick; whether or not this was Palladio's intention, its plainness may have been a reflection of the hierarchical ordering of villa life, with the functional nature of the lowest floor expressed in brick and mortar. For the main stories and the porticos, Palladio employed his typical rendering on the plaster to give the appearance of stone, in this case with a smooth rustication or *bugnato gentile.* The rustication provides just enough of an accent to enliven the surface of the facades, with the creation of blind arches and voussoirs above the windows compensating for the absence of stone moldings. In sunlight this technique, which is even more brilliantly exploited with the Villa Malcontenta, gives a sparkling texture and nuance to the building's appearance.

Palladio's approach to villa design matured rapidly in the 1550s, but he does not yet appear to have developed a clear distinction between villas and palaces. He himself would later write: "The owner's house should be built with regard to his household and status, and one builds as one does in the city."[32] Evidence of this conflation of urban and rural can be seen not only in the overlapping of the Palazzo Porto's plan with those of several villas but also in the design and appearance of the Palazzo Antonini in Udine (plate 173). This building has occupied a peripheral place in Palladio's career, both geographically and metaphorically.[33] Built for an Udinese nobleman, the palace was probably designed between 1554, when Palladio met Floriano Antonini through the offices of Daniele Barbaro, and 1556, when construction began. At that time Palladio was present in Udine for the erection of a triumphal arch in honor of Domenico Bollani, the Venetian governor, and could have supervised the initial stages of work on the palace.[34] Udine was too far from Vicenza to allow for the occasional trips that Palladio is known to have made in similar cases, and construction of the palace would have been supervised by a local architect. Hence only the general plan of the building and its central loggias actually conform to Palladio's plate in the *Quattro Libri.* Though the kitchen wing was never built, it is similar in conception to those of the Villas Pisani and Cornaro as they appear in plan in the *Quattro Libri.*[35]

Today the palace has been engulfed by the urban fabric of Udine, but in the sixteenth century it stood on the edge of the city in a setting of gardens and open spaces rather like the Palazzo Civena or Palazzo Chiericati in Vicenza. This earlier context can still be seen in the late seventeenth-century bird's-eye view of Udine.[36] The location of the Antonini palace no doubt reminded Palladio of his recent suburban villa, the Villa Pisani. Though close in style, the Palazzo Antonini is not a simple repetition of earlier works. The town facade shows a deliberate

exploration of rustication with a ground-floor Ionic order reminiscent of Sansovino's Mint in Venice.[37] The upper floor is plain, by contrast, while the garden facade has a portico *in antis* like the Villas Cornaro and Pisani. No pediment was ever built here, nor do the window frames or balustrades, which must be later interpolations, conform to Palladio's style. On the inside the *salone* has four Ionic columns bearing a flat-beamed ceiling, the Ionic capitals with canted volutes as was the case in the Villa Cornaro. Otherwise, the decoration stems from the seventeenth and eighteenth centuries.

Palladio was obviously pleased with the design of the Palazzo Antonini. His decision to place it first among the palaces in the *Quattro Libri* grants it significance as a prototype for contemporary villas and later palaces like that for Giovanni Battista Garzadore.[38] Here he is setting forth the kernel of his domestic architecture, the basic nucleus of a house on which he wrought innumerable changes. Above all, the Palazzo Antonini is a cogent reminder of the interplay of ideas and the merging of typologies in Palladio's domestic architecture, especially in this period.

Not all of Palladio's villas were designed along this pattern. He also created a solution for villas with a single main story, an approach that proved equally influential with later architects. Its earliest appearance seems to have been in the villa planned for Giovanni Chiericati, brother of the patron of the Palazzo Chiericati. Not mentioned in the *Quattro Libri*, the villa is nonetheless closely related to a drawing by Palladio and bears enough hallmarks of his style for the attribu-

92. Portico of the Villa Chiericati, Vancimuglio di Grumolo (Vicenza).

tion to have gained general acceptance (plate 92).[39] Chiericati inherited the property in 1546, and Palladio's project may well date from a few years later. The villa shows affinities with motifs explored in Palladio's earlier houses such as the Palazzo Civena and the Villa Pisani at Bagnolo, not to mention the Palazzo Chiericati. Its most striking feature is the temple portico, which resembles, in plan, the courtyard loggia of the Palazzo Chiericati. Inside, the dominant feature is a large biapsidal *salone* with cross vaulting flanked by identical staircases and terminating in a Serlian arch with hemicyclical stairs. Here Palladio returned to previously unrealized ideas with motifs that all recall preliminary studies for the Villa Pisani at Bagnolo. Like the Pisani, Chiericati opted for a less ambitious solution, without vaulting or elaborate staircases.

Work on the Villa Chiericati began around 1554, but little more than the foundations were complete at Giovanni Chiericati's death four years later. The house remained incomplete until 1574 when it was finished by the local mason Domenico Groppino. To what extent the simplification of the *salone* and the stairs was intended by Palladio remains moot. Enough of the original design survives, however, to allow the charm of Palladio's concept to shine through. Above all it is the well-proportioned block of the villa combined with a colossal Ionic order and temple pediment that gives the facade its impact and distinguishes it from such earlier villas as that at Bertesina (plate 57). It was this sense of the right proportions for the portico that the architect put to good effect subsequently.

Palladio soon had the opportunity to refine his ideas further with another villa for a Venetian nobleman, this one for Francesco Badoer at Fratta Polesine (plates 93–97). Fratta lies

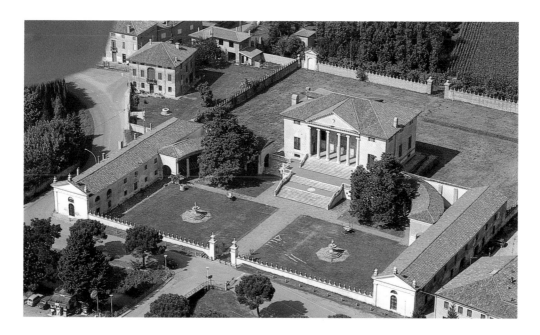

93. Aerial view of the Villa Badoer, Fratta Polesine.

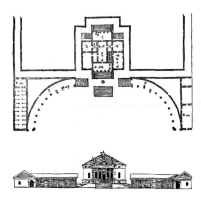

94. Woodcut of the Villa Badoer from the
Quattro Libri.

in the great plain of the Po Valley on the southernmost tip of the *terraferma* dominions of Venice. The region of the Polesine had only been wrested from Ferrara by Venice in 1482, and with its flat fields and numerous canals it was ideal for land reclamation. Francesco Badoer inherited land in Fratta through his wife, Lucietta Loredan. Her family in turn had acquired land near there as early as 1519 when the Venetian government sold its holdings in Polesine to raise capital after the War of the League of Cambrai.[40] A map of 1549 shows only cottages on the site of Fratta, although another map of the area from 1556 shows the villa's boundary walls as standing, an indication that the acquisition of the land and the initial work on the villa complex must have taken place between 1549 and 1556.

In plan, the Villa Badoer is similar to the Villa Poiana of half a decade earlier, but with Badoer the hierarchical structure of the villa found its classic form (plate 71). The plate in the *Quattro Libri* explains Palladio's intentions concisely (plate 94).[41] The villa's forecourt is framed by stables and farm buildings linked to the central block by a simple Tuscan arcade. These end at the foot of an imposing staircase, which rises in two stages to the portico of the *casa padronale,* or owner's house, itself ennobled by an Ionic portico *in antis* surmounted by a pediment with a coat of arms.[42] Although only six bays of the arcades were constructed, the executed villa remains faithful to Palladio's project and embodies the habitual attention to the functional and aesthetic that was the hallmark of his architectural practice.

With the Villa Badoer, Palladio put the definitive touches on his reorganization of the structures associated with villa life, which he achieved through practical and symbolic adjustments to conventional building. By employing quadrants for the form of the arcades, Palladio visibly linked the outbuildings with the owner's house at the center of the estate. He thus made an integrated composition of the various farm elements, unlike the haphazard arrangement of arcades and outbuildings that often prevailed (plate 95). The idea of quadrants probably occurred to him through his study of classical architecture, the hemicycles of Trajan's Forum in Rome presenting a handy point of departure for this motif. The choice of the Tuscan order for the farm arcades conveyed a message in reference to the five orders, for the Tuscan was recognized by Renaissance theorists and architects as the most primitive and hence the lowest of the orders.[43] In the first book of the *Quattro Libri,* Palladio explains its properties in this manner: "When one wishes to make a simple colonnade with the Tuscan order, one can make the spaces between the columns very wide, as their architrave is made of wood. Because of this, the columns are extremely suitable for the needs of villas since carts and farm implements can be left under them; their cost is also low."[44] The grounds for applying the Tuscan order to the farm arcades of the Villa Badoer were thus both practical and aesthetic. Palladio made the walkway the same length

as the columns, and as the intercolumniation sanctioned for the Tuscan order was exceptionally wide he placed a distance of five modules or five column diameters between each. This gave more space and maneuverability for wagons. The result was an attractive arcade with classical overtones that was efficient and cheap to build.

95. Arcades of the Villa Badoer.

Palladio also turned the peculiar nature of the site to the owner's advantage by exploiting the remains of a medieval castle. This became the substructure of the new house and can best be seen from behind (plate 97). Approximately three meters high, its function was to provide a podium on which the ground floor of the villa was built, a decision that not only saved money in terms of laying foundations but, in an area conspicuous for its flatness, provided a vertical thrust to the building. The raised ground floor is placed upon the medieval foundation; as it was essentially a service area, Palladio diverted attention from that level through the elaborate stair-case, which recalls some of Palladio's reconstructions of ancient temple complexes. The visual importance of staircases for villas was being recognized about this time, and in his essay on villas, Anton Francesco Doni recommended for the villa of a prince a staircase like Michelan-gelo's at the Laurentian Library in Florence together with an imposing loggia.[45] The Badoer were not princes but they did exercise feudal control over their estates; the staircase and elevated

96. Detail of portico of the Villa Badoer with wooden architrave.

piano nobile thus assume a symbolic role here in what has aptly been termed "the architecture of political dominion."[46] In this context, the choice of an Ionic order for the portico has a particular significance. Tall, slender, graceful, and thus appropriate for a nobleman's house, the order serves as a foil to the lowly Tuscan of the farm buildings at the Villa Badoer while proclaiming the higher status of the patron.

Like the Villa Chiericati, the columns of the Badoer's portico support a wooden architrave, a traditional Venetian solution

97. The Villa Badoer with its base of medieval ruins.

for a post and lintel system, which combined structural flexibility with economy of materials (plate 96). But these conventional features have been transformed by the application of a classical formal vocabulary. The Ionic order, surmounted by the temple pediment, is enriched by a convex or pulvinated frieze, a motif more strictly associated with the Composite order but previously employed with the Ionic by Raphael on the Villa Madama.[47] The classical feel of the portico is carried through to its ceiling, which has a wooden coffering like that of Palazzo Chiericati. This inexpensive solution again reflects the thoroughness of Palladio's assimilation of classical motifs.

The walls of the portico and some of the interior rooms still preserve the remains of frescoes by Giallo Fiorentino, whom Palladio praised for his grotesques.[48] Though they survive only in part, the frescoes go some way toward explaining the underlying concept of villa decoration. They were conceived essentially as a comprehensive scheme of wall painting with a fictive socle supporting fictive architecture or herms dividing the upper walls into panels of grotesques or of mythological landscapes. The frescoes, with their reliance on grotesques and classicizing landscapes, bear an obvious relationship to Central Italian villa and palace decoration, of which the work of Giovanni da Udine and his circle in Rome as well as Giulio Romano's frescoes in Mantua were the principal frame of reference. Such frescoes were intended as the main embellishment of the interior, for furniture would have been minimal. At the Villa Badoer the ceilings of the rooms are roofed in the conventional manner with wooden beams that still bear traces of their original polychromy. Tucked away to the left of the *salone*, the interior stairs are more utilitarian than in the two-story villas and receive light from the portico and *salone*; holes between the stairs also provide additional lighting down to the ground floor. There, as in most of Palladio's villas, the plan conforms to the room distribution above, but the floors of the rooms are elevated above rather than situated on ground level and are lit by windows placed in lunettes within the handsome brick vaults of their ceilings.

Like many of the earlier villas, the Villa Badoer presents only one formal facade to the out-side world, for both the lateral and rear facades are simply functional, punctuated only by win-dows and fireplaces (plate 97). This was doubtless bound up with the utilitarian nature of the villa as a working farm, a situation that aligns it more with the earlier villas than with later ones like the Villa Barbaro or the Malcontenta. Probably the impression today is more sober than was originally the case, for the facades were rendered then in a smooth rustication. As with the Villa Pisani at Montagnana, the absence of fictive moldings and voussoirs here makes for a more "neo-Palladian" effect than originally was intended by Palladio.

The Villa Badoer presents a fully developed version of one of Palladio's most important contributions to domestic architecture, the temple pediment. Much has been written about this citation from antique architecture and how it came about. Palladio himself explains it in the *Quattro Libri,* saying that the ancients, meaning the Romans, employed the pediment in sacred and secular buildings. As the passage is important, it would be helpful to cite it at length:

> In all of the villas and some palaces, I have placed a pediment on the principal facade, where the main entrance is. Such pediments give emphasis to the entrance and render the building grand and magnificent, as well as making the front more eminent than the other parts of the house. In addition, the pediment is highly suitable for the emblem or arms of the patron since they can be set in the center of the facade. The ancients employed them on their buildings as one can see from the remains of their temples and other public buildings. As I said in the introduction to the first book, it is very likely that they took the design and concept from private buildings, that is, from houses. Vit-ruvius, in the last chapter of his third book, explains how they [pediments] are made.[49]

Palladio develops here a specific argument concerning the interrelationship of public and private buildings in ancient times, basing his opinion on Vitruvius's notion of architecture originating with the first shelters of primitive man. He may have been encouraged in this line of thought by Alberti, who argued that the houses of leading citizens could be embellished with loggias, columns with entablatures, and even pediments, though he added that this last motif should not rival the grandeur of pediments on temples.[50] Then, too, Palladio's collaboration with Barbaro on the latter's edition of Vitruvius apparently confirmed this view of classical architecture. For their account of the house of the ancients, Palladio made a reconstruction showing a pediment in the center of the facade, and Barbaro evidently had no reservations about it. In recent times, the discussion of Palladio's use of the pediment in secular architecture has centered upon what modern scholarship has seen as the erroneous nature of his assumptions.[51] Leaving aside the correctness of Palladio's assumptions, it would be more fruitful to inquire about what evidence may have led Palladio, and indeed Barbaro, to such a conclusion.

Various factors may have directed Palladio's thoughts along such lines. One would have been the mosaic in Sant'Apollinare Nuovo, Ravenna, of Theodoric's palace.[52] Palladio was familiar with Ravenna and had studied its antiquities, so it is very likely that he knew the mosaic in the nave of Sant'Apollinare that identified the building as Theodoric's palace. The most conspicuous features of the palace are precisely those that would have commended it to Palladio's attention, namely a portico and pediment. There are other such pieces of equivocal evidence, but probably the most telling can be found among his drawings after the antique.

Guided by his belief in the common origins of religious and secular architecture, Palladio also seized upon the ground plan of the Temple of Hercules at Tivoli as an element in his overall concept of the ancient villa. He made two drawings of the remains of the temple, both of which are preserved in London.[53] One is a working study, drawn on the spot, while the other is a fair copy (plate 98), revised at the architect's drawing board. Though the site has since been built over, it remained substantially clear in the sixteenth century, allowing Palladio to map out the temple precinct as a large rectangular court surrounded by arches. The center of the precinct is dominated by the substructure of the temple proper, with the foundations of the cella and stylobate visible. Palladio's reconstruction of the layout shows an obvious affinity with his villa designs, particularly one like the Villa Badoer, and he wrote on the fair copy: "This is an ancient palace and is at Tivoli." With such a model before his eyes, it is not surprising to find Palladio adapting and organizing villa complexes on a similar pattern (plate 99). Hence, the temple arcades became those of the villa's farm buildings, and the temple and its steps served as the pattern for the villa proper. In this way, Palladio's creative "borrowing" of motifs from sacred architecture for secular purposes can be seen as part of a general theory concerning the interchangeability of both kinds of architecture in the classical world.

Of course Palladio was not the first architect to apply the temple portico to domestic architecture. Already in the late fifteenth century, Giuliano da Sangallo placed columns and a pediment with the Medici arms at the center of the facade of Poggio a Caiano, and the Villa Giustinian at Roncade showed a more ambitious version of the same theme around 1511 (plate 44). In Venice, too, the Palazzo Contarini delle Figure marked a rare example of the application of this motif in Venetian domestic architecture about midcentury.[54] Undoubtedly Palladio knew some if not all of these buildings, but the differences between his approach to this theme and that of his predecessors is notable. It lies, essentially, in finding the correct scale and proportion for the portico so that it no longer looks like an *appliqué* to the facade rather than an integral part of it. Indeed, Palladio's approach to the portico is indicative of his approach to the villa as a whole, for he has taken the various requisites of a farm complex and combined them in a well calculated ensemble that, through a classicizing vocabulary of forms, has elevated villa life onto a higher plane. To paraphrase Alberti, one could not remove any part of his buildings without spoiling the whole.[55]

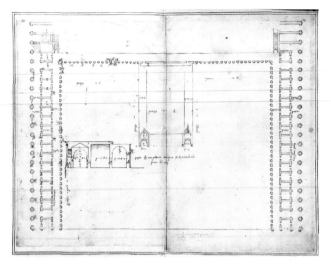

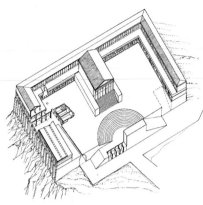

Palladio could not personally follow the villas built after his designs, and as with Christopher Wren's London churches, variations in style and quality can be notable. In some cases, a determined patron could put his own stamp on the building, nowhere more so than at the Villa Repeta and the Villa Barbaro. The Villa Repeta is the most unusual and, by virtue of its early destruction, one of the most tantalizing of Palladio's creations.[56] Its patrons, the Repeta, were a Vicentine noble family with an estate at Campiglia in the Monti Berici south of Vicenza. They had owned this property since 1217 and earlier in the sixteenth century had used it as a retreat for licentious behavior, rather like an Italian version of the English Hell-Fire Club. Palladio states that the new villa was designed for Francesco Repeta, who died in 1556, but the construction was actually carried out by his son Mario. Something of a firebrand, Mario Repeta was arraigned by the Inquisition in 1569; despite this, he continued to draw attention to himself by criticizing the governance of Vicenza and was finally killed by another local noble, Secondo Poiana, in 1586.[57] Our only evidence of the villa's appearance comes in Palladio's woodcut (plate 100), which is conspicuous by virtue of its minimal resemblance to any other of his works. Built around a courtyard with a Doric arcade and corner towers, the villa had an unusual distribution of rooms, with no central block for the owner, a large number of small box rooms, and a total absence of symmetry. Palladio explains that since everything was on one floor, residents could walk about always under cover; though the owner's portion lost some of its usual grandeur, the remaining parts of the villa were thus enhanced.[58] The most eccentric feature of this unusual house, however, was the decorative scheme, whereby each room was dedicated to a particular virtue and frescoed with appropriate scenes and inscriptions. The work of

98. *(left) Plan of the Temple of Hercules, Tivoli.* (RIBA X/16r.) Pen, ink, and wash over chalk underdrawing and incised lines, 42.4 x 56 cm.

99. *(right)* Modern reconstruction of the Temple of Hercules, Tivoli.

Palladio's friend Giambattista Maganza, a poet as well as a painter, it probably reflected the owner's idiosyncratic ideas expressed in a private language understood by his intimates. Whether or not the frescoes had to do with Repeta's heretical leanings, they clearly show Palladio in the role of a coordinator and organizer of other people's ideas.[59]

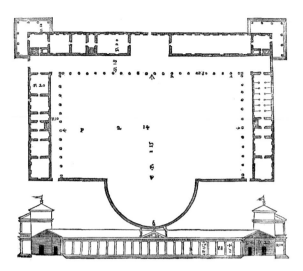

100. *Plan and elevation of the Villa Repeta* from the *Quattro Libri*.

The Villa Repeta was a one-time project while the Villa Barbaro at Maser, similar in format to the Villa Emo at Fanzolo, is more recognizably Palladian. Both were constructed in the area around Treviso, the preferred site for the villas of Venetian noblemen, and share common features, the most obvious being the presence of outbuildings at right angles to the raised main block. This is a feature that can be seen in earlier Trevisan villas like the Villa Agostini at Arcade of c. 1516, suggesting that the architect may have tailored the design to meet local building conventions.

Maser lies in a striking natural setting on a ridge below the Dolomites and above the plain that sweeps towards Asolo and Treviso. The Barbaro had held an estate there from the fifteenth century, and an earlier house is probably incorporated into the present one. Certainly the situation and presence of a natural spring commended the location to Daniele and Marc'antonio Barbaro, who together with Palladio must take credit for the finished product. In the *Quattro Libri*, Palladio observes that the spring provides water for a fountain or nymphaeum cut out of the hillside.[60] The water also creates a fishpond and is then diverted to the kitchen of the villa; it runs through the gardens, farm buildings, and kitchen garden below.

The sloping site is well exploited by the house, which is one story at the rear and two stories at the front. Its main facade is adorned with an engaged giant Ionic order, possibly its first appearance in Palladio's domestic architecture. It is surmounted by a pediment bearing the Barbaro arms, and the main block is flanked by low arcades, terminating in dovecotes. It is ironic that the fame this villa enjoys is virtually in an indirect proportion to its "Palladian" content.[61] While it bears a superficial resemblance to the Villa Emo and other works by Palladio, the eccentricities of Villa Barbaro stand out on closer inspection (plate 101). To begin with, the proportions of the flanking wings are ungainly in relationship to the main block, the result of those wings containing further living quarters on the upper floor—unlike the Villa Emo's, which existed only for farm purposes. Similarly, the elaborate use of sculpture on the main facade, the arcades, and the nymphaeum strikes a discordant note in terms of Palladio's other villas; so, too, the treatment of the main block, which projects much farther forward than the

IOI. Villa Barbaro, Maser (Treviso).

Villa Emo's. The Villa Barbaro's lateral facades also create an awkward transition between the wings and the main facade, something accentuated by the sudden change in decoration. The entablature of the Ionic order ends abruptly at the corners of the main front, and the lateral pediments lack conviction.

In detail as well, many elements suggest that more than one hand played a part in the villa's design. Thus, the rustication presents an unrelieved pattern atypical of Palladio's handling. Likewise the window frames are unlike any in Palladio's oeuvre, too small and fine in detail for the scale of the facade with the upper ones abutting the architrave. The balusters of the central balconies on all three sides constitute another interpolation, this one lifted from Michelangelo's balconies for Saint Peter's in Rome.[62] On all three sides, the central round-headed windows break awkwardly into the entablature, another indication of a design process in which the various elements were not thoroughly assimilated. The composite nature of the exterior is matched by the additive nature of the interior of the villa. While the large cruciform *salone* can be compared with those found in the earlier Villa Pisani at Bagnolo or the roughly contemporary Villa Foscari, its proportions and uneasy relationship to the surrounding rooms stand out against the surer solutions employed by Palladio elsewhere.

It would be wrong, though, to conclude that the Villa Barbaro has little to do with Palladio or should be purged from his works. Its presence in the *Quattro Libri* alone would indicate that Palladio felt it to be his, although, like the case of the Palazzo Thiene, his notion of an "autograph" building would have been freer than ours.[63] The differences between the Villa Barbaro and other works by Palladio are not simply ones of kind but also of degree. If the Malcontenta and the later Loggia del Capitaniato are anything to go by, Palladio was not averse to broken pediments nor to facades that did not correspond to one another.[64] So too the giant order would reappear later on several palace and villa facades, and the use of a canted corner volute on the Ionic columns is definitely a Palladian mannerism.

As Huse and Burns independently observed, Palladio's role here was one of coordinator, reconciling and putting a professional gloss on the intentions of two patrons who knew their own minds. These intentions led to a building that had more in common with contemporary Roman villas than with the villa farms typical of the Veneto. Already in Palladio's lifetime, Vasari likened the nymphaeum (plate 102) to that of the Villa Giulia, and it is a telling comparison.[65] Daniele Barbaro had many ties with Rome, both as an ecclesiastic and as a student of classical architecture. His translation of Vitruvius was dedicated to Cardinal Ippolito d'Este and contained praise of his antiquarian-minded architect, Pirro Ligorio. The nymphaeum and other classical resonances at the Villa Barbaro, the taste for plastic decoration, and the exploitation of its hillside site finds parallels in Cardinal Ippolito's villas at Tivoli and on the Quirinal in Rome, not to mention the Villa Giulia or the later casino of Pius IV in the Vatican.[66] These similarities, as well as the aspects of the facades previously discussed, indicate the patrons' orientation towards the tastes of their Central Italian contemporaries.

The same holds true for the interior decoration. Paolo Veronese's frescoes and their relationship to the design of the villa as a whole have been endlessly discussed.[67] Clearly they should not be seen in isolation from earlier villa decorations by Veronese and his circle, but rather as the culmination or, better, the apotheosis of that style. That the frescoes at Maser were conceived independently of Palladio's work seems unchallengeable in the light of Huse's analysis. As with Giambattista Zelotti's frescoes at the Villa Godi or Giallo Fiorentino's in the Villa Badoer, the architectural forms depicted are alien to Palladio's style. The introduction of a stucco cornice must have been at Veronese's suggestion in order to heighten the illusionistic quality of the fictive architecture (plates 103, 104). The themes of the frescoes—the gods, landscapes, and a celebration of country life—were by this date unexceptional; instead it is Veronese's bravura that raises them beyond the customary level for such work. Long ago Burger suggested that the *salone* of Maser may have been inspired by Pliny's description of the triclinium or dining room of his Laurentine villa—indeed the views from the three windows are reminiscent of Pliny's account of his villa, and the juxtaposition of frescoes of landscapes and ruins embodies the kind of comparison often made in descriptions of Roman villas.[68]

Still, the question remains: What did Palladio make of this? His omission of any reference to the frescoes in his description of the villa in the *Quattro Libri* can be interpreted as a sign of

102. The nymphaeum at the Villa Barbaro.

disapproval, or simply if more prosaically as a lapse.[69] Almost immediately afterward he was at work with Veronese in the refectory of San Giorgio Maggiore, and his relations with the Barbaro brothers do not appear to have suffered. If anything the celebrity of Maser has given undue emphasis to Palladio's silence, exaggerated also by the tendency to consider Veronese's work here in isolation. But it raises an important question: to what extent did Palladio participate in the interior decoration of his villas?

A thorough review of villa decoration in the Veneto lies beyond the scope of this chapter, but some general remarks can be made. Villa and palace decoration were well-established modes

103. *(above)* View through lateral rooms at the Villa Barbaro.

104. *(opposite)* Paolo Veronese (1528–1588). Frescoes in the central *salone* at the Villa Barbaro.

by Palladio's day, and Serlio and Alvise Cornaro could refer to frescoes as a commonplace of private interiors in their writings on architecture. Serlio advocated a total control over decoration on the part of the architect in order to avoid color schemes or subject matter inappropriate to the character of a house.[70] Cornaro predictably took a pragmatic view of the subject, recommending frescoes as a cheap and effective alternative to tapestries and costly hangings; he also preferred grotesques and landscapes since good figural painters were always hard to come by.[71] Palladio's attitude, as far as can be discerned from the *Quattro Libri*, is a good deal more laissez-faire than Serlio's: "One decorates according to various styles, but absolute rules cannot be laid down in this matter."[72] He realized that it was for the patron and his artists to determine what sort of decoration would be suitable for a given house, often but not invariably with the advice of the architect.

Most of the artists who worked in Palladio's buildings came to maturity during the 1540s and early 1550s, as did Palladio himself. This was especially true of the Veronese artists promoted by Michele Sanmicheli.[73] The decoration of Sanmicheli's Palazzo Canossa was underway in the latter part of the 1540s, and the artists involved included Battista dal Moro, Domenico Brusasorzi, Eliodoro Forbicini, and the stuccoist Bartolomeo Ridolfi. Shortly thereafter, Paolo Veronese and Giambattista Zelotti made their debuts as fresco painters in Sanmicheli's Villa Soranza. Sanmicheli's palaces and villas had an obvious impact on Palladio's work during these years, and thus it is not surprising to see the same artists appearing in Palladio's Vicentine palaces in the 1550s: Ridolfi, Forbicini, Bernardino India, and Anselmo Canera in Palazzo Thiene; Ridolfi, Brusasorzi, and Veronese in Palazzo Porto; Ridolfi, Forbicini, Brusasorzi, and Zelotti in Palazzo Chiericati.[74] Many of these artists participated frequently in the decoration of Palladio's buildings, but the extent to which he determined their work within a villa or palace is less easily answered. Palladio's comments on artists in the second book of the *Quattro Libri* show an enthusiasm for their work. In certain instances, such as the ceiling decorations in Palazzo Thiene or the facades of Palazzo Valmarana and Palazzo Barbaran da Porto, the architect must have had an idea of the kind of decoration appropriate, even though the details would have been left to the painter or stuccoist. Sansovino and Alessandro Vittoria collaborated in much the same way on the *scala d'oro* of the Doge's Palace in Venice, where the former designed the staircase and left its stuccoing to his colleague's discretion.[75]

In a few instances Palladio's role seems to have been a more active one. For example, rooms like the *sala degli imperatori* in Villa Poiana (plate 172) or the *salone* of the Villa Pisani at Montagnana (plate 88) bear such close resemblance to Palladio's reconstructions of ancient rooms as to suggest that here the artists worked closely with the architect.[76] But these are exceptions to the rule. The frescoes of Zelotti in the Villa Godi, those by Giallo Fiorentino at Badoer, Veronese's at Maser, Giovanni Antonio Fasolo's at Caldogno, or Battista Franco's and Zelotti's at the Malcontenta, have little in common with Palladio's architectural style and are virtually independent works. In the *Quattro Libri* he never speaks of furnishing designs for interior decoration, which would also indicate a certain distance from this aspect of his buildings.[77]

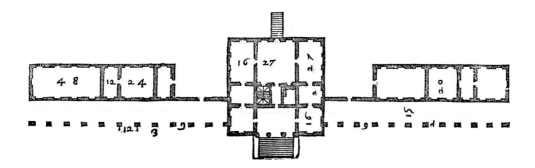

If total control over his projects lay beyond Palladio's reach, there are nonetheless times when design and decoration combine perfectly. One such case is the Villa Emo (plates 105–108), a house that could be interpreted as a refinement upon if not an answer to the villa pattern essayed at Maser. Here again, as with the majority of Palladio's villas, the features of an agricultural holding come more into prominence.[78] Like the Barbaro, the Emo were Venetian nobles who held land at Fanzolo near Treviso from the middle of the fifteenth century; there was already a *casa padronale* on their property by 1509. By 1535 a foundry had been established, though it was probably not until the end of the 1550s, when Leonardo Emo was in his late twenties, that Palladio was called upon to provide designs for a new house. The villa, mentioned in Palladio's draft manuscript for the *Quattro Libri* of 1561, would probably have been finished by 1565, when Emo married Cornelia Grimani.[79]

The Emo had introduced the cultivation of grain to this area, draining much of the land to make it arable, and their success was subsequently translated into one of the most substantial villa complexes erected by Palladio. The villa is foursquare in plan and conforms unusually closely to the woodcut in the *Quattro Libri*.[80] Simple arcades terminating in dovecotes mask the service buildings and elide neatly with the main block, which dominates the estate. The central block is raised in height by a ground floor, as was the case with the Villa Badoer, but here a ramp rather than an elaborate staircase leads to the entrance. This may have been designed to facilitate access to the *piano nobile* by horse, though it could also have served for threshing grain during the harvest.[81] The portico itself provides the one decorative feature in the whole of this extensive facade. Although the order is Doric the effect is somewhat strained, with column spacing more in keeping with that used by Palladio for the Ionic order.[82] The total absence of decorative features on the exterior with the emphasis on planes and volumes could hardly be less like Maser, and its Hellenic purity of design enhances the impact of the Villa Emo.

The simplicity of the exterior is matched by the plan of the main villa block, which is among the least complex in Palladio's domestic architecture. The portico, vestibule, and stairs occupy half of the center of the *piano nobile*, the other half becoming a square *salone*. The same tripartite division is reflected in the lateral suites of rooms. Exceptionally, doors from the por-

105. *Plan of the Villa Emo* from the *Quattro Libri*.

106. Detail of the main facade of the Villa Emo, Fanzolo (Treviso).

107. Giambattista Zelotti's frescoed pergola in the entrance hall of the Villa Emo.

tico lead on to these suites, making them easily accessible from the outside.[83] The shallow vestibule goes directly into the *salone*, which is very much the focal point of the main floor. Its privileged position is emphasized by the height of its ceiling, which is roughly twice that of the vestibule and surrounding rooms. The lower ceilings of the lateral suites are not only in keeping with their proportions but also allow space for a mezzanine floor above them. Compact stairs to either side of the vestibule give access to the mezzanine and down to the service area on the ground floor. Like the Villa Godi, the ceilings of the *piano nobile* are all beamed. That of the *salone* is a handsome coffered ceiling like those found under the porticos of the Villa Badoer or Palazzo Chiericati; it is the only one of its kind in the interior of a Palladian house.

Like earlier villas such as Godi, Poiana, and Caldogno,[84] the interior of the Villa Emo is as opulently decorated as the exterior is plain—just the kind of contrast of which Inigo Jones would have approved. The frescoes are the creation of Veronese's sometime collaborator Giambattista Zelotti, and though not as splendid as Maser's, they are nonetheless striking (plates 107, 108).[85] In the *salone*, the harmony of real and fictive architecture makes a pointed contrast to Veronese's handiwork at Maser, for Zelotti strove to align his Corinthian columns with the beams of Palladio's ceiling. In the lateral rooms, too, the interaction of real and fictive space is evident, although unlike the Villa Barbaro the architecture has not been overwhelmed by frescoes. This is not to say

108. View of the *stanza delle arti* at the Villa Emo, with frescoes by Giambattista Zelotti.

that Palladio took part in planning Zelotti's work here; on the contrary, the decorative scheme is eclectic, drawing on elements from Serlio and Sansovino more than Palladio. In addition, the frescoes from Roman history recall Zelotti's earlier work at the Villa Godi while the smaller rooms, dedicated to Hercules, Venus, the Liberal Arts, or decorated with grotesques, reflected a taste that was by now fashionable. The success of the Villa Emo lies in the secondary role played by the frescoes: because they do not compete as willfully for our attention as do Veronese's, the resulting equilibrium is more in harmony with the lines of Palladio's architecture.

Nothing could offer more of a contrast to the Villa Emo than the Villa Foscari, better known as La Malcontenta (plate 109).[86] Here one encounters for the first time in Palladio's architecture a new type of villa, something much closer to Doni's description of the princely *villa civile*, for the Malcontenta is conceived on a giant scale with an imposing staircase and a stupendous loggia. The patrons of the villa, Nicolò and Alvise Foscari, were descended from the most famous, or infamous, of the fifteenth-century doges, Francesco Foscari, whose architectural patronage in the shape of the Porta della Carta, the Arco Foscari of the Doge's Palace, and the Palazzo Foscari on the Grand Canal was nothing less than regal.[87] Though hardly conspicuous political figures, the Foscari brothers evidently felt they inherited the mantle of their distinguished ancestor when it came to building. Their villa mirrors their social pretensions even as it ushers in a new phase in Palladio's villa designs—the villa as an autonomous, nonagricultural country house.

The Villa Foscari could play out this role because, like the later Villa Rotonda, it was effectively a *villa suburbana*, close enough to Venice to allow the owners easy access but without the demands imposed by a working farm. The villa must have been largely complete by 1560 since the name of Nicolò Foscari, who died that year, appears prominently on the portico frieze together with that of his brother. The interior of the *piano nobile* must have been finished by that date as well, for the painter Battista Franco died while frescoing the main *salone* in 1561.[88] Thus the villa stands at the end of the decade that began with the Palazzo Chiericati and in many ways can be viewed as a résumé of motifs and sketches developed by Palladio over the previous years. Its plan with a central cruciform *salone* recalls the much earlier Villa Pisani at Bagnolo or one of the drawings sometimes associated with the Villa Chiericati, in which a portico reminiscent of the Pantheon is combined with a cruciform cross-vaulted *salone*.[89] In much the same way, the fenestration of the south facade recalls that of the Villa Poiana (plates 75, 110); yet what an immense gulf lies between them! For the first time in his private practice, Palladio was able to build on a scale comparable to an antique temple, with patrons whose purses were equal to the cost of novel effects. And produce such effects is just what Palladio did.

The gestation of the Villa Foscari was obviously long, and Palladio certainly pondered many of its features long before he ever put them into concrete form. The nucleus of the villa can probably be traced back to one of his earliest villa studies (plate 59) in which the cubic structure of the house rests on a high basement, its facade enlivened only by a Serlian arch and a thermal window.[90] Its very plainness masks the audacity of its design, for the central *salone* is

109. Main facade of the Villa Malcontenta, Gambarare di Mira (Venice), from the canal.

cross-vaulted and lit from a thermal window above. Like some early villa and palace projects, several features of the Villa Foscari were probably dictated by the fact that the patrons were two brothers who required separate though comparable facilities; hence, the twin staircases and gardens, and the large suites separated by the *salone*.[91]

The site of the Malcontenta at Gambarare di Mira is low-lying and faces the Brenta Canal, then a busy means of transport between Venice and mainland sites. As the land was prone to flooding, Palladio took the unusual step of raising the ground floor on a base several feet high so that it would remain dry. This in turn emphasized the height of the ground floor and *piano nobile*, making them similar to the proportions of a Venetian palace. The ground floor can be entered from a central door in the podium of the portico or from side doors that led into the

110. *(above)* Staircase on the main facade of the Villa Malcontenta.

111. *(opposite, top)* Rear facade of the Villa Malcontenta.

112. *(opposite, bottom)* Vaulted *salone* of the Villa Malcontenta with frescoes by Battista Franco and Giambattista Zelotti.

private gardens. As with other villas, the distribution of rooms on the ground floor corresponds to that of the floor above, but the scale is massive, the vaulted ceilings and walls of this floor perhaps costing as much as many smaller villas.

The main facade overlooks the canal. Its scale and towering Ionic portico have an almost theatrical quality calculated to overwhelm the approaching visitor. This would have been even more the case since anyone traveling by boat would have first seen the villa from an even lower viewpoint in the canal. The double stairs and octastyle portico (plate 110), rare in Palladio's oeuvre, were lifted directly from a single classical source: the unusual temple of Clitumnus near Spoleto.[92]

Palladio may only have known of this structure indirectly through a drawing by Pirro Ligorio, which he copied, for like Ligorio he reconstructed it with paired staircases although the temple had only one. The temple must have come to mind when Palladio was searching for a way to combine the traditional portico features with a central entrance on the ground floor, but the diminutive nature of the original lacks the grandeur with which the Malcontenta has been invested. Here, the stairs rise in three stages, with spacious landings imposing upon the visitor a deliberately measured cadence that magnifies the distance involved.[93] The scale of the portico and its outsized temple portal are related to the dimensions of the *salone* behind them, which is itself one and a half stories high. Palladio employed his preferred Ionic order here with the characteristic canted corner volute. Since the facade faces north and most of the light would come from the other three facades, Palladio could afford to devote such a conspicuous amount of space to the portico at the expense of windows.

The lateral facades of the Malcontenta are extremely plain, relieved only by the rendering of the brickwork and the moldings. But it would be wrong to describe them as simply functional, like the corresponding sides of the Villa Badoer (plate 97), since no chimney flues violate their lines. The pattern of the rustication creates a bold and suitably noble effect, especially when viewed in conjunction with the rear facade (plate III). Facing south, this facade too was conceived not only to maximize lighting for the villa but also to be admired. It displays a rhythmic fenestration similar to a Venetian palace, with its clustering of windows about the central *salone*. Palladio did not simply leave these elements as such but integrated them into a coherent pattern. The central motif becomes the three mullioned windows and thermal window above. They light the *salone*, and as the *salone* is half a story taller than the surrounding rooms, the curve of the thermal window breaks into the floor above, thus giving rise to the broken pediment. This reflects the portico on the opposite side of the house, which the line of the south facade is brought forward to emphasize. Above the main block of the house a third story can be seen, straddling the roof of the building and echoing the pediments underneath. It owes its existence to the unusual proportions of the *salone* below, and is half a story above the rooms to either side.[94] The skyline is further punctuated by slender Venetian chimneys terminating in caps to prevent embers from setting fire to the roof. They serve as an effective foil to the upper story and are another reminder that Venice is not far away.

Palladio's attention to surface textures is better known from his palaces than his villas, but the Malcontenta, which was obviously meant to be seen from all angles, received an unusually rich surface treatment. The architect exploited a gamut of effects, from bare brick around the base of the building, to *sgraffito* for the ground floor and tympanum of the pediment of the portico, to the bolder pattern of rustication, similar to that of the Villa Cornaro, for the principal stories. The recent restoration of the villa has also brought back another aspect of its original appearance long forgotten: color. Some years ago, Cevese drew attention to the singular state of the columns of the Malcontenta's portico[95]—where the surface stucco had peeled off, the bricks of the column shaft could be seen to join exactly with their stone bases. If they were meant to receive a coating of plaster, he pointed out, the bricks would not have met the top of the stone base; instead, they would have been set back to allow space for a thin coating of plaster. Cevese concluded that the contrast between brick and stone was the effect Palladio wanted, and the stucco coating represented a later accretion. He also pointed to the similar contrast of stone and brick on the giant order of the Loggia del Capitaniato in Vicenza (plate 195), a technique Palladio employed on the columns of the cloister of the Carità in Venice (plate 115), which was approximately contemporary with the Malcontenta.[96] There can be little doubt that this bichrome aspect of ancient buildings appealed to Palladio, and he introduced it into his buildings for much the same reasons that Borromini did a century later. Above all, the study of ancient brickwork gave architects scope to introduce new effects into their buildings, effects that could be sanctioned by an appeal to ancient authority. At the Malcontenta its impact is amplified by the play of brick and plaster on the rest of the facade. The horizontal bands between the ground and the first floor and the entablature encircling the building above the *piano nobile* break up the potential monotony of the rear and lateral facades while serving to distinguish the parts of the building. Thus Palladio exploited color as a means of underlining the divisions of the house.

The interior of the *piano nobile* is dominated by the cruciform *salone*, which rises in a fusion of cross and barrel vaulting to a height of over eight meters (plate 112).[97] The height of the vault, enhanced by the faded colors of Franco's and Zelotti's frescoes, creates one of the most diaphanous spaces in all of Palladio's architecture. As one moves from the *salone* to the suites of rooms, Palladio's attention to scale and the variety of vaulting and dimensions makes a deft contrast to the more imposing dimensions of the central room. At the end of the lateral suites come the staircases. Like those in previous two-story villas, they take their light from the south front and from the adjacent *camerini*, which must formerly have been dressing or service rooms.

In 1574, the French king Henry III was received at the Malcontenta. It is easy to imagine the scene of barges arriving in state from Venice, the servants in livery stationed on the staircases, and the Foscari posed beneath the portico.[98] Indeed for this kind of gesture the Malcontenta was conceived—for representational functions and for status. In this sense, it is more comparable to an English country house of the eighteenth or nineteenth century than any other of Palladio's villas. Far removed from the simplicity and severity of Palladio's earliest villas and on a different plane from even the grander farm villas like Emo and Cornaro, the Malcontenta marked the way to the more ambitious villa projects of the next decade, notably the Villa Sarego, the Villa Rotonda, and the Villa Trissino at Meledo.[99] By the end of the 1550s, Palladio had found his stride and had located a group of patrons willing to give scope to his talents. The opportunities this afforded led Palladio to articulate a new type of house, which became the forerunner of country houses and even palaces around the world.

VI
RELIGIOUS ARCHITECTURE

SﾀTANDING BY THE PUNTA DELLA DOGANA, THE OLD CUSTOMS HOUSE AT THE ENTRANCE TO the Grand Canal, one takes in the most miraculous of all views of Venice: the Doge's Palace and Sansovino's Library of San Marco stand to the east with San Giorgio Maggiore across the bay, while the Redentore closes the scene triumphantly to the west. The churches, of course, were designed by Palladio and represent his contribution to the city's appearance. They also embody his mature statement on what he would call Christian temples, a merging of the classical and contemporary in a new kind of architecture comparable to his achievement with villas and palaces.

Although churches occupied Palladio in the last two decades of his life, his ideas about them were fully formed by 1558. In that year a contract was drawn up for the execution of a new facade for a patriarchal cathedral of Venice, San Pietro di Castello.[1] According to this document, the facade was to be constructed of Istrian stone with a giant order of six engaged Corinthian columns fronting the nave and a smaller order of pilasters, three each for the side aisles—a formula consistent with his later church facades. Two Venetian noblemen, Marc'antonio and Daniele Barbaro, stood surety for the project. The document is highly significant for several reasons. As detailed in the contract, the overall concept and particulars correspond to the kind of solution employed by Palladio on his executed church facades, some four years before he first put it into effect at San Francesco della Vigna. The presence of the Barbaro brothers is also telling because Palladio had just finished an intensive collaboration with Daniele on the latter's translation of Vitruvius and had recently acted as coordinating architect for the brothers' villa at

113. Nave of San Giorgio Maggiore, Venice.

Maser.[2] As patriarch-elect of the town of Aquileia, Daniele was well placed to launch Palladio's career as a church architect, and he would later support his work at San Francesco della Vigna much as his brother played a decisive role in the deliberations concerning the Redentore. Unfortunately the patriarch of Venice, Vicenzo Diedo, died before serious work could begin, and the project was deferred until the 1590s when the old facade was replaced by a new "Palladian" one under Francesco Smeraldi. Though Palladio's design was obviously modified, presumably by Smeraldi, the integration of large and small orders and their relationship to the proportions of the nave and aisles remain faithful to Palladio's project of 1558.

Palladio did not have to wait long before he was employed on another major ecclesiastical project, this time not a church but a monastery. The work in question was the convent of the Lateran canons known as Santa Maria della Carità.[3] The canons had moved to Venice from Ravenna in 1134, and over the centuries established a close relationship with the confraternity of Santa Maria della Carità, which occupied part of their site and shared a common entrance with the monks. By the early fifteenth century moves had been made to rebuild the complex, which stood on a large swath of land between the Grand Canal and the wharf of the Zattere. After the church of the Carità was rebuilt in the 1440s, the monks attempted to acquire a street behind their immediate property in order to enlarge their site. Nothing came of this, but unspecified work was underway at the site during the 1540s, and a project for the whole complex was drawn up in the 1550s, though not by Palladio.[4] His involvement must have come by the end of that decade, since in March 1561 he received ten *scudi* for a new model. Work centered on the construction of a new atrium, some adjacent rooms, and a cloister up to 1569. After that, construction trailed off, although a new refectory was begun on the far side of the cloister in the 1570s.

Only a fraction of the project published in the *Quattro Libri* was ever built, much of it only to be swept away by a fire in 1630. Now all that survives is a magnificent fragment: the sacristy, an oval staircase, and one side of the cloister (plates 115, 116). To appreciate the architect's intentions, one must turn back to the words and images in the *Quattro Libri* (plate 114). Characteristically, Palladio published the Carità not with the temples in Book IV but with the private houses in Book II. This was not so strange as it might seem because he explains that the plan of the convent illustrated his concept of the house of the ancients.[5] Although Vitruvius indicated that these were often rambling structures, extending over courtyards and with a variety of rooms, Palladio and Barbaro could only conceive of them in terms of large, well ordered complexes like the Roman baths. Consequently, they invested classical domestic architecture with a monumentality and

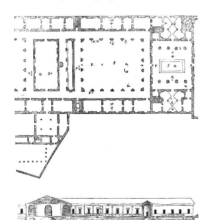

114. *Plan and elevation of the Carità* from the *Quattro Libri.*

a symmetry it never possessed. It was a style that also lent itself to the creation of great monastic complexes. In this, Palladio followed a pattern already established by fifteenth-century architects like Giuliano da Sangallo, Francesco di Giorgio, and Bramante, but Palladio's Carità is even more thoroughly imbued with a sense of classical prototypes.[6]

If completed, the Carità would have been Palladio's most impressive Venetian commission, and the boldness of its design marked him as a promising new architect. Giorgio Vasari was struck by it when he met Palladio in Venice in 1566, describing it in more detail than any other of the architect's buildings in the second edition of his *Lives of the Artists*.[7] For his part, Palladio gave three plates to it in the *Quattro Libri*, and with these he set out his vision of the complex. The plan in the *Quattro Libri* was undoubtedly ideal, but it was drawn with an eye to the potential expansion of the convent beyond its existing confines. Like many of Palladio's projects, it was planned for a piecemeal construction.

Next to the church, Palladio designed a grand atrium with a colossal order of columns supporting a terrace; the concept derives from Vitruvius's Corinthian *sala* but substitutes Palladio's preferred Composite order. This was the first colossal order employed by the architect in his domestic architecture, and it would become a standard feature of his palace and villa designs in subsequent years. Adjacent to the atrium is the only surviving interior suite of rooms, the sacristy (called a *tablinum* in imitation of a corresponding room in a Roman house). Compact of proportions, the *tablinum* refines the theme of a columnar hall in Palladio's earlier houses, for here the Doric columns punctuate the room, dividing it into a biapsidal entrance and a rectangular space, both with handsome cross-vaulting (plate 116). The use of colored paving stones, inspired by the patterns sometimes found in Roman floors, reinforces the spatial effect. Another remarkable feature is the oval staircase connecting the sacristy to the upper floors of the building. This could be constructed without a central support because each stair supports the one above, rather like the trajectory of an arch that describes a spiral instead of a semicircle. The invention of the stairway, which had the virtue of compactness, was credited to Marc'antonio Barbaro by Palladio, who also commended its utility in providing overhead lighting.[8]

Beyond the atrium lies the one remaining side of the cloister (plate 115). Its first two floors were originally arcades and the third held the monks' cells. The arcades were to have formed opposite sides of the cloister with the refectory serving as a link building; the design replaced the prior structure by abolishing a wing that divided the area into two smaller courts. The surviving wing is uncompromisingly Roman in appearance, reminiscent both of ancient structures like the Coliseum and modern palace courtyards like Baldassare Peruzzi's for the renovation of the Theater of Marcellus or Michelangelo's adjustments to the Palazzo Farnese. The courtyard facade contains further touches of Palladio's new style in its combination of unadorned brick— imported at great expense from Ferrara—and stone, as well as the unorthodox combination of a Corinthian frieze from the Temple of Vesta at Tivoli with the Doric order.[9]

The Carità remains a torso, albeit a beautiful one. Its boldness and thorough saturation in the classical style distinguished the Carità from any contemporary religious building in Venice and could only draw attention to its creator's gifts. Thus, it is not surprising to see Palladio drawn into two other ecclesiastical projects shortly after the Carità was begun.

The present church of San Francesco della Vigna had been rebuilt in 1534 according to a model by Jacopo Sansovino.[10] Doge Andrea Gritti, whose family palace stood adjacent to the

115. Cloister of the Carità.

church, laid the foundation stone and probably had some role in the commission coming to Sansovino. The eminent Franciscan friar Francesco Zorzi acted as procurator in the early stages of construction and intervened at critical moments, furnishing a memorandum on Sansovino's model and negotiating the paving and enlargement of the *campo* before the convent. The new church subscribed to a pattern typical of the reformed Franciscan order by having a single nave with side chapels, a suppressed transept followed by a presbytery, and a retro-choir, all elements similar to the earlier churches of San Giobbe in Venice or San Salvatore al Monte in Sansovino's native Florence.[11] Sansovino's facade is known only from foundation medals, but it probably resembled a slightly earlier Venetian church facade like Santa Maria Mater Domini; that is, it would have had a simple brick front articulated by columns or pilasters and a mezzanine story with a three-light window surmounted by a small pediment. Sansovino's solution was reminiscent of Roman church facades of the 1520s, but it must have looked increasingly out of date by the late 1550s when work was being contemplated.

After the death of Andrea Gritti in 1538, the Grimani family became the dominant force at San Francesco della Vigna by acquiring the rights to erect family memorials on the external and internal facades as well as to create a family chapel. Following an established Venetian tradition

116. The small sacristy of the Carità.

Vettor Grimani, a procurator and influential supporter of Sansovino, wished to create a monument to his grandfather Doge Antonio Grimani on the main facade and other family memorials on the interior.[12] A lawsuit prevented any work from being carried out before Vettor Grimani's death in 1558, and the commissioning of the facade fell to his younger brother, Giovanni, patriarch of Aquileia. Giovanni Grimani had other plans for San Francesco and abandoned the memorial to Doge Antonio Grimani on the exterior as well as the interior memorials; moreover, he appropriated the family chapel as his own and dropped Sansovino as architect in favor of Palladio. Palladio thus established himself as the most powerful and respected architect in Venice. There may well have been an element of family rivalry spurring Giovanni Grimani to drop his elder brother's model for the church facade in favor of a newer, more ambitious design, which is exactly what Palladio gave him.

The commission for San Francesco marked a turning point in Palladio's career, even as it signalled a change of taste among the patriciate. Giovanni Grimani was an architectural amateur and doubtless took counsel from Daniele Barbaro, who was Grimani's designated successor as patriarch of Aquileia as well as protector of the Franciscans in Venice.[13] Having backed Palladio at San Pietro di Castello, Barbaro must have urged consideration of his protégé in this case. Both Barbaro and Palladio represented a younger generation now on the threshold of power and influence. But Barbaro died before he entered into his ecclesiastical career, while Palladio established himself as the premier Venetian architect with his remarkable design for San Francesco della Vigna.

Begun around 1562, the base of the facade had been laid when Vasari saw it four years later (plate 118).[14] Vasari was taken with the design and rightly so, for not since Mauro Codussi had anyone produced such an imaginative contribution to Venetian church architecture or such an authoritative recreation of a classical temple front. Visitors to the remote *campo* of San Francesco are still impressed by the assurance with which classical orders are used on a scale comparable to classical architecture and by the apparent ease with which Palladio resolved the problem of adapting the orders to Christian church facades. The unusually high base has drawn criticism, but it enabled the architect to place large and small columns on the same level while imparting a more monumental feel to the facade as a whole. Rising above this socle and defining the center of the facade, four engaged, colossal Corinthian columns support the pediment, assuming the function of an applied portico. A smaller Corinthian order flanks the main portal and the lateral portions of the facade, setting up a counterpoint with the larger order and closing the facade on either side. The linear quality of the design seems to have been etched into the Istrian stone. The main entrance is unusually wide and is surmounted by a thermal window instead of the abandoned monument to Doge Antonio Grimani. The overall effect is strongly reminiscent of Palladio's reconstructions of Roman temples, especially the Temple of Minerva in the Forum of Nerva (plate 120).

Employing combinations of orders and entablatures, Palladio's church facades were unusual by the standards of his day. They have engendered a great deal of discussion, much of it centered on Wittkower's famous analysis of what he termed the "double pediment" motif found on Palladio's three most famous church facades (plate 117). According to Wittkower, the merging of the larger and smaller pediments at San Francesco della Vigna and all of Palladio's other church facades creates the illusion of two superimposed temple fronts, an effect inspired by Vitruvius's account of the basilica and temple he built at Fano.[15] Though long since vanished, the basilica was described in some detail in his treatise and became the subject of numerous reconstructions from the Renaissance onward, even by Barbaro and Palladio (plate 200). Wittkower wanted to see the juncture of the entablatures of the larger and smaller orders of Palladio's church facades as reflecting "the double arrangement of gables" at Fano, but what Vitruvius actually discussed was the way in which the gables of basilica and temple ran in two directions, forming the letter *T.* Moreover, the reconstructions of the building at Fano published by Cesariano in 1521 and by Barbaro in his Vitruvius do not remotely resemble Palladio's church facades, nor does Barbaro's translation of this celebrated passage mention pediments or any part of the facade.[16] In all probability, the explanation for the appearance of Palladio's church facades lies elsewhere—in particular, in his draftsmanship. Proof of this can be found in a drawing that is generally accepted as a preliminary project for San Francesco della Vigna (plate 119). Here, the center of the facade has been conceived as a triumphal arch, presumably with places for Grimani busts. The wings still support fragments of pediments even though this motif does not correspond to the main triumphal arch motif.[17] In one of his later proposals for San Petronio in Bologna, Palladio even juxtaposes the temple and triumphal arch motif on the same sheet, though the lateral semipediments remain constant on both sides (plate 203). If double pediments were the basis of Palladio's facades, one would expect them to be a constant feature in all such drawings.

Any explanation of Palladio's church facades must take account of his design procedure and the way in which he habitually rationalized spatial effects in his drawings. As we have seen, this was a by-product of the orthogonal elevations that he employed in his reconstructions of antique buildings and in his own projects.[18] The elevation of the Temple of Minerva in the Forum of Nerva (plate 120), mentioned above, is a good example of this process. The graphic evidence there can be interpreted in any number of ways without reference to a ground plan: thus, one could be looking at pilasters and engaged columns instead of columns flanking a precinct wall and a freestanding portico, as was, in fact, the case. When Palladio reviewed his drawings in his study, he could take motifs such as

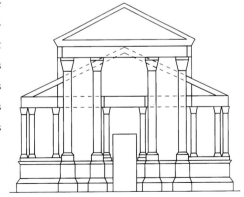

117. Rudolf Wittkower prepared this diagram to explain the genesis of Palladio's church facade.

these and tailor them to suit the requirements of San Francesco, or indeed San Giorgio Maggiore. But he obviously delighted in reproducing the spatial ambiguity of orthogonal elevations in his architecture, especially in the 1560s. The facade of Palazzo Valmarana in Vicenza (plates 187, 188) displays a similar compression of spatial layers through the juxtaposition of large and small orders, an effect heightened by the entablature of the smaller order running behind the larger one. The result at San Francesco was a facade far in advance of any contemporary church in Venice, or indeed elsewhere in Italy.

Almost simultaneously with his work on San Francesco, Palladio was drawn into two other projects, one the rebuilding of the small convent church of Santa Lucia, the other one of the grandest works of his career at San Giorgio Maggiore. In both cases, Palladio pitched his proposals to suit the scale of the commission and the patron's pocketbook.

The church of Santa Lucia is often overlooked in discussions of Palladio's architecture, in part because it no longer stands; yet it was an ingenious response to a compact site and a commission from a wealthy and powerful nobleman, Leonardo Mocenigo.[19] The Mocenigo family

118. *(opposite)* Facade of San Francesco della Vigna.

119. *(above) Project for San Francesco della Vigna.* (RIBA XIV/10.) Pen and ink over incised lines, 31.5 x 41.4 cm.

inherited burial rights in the presbytery of Santa Lucia in 1507, and Leonardo Mocenigo ordered the rebuilding of the church from Palladio in 1565. Palladio was Mocenigo's preferred architect, for he also commissioned two villa projects from him near Treviso and on the Brenta Canal, the latter being an especially ambitious project.[20] Work began on the presbytery but was interrupted by the patron's death in 1575, and although an inscription on the facade stated that the church was rebuilt to Palladio's design, it was completed only in 1617.

Our knowledge of the church derives chiefly from eighteenth-century sources like Bertotti Scamozzi, Antonio Visentini, and paintings by Antonio Canaletto (plates 121, 122). These indicate that it had a drab functional facade, probably not by Palladio; the interior was a brick box in plan, subdivided into a small narthex and rectangular nave with three chapels at the east end. The narthex contained the raised choir of the nuns, a traditional solution for small monastic churches in Venice, and piers with engaged columns separated the narthex from the nave. These piers found correspondence in those of the presbytery, which was the most ambitious part of the design, conceived as a pseudo-oval punctuated by niches. Santa Lucia marked Palladio's first attempt to recreate an antique interior in a contemporary church and also served

120. *Elevation of the Temple of Minerva in the Forum of Nerva.* Museo Civico, Vicenza (Vic. D 21r). Pen and ink over incised lines, 43 x 56.2 cm.

to advertise his talents in this sphere. The plan harkened back to the Veneto-Byzantine pattern of a Greek cross inscribed within a square, such as that of San Giacomo di Rialto or Mauro Codussi's San Giovanni Crisostomo, but the feeling for space was closer to the Roman architecture of Bramante and his circle, which Palladio so admired. In elevation, the interior resembled Palladio's later projects for the Redentore (plate 134) or his reconstruction of Vitruvius's Corinthian hall (plate 171) though here conceived as a two-story solution with an Ionic and a Composite order as well as thermal windows. The whole was crowned by a barrel vault made of cane and plaster.[21]

In this same period Palladio became involved in his largest ecclesiastical project, the rebuilding of the church and convent of San Giorgio Maggiore. The antiquity and setting of San Giorgio made it central to the history and ceremony of the city.[22] A church had existed from 790 on the island of San Giorgio, which Doge Tribune

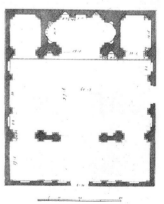

121. *(above)* Antonio Visentini (1688–1782). *Longitudinal sketch of Santa Lucia, Venice.* (RIBA, Visentini 118 [4].) Pen, ink, and wash over incised lines, 50.3 x 76 cm.

122. *(right) Plan of Santa Lucia* from Ottavio Bertotti Scamozzi, *Le fabbriche e i disegni di Andrea Palladio,* 1796. (RIBA V. 36 [1].)

Memmo gave to the Benedictine order in an act of donation in 982. The doge and government officials visited the church every year on the feast of Saint Stephen to venerate his relics, a ceremony dating from the twelfth century. The original monastic complex was extensively restored in the thirteenth century and again in the early fifteenth. Shortly before 1500 a large dormitory wing had been begun behind the pre-Palladian church, the architect for which was Giovanni Buora, a sometime follower of Pietro Lombardo. Buora or his son Andrea may have been the author of a comprehensive project for renewal of the monastery and church proposed around 1521–22.[23] This project included a new cloister already begun in 1516, but little else was accomplished except for laying out a new refectory. An oblong room some ten by thirty meters, the refectory had only been constructed up to the height of its roundheaded windows upon Palladio's arrival in 1560. He then transformed what would have been a conventional room into something more dramatic by endowing it with a classical cornice, cross vaulting, and three thermal windows (plate 123). These interventions turned the room into something reminiscent of a Roman bath, and the interior was further embellished by Paolo Veronese's *Marriage at Cana,* which originally stood at the far end.[24]

Equally important and even more dramatic are the sequence of spaces that bring the visitor from the cloister to the refectory. Here the main problem facing Palladio was to provide a transition within a confined area to the refectory half a story above. This he achieved by raising the height of the small vestibule and filling it with a staircase dominated by an imposing portal

123. *(left)* Refectory of San Giorgio Maggiore, Venice.

124. *(right)* Vestibule of the refectory, San Giorgio Maggiore.

(plate 124). The doorway is based upon a classical portal in Spoleto, one that Michele San-micheli occasionally employed in his architecture, but Palladio has enlarged it to a superhuman scale that rivets our attention.[25] Vasari must have been struck by this vestibule when he visited Venice, for he called it a *ricetto* in his biography of Palladio, a distinctive word that he also used to describe the similarly proportioned vestibule of Michelangelo's Laurentian Library.[26] The comparison is interesting because Michelangelo treats the staircase and wall as a sculptural unit while Palladio achieves his desired effect through the contrast between the elongated propor-tions of the bare vaulted room and its richly carved portal. The adjacent room serves as an antechamber to the refectory and is distinguished by a slightly simpler portal flanked by two ele-gant washbasins in pink Verona marble. The washbasins are particularly striking examples of Palladio's ability to combine classical with contemporary, in this case Michelangelesque, motifs.[27]

Palladio's flair and ingenuity here convinced the Benedictine monks to entrust him with providing a model for their new basilica in 1565. By this date the dilapidated nature of the old church would have been glaringly apparent, especially since the other main monastic churches in Venice had been rebuilt in the fourteenth and fifteenth centuries. Early maps of the island of San Giorgio indicate that the pre-Palladian basilica consisted of a nave with side chapels, but it stood further back and to one side of a small *campo.* An old cloister planted with cypresses and an atrium stood in front of the church, but the cloister was removed to its present location in 1516, which implies that plans for enlarging the church and *campo* were entertained at that time.[28] The plan of the new church in the 1521–22 project, perhaps by Buora, called for a broad nave, two aisles, six chapels on either side, and a transept defined by three domed bays fol-

125. Aerial view of the *campo* and facade of San Giorgio.

lowed by a domed presbytery with flanking chapels. The design conformed to the norms for new churches laid down by the Benedictines, who distinguished themselves from other religious orders at this date by their precise standards for new monastic churches. The project also corresponded to Alessandro Leopardi's new plan for the church of Santa Giustina in Padua, the mother church of the Monte Cassinese congregation to which San Giorgio belonged.[29] Representatives of the congregation met periodically to discuss their affairs, including any new building programs; hence the similarities between the two projects would have been dictated by the congregation's guidelines.

Some features of Palladio's church were anticipated here, but he transformed this foursquare model through his incomparably greater artistic gifts. Bricks and mortar were the basic ingredients; yet it was the quality of design that must have impressed his patrons. As Palladio wrote in 1567, buildings were praised "more for their form than for their materials."[30] A wooden model of the new church was fashioned by March 1566 and work began soon afterwards. The Venetian Senate encouraged the project by authorizing the monastery to fell one thousand oaks from one of its estates near Treviso to provide foundations for the new building.[31] The foundation stone was laid in 1566 in the presence of the doge, the patriarch, and the abbot Andrea

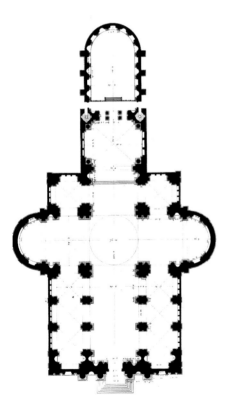

Pampuro, then acting head of the Cassinese congregation. One year later the piers were being constructed, and contracts were issued for the walls, chapels, and vaulting in 1568. The cupola was underway when the French king Henry III inspected San Giorgio during his visit of 1574, and the body of the church was finished the following year. The choir was begun the year of Palladio's death and finished in 1589. Decoration of the interior continued through the 1590s with paintings by the Tintoretto and Bassano workshops as well as sculptures by Girolamo Campagna and Niccolò Roccatagliata. In 1597 the chapter again petitioned the Senate for permission to fell thirty oaks for the facade, but work only began ten years later. At that time a contract was drawn up with a stonemason, Giulio di Bortolo, in which the facade was to be executed "in conformity to the model." The whole project was finished four years later.[32]

126. *Plan of San Giorgio Maggiore* from Ottavio Bertotti Scamozzi, *Le fabbriche e i disegni di Andrea Palladio*, 1796.

San Giorgio Maggiore offered Palladio the opportunity to establish himself as the major architect in Venice. The Carità, San Francesco della Vigna, and Santa Lucia were markers along the way, but the Benedictine project gave him the scale and means to realize his ideas. San Giorgio sometimes suffers by comparison with the Redentore, as if churches, especially church facades, were abstract exercises in problem solving. Such an approach ignores the differences in function and scale between Palladio's churches. A large Benedictine monastery had specific needs that made for a complex brief, and Palladio's solution was as masterful as it was unexpected (plate 126). The beauty of the design lies in his ability to reconcile potentially conflicting elements while endowing them with a style at once saturated in a classical vocabulary and yet not completely unconnected with Venetian traditions. The main body of the church is conceived as a classical basilica, inspired by Palladio's reconstruction of the Basilica of Maxentius, which he ranked among the most beautiful in Rome.[33] The Basilica suggested to Palladio the combination of a large rectangular hall divided by piers into a nave and aisles. The twin apses featured in his reconstruction of the Basilica probably suggested the transept arms of San Giorgio, although he moved them one bay from their customary location by the presbytery in order to provide a second nave for the great occasion when the doge and government officials came to venerate the relics of Saint Stephen.[34]

In elevation, a precise logic informs every part of the design (plates 113, 129). A giant Composite order frames the nave while supporting a barrel vault above, and a smaller Corinthian order articulates the aisles, which have cross-vaulting. Piers, column bases, capitals, and moldings are of stone, although brick and plaster give a similar illusion to the rest of the structure as well. The side chapels are uniformly designed and elevated three steps above the floor; their tabernacles have a Corinthian order, and the principal altars in the transept are further distinguished by column shafts of colored marble. The presbytery is also elevated three steps above floor level and has vaulting supported by Composite piers and fluted columns. A screen of Corinthian columns marks a caesura between the presbytery and the monks' choir. It, too, is raised above the presbytery and charged with a richer decorative effect inspired by Palladio's reconstruction of the court of the temple on the Quirinal.[35] In the choir, the scale and style change, this time to a more intimate effect with alternating niches and aedicules above the richly carved walnut stalls. Though built after his death, the choir must reflect Palladio's original intention as well as the reformist tendencies of the Cassinese congregation, which advocated retro-choirs so that the celebration of mass could be seen by all present rather than exclusively by the monks.[36]

As an experience, the interior of San Giorgio overwhelms any visitor through its scale and the grandeur of its architect's imagination (plates 127, 129). The stone bases of the Composite piers tower overhead, and their entablature projects sharply forward, framing the lunettes that pierce the barrel vault. The initial quadrilateral impression of the basilica is unexpectedly broken up by the cross-axis of the transept, equal in length to that of the nave. At the crossing, the cupola appears to float overhead, an effect enhanced by the slender dimensions of the piers (plate 127). Palladio could afford to make them much slenderer than in a Central Italian church because the cupola is built in the Veneto-Byzantine tradition with a low drum supporting a light timber construction, unlike, for example, the masonry dome of Saint Peter's. Though the church

is dominated by its two main axes, subsidiary views open on all sides, and the interplay between parts means that clarity and rationality prevail over confusion or clutter. In his orchestration of different scales and spaces, Palladio applied the lessons learned from his study of the baths: each component is distinguished from the others, and all interlock in a tradition that looks back through Codussi to Brunelleschi.

More controversy has surrounded the facade of San Giorgio than any other aspect of Palladio's religious architecture (plate 128). There has been a persistent tendency to see the extant facade as a departure from the architect's intentions even though an early elevation shows a clear connection with his experience at San Francesco della Vigna as well as with the finished project. According to this drawing, Palladio initially opted for a solution with a common base for the large and small orders, the latter framing monuments to two doges who were early benefactors of the convent. The study has also been connected with a later plan of the church and cloister indicating a freestanding portico on the steps in front of the church; however, the earlier elevation shows no step and its main order must be read as applied while the plan with portico has been shown to date from the 1590s, ten years after Palladio's death.[37] Palladio may have toyed with the idea of a portico for the facade,

127. (above) Cupola of San Giorgio Maggiore.

128. (opposite) Facade of San Giorgio Maggiore.

129. Detail of crossing,
San Giorgio Maggiore.

130. Leon Battista Alberti (1404–72). Facade of Sant'Andrea, Mantua.

but he would have soon appreciated that such a scheme could not work effectively since it would have consumed too much of the small *campo* in front of the church and would have proved awkward in relation to the body of the church. As built, the facade combines the illusion of a portico, when seen from across the water, together with a dynamic overlapping of engaged columns and pilasters, when seen from nearby (plate 125).

Palladio eventually discarded his early project for a solution with individual bases in proportion to the different orders, presumably because this reflected the arrangement of the orders on the interior. He patterned his solution on Alberti's Sant'Andrea in Mantua where the division of the facade into three bays by large and small orders reflects the basic module of the nave wall (plate 130). The lucidity of Alberti's solution clearly impressed Palladio since he incorporated similar correspondences not only in his own churches but also in his detailed critique of the proposed model for a new cathedral in Brescia.[38] In his report of 1567, Palladio wanted to alter Lodovico Beretta's model so that the nave would have piers with an engaged colossal order in place of columns while the aisles would have smaller piers in keeping with their scale. Palladio advocated the same solution with large and small orders for the central and lateral portions of the facade, respectively. Though rarely mentioned in accounts of Palladio's churches, the report to Brescia offers the clearest statement of his "system" of church design, revealing it as fully articulated by the early stages of San Giorgio. In designing San Giorgio, Palladio also recalled the unusual facade designed by Falconetto for the parish church at Codevigo (plate 131) where the comparable tabernacles were framed by a Doric order on high bases. Behind both Falconetto's and Palladio's facades lay the influence of the unusual Temple of Minerva at Assisi (plate 182), where the portico columns were given individual socles, but Palladio has raised the motif to a scale rivaling antiquity itself.[39] Forceful and unorthodox, the facade of San Giorgio Maggiore more than lives up to the demands of its setting.

The church of the Redentore was the product of a very different type of commission, one that involved the highest councils of the Venetian Republic, and it owed its existence to one of

the most devastating bouts of plague suffered by Venice since the Black Death of
the Middle Ages.[40] The first outbreaks
occurred in the latter part of 1575 and
flared until July 1577, by which time more
than fifty thousand people had perished.
The losses amounted to a quarter of the
city's population, and as the poor were dis-
proportionately affected by the epidemic,
the social and economic fabric of the city
underwent acute strain. To make matters
worse, there was no common agreement on
the plague's origins or on procedure against
it. Rather like contemporary debates over
the economy, informed opinion of the day
split between the classicists, who adhered to
theories of bad air and astrological conjunc-
tions laid down by ancient writers, and the
empiricists, who believed in a theory of
contagion and argued for improving social
conditions as a means of combating plague.
Gradually inertia gave way to action by the

131. Giovanni Maria Falconetto (1468–1535). Facade of parish
church, Codevigo (Padua).

government; quarantine was ordered for the ill, mass burial in lime pits for the dead, and food
and medication were procured for the needy. The Church was also called upon to organize peni-
tential processions and services to appease the wrath of God, and the Venetian Senate resolved
to erect a church as an offering against the cessation of the plague. Down to the seventeenth
century outbreaks of plague were commonly associated with God's anger, a connection rooted
in the Biblical plagues visited upon the Israelites in the wilderness and those that resulted from
David's pride.[41] Whenever there was an outbreak of plague there was a revival of devotion of
saints like Roch and Sebastian as well as the veneration of Christ the Redeemer, to whom the
votive church of 1576 was dedicated. An annual pilgrimage by the doge and government on the
feast of the Redeemer was decreed, and ten thousand ducats were initially set aside for the
church, "not using stones or marble but making a solid structure appropriate to a devotional
church."[42] Two noblemen were entrusted with the task of selecting a site, and one owned by the
Capuchin friars on the Venetian island of Giudecca was chosen, probably because it was unbuilt
and presented no prospect of interference by the local clergy. As soon as the site was chosen,
Palladio received the task of preparing models for the new church.

The choice of Palladio is not explained, but his extensive experience in public architecture made him the obvious candidate. Two projects, one centralized and one "quadrangular," or cruciform, were presented to the Senate for review in February 1577. Accounts of the debate show that Marc'antonio Barbaro played a prominent role. By this date he had established himself as notable diplomat and an arbiter of questions about architecture, but although Barbaro argued strongly in favor of a *rotunda,* he remained in a minority.[43] Judging by Palladio's remarks on church design in the *Quattro Libri,* this would have been the architect's preferred solution as well.

A suite of drawings can be connected with Palladio's ideas about a centralized plan, which typically range from a less expensive design without a cupola and portico to a more elaborate version with Pantheonic portico and domed, centralized interior.[44] Constant features, all of which would be translated to the definitive project, include the division of the church from the choir by a columnar screen, the presence of twin sacristies, and the use of small spiral staircases. The Senate, however, preferred a cruciform design, partly for liturgical reasons, partly for practical considerations of more space. The site, too, was enlarged in length and breadth to provide more space for the building. The foundations were begun in May 1577, and the church was consecrated fifteen years later.

Although the Redentore is neither so large nor so opulently appointed as San Giorgio Maggiore, it pays handsome tribute to the investment by the Venetian government, which finally amounted to some sixty thousand ducats. It also reflects the triumphalist mood of church and state in the first years of the Catholic Reformation. The Capuchins protested against the church's splendor but their complaints were ignored, much as the Jesuits' preferences for a simpler design were set aside by Cardinal Farnese, who paid for the Gesù in Rome. Like San Giorgio, the Redentore demonstrates Palladio's ability to tailor his style to the site of the building, as well as to its functions, which in this case were ceremonial, votive, and monastic.[45]

The Redentore's ceremonial quality is the first called to mind as one approaches the church today, and it is easy to conjure up the procession of dignitaries who visited there on its feast day. The facade was conceived for the view across the Giudecca Canal and is built up of a variety of elements, from the Corinthian pilasters and segments of pediments to the frontispiece proper, which modulates from colossal Composite pilasters to engaged columns (plate 132). The colossal order supports a pediment set into the attic but conveys the illusion of a portico *in antis*, much as was the case at San Francesco della Vigna and San Giorgio. This illusion continues above the attic where the triangular form of the hipped roof echoes the pseudo-pediment and rises toward the dome and flanking bell towers. The compactness and smaller scale of the facade is the key to its popularity over San Giorgio. Not only is the total effect more integrated, but the common base for both orders also avoids the stark contrast in pedestal heights found at San Giorgio. The staircase, too, frames the center of the facade while masking the transition from basement to entrance.

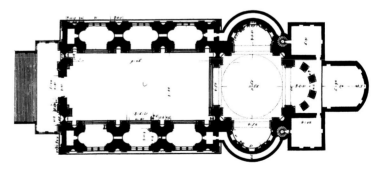

132. (*opposite*) View of the Redentore from across the canal.

133. (*above*) *Plan of the Redentore.* Begun in 1577, the church was finished by 1592.

134. Interior of the Redentore.

On the interior one finds the same clear and rational arrangement of elements as in San Giorgio, here allied to a plan of equal ingenuity (plate 133). The Capuchins were a preaching order, an offshoot of the Franciscans, and their basic need was for a large, uninterrupted nave for sermons. Lateral chapels were required for private devotions and smaller masses. These functions are served by the rectangular block that marks the first section of the church, a space articulated by paired, engaged Corinthian columns that flank the chapels and turn in toward the crossing, thus defining the boundary of nave and transept (plate 134). As at San Giorgio, the chapels are raised three steps above the floor of the nave but have a biapsidal plan. This motif derives from the Roman baths but was filtered through Palladio's study of Raphael's Saint Peter's and works inspired by it, most notably Girolamo Genga's church of San Giovanni Battista in

Pesaro (plate 136).[46] As Burns observed, Palladio would have known Genga's church firsthand and was obviously taken with the elegance of its plan, although its elevation lacks the quality of detail found at the Redentore. Palladio's choice of a similar plan with a suppressed transept here has sometimes been linked to contemporary churches like the Gesù in Rome, but this was a fairly common plan, particularly for urban sites where extended transepts were not always feasible.[47] At the Redentore, the walls between the chapels serve a double function as piers, rising to form buttresses for the nave vault in the manner of Alberti's Sant'Andrea in Mantua. On the exterior, Palladio allied this structural element to a strategic repetition of pilasters and thermal windows, thereby creating a coherent lateral facade (plate 137).

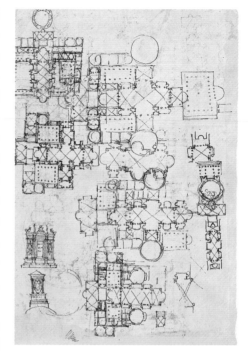

At the crossing, the ceremonial and votive functions of the church are expressed by the statelier style defined by the triconch surmounted by the dome (plate 138). Similarly compartmentalized solutions can be found in Palladio's reconstructions of the Roman baths (plate 135), and the triconch formula had been anticipated by Bramante's choir of Santa Maria delle Grazie in Milan as well as Sanmicheli's votive church of the Madonna di Campagna near Verona.[48] This area gains a distinctly antique resonance through its separation from the sacristies and choir by the columnar screen, a favorite motif from the baths. Palladio opened out the crossing to the width of the side chapels and extended it the same length behind the high altar, thus encouraging a flow of pilgrims around its perimeter. As a whole, the layout encourages a progression from nave to transept and back again, a sense of movement underscored by Palladio's manipulation of those horizontal and vertical elements that contrive to be in counterpoint. The colossal order itself changes from engaged columns to pilasters to freestanding columns while minor motifs like the Vitruvian scroll running between the engaged columns reappear on the chapel walls (plate 134); base

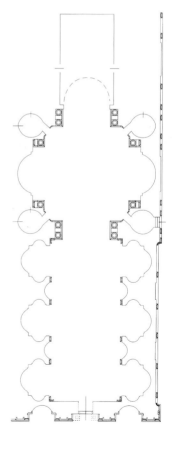

135. *(above)* *Sketches of the Baths of Agrippa.* (RIBA VII/6v.) Pen and ink, 21.5 x 31.2 cm.

136. *(right)* Girolamo Genga (c. 1476–1551). *Plan of San Giovanni Battista, Pesaro.*

moldings are also linked from column to column. Palladio selected the intricate profile of the columns in the Temple of Diana at Nîmes to set off the colossal order of the Redentore.[49]

Like San Giorgio, the Redentore reveals Palladio's intensive study of the baths, but the church is much more than a compendium of motifs or "influences." Instead, it is a harmonious blending of many elements into an organic whole, something that makes the experience of a Palladian church as complex and satisfying as a church by Borromini.

If Palladio felt any disappointment that a centralized plan was not chosen, he was soon able to compensate with the creation of the church at Maser, which was very much a joint effort with Marc'antonio Barbaro. The Tempietto, as the church at Maser is commonly called, was one of the last works planned by Palladio and bears the names of patron and architect as well as the date of 1580 in its lateral frieze (plate 139). A bull by Pope Sixtus V from 1585 refers to the church as having been newly built by Marc'antonio Barbaro in the middle of the village of

Maser at a cost of six thousand ducats.[50] The same document indicates that the Tempietto was to have replaced the old parish church of Maser, but the transfer was never achieved. The bull tells a great deal about the purpose of the building and the site chosen for it. The church was designed to fulfill the twin functions of villa and parish

137. (*above*) Right flank of the Redentore.

138. (*left*) Crossing of the Redentore.

139. (*opposite*) The Tempietto at the Villa Barbaro.

MARCVS·ANTONIVS·BARBARVS·PROCVRATOR·FRANC·FILIVS

church, and thus it was set on a prominent site on the road from Asolo to Treviso, bordering both the Barbaro estate and the village. This site corresponded to Palladio's recommendation that churches could be placed outside cities and facing onto roads so that passersby would be encouraged to say their prayers; it also helps to explain why the church has one principal viewpoint.[51]

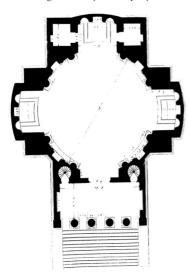

The church has a centralized plan, in the tradition of chapels like Sanmicheli's Cappella Pellegrini or Vignola's Sant'Andrea on the edge of the Villa Giulia in Rome, but it is capacious enough to house the village inhabitants as well as the villa household.[52]

The Tempietto is also unusual insofar as its Christian dedication has been subsumed under a nickname redolent of pagan temples. Even from the earliest printed accounts it has been called a *"bel tempio rotondo"* or *"piccolo Pantheon,"* just as Paolo Almerico named his villa "La Rotonda."[53] In both cases, the

140. *(above)* Interior of the Tempietto at the Villa Barbaro.

141. *(left) Plan of the Tempietto,* Villa Barbaro.

names pay tribute to the derivation from one of Palladio's most favored antique buildings, the Pantheon, which often figured in his reconstructions of ancient temple complexes (plate 206). An obvious link exists between the Tempietto and Palladio's early studies for the Redentore, but the relationship between the Tempietto and the Pantheon is more in spirit than detail. Its Corinthian portico and stepped, hemispheric dome proclaim an affinity with the great rotonda in Rome, but the plan of the church is novel in its combination of cylinder and Greek cross (plate 141). The perimeter of the nave is defined by a circle while the three chapels are pulled back far enough to indicate the arms of the cross; the chapel walls double as buttresses for the dome, which rests directly on the cylinder.

The stucco decoration of the exterior and interior is perhaps even more a reflection of Marc'antonio Barbaro's taste than Palladio's.[54] The principal interior motif is a triumphal arch formed by engaged Corinthian columns that flank the entrance and altar recesses (plate 140). The walls are given aedicules, a common motif in Palladio's later architecture, and they and the principal altars contain stucco figures commemorating the patron saints of the Barbaro family.[55] Unlike Palladio's other churches, the Tempietto is dimly lit, but this conforms with its purpose as a mortuary chapel for the patron and his family. In fact the whole church can be interpreted as a family memorial despite the absence of epitaphs. Marc'antonio Barbaro presumably shared his brother Daniele's dislike of funerary monuments in churches and sought through his villa and the Tempietto to leave a monument to himself, his brother, and, indirectly, their architect.[56]

Legend says that Palladio died at Maser in August 1580, probably when planning the Tempietto. At that date none of his major churches was finished, and the Zitelle, the modest neighbor of the Redentore on the Giudecca Canal, had only been begun.[57] Nevertheless Palladio's achievement in this field was as notable as in any other aspect of his career. Although the influence of his churches was largely confined to the Veneto, the Carità, San Giorgio Maggiore, and the Redentore all gave him scope for expressing his vision of architecture on a scale rivaling the monuments of antiquity.

VII

BRIDGES

PALLADIO IS NOT NORMALLY CONSIDERED AS A DESIGNER OF BRIDGES, BUT THEY OCCUPIED HIM throughout his career and form a distinctive category within his work. In addition, he was the first modern architect to publish extensively on the subject of bridges and his designs are fascinating, not only because of the insight they give to his thought processes but also for the clear division they demonstrate in his use of wood or stone. Bridges also constitute the only part of Palladio's architectural practice that anticipated future trends as much as it returned to classical precedent.[1]

Bridge building was always an area of expertise in which architecture, engineering, and the skills of carpenter and mason overlapped. Especially in Italy, ancient bridges and aqueducts remained as testimonials to Roman engineering, and since most towns were on or near water the maintenance and construction of bridges became a focal point of civic concern. While the Ponte Vecchio in Florence and the Ponte Scaligero in Verona (plate 145) remain picturesque if isolated examples of early bridges, Venice still shows how significant they can be in urban life.

Techniques of building bridges hardly advanced between Roman times and the eighteenth century. Leonardo drafted wooden bridge designs for Cesare d'Este and a 240-meter single-span stone bridge for Constantinople; Palladio's patron Daniele Barbaro made a study of old London Bridge (plate 146) while he was ambassador to England in the late 1540s. But the general approach to bridges was more empirical than theoretical, and it was not until the age of Galileo that arch spans and tensile strength became subjects of scientific research.[2]

Girded by two rivers, Vicenza boasted a number of medieval as well as the remains of two Roman bridges. One of Palladio's first public acts as an *inzegnere* or architect was to give an opinion on the state of a wooden bridge over the Tesina River at Torri di Quartesolo on the edge

142. The wooden bridge at Bassano del Grappa.

of Vicenza.³ This occurred in 1544, and Palladio's name appeared in the documents together with that of his erstwhile master, Giovanni da Porlezza, and Guglielmo Marchesi, a local carpenter whose sons later worked under Palladio on the Basilica arcades and on his wooden bridge over the Bacchiglione River at Porta Santa Croce. The early stages of the new arcades for the Basilica also meant close collaboration with Martino Dezin, a carpenter from Bergamo and son-in-law of Giovanni da Porlezza who made the model of the loggias in 1549 and subsequently worked with Palladio on two of his wooden bridges.⁴ Palladio's contacts with carpenters were a necessary part of his normal trade, and his work on houses and villas gave him ample opportunity to observe the basic structural systems used in roofs (plate 74) and in constructing arches. Such help was especially pertinent for bridges where questions of span and load-bearing capacity would be critical. But Palladio didn't simply rely on advice here; rather, he made his own studies, something that the third book of the *Quattro Libri* demonstrates.

As most of our knowledge of Palladio's bridges derives from his treatise, it is best to refer to it as a guide to his thoughts. His engagement with the subject becomes even more apparent when one compares Palladio's treatment of bridges in the *Quattro Libri* with Alberti's.⁵ On a philosophical level, Palladio follows Alberti's discussion of bridges as an extension of roads and separates them according to materials employed. But while Alberti gives a highly compressed account of bridges in a few paragraphs, Palladio awards them several chapters and writes with a familiarity bred of practical experience. Exceptionally, it is Palladio who culls the classical sources on antique bridges, such as the legendary one erected by Hercules on the future site of Rome, or the Pons Sublicius, an easily dismantled wooden structure made famous by Horatius Cocles' defense of Rome against the Etruscans. Equally characteristic of their different approaches is the two authors' account of Julius Caesar's bridge over the Rhine. In his *Commentaries,* Caesar described in some detail a wooden bridge assembled in ten days during one of his campaigns in Gaul.⁶ Some forty meters long and three and a half meters wide, the bridge elicited great interest in the Renaissance. Palladio certainly would have considered it when he studied the *Commentaries* as a young man under Giangiorgio Trissino—he later published an illustrated translation of them, suggesting a more than casual interest.⁷

Alberti's account of Caesar's bridge over the Rhine was little more than an extended quotation of Caesar's own words, with slight amendments. Palladio obviously knew the passage in Alberti, and he could compare it with the illustrated edition of Caesar published by Fra Giovanni Giocondo in 1513; with a more recent edition translated by Francesco Baldelli and illustrated by the architect Giovanni Antonio Rusconi; and with an illustrated edition of Alberti first published by Cosimo Bartoli in 1550 and reprinted in 1565.⁸ The earlier woodcuts were of some help although the ones in Fra Giocondo's and Bartoli's editions were extremely approximate and offered little guidance for Palladio; that by Rusconi was clearer and more considered though surpassed by Palladio's in terms of detail and precision. Indeed, Palladio employed here the method of exposition used by Daniele Barbaro in his edition of Vitruvius—that is, the original text is given, followed by a commentary with illustration. It is noteworthy that Palladio's translation of Caesar differs from those then available in print, which would indicate an independent line of inquiry on his part.

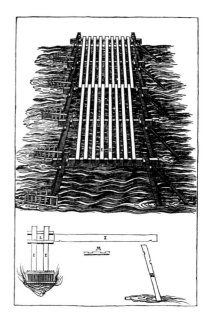

Palladio interpreted the bridge as a trapezoidal structure, composed of a series of A-frames over which interlocking planks formed a road (plate 143). Pairs of opposing uprights were hammered into the river bed some forty Roman feet apart and angled toward and against the current. They were then bound together by planks that were fitted into the uprights for greater stability. This frame was overlaid by further planks and then by rods and wickerwork. The whole structure was reinforced upstream by stakes that were bent to form bastions at the foot of the frames and by single struts downstream to absorb the force of the current. Palladio departed from his customary practice by illustrating the bridge with a bird's-eye view, which made sense here in terms of conveying to the reader the overall nature of the bridge.[9] As it happened, the architect had the opportunity to test his reconstruction in 1559 when a flood destroyed the old wooden bridge at Santa Croce in Vicenza. He mentioned this bridge in the *Quattro Libri*, but it was replaced by another shortly after his death.[10]

We are on firmer ground with Palladio's other bridge designs in timber since he illustrates them in the successive chapters of book three. These form a remarkable series of projects related to a single-span bridge over the Cismon River, commissioned by Palladio's close friend and patron Giacomo Angaran.[11] Angaran held large estates in the region of Bassano and acquired the rights of passage over the Cismon on the road between Trent and Bassano del Grappa in the 1540s. This was not far from the villa that Palladio projected for Angaran about 1548.[12] As Palladio explained, the Cismon came down from the mountains and entered into the Brenta River above the town of Bassano. More a torrent than a river, it could move with extreme velocity and was also used by lumberjacks for sending logs down stream. Both the strength of the current and the volume of logs and stones carried with it rendered conventional wooden bridges inadequate, and earlier bridges on the site had to be restored annually. Angaran turned for advice to Palladio, who produced four solutions that resolved the problem in unusual ways (plates 144, 147, 148).

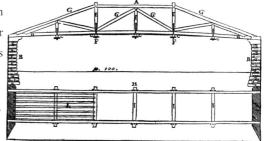

143. *(above) Reconstruction of Caesar's Bridge* from the *Quattro Libri.*

144. *(right) Bridge over the Cismon River* from the *Quattro Libri.*

Essentially Palladio created a single-span bridge, thus avoiding the necessity for intermediate supports set in the water. While this may seem the obvious solution, it had its daring aspect, for the span involved was one hundred Vicentine feet or approximately thirty-five meters, far more than the normal span of such bridges. In extending the span beyond the customary length of twenty-five or thirty feet, the problem lay in devising a system largely composed of members appreciably shorter than the gap to be spanned. Palladio seems to have been the first to devise such a system, thus enabling larger single-span bridges to be built.[13] He did this by employing a trussed or triangulated configuration in which the individual members were joined together with iron straps and pins where they would otherwise tend to pull apart. Triangulation allows greater distances to be spanned by creating a new pattern of equilibrium with most members acting solely in compression or in tension rather than by bending. Ideally only the timbers directly carrying the roadway need act as beams, passing on their loads to the triangulated members where they meet one another.

Palladio had already had experience with analogous systems in roofs, and he could have observed similar, albeit simpler, triangulation in timber-roofed early Christian basilicas. There the basic triangle was formed by a pair of rafters joined at their feet by a horizontal tie and was typically stiffened by means of a secondary system of inclined struts carried by a central vertical tie.[14] Palladio adapted this system for use in his own buildings such as the Teatro Olimpico and he adapted it further for the first of his four Cismon River projects.

Before the bridge was constructed, the banks were strengthened by stone abutments to provide firm support at each end for two trusses to carry the roadway. Each truss was divided into

145. Architect unknown. Ponte Scaligero, Verona, built around 1375–76.

six equal bays by vertical timbers that were fastened to the bottom chords by iron straps. Three further timbers constituted the top chord of each truss, linking the tops of the vertical timbers to one another and, over each abutment, to the bottom chord. To complete the triangulation, diagonal struts connected the feet of the vertical timbers to the top chords at the points of connection with adjacent verticals. Five cross-beams then connected the bottom chords at their points of connection with the vertical timbers, and over these were laid the longitudinal beams of the roadway. At first sight the principles behind this seem simple enough—based, as Pane observed, on the "fundamental intuition of the non-deformable structure of the triangle."[15] But how was the structure intended to work? Closer inspection soon discloses ambiguities: how, in particular, are we to understand the bottom chords? All that can be said with certainty is that the trusses would collapse if these chords were not effectively continuous from end to end, capable of transmitting from abutment to abutment the tensions necessary to resist the compressions in the top chords. The plan in the woodcut shows them as single continuous lengths, although finding, transporting, and setting in place single timbers of around thirty-five meters' length would have posed considerable difficulties (plate 144). Still, these difficulties could have been avoided by scarfing together three shorter lengths for each chord, a procedure that could also have made it easier to achieve the definite upward curve seen in the side view.

The three illustrations that follow in the *Quattro Libri* present two variations on the first solution as well as a more interesting alternative (plates 147, 148). The first is the most traditional, composed of eight small bays with the chords formed of superimposed timbers, each projecting farther than the previous one until the central gap could be spanned by a short beam. Palladio reports that Alessandro Picheroni, who was an expert in carpentry and a designer of ships, had seen a similar bridge in Germany, meaning probably in the Tirol, but this type of pseudoarch would have offered little resistance to heavy loads.[16] The second woodcut is more of a variation on the original design, with cross-diagonal struts and further buttressing by beams running between the first posts and the stone abutments. Here as in the

146. Claude de Jongh (fl. 1626–63). *Old London Bridge*, c. 1630. Iveagh Bequest, Kenwood House, London. Oil on panel, 51.3 x 170.3 cm.

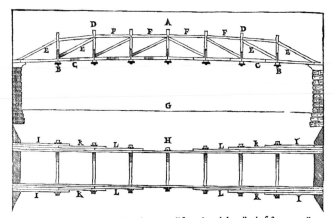

LA inuentione del ponte, che fegue; ha la parte di fopra, laquale è quella, che fostenta tutto il
carico; fatta di portione di cerchio minore del mezo circolo, & ha le braccia, che nanno da un co-
lonnello all'altro, cofi ordinate, che nel mezzo de' fpacij, che fono tra i colonnelli, s'incrocciano. Le
traui, che fanno il fuolo del Ponte; fono incatenate à i colonnelli cō arpefi, come nelle inuentioni,
di fopra. Per maggior fortezza fi potrbbono aggiogner due traui per ogni capo del ponte, lequali affermate ne' pilaftri con un capo, con l'altro arriuaffero fotto i primi colonnelli, percioche aiu-
terebbono molto à foftentar il carico del ponte.

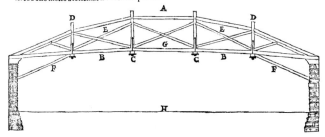

CCC   A, E'

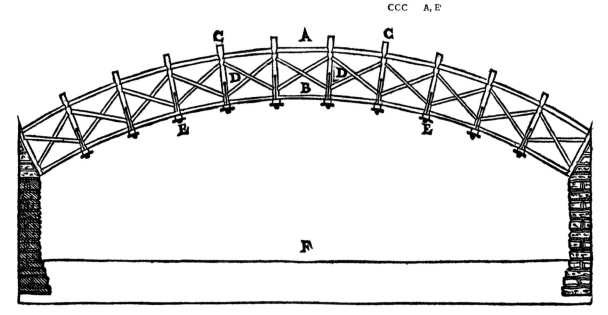

147. *(top) Two variations on the Cismon River design from the* Quattro Libri.

148. *(above) Final variation on the Cismon River design from the* Quattro Libri.

subsequent design the number of bays is odd (five as opposed to eight or six in the previous designs) so that a bay rather than a post marks the center of the bridge; in the second and third designs, each bay is reinforced by diagonal struts. The third (plate 148), however, represents more of a departure since it describes a shallow arch. The advantage here is that the arch could be varied according to the distance involved. The abutments have also been built up at an angle to conform better to the curve of the arch. Here, Palladio has adapted the system used for constructing brick and stone arches, applying it to a timber bridge.[17] Since the design married the basic concept of the arch with that of the diagonally braced truss, Palladio obviously felt it merited serious consideration in its own right. Although only the first of the four timber projects was carried out, he took the unusual step of publishing the alternatives as a means of "copyrighting" his inventions.

The bridge over the Cismon River was built between 1550 and 1552. Scamozzi later credited the design to the carpenter Martino Dezin, an incorrect assumption though one cannot underestimate his role in putting Palladio's design into effect.[18] The total cost to Angaran came to five hundred ducats, yet the bridge lasted half a century, and even as late as the eighteenth century the stone piers were still standing.[19] The episode was definitely not tangential to Palladio's career; rather, it was the fruit of more than a decade's experience with carpentry and bridge building. He was justifiably proud of his designs, and although wooden bridges were regarded as inherently less noble than stone ones, they could, in Palladio's eyes, be similarly durable, beautiful, and convenient. Wood also had the advantage of lightness, cheapness, and flexibility. Rather surprisingly, Palladio also saw such designs, which reduced a bridge to its essential structure or *tessitura,* as possessing an intrinsic beauty.

The bridge at Bassano del Grappa, the other wooden bridge executed to Palladio's design, represented a different kind of structural problem, one in which Palladio was basically called upon to make refinements to a traditional design. This occurred late in 1567, after a terrible flood destroyed the covered bridge that spanned the Brenta River and connected Bassano with Vicenza. The bridge was of strategic importance, not only for Bassano but also for communications between Venice and the north.[20] The earliest mention of a bridge on this site dates from 1209, but this was probably not the first. The structure had already been restored and replaced several times by 1498, when it is recorded as being rebuilt in wood "as before." In 1511 the War of the League of Cambrai witnessed further destruction of the bridge, and thereafter several proposals came and went, including an attempt to build a two-bay stone bridge. Only in 1530 was a new wood bridge finally constructed; initially it was supported by two piers, later augmented to five, and lasted until October 1567.

Records of this pre-Palladian bridge show that it followed a conventional design for a covered bridge, resting on large piers resembling spurs. Covered bridges were more common in mountainous areas where weather and winds were less clement, and this one was placed obliquely across a bend in the Brenta at a point where the river was narrowest and the current less treacherous.[21] The rebuilding of the bridge after its destruction in 1567 was not simply a matter of urgency but also one of local pride. By that date the covered bridge at Bassano had assumed a symbolic importance in the identity of the town and even figured prominently in a fresco that once adorned the Palazzo Pretorio, the civic palace of Bassano. No doubt the selection of Palladio as consultant engineer was related to his recent success at Cismon and to the support of Giacomo Angaran, whose recommendation obviously carried weight in Bassano. Palladio received payment for a design as early as January 1, 1568, and the city council decreed that the new bridge should be constructed like its predecessor, though "with those additions deemed necessary by the architects and masters who will build it."[22] This gave some flexibility but effectively channeled Palladio's work along predetermined lines.

Meanwhile, money was raised, timber purchased, and Palladio's model was fetched from Vicenza in July 1569. At the same time, Giacomo Angaran intervened in favor of Battista Marchesi as the executant carpenter of the new bridge. Marchesi was a member of the Vicentine family of carpenters whom Palladio frequently employed, and he had built the wooden bridge at Santa Croce in Vicenza after Palladio's design only a few years before.[23] In October 1569 Palladio was reimbursed for the model, and for coming to Bassano to inspect the work. Construction proceeded swiftly and the bridge was finished in 1570.

So closely did the project anticipate the publication of the *Quattro Libri* that it only appeared with a partial illustration, though with a lengthy verbal account (plate 149).[24] Palladio tells us that he "ordered" the bridge, rather than designing it, probably to indicate that it wasn't purely his own invention. Nevertheless, there are touches that reflect his personal approach. As he describes it, the bridge spanned 180 Vicentine feet (65 meters) and was divided into five bays by four piers, one less than in the previous bridge. This reduction in piers, which could be done because Palladio reinforced the end piers with oak and larch posts, meant that the bridge was less vulnerable to damage from the impact of strong currents. Again to minimize possible damage the piers were reduced to a skeletal structure consisting of eight uprights thirty feet long, one-and-a-half by one-and-a-half feet thick. These were placed two feet apart, and the total width of each group of eight came to twenty-six feet. The piers were driven into the river bed and reinforced on either side by spurs that extended outward at a forty-five-degree angle and resembled arrowhead bastions

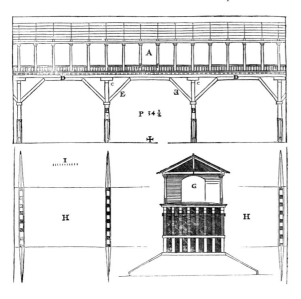

149. *Bridge at Bassano del Grappa* from the *Quattro Libri.*

found on stone bridges. These skeletal piers were covered with large planks as protection against the effects of water while the eight uprights were bound above by a single beam. It took eight beams to reach the distance between one pier and the next. Over them was laid the bed of the roadway, and inclined struts were added underneath to each bay; this last element constituted an improvement on the previous structure and must have been related to Palladio's earlier experiments with bridge design. The bridge was topped by a covered walkway as before, and here Palladio added another new touch in the form of wooden Tuscan columns with an architrave. The architect would have been prompted to introduce this classical touch through his sense of decorum, given that the Tuscan order was the most primitive of the standard columns and had the largest intercolumniation.[25] In any case, the success of Palladio's design was proved by the the fact that despite numerous repairs it lasted until 1748 when an especially bad flood carried it away (plates 142, 150).

On the strength of this achievement at Bassano, Palladio received a summons from the city council of Belluno in 1579 to advise on rebuilding a wooden bridge there.[26] The invitation to Belluno led to the presentation of two alternative designs for the new bridge, one in wood and

150. Roberto Roberti (1786–1837). *View of Bassano*, c. 1813. Museo Civico, Bassano del Grappa. Oil on canvas, 54 x 84 cm.

the other in stone. It has been argued for some time that Palladio presented similar alternatives to the council of Bassano and that the three-bay stone bridge illustrated in the *Quattro Libri* was the unsuccessful project in stone (plate 151). Certainly Palladio left enough evidence for a careful reader to put two and two together: the measurements are identical, even down to the water level against the piers, although the author makes no mention of the intended site—which, as we shall see, happened with the even more notorious case of the Rialto Bridge project. The ultimate purpose of this project has been called into question because of its similarity with another project for a stone bridge that Palladio prepared for the Tesina River at Torri di Quartesolo near Vicenza, although the Tesina project called for a smaller span.[27] What is noteworthy, however, is the consistency of Palladio's approach and the striking difference between his wooden and stone projects. At first sight this difference may seem so great as to rule out the conclusion that both plates 149 and 151 were intended for Bassano, but the cleft between alternatives is typical of the divergent values that the architect ascribed to each type of material. Although some hints about Roman timber bridges were available through written sources and occasional images such as those found on Trajan's column, Palladio generally relied on his own intuition and the basic structural tradition with which he was familiar. Without classical precedents, his imagination was freer to develop along a different aesthetic from that which obtained when there were classical prototypes before his eyes.

This is abundantly clear when one looks at his designs for bridges in stone. Here Palladio—and Alberti before him—was on firmer ground, and the achievements of the Romans more than fulfilled the Vitruvian triad of *firmitas, utilitas,* and *venustas,* or durability, usefulness, and beauty. In his treatise Palladio prefaced his account of individual bridges with general observations on the nature of their construction, borrowed specifically from Alberti.[28] He advised building where the river banks are of stone or similarly solid. Special care should be taken that the end piers are robust, he explained, and an even number of piers should be used because nature endows every creature with an even number of legs to support its weight. This last observation is typically Palladian in its appeal to the natural world as a justification for what was simply an aesthetic preference, and such comparisons often appear in Palladio's writings.[29] The piers should be built where the current is least turbulent, he continued, and they should be constructed in the autumn when the water is at its lowest. He also recommended that the thickness of the piers should fall between one-fourth and one-sixth of the width of the arch; large blocks of stone should be employed for them, bound together by metal cramps. The arches should be semicircular, the form Palladio believed to be the strongest, but if this would make the way across the bridge uncomfortably high then a segmental form was advisable. Here, too, the preference for semicircular arches reflected a typical Renaissance bias, but Palladio also knew that when the span was large, the height of the arch could render the bridge less useful.[30]

Palladio supported these general observations with a rapid survey of Roman bridges, focusing chiefly on the bridge erected by the emperor Augustus at Rimini (plate 152). This he felt to be the most beautiful of the Roman bridges he knew, and his illustration shows a careful study of it. The bridge has five roundheaded arches, the central ones of equal width, the end ones slightly smaller; the piers are slightly less than half the width of the central bays and have spurs at right angles.[31] Each of the four main piers has a tabernacle for statuary and additionally a cornice running along the top, a detail Palladio found especially handsome. The bridge at Rimini receives privileged treatment here because it was the architect's *beau ideal* and the touchstone for his essays in this field. For balance, two other ancient bridges are also reproduced, both in Vicenza and both sharing a similar design and scale.[32] The two bridges had elliptical arches and an unusual feature in the form of projecting stones below the imposts of the arches. Palladio noted that these served as a base for the timber structure used when constructing the arches; in this manner, he reasoned, the timber rested on the piers and was not built in the water, thus rendering it less subject to changes in the current. Palladio borrowed this feature for his unexecuted Bassano project and for the bridge at Torri di Quartesolo. Although he added a fourth bay to the Roman bridge over the Bacchiglione River, he preferred to reproduce the bridge's original appearance, noting that two of the three bays were later replacements.

Sandwiched between these illustrations of ancient Vicentine bridges comes the most

famous of Palladio's designs for a stone bridge, that for the Rialto in Venice (plate 153). In many respects it only amplifies the principles observed by Palladio in his unsuccessful stone project for Bassano, but it also touches on a major episode in the urban history of Venice, one that needs to be placed in context before Palladio's design can be analyzed. After Piazza San Marco, the Rialto was the second most important area in Venice, a center of financial dealings as well as the major market of the city.[33] The Rialto was also the only point at which the Grand Canal was crossed by a bridge, and it was the nature of that bridge that preoccupied Venice for half a century before Palladio delivered his first project.

Although a bridge may have existed at the Rialto as early as the twelfth century, one was certainly standing by the first years of the thirteenth.[34] Rebuilding and restoring the wooden structure are recorded at regular

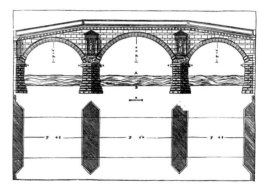

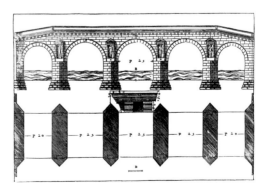

151. *(top) Alternative project for a stone bridge at Bassano* from the *Quattro Libri.*

152. *(above) Bridge of Augustus at Rimini* from the *Quattro Libri.*

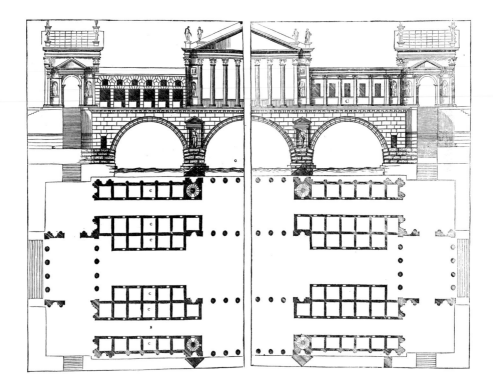

intervals, at least from the fifteenth century, and a proposal to place shops on the bridge, as a revenue-enhancer for the state, sparked a lively debate in 1458. The proposal carried, although the question of the bridge's appearance remained an issue. Our image of the old wooden bridge at the Rialto derives from a painting by Carpaccio of the 1490s and from Jacopo de' Barbari's famous bird's-eye view of Venice published around 1500. The bridge then consisted of larch ramps with two rows of shops separated by a wide passageway, all supported by six rows of piers composed of eight beams bound together transversely. At midpoint the bridge contained two movable sections, which could be raised or lowered by chains. This allowed galleys and above all the doge's barge, the *Bucintoro,* to pass up the Grand Canal on state occasions.[35]

By the turn of the century, with the old wooden structure in a rickety state, the first signs of interest in stone bridges began to emerge. As early as 1471, Doge Cristoforo Moro left money for the erection of a stone bridge over the Cannaregio Canal, a distance comparable to the width of the Grand Canal at the Rialto. His motive was to make access easier to the hospital and friary of San Giobbe, of which he was the major patron, and the bridge was finally constructed by 1503.[36] That same year, Verona petitioned Venice for funds to rebuild and fortify a stone bridge called the Ponte della Pietra, a project that dragged on until 1508. Another stim-

153. *Rialto Bridge project* from the *Quattro Libri.*

ulus came from Paris, where the replacement of the old wooden Pont Nôtre-Dame with a stone bridge excited the interest of the Venetian ambassador. After the new Parisian bridge was constructed between 1499 and 1507 by the Veronese Dominican Fra Giovanni Giocondo, the Venetian government began sounding him out about acquiring his services. Fra Giocondo, who had gained international fame as an architect and as an expert on hydraulics, offered his assistance to the Republic in 1506, stipulating a stipend of only one ducat a day.[37] The offer was accepted by Venice, and it may not be coincidental that the first recorded reference to a stone bridge for the Rialto dates from the following year. It is not clear whether the project originated with Fra Giocondo or with a local architect like Giorgio Spavento, the *proto* or chief architect of San Marco, but in 1507 the Venetian diarist Marin Sanudo recorded the existence of such a model, which was entirely of stone though with a drawbridge mechanism at the center.[38] The description suggests a hybrid structure, a cross between a traditional Roman bridge and the wooden drawbridge then in place. The project also anticipated the difficulties that would plague later generations in trying to reconcile the divergence between classical models and the reality of the bridge as it had evolved in the fifteenth century.

Instead of rebuilding, however, the Venetian government opted for a modest rehabilitation of the old structure, a gesture that would become a leitmotif of the Rialto's history for decades to come. Even the great fire of 1514, which destroyed the market section of the Rialto area, only served to shift attention away from the bridge to the more urgent task of reconstructing what had been lost.[39] The fire occurred in January and consumed the whole of the market area in less than six hours. The tightly packed buildings and stalls burned like tinder, and some contemporaries compared the scene with the Sack of Troy. In the aftermath, several projects for rebuilding the area were presented to the Venetian Senate, of which the most interesting was that by Fra Giocondo. Vasari apparently knew Fra Giocondo's model, and described it in some detail.[40] The project called for a square surrounded by canals on all four sides. The outer embankments of the square were to be reserved for the sale of food but the main part given over to higher forms of commerce. These would take place in two ranges of buildings running around the square and set one within the other. The outer range was designated for drapers' shops with room for storage above while across an internal street lay the inner range, faced with loggias on two floors (plate 154). The space behind the loggias was reserved for jewelers, goldsmiths, and bankers, and a church dedicated to Saint Matthew would stand in the central square. As an alternative, there could be two churches under the loggias— a concession, perhaps, to the presence of San Giovanni Elemosinario as well as San Giacomo on the Rialto site. Boldly imaginative, Fra Giocondo's proposals had the virtues of a lucid and hierarchical rearrangement of the disorderly sprawl of the old market. Its buildings could be self-contained, and they shared a uniformity consonant with Vitruvius's and Alberti's thoughts on public squares. Moreover, it can be seen as the latest example of an urbanistic trend that found earlier expression in Bramante's reordering of the square in Vigevano or his

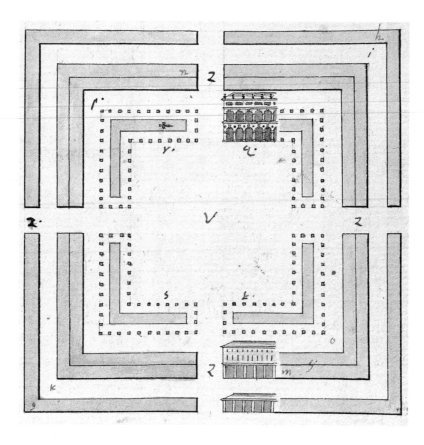

more recent project for the papal tribunal in Rome, which incorporated the church of San Biagio della Pagnotta.[41]

However, Fra Giocondo's plan was doomed to failure through the pressures of time and money, not to mention the consequences such a drastic intervention would entail for the rest of the city. The solution eventually adopted was a more modest one submitted by Antonio Abbondi, called Scarpagnino, who had already proved himself an able technician with the rebuilding of the Fondaco dei Tedeschi, the German warehouse on the opposite side of the Grand Canal, and with recent repair work on the Rialto Bridge.[42] Scarpagnino's project clothed the main buildings around the Campo San Giacomo with uniform facades of ground-floor shopping arcades and two upper floors for government offices. He reduced the area of the market proper almost to the form of a square, giving it a new pavement. The consistency and rationality of his approach may well have been influenced by Fra Giocondo's ideas, but it also followed upon the recent reconstruction of the houses on the north side of Piazza San Marco where the facades were uniform.

154. Fra Giocondo (c. 1433–1515). *Project for the Rialto*, 1792. *Convito Borgiano*, manuscript in the Biblioteca Civica, Treviso.

Financial constraints and the disruptions caused by the War of the League of Cambrai meant that the restoration of the Rialto Bridge limped along until 1537, but Scarpagnino's flexible and utilitarian concept obviously appealed to a majority within the Venetian government, a majority determined to avoid major expense and chaos in such a vital part of the city. The same attitude governed the city's response to the ever parlous state of the bridge.[43] Even its partial collapse in 1528 only resulted in further temporizing and patchwork. This was perhaps inevitable, given the lack of expertise in bridge building and the Venetian system of government by committee. Periodic attempts to revive interest in a new bridge met with limited success. The most notable contribution to the debate came in 1547 when a design was submitted for a single-span wooden bridge.[44] Pietro di Guberni, its author, presented an ingenious scheme that contained a double row of shops separated by a street, with two landings in the middle and at the summit of the bridge. Though the arch was not fully semicircular it was high enough to allow the *Bucintoro* to pass underneath, and the component parts of the bridge were so arranged as to allow a piecemeal replacement as finances allowed. Di Guberni further calculated a lifespan for the bridge of eighty years. Unfortunately, opinions were divided on the feasibility of the design, some feeling the architect had underestimated the width of the canal, others believing the ascent would prove too steep, and still others suggesting that the constituent sections could not be so easily replaced.

Although the proposal was not accepted, it did stimulate a new initiative by the government. Three new overseers were appointed in 1551, charged with taking soundings and commissioning projects for a new bridge as well as further building in the area. Two of the new appointees, Vettor Grimani and Antonio Capello, were proven partisans of contemporary architecture and had been staunch supporters of Jacopo Sansovino's projects for the Piazza San Marco.[45] The one concrete result of their endeavors was a utilitarian new market building, the Fabbriche Nuove, designed by Sansovino and executed between 1555 and 1559, but according to a subsequent account by Palladio's patron Marc'antonio Barbaro, the overseers also solicited models for a new bridge from architects all over Italy, including Vignola, Michelangelo, and Sansovino. By 1554 these models had reached Venice, although the sources are silent about their reception.

Here Palladio enters the story as one of the competitors, and his submission survives in the form of a drawing now in Vicenza (plates 155, 156).[46] As the architect of the Basilica loggias and as the designer of the thirty-five-meter timber bridge over the Cismon River, Palladio was a serious contestant and was also eager to make a name for himself in Venice. In 1554, he competed unsuccessfully for the post of architect to the Salt Magistracy and submitted a model for the new staircase in the Doge's Palace the following year.[47] The proposals that Palladio laid before the Venetian government were radical and uncompromising in their design, but they were also calculated to draw attention to their author as a rising figure in Venetian architecture.

What Palladio did was to return to the project of Fra Giocondo, refining it and combining

it with a new stone bridge according to his aesthetic criteria. The plan shows the bridge as the link between two compact, rectangular forums (plate 156). As orientation, the names of the Fondaco dei Tedeschi, Campo San Bartolomeo, and the church of that same name are indicated on the right-hand side of the sheet, and measurements are given to establish the dimensions of the project as a whole.[48] According to the plan, the bridge would have been approximately forty-six meters long and the forums would have been some fifty-five by thirty-eight meters. The main entrances to the whole complex lie at either end through a tetrastyle atrium or through the passageways punctuating the blocks of shops. Internal stairs indicate the blocks of the forums were intended to have two stories, with the ground-level shops opening outward and presumably with the upper floor reserved for offices or storage. This left the interior of the square as a columnar arcade on three sides and dominated by the entrance to the bridge on the fourth. The effect would have been like Palladio's reconstruction of the Forum of Nerva, where the Temple of Minerva became the focal point (plate 120). In Palladio's project, the bridge could be reached either from the wide ramp entering the forums or by means of narrow stairs leading directly up from the canal banks. Both ramps and stairs converge on a landing at which the bridge proper begins, and a further four steps lead to the main body of the bridge, which is flanked by shops except for the central loggia.

The elevation of the bridge appears on the other side of the sheet (plate 155). Here Palladio

155 and 156. *Early project for the Rialto,* 1554. Museo Civico, Vicenza (Vic. D 25r-v). Pen, ink, and wash, 47.7 x 76 cm.

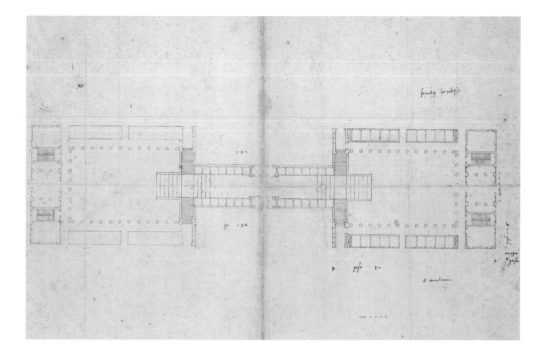

follows the pattern later to be articulated in the *Quattro Libri*: a bridge of five semicircular bays (the lateral ones two-thirds the width of the central ones) is supported by an even number of piers, the central four being decorated with aedicules framed by Ionic columns. The stonework makes a study in rustication, bolder and rougher at the water line, smoother in the spandrels and along the walls of the shops above. The extended use of rustication was not only prompted by decorum, but was also necessary since the walls of the bridge merely enclosed the backs of the shops. There was no existing classical precedent for this feature, and Palladio later defended their presence by an allusion to the Pons Aelius, now known as the Ponte Sant'Angelo in Rome.[49]

The central feature of the elevation is a loggia with six Corinthian columns supporting a triangular pediment. The spacing of the columns and the general impression is reminiscent of the Temple of Clitumnus near Spoleto, which Palladio knew from drawings, and the analogy extends as far as the functions of the loggia, which Palladio's design casts as a temple portico.[50] The drawing, festooned with figures sketched by another hand, pays tribute to Sansovino's Loggetta in Piazza San Marco (plate 157) through its combination of sculpture and architecture. Here, the aedicules contain statues of virtues in classical guise and are surmounted by other figures representing river gods. With more virtues adorning the central pediment, the total effect would have been to convey once again the "myth of Venice," that carefully rehearsed image of itself that the Republic wished to project.[51] The decoration was a gesture on Palladio's part toward the prevailing taste in Venetian public architecture as he understood it.

Palladio's first Rialto project marks one of the rare occasions on which the architect created a large urban complex, and as such it is of great interest. Naturally, it has some affinities with earlier villa complexes like the Villa Pisani at Bagnolo or the Villa Thiene at Quinto (plates 61, 67), but it shares even more features with his studies of classical forums and with his project for the Convent of the Carità (plate 114). As we have seen, the Rialto proposal took as a basic point of reference Fra Giocondo's 1514 project, though refining it in the light of Palladio's own aesthetic concepts. Instead of one self-contained "island" there were two symmetrically placed on either side of the canal, these combining the subdivisions of Fra Giocondo's market with the appearance of an ancient forum linked by a classically inspired bridge. Palladio modeled his ideas on the bridge of Augustus at Rimini but overlaid it with the pattern of the old Rialto Bridge, with its twin rows of shops and central opening, which here is translated into a permanent loggia. The layout envisaged a total of sixty-eight shops distributed between the bridge and the squares, improvements whereby the architect hoped to justify the extensive rebuilding his project would have provoked. This was one of the two points on which the project foundered. By any reckoning, to create two large squares would have entailed enormous upheavals in an area as densely constructed as the Rialto, and Palladio was being excessively optimistic in thinking that the authorities would have allowed it.[52] By the same token, the introduction of five stone arches across the canal would not have permitted the passage of the *Bucintoro* nor any other large ships. Here, and not for the only time, Palladio's tendency to follow the internal logic of a design led to an attempt to correct the existing situation rather than to work with it. The same procedure can be seen in the case of the Convent of the Carità, the rebuilding of the Doge's Palace, and the designs for San Petronio.[53]

The drawing in Vicenza was not Palladio's last word on the subject of the Rialto Bridge. He returned to the argument a few years later with a revised version, published over three pages of the *Quattro Libri*. Though not designated as such, the plates have long been recognized as for the Rialto Bridge.[54] Palladio's reluctance to name the site for this bridge parallels the case of the stone bridge design for Bassano, which Palladio published on the following page of the *Quattro Libri*. In each case the history of the project was suppressed in favor of a more general presentation whereby Palladio preserved his ideas through publication. With the published Rialto design, Palladio dropped the twin forums but enlarged the dimensions of the bridge to accommodate more shops than were planned in the earlier drawing. The basic touchstone again is Augustus's bridge at Rimini, expanded in width to carry a substitute forum. This is clear in the plan where three streets separate the six rows of shops and the columnar screens. Both the entrances and the center of the bridge have been turned into porticos with a giant order of Corinthian columns, statues in niches, and acroteria. On the left side of the elevation, a section through the first street is given, rendering the facades of the shops; on the right side, the external walls of the shops are shown as they would have appeared from the water. Here, the use of an engaged order marks an improvement on the plain rusticated walls, and every aspect of the bridge has been embellished. Even more than his first proposal, this is sovereign architecture reminiscent of Palladio's contemporary project

for the villa of Leonardo Mocenigo on the Brenta or of his work at San Giorgio Maggiore (plates 113, 129).[55]

Palladio gives us no information about the entrance facades to the bridge in the woodcut but some information is conveyed by two drawings in Vicenza. Previously interpreted as triumphal arches, they have recently been connected with the Rialto project by Burns.[56] Both drawings represent intermediate phases between the simpler project of the mid-1550s and the woodcut published in 1570. They are conceived as triumphal arches with a giant Composite order and statuary alluding to a Venetian setting. The frontal and lateral stairs in one of the drawings (plate 158) correspond to the entrance to the bridge as given in the first project and as shown in the *Quattro Libri* plate; in both drawings, the stairs are too many and too steep for a public loggia, but they would have been suitable for bringing pedestrians up to the level of the bridge. The powerful nature of the two facades offers an insight into what

157. *(above)* Jacopo Sansovino (1486–1570). Loggetta in Piazza San Marco, Venice, 1537–42.

158. *(right) Project for entrance to the Rialto Bridge.* Museo Civico, Vicenza (Vic. D 20r). Pen, ink, and wash, 50.7 x 43 cm.

Palladio's public architecture in Venice might have resembled if his ideas had chimed with the majority opinion inside the Venetian government. At the same time the absence of a frontal view of the bridge entrances in the *Quattro Libri* suggests that Palladio was not happy with either drawing, and by the time of publication, the triumphal arch solution had been discarded in favor of a temple facade with a Corinthian order.

Palladio's second project for the Rialto Bridge suffered from the same optimism and inflexibility as the first. As Burns noted, the absence of any measurements in the woodcut draws a veil over its impracticability. Since the distance between the columns of the porticos was only three feet, the passage of goods would have been restricted; then, too, the sinking of two large piers into the water would have had a similar effect on water traffic.[57] When a similar design was proposed by Vincenzo Scamozzi in 1588, it was turned down for similar reasons, and the authorities finally opted for a single-span bridge of a more modest but practical design by Antonio da Ponte, then chief architect of the Salt Magistracy (plate 159).[58] Da Ponte's solution left ample space for water traffic while providing revenue from the two rows of shops on the bridge. In avoiding the pomp and expense of Palladio's projects, he also came closer to the interests of his masters than did Palladio or Fra Giocondo before him.

The tangible results of Palladio's bridge designs are few, although his projects experienced a

159. Antonio da Ponte (c. 1512–1597). Rialto Bridge, 1588.

revival in the eighteenth century when bridge building became an industrial preoccupation. This was especially the case with the timber designs, which were actively studied and dutifully recorded in treatises by Gauthey and others.[59] Their fascination is not surprising given that the *Quattro Libri* still represented the best and most concise treatise on modern architecture. Palladio's wooden bridges offered possibilities of extending the span of timber constructions beyond the twenty to twenty-five feet then possible, and his treatise was the first printed source to describe bridges in theoretical as well as practical terms. Although in the eighteenth century the term "Palladian bridge" was often applied to simple truss structures frequently designed for gardens, they were held in high esteem, as this remark by Sir William Chambers to a client suggests:

160. William Etheridge (d. 1776). Mathematical Bridge, Queens' College, Cambridge, England, originally constructed after Etheridge's design in 1749; rebuilt in 1867 and again in 1902.

"... I have sent you a design of a Bridge which has scarcely any rise at all. It is a thought of Palladio's and provided you have it framed by a skilful carpenter will do very well and look very handsome." A number of voussoir bridges were also created such as William Etheridge's mathematical bridge at Queens' College, Cambridge (plate 160), or that built for the anglophile prince of Anhalt-Dessau at Wörlitz, south of Berlin.[60]

Ironically, it was the stone bridges, those by which the architect set more store, that proved less influential in the long run. Though they were admired they were only occasionally imitated, and then only in the form of miniature versions like that built by Lord Pembroke and Roger Morris at Wilton or subsequent copies at Prior Park and Stowe.[61] No doubt it would have irritated Palladio intensely to learn that his Rialto Bridge had been reduced to the scale of a garden folly, but it was probably the only feasible way for it to be realized in three dimensions. The Rialto Bridge became its own monument and is now best known through

161. Canaletto (1697–1768). *Caprice with Palladian Bridge at the Rialto*, 1743–44. Royal Collection, Windsor Castle. Oil on canvas, 90.8 x 130.2 cm.

Canaletto's *caprices*—a group of overdoor paintings of Venetian monuments by Palladio, including one of the Rialto area in which da Ponte's bridge has been replaced by Palladio's (plate 161). Painted between 1743 and 1744 for the English consul, Joseph Smith, the works probably reflect the patron's interest in Palladio's architecture more than the painter's, but they proved popular enough to stimulate copies by Francesco Guardi and one ordered from Canaletto by no less a connoisseur and critic than Francesco Algarotti.[62] Not only did Algarotti have the artist paint Palladio's bridge in place of da Ponte's but he also had Canaletto include Palazzo Chiericati on one bank and the Basilica, set in a large square, on the other. In a letter to a correspondent, Algarotti explained his motives in words that would have been balm to the architect's heart: "You will know that the Rialto Bridge, for all its reputation, has no other virtue than that of being a great pile of stones, shaped into a big arch about one hundred feet wide, and on top of which it carries two rows of shops of the heaviest and squattest architecture one can possibly imagine. . . . For this reason, in place of the Rialto Bridge . . . we put the bridge designed by Palladio for that same location and which is the most beautiful and decorated building one could wish to see."[63]

DE' CINQVE ORDINI, CHE VSARONO
gli Antichi.   Cap. XII

INQVE sono gli ordini de' quali gli Antichi si seruiro-
no, cioè il Toscano, Dorico, Ionico, Corinthio, e Composito. Questi si deono così nelle fabriche disporre, che'l più
sodo sia nella parte più bassa: perche sarà molto più atto à
sostentare il carico, e la fabrica venirà ad hauere basamen
to più fermo: onde sempre il Dorico si porrà sotto il Ionico: il Ionico sotto il Corinthio; & il Corinthio sotto il Composito. Il Toscano, come rozo, si vsa rare volte sopra terra, fuor che nelle fabriche di vn'or
dine solo, come coperti di Villa: ouero nelle machine grandissime, come
Anfitheatri, e simili: lequali hauédo più ordini questo si ponerà in luogo del
Dorico sotto il Ionico. E se si vorrà tralasciare vno di questi ordini, come sa
rebbe, porre il Corinthio immediate sopra il Dorico; ciò si potrà fare, pur
che sempre il più sodo sia nella parte più bassa per le ragioni già dette. Io por
rò partitamente di ciascuno di questi le misure, non tanto secondo che n'inse
gna Vitruuio, quanto secondo c'ho auuertito ne gli edificij Antichi: ma pri
ma dirò quelle cose, che in vniuersale à tutti si conuengono.

DELLA GONFIEZZA, E DIMINVTIONE DELLE
Colonne, de gli Intercolunnij, e de' Pilastri.   Cap. XIII.

E COLONNE di ciascun'ordine si deono formare in
modo che la parte di sopra sia più sottile di quella di sotto, e nel mezo habbiano alquanto di gonfiezza. Nelle di-
minutioni s'offerua, che quáto le colonne sono più lúghe,
tanto meno diminuiscono, essendo che l'altezza da se fac-
cia l'effetto del diminuire per la distanza: però se la colon
na sarà alta sino à quindeci piedi; si diuiderà la grossezza da basso in sei parti
e meza, e di v. e meza si farà la grossezza di sopra: Se da xv. à xx. si diuiderà la
grossezza di sotto in parti vij. e vj. e mezo sarà la grossezza di sopra: similmen
te di quelle, che saranno da xx. sino à trenta; si diuiderà la grossezza di sotto
in parti viij. e vij. di quelle sarà la grossezza di sopra: e così quelle colóne, che
sarãno più alte; si diminuirãno secódo il detto modo per la rata parte, come
c'insegna Vitruuio al cap. ij. del iij. lib. Ma come debba farsi la gófiezza nel
mezo; non habbiamo da lui altro che vna semplice promessa: e perciò di-
uersi hanno di ciò diuersamente detto. Io sono solito far la sacoma di detta
gonfiezza in questo modo. Partisco il fusto della colonna in tre parti egua-
li, e lascio la terza parte da basso diritta à piombo, à canto l'estremità della
quale pongo in taglio vna riga sottile alquanto, lunga come la colonna, ò
poco più, e muouo quella parte, che auanza dal terzo in suso, e la stor-
co fin che'l capo suo giunga al punto della diminutione di sopra della colonna sotto il collarino; e secondo quella curuatura segno: e così mi vie-
ne la colonna alquanto gonfia nel mezo, e si rastrema molto garbatamen-
te. E benche io non mi habbia potuto imaginare altro modo più breue,
& espedito di questo, e che riesca meglio; mi son nondimeno maggior-
mente cófermato in questa mia inuentione, pòi che tanto è piaciuta à messer
Pietro Cattaneo, hauendogliela io detta, che l'ha posta in vna sua opera di
Architettura, cóla quale ha non poco illustrato questa professione.

     A, B, La terza parte della colonna, che si lascia diritta à piombo.

     B, C, I due terzi che si vanno diminuendo.

     C, Il punto della diminutione sotto il collarino.

     Gli intercolunnij, cioè spatij fra le colonne si possono fare di vn diametro
e mezo di colonna, e si toglie il diametro nella parte più bassa della colonna; di due diametri; di due, & vn quarto; di tre, & ancho maggiori:

VIII
THE
QUATTRO LIBRI

I F NO BUILDING BY PALLADIO HAD SURVIVED, HE WOULD STILL BE NUMBERED AMONG THE MOST influential of architects simply by having published the *Quattro Libri dell'Architettura*. With its appearance in 1570, he created a new kind of architectural treatise, one that neither rewrote Vitruvius nor sought to discuss architecture on a purely theoretical level as other Renaissance books had done. Instead, the *Quattro Libri* offered a systematic account of architecture, literally from the ground up, together with Palladio's own projects for houses, bridges, and reconstructions of the best examples of ancient temples. Although an incomplete work—at least two further books were planned to accompany the first four—Palladio's treatise exhibited his greatest qualities: his innovative approach to domestic architecture and his profound knowledge of antiquity.[1]

Ever since Poggio Bracciolini retrieved Vitruvius's *Ten Books on Architecture* from comparative neglect in 1414, the Latin text became an object of study for Renaissance humanists and architects alike. Vitruvius endeavored to give his profession an intellectual respectability by stressing the rational principles and theoretical aspects of architecture, but his prose was far from clear and left many topics untouched. Nevertheless, the survival of such a text from antiquity meant that Vitruvius acquired a sacral aura for the Renaissance reader and inevitably served as a model for contemporary writers. Thus, when Leon Battista Alberti composed his treatise on architecture, he divided it into ten books and consciously echoed his Roman source in subject matter and precepts, but Alberti also adopted a critical attitude toward Vitruvius and referred to his opaque language as "midway between Latin and Greek."[2] Stressing the importance of checking

162. *Illustration of entasis* from Book I of the *Quattro Libri.*

what Vitruvius said or did not say against the evidence of Roman architecture, Alberti also turned to a wide variety of literary sources, including Plato and Aristotle, in order to weave together a sociology of architecture.

Alberti's aims were largely successful. His *De re aedificatoria,* which was finished by 1452, set the tone for debates on architectural method down to the eighteenth century. Yet Alberti wrote in Latin, thus limiting his potential audience, and did not intend that his magnum opus should be illustrated. The advent of printing meant that Alberti and Vitruvius gradually became more accessible, the two being first published in 1485 and 1486 respectively; indeed by the sixteenth century, Rabelais could rank them equally as architectural theoreticians.[3] A general interest in architecture during the fifteenth century prompted professional architects to put pen to paper. One of the first of these was Antonio Averlino, better known as Filarete, whose elaborately illustrated manuscript was produced in the mid-1400s (plates 165, 166). Dimly aware of Alberti, Filarete seems more indebted to medieval romances than to contemporary architectural discourse, but even within this context he grappled with the broader urbanistic concept of architecture in his description of his imaginary island city of Sforzinda, where all buildings from cathedral to cottage were surveyed.[4]

More important and more directly bearing upon Palladio's writings were the ideas of the Sienese architect Francesco di Giorgio Martini. Completed in Urbino around 1482, his manuscript was also written in the vernacular, although never published, but it had a more practical scope and was more widely read than Filarete's.[5] His writings attempted to come to terms with Vitruvius although he was incapable of disentangling the Roman architect's comments on the orders and on proportion. In any case, Francesco di Giorgio did place considerable emphasis upon Roman buildings and their measurements as a check against Vitruvius's theories. He also devoted space to military architecture, and there he boasted that the modern age was faced with problems like artillery unknown to antiquity.[6] Another feature of his manuscript that had a bearing on Palladio lay in the introduction of his own designs for houses. These ranged from plans and elevations of artisans' houses to those of the nobility and princes. In both these areas, military and domestic architecture, Francesco di Giorgio foreshadowed Palladio's own approach in the *Quattro Libri* in his emphasis upon problems untouched by Vitruvius and on the promotion of his own designs.

Architectural publications increased markedly in the sixteenth century. In 1511, the Veronese friar Fra Giocondo published an improved text of Vitruvius, together with some mediocre woodcuts (plate 164); a decade later, an elaborate Italian translation with more than one hundred illustrations appeared from Cesare Cesariano in Milan. Pietro Lauro's Italian translation of Alberti, the edition read by Palladio, was published in Venice in 1546, and a second version was printed by Cosimo Bartoli in Florence four years later.[7] The publication that had the greatest impact on Palladio, however, was undoubtedly Sebastiano Serlio's multivolume handbook, which appeared at intervals starting in 1537. Serlio had studied under Baldassare

Peruzzi and inherited much of his master's material on classical architecture.[8] In the preface to book four, the first volume to be published, Serlio outlined the content of his seven books. The range of material was encyclopedic, from the correct use of the orders to a presentation of the "classic" buildings of ancient and modern times, a volume on geometry and perspective, and his own designs for temples and houses. But Serlio's books lacked coherent structure and measurements, and were old-fashioned in their reliance on perspectival renderings of buildings and moldings. Although his presentation resembled manuscript treatises more than printed books, his work found a receptive audience indicative of the market for such do-it-yourself manuals.

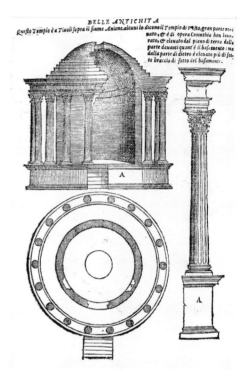

As a young man Palladio copied Serlio's woodcuts and similar drawings of Roman monuments (plates 6, 163) and probably had occasion to meet Serlio through the circle of Alvise Cornaro.[9] Clearly Serlio's popular success indicated the potential for well-illustrated architectural books in the vernacular, and it has been argued that a number of Palladio's early villa and palace drawings were made with publication in mind (plates 28, 29).[10] Evidently the idea emerged from his early trips to Rome in the 1540s and from his acquisition of a corpus of drawings after the antique as well as from his own designs for domestic architecture. Other architects like Serlio, Antonio Labacco, and Philibert de l'Orme all testify in their writings to the difficulty and expense of studying ancient buildings and to the consequent desire to preserve their labor by publishing their works. Palladio echoes this sentiment in the dedication of the first two books of the *Quattro Libri* to his Vicentine patron, Giacomo Angaran.[11]

Palladio had assimilated enough material by 1555 for the popular writer Anton Francesco Doni to remark that he had made many designs of all sorts of build-

163. (*top*) Sebastiano Serlio (1475–1554). *Round Temple at Tivoli,* from Book III of *L'Architettura.*

164. (*right*) Fra Giovanni Giocondo (c. 1433–1515). *Doric entablature* from his edition of *Vitruvius,* Venice, 1511.

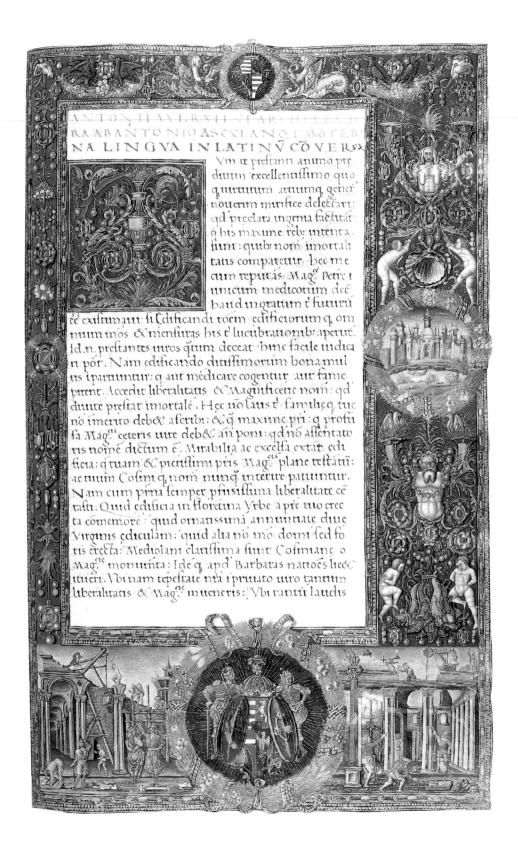

ings for a future publication, adding, "the man came into the world to put architecture to rights. His book has no title, but from its contents it could be described as a guide to good architecture."[12] Palladio's concern with a normative architecture and his intentions to publish his own projects are clearly recognizable from Doni's remarks, and another component in his future treatise was mentioned in print the following year. This came in Daniele Barbaro's famous tribute to Palladio's collaboration in his Italian edition of Vitruvius: "I should have exerted myself to describe in detail many things, measurements and styles not mentioned by Vitruvius, but knowing that a book will soon appear on private houses composed and designed by Palladio and having seen that it lacks nothing, I have not wished to use the work of another as my own."[13] Barbaro went on to add that Palladio's book gives a complete guide to building from the foundations to the roof, a comprehensive survey of the orders, parts of the house, and his own palace designs, as well as some excellent drawings of ancient buildings. Barbaro, too, suggests that the text was at a fairly advanced stage by then, and he draws attention to Palladio's working procedure, which consisted of choosing the best elements from ancient architecture—not necessarily from Vitruvius so much as from the extant buildings themselves (plates 168, 200).

Piecing together the evidence, one can say that the early stages of the *Quattro Libri* probably emphasized the principles of correct building and the architect's projects more than the antique. Palladio would have been encouraged in this approach by two early mentors, Giangiorgio Trissino and Alvise Cornaro. Both embarked upon architectural treatises themselves, with an

165. *(opposite)* Antonio Averlino, called Filarete (c. 1400–1469). Illuminated first page of *Architecturae Libri XXV,* Book I, fol. 5r. Biblioteca Nazionale Marciana, Venice.

166. *(above)* Filarete (c. 1400–1469). *Origins of building* from the *Architecturae Libri XXV,* Book I, fol. 10v. Biblioteca Nazionale Marciana, Venice.

emphasis upon educating a broader public allied with a robust skepticism towards Vitruvius's text.[14] Trissino's is the shorter, merely a few sheets of pithy remarks insisting on security, convenience, and decoration in buildings, and it was obviously abandoned by its author. Cornaro's remarks go much further and are closer to several strands in Palladio's book. He writes plainly and eschews discussions of churches, public buildings, and the planning of cities—all topics dear to the hearts of Vitruvius and Alberti. Cornaro's pragmatism leads him instead to discuss the renovation of older properties and the creation of what we would call middle-class housing since this forms the bulk of buildings in any city. He also avoids dealing with columns—other books explain them, he remarks—and insists that buildings can be beautiful without them. Most of Cornaro's comments are commonsensical and touch on practical aspects of houses like the widths of doors, stairways, number of windows, and vaulting. But though it reached a fair degree of completion, the treatise remained unpublished until this century.

Surveying Palladio's predecessors only makes the achievement of the *Quattro Libri* seem all the more remarkable. Palladio was able to draw upon the various strands of architectural writings in his own milieu and transform them into a fluent and well organized handbook. The twenty or more years of its preparation allowed him to refine his ideas and gradually broaden its scope. The initial bias toward the orders and his own projects was balanced later by Palladio's reconstructions of ancient buildings. As late as 1570, when Palladio petitioned the Venetian Senate for copyright, only three books were envisaged. The change to four books occurred at the eleventh hour, and the earliest copies were issued in two volumes: in one, the first two books on the elements of building along with Palladio's own house projects, and in another, the third and fourth books on public architecture and the antique.[15] Subsequently the four books were bound together in the format that came to be definitive, but it is clear from the text that Palladio saw the four books as only the first in a series, like Serlio's multivolume publication.

The different focuses of the two halves of the treatise are brought out in their dedications: the first two volumes on domestic architecture are inscribed to the architect's close friend and Vicentine patron Giacomo Angaran, while the latter volumes on public and monumental building are dedicated to Emanuele Filiberto, duke of Savoy, whom Palladio met in Vicenza in 1566. In his dedicatory epistle to Angaran, Palladio sets forth his motives for undertaking such a work. He glances at his long years of practice, his intensive study of ancient architecture in Rome and elsewhere, and his hope that by publishing the fruits of his labors "those who will come after me can, by following my example and using their wits, raise their own buildings to the standards of beauty and grace found in ancient ones." In a second preface to the general reader Palladio goes on to explain more of his purpose, allying himself to the tradition of good architecture practiced by Vitruvius, Alberti, and their followers. He particularly singles out Sansovino in Venice and a number of Vicentine contemporaries, among them Trissino, the Thiene brothers, and the Belli family. Palladio briefly outlines the contents of the four books and glances at future volumes on triumphal arches, baths, and amphitheaters.[16] Although he does not remark on it explicitly, his purpose is also illuminated by his decision to write in the vernacular and to avoid long words or technical terms other than those commonly employed by builders, for in this way he could expand his readership to all levels of society, from gentlemen amateurs to practicing architects with no knowledge of Latin.

The exposition of the first book reflects very much the workings of Palladio's mind. Lucidly written and well organized, it moves smoothly from the general to the particular. It avoids the speculative and abstract, instead fastening upon the empirical. The Vitruvian triad of durablity, usefulness, and beauty is amplified by specific advice on building—Palladio has so absorbed the precepts of Vitruvius, Alberti, and a host of Roman authors that he can weave their observations into his own prose. His practical bent can also be seen in his reduction of Alberti's three books on the preparations for building and selection of material into a few succinct pages.

Palladio takes his reader through the process of building from the foundations up. Unlike his predecessors, he does not speculate on why men first built shelters (plate 166), neither does he have time for the anthropomorphic origins of columns, nor, for that matter, does he indulge in the elaborate theories of harmonic proportions of rooms and vaults that are such a conspicuous feature of Alberti's treatise. Indeed, Palladio's approach to this subject is the opposite of Alberti's, the architect paring down the two chapters devoted to this topic in the manuscript draft of the *Quattro Libri* to a single one and reducing the examples only to concrete ones.[17] Wittkower's influential interpretation of harmonic proportions in Palladian buildings has invested the architect's treatment of this subject with an excessive theoretical ballast more worthy of Alberti or Daniele Barbaro, the latter having grappled with the subject in his commentary on Vitruvius.[18] Certainly Palladio's printed remarks are much more practical and closer to Alvise Cornaro's brief treatment of proportion. He subscribed to the ancient topoi that the macrocosm of the world was reflected in the microcosm of man and that the rules of architecture refer to the rules of nature, but there is very little evidence that Palladio treated such concepts as more than metaphors. Indeed he once remarked appositely that "just as the proportions of voices are harmony to the ears, so those of measurement are harmony to the eyes, which according to their habit delights [in them] to a great degree, without it being known why, save by those who study to know the reasons of things."[19] Many of the proportions employed in Palladio's domestic architecture are traditional (e.g., 1:1, 2:3, 3:4), yet others are neither rational nor encompassable within Wittkower's framework. Given the brief treatment of proportion in Book I of the *Quattro Libri*, it is also surprising that the subject is not mentioned in Book II where room dimensions are given but rarely commented upon.

The heart of the first book deals with the orders, and here Palladio's approach can be seen as the culmination of attempts to rationalize the classical use of columns.[20] Palladio begins his account of the orders with his explanation of how to obtain the curvature of a column shaft (plate 162). In keeping with his principles, he does not employ the technical term *entasis* but

simply refers to "the swelling in the middle of the column"—an artificial curvature first applied to columns by the Greeks in order to correct the optical illusion of concavity that a perfectly straight column would give from a distance. Vitruvius never explained how *entasis* was achieved; therefore Palladio gave his own solution. He explains how to divide the height of the shaft into three parts with the lower third of the shaft straight while a flexible rule is placed against it and used to describe the curvature of the upper two-thirds. His verbal explanation is matched by a visual diagram of a Corinthian column; indeed the integration of words and pictures is one of the major ingredients in the success of the *Quattro Libri*.[21]

The five orders as presented by Palladio represented a fairly recent codification. Though Pliny mentioned five orders (the fifth being the Attic) in his *Natural History,* Vitruvius mentioned only four. Closer to Palladio's own day, Alberti did not describe the Tuscan order but introduced the Composite order as the Italic. Filarete and Francesco di Giorgio discussed the orders in terms of the proportions of columns, but Filarete gave all his columns Corinthian capitals while Francesco di Giorgio favored Ionic. Only with the sixteenth century did a correct sense of the proportions and what might be called the identities of the orders come into common use. Raphael defined the five orders as used by later architects in his letter to Leo X, and Serlio first published the total order with all its parts, doorways, and fireplaces en suite. Serlio's arrange-

167. Paolo Veronese (1528–1588). *Daniele Barbaro.* Rijksmuseum, Amsterdam. Oil on canvas, 121 x 105.5 cm.

ment of the orders in terms of increasing height became canonical in all subsequent publications (plate 169). However, he showed little of the critical stance toward Vitruvius that informed Palladio's handling of the same theme. Palladio, on the other hand, goes so far as to say that his "orders are given after the ancient buildings rather than Vitruvius."[22]

A stronger influence still on Palladio's presentation of the orders was a short text published by the Bolognese architect Giacomo Vignola in 1562 (plate 170).[23] Vignola's *Regola degli cinque ordini* was a deluxe engraved book aimed at a more limited scholarly audience. It presented the orders more clearly than did Serlio, giving illustrations of freestanding and engaged columns, and explained their proportions in terms of the diameter of the shaft as Vitruvius had done. Vignola's book appeared just as Palladio was writing his own and probably spurred him to revise his thoughts on the orders. In any event Palladio deals with the orders in a very similar way, although he adds his own refinements to the hierarchy of the five.

For the proportional system adopted by Serlio, Vignola, and Palladio, Vitruvius offered few clear ideas. He did prescribe proportions of 1:7 (diameter to height) for the Tuscan and Doric orders and 1:9 for the Ionic, but he did not consider the Corinthian or Composite orders. Characteristically, Palladio and his immediate predecessors were guided by their own aesthetic bias when they came to this topic. Serlio gave proportions of 6, 7, 8, 9, and 10 for the heights of the Tuscan, Doric, Ionic, Corinthian, and Composite orders while Vignola advised 7, 8, 9, 10, and

168. Palladio. Frons scenae *of an ancient theater* in Daniele Barbaro's edition of *Vitruvius* of 1556.

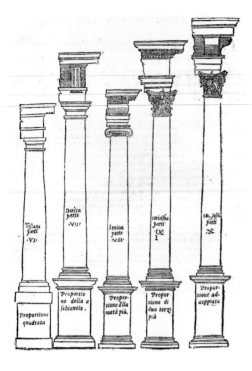

10 for the same sequence. Palladio adopted a different course. He followed Vitruvius's rule for the Tuscan and Ionic orders (i.e., 1:7 and 1:9, respectively), but he adjusted the Doric order to 1:7.5 and graded the Corinthian and Composite orders as 1:9.5 and 1:10, respectively. Not only did he present the orders as a neater package than was the case in classical architecture, Palladio also followed a general trend in sixteenth-century architectural thought by placing the Composite at the apex of the five orders, even though the evidence of antiquity was again equivocal. When Vincenzo Scamozzi came to publish his treatise on architecture in 1615, he reversed the positions of the Corinthian and Composite columns—and with convincing arguments.[24]

Like Alberti and Barbaro before him, Palladio demonstrated a Renaissance bias by expecting Roman architecture to be more systematic than it actually was. Nowhere is this more apparent than in his linkage of the orders with Vitruvius's observations about intercolumniation. Vitruvius expressed the variety of distance between columns in temple porticos in terms of column diameters, seeing some like the araeostyle as too wide, others like the pycnostyle as too close, and the eustyle as just right. Vitruvius saw intercolumniation as a separate issue from the height of columns, but his use of column diameters in this context led to an assumed link on the part of his Renaissance readers. The connection between types of columns and columnar spacing had been introduced into Renaissance treatises with Cesare Cesariano's Italian edition of Vitruvius of 1521. Palladio, however, was aware of the distinction between the two issues and

169. *(top)* Sebastiano Serlio (1475–1554). *The Five Orders* from Book IV of *Le Regole generali dell'architettura,* 1540.

170. *(left)* Giacomo Barozzi da Vignola (1507–1573). *The five orders* from the *Regola degli cinque ordini,* 1562.

prefaced his own account of the proper distances between types of orders as only examples of what Vitruvius had in mind. Thus the Tuscan order, which was *"bassa, larga et umile"* (low, wide, and humble) and carried a wooden entablature, was matched with the araeostyle intercolumniation of 4 diameters; the Doric was aligned with the diastyle of 2.75 diameters, as against 3 diameters in Vitruvius, in order to avoid cracking the architrave; the Ionic order, which held central place in the sequence, was matched with the eustyle of 2.25 diameters; the Corinthian went with the sistyle of 2 diameters; and the Composite keyed to the pycnostyle of 1.5 diameters.[25] Palladio pieced together this system from his study of temple porticos as well as from a creative reading of Vitruvius's text, and his plates of the five orders manage to present a progressive view of them, from the lowly Tuscan to the Composite. As the orders grow taller and slenderer, so too the intercolumniation grows smaller.

Palladio's plates furnish a handsome series of detailed and complete views of each order, a feature reflecting the author's own conclusion about the best forms he employed in his architectural practice. The plates, which are of a much higher quality than Serlio's woodcuts, are clearly labeled and were intended to serve as templates for aspiring builders. The orders are standardized in Book I, while learned topics such as the composite base or the Vitruvian Ionic base—the latter being a feature of Serlio's and Vignola's accounts of the orders—are here downplayed. The eccentric or unusual classical variations in capitals and bases are reserved for Book IV.

Book II represents something of a novelty among contemporary published treatises, for here Palladio's own buildings take center stage. Of course earlier architects like Francesco di Giorgio and Serlio had made designs for all types of houses, but their projects, which were essentially abstract and not based upon specific commissions, were not published before the first edition of the *Quattro Libri*. Only the Frenchman Jacques Androuet du Cerceau's *Livre d'architecture* of 1559 offered a precedent, but its dry text and distinctly French designs would have said little to an Italian public.[26] Palladio's second book lies at the very heart of his approach to architecture: if one can use the word "system" to describe his work, that system is implicit in his presentation of his own projects.

Palladio begins by reelaborating Vitruvian and Albertian notions of decorum or the appropriateness of a house to its owner's status. A correspondence should also exist between the scale of a building and its internal divisions, he adds, because a large house with only small rooms or a small house with only a few large spaces provokes irritation. Palladio often appeals to nature for the rationale behind his approach to building: walls and columns should taper as they rise, he remarks, just as trees do, and the divisions of a house should resemble the human body in that the most beautiful members should be visible while the more functional parts should not be on display.[27] Thus, he prefers to place the functional parts of the household—kitchens, ovens, storerooms, servants' hall—in the basement while the main floors are rendered free for habitation and the patron's use. The main living area should be further divided into small, medium, and large rooms with the smaller reflecting the more intimate functions and the larger the more

public ones. Above all, these suites of rooms should be symmetrical so that one part of the building accords with the other, resulting in a graceful and beautiful whole. Anyone possessing a superficial acquaintance with Palladio's work would recognize these points as commonplaces of his architecture, and the subsequent plans and elevations illustrate them.

"I shall be considered fortunate," Palladio states early on in the second book, "in having found gentlemen of such noble and generous spirit and of such excellent judgement that they have believed my arguments and abandoned that old style of building that had no grace or beauty." Book II is as much a testimonial to Palladio's patrons as it is a celebration of his genius, and it is the Vicentine nobility who inevitably loom large in the works illustrated. These are the people who made his career possible, and this part of the *Quattro Libri* can be read as a paean to his adopted city. Interspersed between town and country projects are Palladio's reconstructions of ancient domestic architecture, which expand upon passages in Vitruvius but present them in recognizably contemporary form (plate 171). Discussion of columnar atria allows

171. *Corinthian Hall* from Book II of the *Quattro Libri.*

Palladio to introduce his project for the Convent of the Carità (plate 114), which he obviously conceived as a re-creation of a Roman house.[28] Similarly, a Roman villa is presented in chapter sixteen as a foil to the ambitious projects for the Villa Thiene at Quinto and the Villa Sarego at Santa Sofia.[29] Thus the implicit dialogue between ancient and modern architecture is rendered explicit through the juxtaposition of Palladio's projects and reconstructions. In addition, the book betrays signs of last minute changes in policy, such as when Palladio adds a number of unexecuted projects at the end of the book, going against his original intention to deal only with buildings actually constructed.[30] Here, too, the purpose was probably twofold: on the one hand it drew attention to Palladio's latest ideas on domestic architecture while on the other it underscored his close ties with the ruling circles in Vicenza and Venice.

Palladio does not begin his review of his own projects with a Vicentine palace as one might expect, but rather with one of his less well known projects, the palace of Floriano Antonini in Udine (plate 173).[31] This surprising choice can probably be explained because the palace gives the best introduction to Palladio's system by virtue of its compact design. Conceived in the mid-1550s, the house developed from the earlier studies for Palazzo Porto and was also related to the villa-palaces of Francesco Pisani at Montagnana and Giorgio Cornaro at Piombino Dese. The project for Floriano Antonini illustrates Palladio's cubic block with a four-columned atrium, ample stairs leading to the second *piano nobile,* and a garden portico defining the building's spine. Typical suites with three rooms of graded sizes form the flanks while *camerini* for storage or service and toilets occupy the interstices. The same plan is replicated on the upper floor, although space above is given over to grain storage as often occurred in town and country dwellings. The kitchen and services have been placed exceptionally in a wing to the left of the main block, a result perhaps of a suburban site that encouraged horizontal as opposed to vertical expansion. The single lateral wing of Palazzo Antonini was never actually built so its presence in the *Quattro Libri* puzzled later commentators; indeed, the eighteenth-century architect Francesco Muttoni believed it to be an interpolation by the engraver.[32] This was not,

however, an uncommon feature in Palladio's designs and finds a parallel in the twin projects for Montagnana and Piombino Dese as well as in the early studies for the Villa Pisani at Bagnolo.

After showing the "essential" Palladian palace in this first woodcut, the author proceeded to take his reader through a series of variations in the subsequent pages—not, as

172. *Sala degli imperatori* from Villa Poiana, Poiana Maggiore.

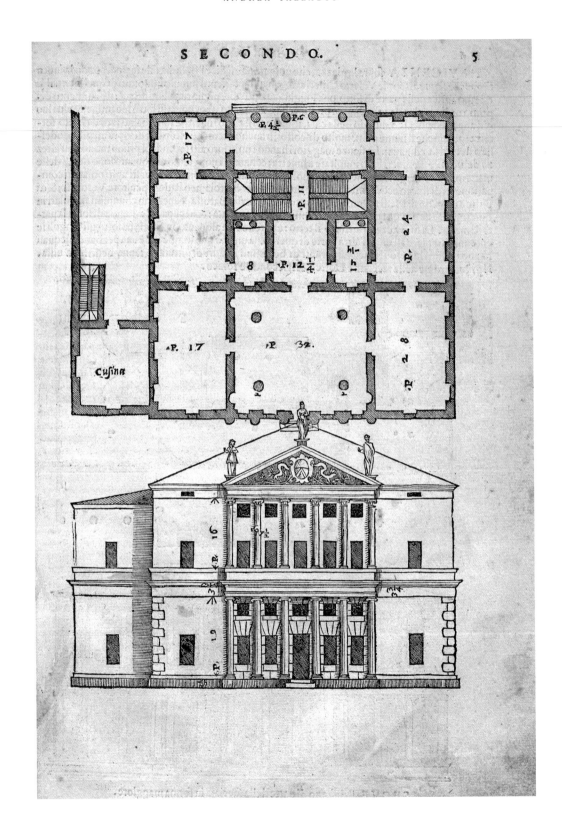

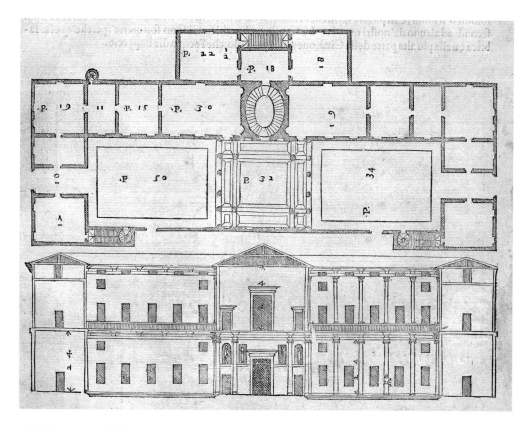

with Francesco di Giorgio, in purely abstract variations on a given theme but rather in response to unusual sites, such as Palazzo Chiericati, which is only one room deep at its center (plate 42), or the unusual lateral expansion of typical Palladian elements around two courtyards in the narrow and awkward site of Palazzo della Torre in Verona (plate 174).[33] The sequence of presentation is also noteworthy in that it sheds light on Palladio's architectural theory. For one thing, it shows that even as late as 1570, Palladio's thinking on the separate natures of palaces and villas was fairly fluid. The Villa Rotonda (plate 175) is placed among the palaces by virtue of its suburban site and lack of an agricultural component, and the juxtaposition of the Villa Pisani at Montagnana and the Villa Cornaro at Piombino Dese was also deliberate. In this last instance, Palladio seems to invite the reader to compare two variations on the type established by Palazzo Antonini in which the basic units are adroitly shifted and two possibilities for lateral expansion are demonstrated. With the Villa Pisani, the addition of wings is expressed in terms that could only be described as utopian, but with the Villa Cornaro, the wings were added some forty years after publication of the *Quattro Libri*.[34]

173. *(opposite) Palazzo Antonini in Udine* from Book II of the *Quattro Libri*.

174. *(above) Palazzo della Torre in Verona* from Book II of the *Quattro Libri*.

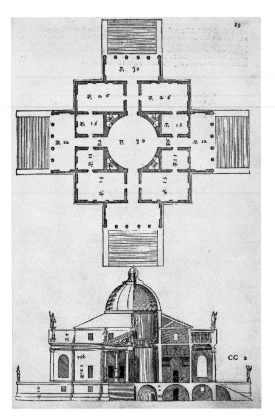

175. *Villa Rotonda* from Book II of the *Quattro Libri.*

Mention of the woodcuts for Book II often raises questions of reliability similar to the one prompted by the unbuilt wing of Palazzo Antonini. The problem was first addressed in the late eighteenth century by Bertotti Scamozzi, who measured Palladio's buildings and reported the notable differences between the *Quattro Libri* plates and the extant works.[35] More recently, the polemic surrounding the illustrations has become polarized between those who reject the woodcuts as totally unreliable and others who see them as the key to the architect's real intentions, however brutally compromised in execution.

Admittedly, there are numerous problems with the woodcuts, some slight, others more serious, and for every accurate rendering of a project there are four or five that materially diverge. These discrepancies became more obvious in the eighteenth century when tourists began to inspect Palladio's buildings. With the plates of the Porto, Thiene, and Valmarana palaces, we are shown projects vastly inflated beyond the actual buildings; the same can be said of the Villas Thiene at Quinto, Sarego at Santa Sofia, and Trissino at Meledo, to mention only the most conspicuous. The Villa Godi receives a pediment and its plan is expanded far beyond the limits of the land available while the Villa Pisani at Bagnolo is given a Doric portico that jars with the rear facade as built (plates 48, 61). While these and other deficiencies can be laid against the woodcuts, outright dismissal of them would deprive us of an essential ingredient in understanding Palladio's thought processes, however unreliable they might be in detail. They are, above all, modal works, presenting us with a snapshot of Palladio's architectural ideas in the years just prior to the publication of his treatise. From a book like the *Quattro Libri* it would be a mistake to expect today's standards of veracity. Although the second book celebrates Vicenza and the discernment of the architect's patrons, it was also addressed to a public hardly likely to have firsthand knowledge of the buildings illustrated. Moreover, the active period of work on this part of the book fell during the 1560s, some twenty years after the earliest projects were begun, at a time when Palladio probably felt justified in bringing works like the Villa Godi and Villa Pisani up-to-date by improvements in keeping with his later architectural style. That such a process was habitual can be seen from Palladio's woodcuts for the exterior and courtyard facades of Palazzo Thiene (plates 176, 177). The drawings date from the 1560s and

do not, therefore, document the initial phase of building.[36] Comparison with the two facades is instructive, for Palladio toned down the elements reminiscent of Giulio Romano by regularizing the rustication and adding an extra fascia between the ground and first floor as he did with the Basilica project about the same time.[37] Similarly, the project for Palazzo Iseppo da Porto illus-trated in Book II is neither the one begun in the late 1540s nor that contemplated by the architect in a manuscript draft of the early 1560s. As Berger observed, Palladio's first manuscript draft of the entry on the palace simply refers to a garden wing planned for kitchens and lodgings for female servants, which corresponds to the kind of structure mooted in early drawings (plate 35).[38] This entry was subsequently crossed out in favor of something closer to the printed text describing the later project with two palaces of similar scale linked by a courtyard with a giant order of columns (plate 190). As with the Palazzo Thiene, the germ of the *Quattro Libri* plate can be found in earlier designs where dotted lines indi-

176. *(above)* Courtyard of the Palazzo Thiene, Vicenza.

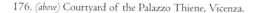

177. *(right) Courtyard of the Palazzo Thiene, Vicenza,* from Book II of the *Quattro Libri.*

cate possible expansions on the rear of the Porto site, but the expansion of the project and the introduction of the giant order follows a trend first manifest in Palladio's architecture during the 1560s, when he began to grapple with the problem of scale and monumentality posed by the Carità and San Giorgio Maggiore.

Palladio's interest in an audience beyond the Veneto also led to the alteration of projects so that the accidental conditions of the site or the actual state of construction could be ignored in order to concentrate on essential qualities of design. Two such examples can be found in the palaces Valmarana and Barbaran da Porto (plate 178). In both cases, the oblique lines of the sites have been concealed in favor of a regularized plan. With the plate of Palazzo Barbaran, Palladio also offers a small view of the original design for the facade with a giant order reminiscent of Palazzo Valmarana. This was dropped in favor of a two-order solution (plate 196), but both are presented here as alternatives. The incongruities in the *Quattro Libri* plates can best be explained by the architect planning his works with one eye on reality and the other on the ideal that found expression in his treatise.[39] Palladio's villas and palaces were also conceived so that they could be executed piecemeal, and many of them never progressed beyond the initial stage (plate 32).

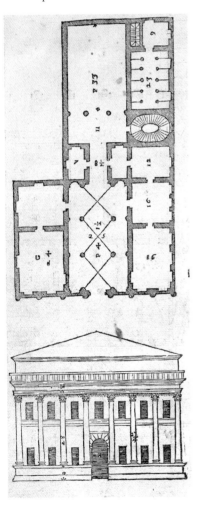

178. *Palazzo Barbaran da Porto, Vicenza,* from Book II of the *Quattro Libri.*

Palladio's intention had been to print three books prior to 1570, although the present third book was hastily cobbled together at the last moment.[40] Many of its elements, such as the Greek and Latin forums, the Basilica in Vicenza and the palestra, or wrestling ground, were originally intended for the second book, but Palladio's growing interest in bridges changed that. From 1567 he had been occupied with the major undertaking of the bridge at Bassano del Grappa, and the designs produced for this and for his other projects led to a recasting of the material now composing book three. The dedication of Books III and IV to Emanuele Filiberto, duke of Savoy, also indicated a shift of emphasis to public buildings and the antique. (Originally these books were published as a separate volume, and they do cohere successfully.)[41] Book III treats urbanistic themes and relies heavily upon Alberti's fourth book for the way in which roads, bridges, and squares are treated. Elaboration of the older writer's arguments is avoided, but Palladio typically displays a keenness for archaeology through his detailed consideration of Roman roads, especially the Via Ostiensis, which connected Rome and Ostia. This is given half a page's description plus a detailed drawing, as against one sentence in Alberti, and Palladio adds further references to other Roman roads that show his profound knowledge of the subject.

Palladio treats bridges by employing the same definition of them given by Alberti, that is, a road over the water. He also adds that they should be constructed with the same attention to usefulness, durability, and beauty that inform other building projects.[42] Here, too, Alberti's one chapter on this subject is expanded by Palladio, in this case to twelve chapters constituting the most comprehensive treatment of the subject before the eighteenth century. Palladio follows Alberti's distinction between wooden and stone bridges but his section on the former is much more detailed because of his numerous commissions in this field. The stark division between his utilitarian approach to wooden bridges and his slavishly classical stone bridges comes across very clearly through the illustrations (plates 149, 151). The stone versions tend to be patterned upon Augustus's bridge at Rimini, and it is notable that the celebrated project for the Rialto demonstrates the same tendency toward the monumental found in the reworking of some of Palladio's palace and villa complexes.

Vitruvius and Alberti are the touchstones for the description of classical forums and their buildings, and this topic appears as a logical extension of the discussion of roads and bridges.[43] Unlike some architectural theoreticians Palladio does not attempt to recreate an ancient city, and his comments on urbanism are more generic than specific, subscribing to Renaissance conventions on symmetry, proportion, and the types of buildings and arches that adorn squares. Only basilicas and palestra are explored in detail, for theaters and baths were to be left for future volumes. Palladio's collaboration on Barbaro's edition of Vitruvius lay behind his reconstruction of the Roman law court or basilica, but his treatment of the subject is much more concise and only refers in passing to Vitruvius's basilica at Fano, which Palladio reconstructed for Barbaro (plate 200).[44] Mention of Roman basilicas allows Palladio to introduce the contemporary equivalent in the shape of the Palazzo della Ragione in Vicenza, which Palladio called the Basilica (plate 179). This continues the ancient-modern comparisons employed in Book II and in the preceding account of bridges, but Palladio's presentation of the Vicentine Basilica cost him a great deal of effort, as the lengthy, corrected drafts testify.[45] Palladio places his work in the context of the Veneto tradition of public palaces, invoking the similar structures in Padua and Brescia. Palladio produced two plates that give the plan and elevation of the Basilica as well as the corner solution, yet no mention is made of the awkwardness of the original structure or the irregular site, both of which are among the chief reasons for its fascination today. Again, this reticence can best be explained by Palladio's avoidance of accidental difficulties in favor of presenting an ideal version of his creation. Following his discussion of the Basilica, Palladio devotes the final pages to the palestra. This discussion stems from Palladio's early interest in Roman warfare and his study of Caesar with Trissino, and culminated in a later publication of Caesar's *Commentaries* in a translation by his sons.[46]

The fourth and last of the *Quattro Libri* is less well known than Books I and II, but Palladio's fame in previous centuries rested as much upon the reconstructions of ancient temples found

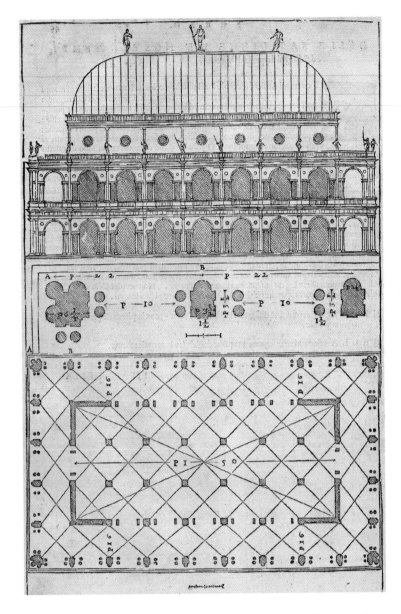

here as upon his palace and villa designs. Temples form the principal theme of the last book, a topic regarded by the architect as a bridge to further books on the antique and on his own architecture. Palladio chose to concentrate on temples because they represented an achievement that could be matched in contemporary ecclesiastical architecture and because some, like the Pantheon, remained among his first loves in classical buildings. In addition, the nature of his reconstructions gave expression to Palladio's imaginative powers, demonstrating a knowledge of antiquity far beyond all but his most learned contemporaries.

179. *Plan and elevation of the Basilica* from Book III of the *Quattro Libri*.

Palladio prefaces his reconstructions with a lengthy introduction again taking up the theme of the overlap between ancient and modern architecture. The ambiguity with which he shifts from classical to contemporary "temples" was inherited from Alberti, whose seventh book on the ornamentation of temples was fundamental to Palladio's general approach just as his influence had been felt by virtually all previous writers on the subject.[47] Like his famous predecessor, Palladio believed churches to be the most important building in a city, and thus his discussion of temples follows logically from the consideration of public buildings and squares in the third book. Sites and forms of temples are discussed, with Palladio expressing a preference for circular plans as being the most beautiful, uniform, capacious, and perfect, demonstrative of the unity and infinite being of the creator.[48] Much less attention is given to the cruciform plan, though he does mention it as the plan of his own church of San Giorgio Maggiore. The Albertian doctrine of decorum or appropriateness of a type of temple and its architectural order to a given deity is also discussed. This concept went beyond Vitruvius's simpler equation of the types of orders with different gods but the idea in general had become a commonplace by the sixteenth century.[49] Thus Doric temples were considered appropriate to Mars or Saint Peter, Ionic for Juno or a matronly saint, Corinthian for Venus and the Muses or for Christ and the Virgin Mary. Palladio also furnishes a detailed account of the divisions of temples and their relationship to each other, much of which stemmed from his measurements of antique buildings.

Palladio offered his reconstructions of Roman temples to the public not only to place his archaeological work on record but also to illustrate how modern churches could be designed in a manner that would evoke comparable awe and inspiration. In fact he grew indignant when he reflected how far superior pagan temples were to churches of the Christian faith, probably an indication of his dissatisfaction with much contemporary church building and with its medieval heritage.[50] Often his reading of Roman ruins was based as much upon an attentive study of Vitruvius's remarks about temples as upon the scant evidence standing or remaining unburied by debris. What distinguished Palladio's woodcuts was the empathy he had for Roman architecture and his painstaking recording of ornamentation as well as his thoughtful conjecture upon the functions of the buildings he recorded. This was quite unlike Serlio, who cheerfully reproduced vague ground plans or fragments of structures without troubling much over their original function. Palladio was also much more visually aware than the purely archaeologically minded writers such as Stephanus Pighius or Fulvio Orsini.[51]

The construction of the fourth book broadly follows a pattern of first illustrating buildings in Rome or on its borders, then within Italy, and finally a few beyond. The criteria for inclusion were that the structures should be temples and that they illustrate as many of the orders as possible. All of the drawings were revised during the 1560s when their measurements were made uniform and the elevations of works like the Forum of Nerva (plate 120) and the Temple of Clitumnus were changed from perspective to orthogonal.

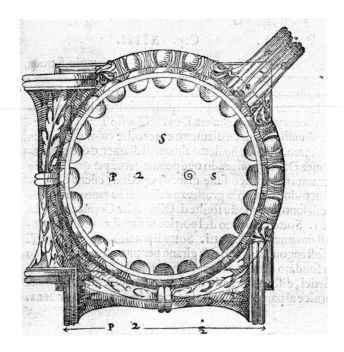

One of the most remarkable elements of the fourth book is what it tells us of Palladio's grasp of Roman architecture. Surprisingly, he displays only a vague awareness of the development of classical buildings, and his reconstructions, whether of Republican or Imperial structures, are in much the same style, governed by those elements he admired in his favorite buildings and that he employed in his own works. He was, of course, conscious of Roman architectural history, but he employed his knowledge selectively. For example, Palladio identified one ruin as the Temple of the Sun and believed it to be an Imperial building because it was not mentioned by Vitruvius. He acknowledged that the Lateran Baptistry and Santa Costanza (which he referred to as the Temple of Bacchus) were postclassical although reflecting a late classical style, yet his illustrations of the Greek house and forum did not differ in essentials from their Roman counterparts.[52] The antique was for Palladio a touchstone or a set of rules, and as he wrote in his first book, "The ancients also varied, but they never departed from those universal and necessary rules of art."[53] He recognized and even illustrated some aspects of this variety, but it was a variety within safely defined limitations, such as the capital with winged horses from the Temple of Mars Ultor, something Palladio never imitated in his own work, or the canted corner Ionic capital of the Temple of Fortuna Virilis, which he did (plate 180).

Some of the works included by Palladio were predictable, like the Pantheon, the Temple of Antoninus and Faustina, or the Basilica of Maxentius, the latter of which he and his contemporaries knew as the Temple of Peace. The interest of Bramante in this last structure guaranteed a

180. *Ionic capital with canted volute at the Temple of Fortuna Virilis* from Book IV of the *Quattro Libri.*

careful study by later generations of architects. Palladio's reconstruction followed the prevailing theory that the basilica had two apses and one entrance rather than two entrances and one apse as was, in fact, the case.[54] Palladio's reconstruction for the *Quattro Libri* was guided by Vitruvius's discussion of Roman temples and by Renaissance expectations of symmetry in temples. His elevation of the basilica essentially corresponds to Serlio's although the proportions of the bays are more ample, on a ratio of 1:2 rather than 1:3.

The conflict between Palladio's love of system and his eye for an unusual motif recurs throughout Book IV, most glaringly apparent in his presentation of the Temple of Minerva at Assisi (plates 181, 182).[55] The building was a late Republican temple with a conventional Corinthian portico but with the distinctive feature of pedestals supporting each column. In a famous passage of his treatise, Vitruvius declared that all parts of a temple must be in propor-

181. Architect unknown. Portico of the Temple of Minerva at Assisi.

tion much as the limbs of a man correspond to one another. Palladio endorsed this concept, paraphrasing it in his general remarks on temples in Book IV, but the stumpy pedestals of the Temple of Minerva, so out of keeping with the scale of the columns, presented him with a dilemma. His solution was to recast the whole facade, making the pedestals as tall as the distance between the middle columns and altering the dimensions of the columns and pediment as well. Less drastic but equally flexible was his reconstruction of the Forum of Nerva in Rome.[56] The forum and temple (plate 120) were only partially intact, and Palladio could not have made a full reconstruction of the site without excavations. Although inevitably his exploration of them was limited, his earlier drawing of the precinct assumed an area of ten bays by five. In the preparatory drawing for the *Quattro Libri* plate, however, the proportions were altered to fifteen bays by five, thus creating a more ideal relationship between the length and width of the forum.

182. *Temple of Minerva at Assisi.* (RIBA XV/9v.) Pen, ink, and wash over incised lines, 42.7 x 29.1 cm.

The same cosmetic attention was given to the facade of the Temple of Minerva within the forum, which shows a ratio of 1:1 for its width and height.

Not even a revered work like Bramante's Tempietto was spared this treatment.[57] Already Serlio had reserved a place for Bramante's works among the classical temples of his third book, and Palladio too affirmed his own allegiance to Bramante's school in his remarks on the round temple. For him, Bramante was "the first to bring back to light the good and beautiful architecture that from antiquity to that time had been hidden," and the Tempietto furnished him with an example of a Doric temple, the only one to appear in Book IV. Palladio's plan and elevation are more accurate than Serlio's, but he still manipulates the heights of the ground and upper stories so that the ground floor has a ratio of 4:5 to the diameter of the portico while the upper floor has the same ratio to the diameter of the temple cella. The end product is svelter than Bra-

183. *Details of Pantheon* from Book IV of the *Quattro Libri.*

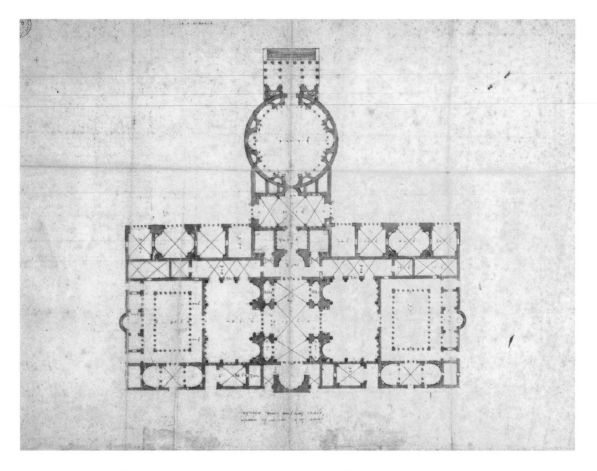

mante's building, but Palladio was not acting eccentrically by making this change. Raphael, too, had both praised and criticized Bramante's work, and he too altered the design of the Tempietto when he introduced a variation on it in the background of the tapestry cartoon, *Saint Paul Preaching in Athens.*[58]

Palladio followed a similarly creative approach in his treatment of the Lateran Baptistry, which he reproduced not as it was but as it might originally have been, with a domical vault, three proportioned stories, and two symmetrical chapels either side of the central octagon.[59] He expressed misgivings about its presence and that of Santa Costanza in Book IV, but he clearly admired their richness of decoration and the fact that both "temples" gave scope for illustrating the Composite order with a convex frieze, a late antique motif he found particularly attractive.

Palladio did not hesitate to correct ancient works or indeed his own for publication in the *Quattro Libri,* especially when they clashed with his architectural expectations. This was a trait that spilled over into his private practice in later years, when he attempted to reorder existing

184. *Finished plan of the Baths of Agrippa.* Museo Civico, Vicenza (Vic. D 33r). Pen and ink over incised lines, 43.5 x 57.5 cm.

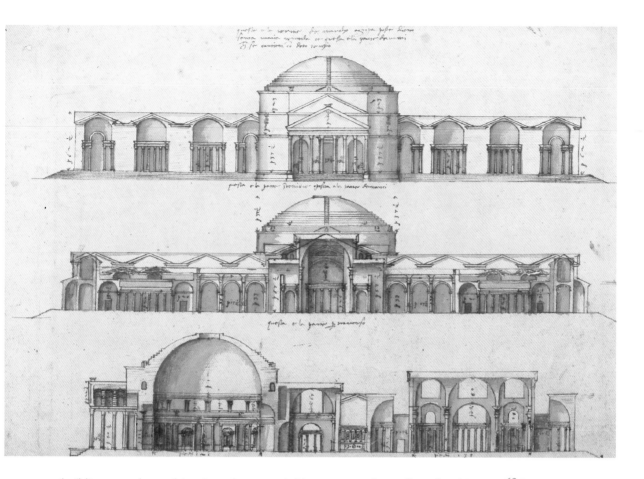

buildings or other architect's projects to suit his preconceptions of good architecture.[60] But on occasion he drew back from this, such as in the woodcut dedicated to the Mausoleum of Romulus on the Via Appia. Only the basement of the tomb survived, as it does now, together with the precinct wall of what was a substantial complex. Palladio's ground plan does not differ very much from Serlio's, but it contains a wealth of detailed measurements not found in Serlio's woodcut. In a preliminary study Palladio extracted from the tomb's substructure a ground plan reminiscent of the Pantheon, a connection that is even more recognizable in the frontal and lateral elevations at the bottom of the sheet. Yet the elaborate elevations were omitted from the published version, in which only hints at the Pantheonic concept are conveyed by the ground plan. Despite his hesitations, the consensus among later archaeologists is that the building was indeed Pantheonic in style, and more modern elevations of the mausoleum followed Palladio's intuition.[61]

The Pantheon is the ancient structure that Palladio felt the least necessity to adapt to his system, not only because it remained relatively intact but also because it embodied an architec-

185. *Elevation of the Baths of Agrippa.* (RIBA VII/3.) Pen, ink, and wash, 28.7 x 42 cm.

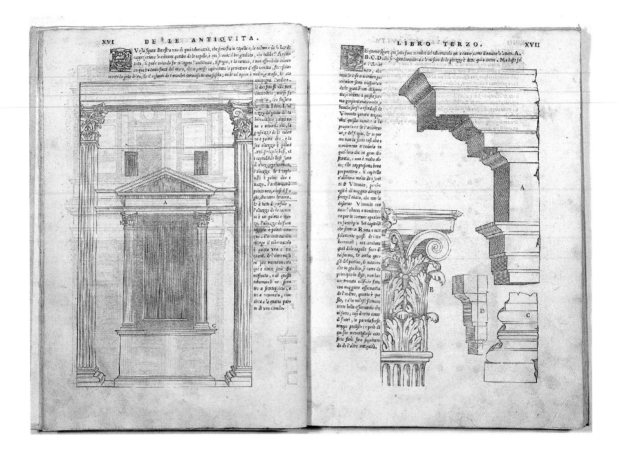

tural ideal that he employed whenever possible. His appreciation of the building is evident from his introductory comments and from the ample space allotted to it: a total of ten woodcuts take the reader through all aspects of the Pantheon's exterior and interior. Palladio's study of the Pantheon was systematic and comparable to the detailed study of the building made by Baldassare Peruzzi in the previous generation. The differences between his approach and that of Peruzzi's pupil Serlio are indicative of the gap between the two treatises (plates 183, 186).[62] Serlio's published treatment of the Pantheon mixed orthogonal with perspectival elements and combined general comments with measurements in a commentary that is fitted in and around the illustrations. The presentation seems calculated to place obstacles in the path of the reader, whereas Palladio's pages are neatly divided between commentary and illustrations, the latter containing measurements and following in a logical sequence from plan to elevation and sections. Details are clearly labeled and either face the sections or are contained within them. The result makes for greater coherence and reflects the logical exposition that distinguishes the *Quattro Libri* from rival publications.

186. Sebastiano Serlio (1475–1554). *Details of the Pantheon* from Book III of *Le Regole generali dell'architettura*, 1540.

Death preempted the expansion of the treatise that Palladio promised in the proem to Book I, where he mentioned further volumes on "theaters, amphitheaters, arches, baths, aqueducts, fortifications, and ports."[63] Numerous drawings, some in a high state of finish (plates 184, 185), testify to his intentions, and Paolo Gualdo, Palladio's earliest biographer, records that the architect was at work on a new edition of the book at the time of his death. Palladio's surviving son and heir, Silla, petitioned the Vicentine Accademia Olimpica for a subvention toward the publication of a new edition in 1581, but nothing came of it.[64] Instead, the original edition was reprinted that year and twice thereafter while foreign editions began to appear, all making the *Quattro Libri* an international best-seller in the seventeenth and eighteenth centuries. While the incomplete nature of the treatise has deprived us of Palladio's thoughts on further aspects of his own buildings and Roman architecture, the achievement of the four books is considerable. The books give us an insight into the architect's mind and demonstrate the clarity of approach that underlay Palladio's projects and his reconstructions after the antique. But above all, the *Quattro Libri* exemplifies in printed form his adherence to the Vitruvian principles of usefulness, durability, and beauty.

IX
PALLADIO'S LATE STYLE

GIORGIO VASARI VISITED VENICE IN 1566 AND THERE HE MET ANDREA PALLADIO, WHO showed him some of his projects and the manuscript of his treatise. Although brief, their encounter was recorded in the second edition of Vasari's *Lives,* where a short sketch of Palladio's career was appended to the biography of Jacopo Sansovino, then considered the unofficial "first architect" of Venice. Vasari listed virtually every major palace and villa by Palladio, referred to his churches and especially to the project for the Convent of the Carità, and rounded off his account enthusiastically by stating, "We can expect greater things from him everyday."[1] Clearly Vasari perceived the forcefulness and creativity in Palladio's architecture, finding in his latest work something akin to the *terribilità* or awesomeness of Michelangelo. Today Palladio is not normally thought to be as inventive an architect as Michelangelo, but this is partly a reflection of the *Quattro Libri*'s influence over our perception of Palladio's achievement: the treatise is heavily weighted toward his earlier architectural style and contains only hints of later developments. The changes and novelty that so impressed Vasari began to appear in the early 1560s and stemmed from the impact of Palladio's religious architecture on his domestic projects. In this final chapter, we shall be examining Palladio's later projects as an index of his development as an architect over his last fifteen years; in particular we shall focus on the way in which his public and private architectural vocabularies began to coalesce.

Palladio returned to palace commissions in the mid-1560s after a hiatus of more than a decade. During this period he had been kept busy by his involvement with numerous villa pro-

187. Palazzo Valmarana, Vicenza.

jects and in the later years by his growing practice in Venice. But Vicenza had not been entirely abandoned by him, and there were forces at work that led to a new spurt of private building in the second half of the sixteenth century. In 1556 Alvise Zorzi, the Venetian *capitano* or deputy rector of the city, estimated that Vicenza's population was close to twenty-eight thousand, if the outlying districts were included, and noted that the city had become so populous that house prices had been driven upwards.[2] Evidently the scarcity of accommodation led to inflation in the housing market, one solution to which involved building homes on a large scale so that various branches or generations of a family could inhabit them at the same time.

Surveying a map of Vicenza, one can appreciate that many of the interventions by Palladio and his patrons throughout the years had the effect of upgrading certain parts of town: the Palazzo Chiericati, the Palazzo Piovene all'Isola, and the Teatro Olimpico were clustered about the eastern end of the *strada maggiore*, today's corso, marking the entrance to Vicenza from Padua, while the Palazzo Porto Breganze, Palazzo Thiene Bonin, and the intended site of the Palazzo Capra were all found in the area of the Piazza Castello at the other end of the corso. In his account of the Palazzo Capra, Palladio remarked that its patron intended to build "more for the ornament of his city than for his own need," sentiments that could have been applied to an even more exacting patron, Montano Barbaran.[3] His palace rose on a deep plot of land just off the corso and opposite the fifteenth-century Palazzo Thiene. Never finished, the palace contributed to the financial embarrassment of Barbaran's family as well as to the imposing image that the Vicentines sought to project of their city. So concerned was the city with its appearance, in fact, that in some cases remodeling the facade of a house was made one of the conditions of obtaining citizenship.[4]

The first signs of Palladio's late style in palace design can be traced to the Palazzo Valmarana, designed in 1565 and begun the following year (plates 187, 188). Palladio refers to the patron in the plural as the *Counts* Valmarana, which probably means that it was a family project. Giovanni Alvise Valmarana is occasionally cited as the instigator of the palace, but there is no mention of it in his will of 1558.[5] His connections with Palladio went back at least to 1543, when Valmarana supervised the decorations for the formal entrance of Cardinal Ridolfi to his episcopal see, Vicenza, an occasion for which Palladio created temporary architecture. He played a more decisive role five years later when he was a member of the three-man committee that recommended Palladio's project for the Basilica arcades. Valmarana evidently took a keen interest in architectural matters, but it was his widow, Isabella Nogarola, who should be credited with pursuing the project for a new palace; she signed the building contract with the foreman, Pietro da Nanto, and what was built seems to have occurred during the next few years.

The novelty of the work is immediately apparent with the facade, where Palladio first introduced the concept of the giant order spanning two stories into his domestic architecture. The facade is conceived in seven bays, the outer ones articulated by a small order of Corinthian pilasters with shield-bearing pages above and the inner bays by Composite pilasters almost twenty-nine Vicentine feet in length. Below this is an imposing pedestal that breaks forward beneath the colossal pilasters, and the whole is crowned by an attic story. The general effect is one of compression, for which each element overlays another in an elaborate layering, an effect heightened by the way in which the entablature of the Corinthian order appears to run behind the dominant pilasters (plate 187). In many details the facade recalls that of San Francesco della Vigna (plate 118), begun shortly before, and like the facade of San Giorgio Maggiore, which was intended to be seen from an angle (plate 128), the Palazzo Valmarana was obviously designed for a raking view from the intersection of the city's principal street and its own.[6]

Palazzo Valmarana is the first instance of that merging of monumental and domestic styles that is so characteristic of Palladio's late palaces. This is not surprising if one bears in mind that the architect was in the middle of a decade of projects that challenged him to think on a larger scale, beginning with the Carità and ending with the plans for San Giorgio. The colossal order enabled Palladio to give a vertical emphasis to palace facades and to make their impact more dramatic. His use of it here had been anticipated by Michelangelo on the exterior of Saint Peter's and in his Capitoline projects as well as by Raphael on the garden facade of the Villa Madama, and the experience of dealing with similar problems of scale in his own ecclesiastical buildings gave Palladio a feel for its potential here.[7]

The intended extension of the Palazzo Valmarana around a courtyard, flanked by loggias on two sides and followed by a walled garden and stables, derives from his reconstruction of Vitruvius's Greek house and invites comparison with the published plan of Palazzo Capra. It can also be seen as a development of early projects for Palazzo Iseppo da Porto (plate 35)[8]— indeed the overlap between Palazzo Valmarana and the *Quattro Libri* project for Palazzo Porto comes across very clearly in the drawings for the woodcut elevations of both palaces (plates 188, 189). Where the actual facade of Palazzo Porto reflects Palladio's early maturity as an architect, the proposal, which shows a courtyard with giant Composite columns and pilasters supporting the balcony, is incompatible with his early drawings for the palace and must date from the mid-1560s, the period when the architect was clearly enamored of the giant order.[9]

The elevation for the courtyard of Palazzo Porto invites comparison with another of Palladio's essays in the monumental, this time his reconstruction of Vitruvius's Basilica at Fano (plate 200). This was one of the few buildings that the Roman architect described in his treatise at some length, and it was an object of great interest for Renaissance architects.[10] The Basilica's central hall was a rectangular space, 120 by 60 feet, with a colonnade separating the central nave from the aisles. Vitruvius gave the columns' proportions as fifty feet long and five feet in diameter; pilasters of one-half these dimensions were attached to each column and supported a gallery. Palladio's reconstruction of the Basilica for Barbaro's edition of Vitruvius shows a giant Corinthian order with a gallery bisecting the column shaft. In plan and elevation, his conception of this antique building contains the genesis of the courtyard of Palazzo Iseppo da Porto and

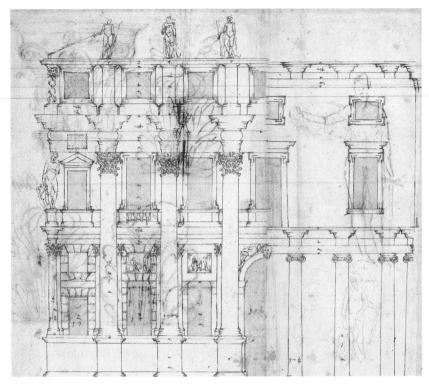

188. *(top) Elevation of the facade and courtyard of the Palazzo Valmarana,* mid-1560s. (RIBA XVII/4r.)
Pen and ink over incised lines, 29 x 31.9 cm.

189. *(above) Elevation of the facade and courtyard of the Palazzo da Porto Festa,* mid-1560s. (RIBA XVII/3r.)
Pen and ink over incised lines, 28.9 x 37.2 cm.

that of the Villa Sarego at Santa Sofia (plates 189, 191). For Palladio, antique architecture was synonymous with grandeur, and his recreations of Greek and Roman houses are largely inspired by the evidence of colossal Roman baths. His formulation of the courtyard and second wing of Palazzo Porto, neither of which were built, were guided by his reading of Vitruvius and by the visual evidence of Roman remains as the commentary in the *Quattro Libri* indicates. The most arresting feature here would have been the colossal Composite columns backed by Corinthian pilasters, which would have risen to a height of thirty-five Vicentine feet and would have been flanked by a grand staircase with views onto the courtyard. Some idea of the effect can be gained by photographs taken of the model of the *Quattro Libri* design made for the Palladio Center in Vicenza (plate 190). In particular, they display an almost Piranesian sense of the overwhelming impact of the Composite capitals.[11]

No progress was made on the courtyard of the Palazzo Porto, but an idea of its potential impact is gained by a contemporary project, the villa of Marc'antonio Sarego at Santa Sofia near Verona (plate 191). Though sometimes judged an early work, the villa is neither mentioned in the manuscript of the *Quattro Libri* nor listed by Vasari, and documentary evidence shows that building activity was underway between 1565 and 1569.[12] Approximately half the project published in the *Quattro Libri* was realized, but it is clear from the orientation of the end capitals of

190. Proposed courtyard of the Palazzo da Porto Festa.

the colonnade that the building was complete as it stands (plate 192).[13] The Sarego family's estate had been famous in the Middle Ages for its fountains, and a palace, farm buildings, and church existed there by the late fourteenth century. Marc'antonio Sarego inherited the property in 1552 but a family quarrel prevented development for some years. During the 1560s several members of the Veronese Sarego and Della Torre families engaged Palladio for villa and palace designs in a burst of competition, and Marc'antonio's villa is the most remarkable of them all. Little more than half the main court was realized, but Palladio achieved here an imaginative essay in the use of rustication. In his account of the villa in the *Quattro Libri,* he notes that villa decoration allowed greater license than town dwellings, glancing back to a similar observation by Alberti.[14] His extensive use of rusticated stone draws upon theories of decorum whereby rough-hewn stone was deemed appropriate for city gates, fortified buildings, and country dwellings. Palladio had, of course, employed this motif before on works like the external facade

of the Villa Pisani at Bagnolo (plate 43); yet here it is the fantastical appearance of the colossal Ionic columns, their shafts composed of uneven blocks of Veronese limestone, that catches the spectator's attention. Unprecedented in the architect's work, they nonetheless conform to the element of fantasy that entered Palladio's work in the 1560s. The motif of these columns may have been prompted by the rusticated columns of the Port of Ostia, which Palladio undoubtedly knew, but there were also strong local

191. *(top)* View of the Villa Sarego, Santa Sofia (Verona).

192. *(left)* Detail of end columns of the colonnade, Villa Sarego.

associations, which may have proved more decisive, because of the extensive use of rustication on the exterior of the amphitheater in Verona.

The Villa Sarego is the only one of Palladio's villas to feature stone to such an extent, and it cannot be coincidental that the quarries from which the stone derived were owned by Marc'antonio Sarego. Here, too, the columns are backed by pilasters that support the gallery, creating a contrast between the roughly worked stone and smooth moldings that obviously delighted the architect. The effect of the courtyard on the Villa Sarego is like Palladio's reconstruction of the Basilica at Fano, and, as with the courtyard of the Palazzo Porto, emulation of the antique was the architect's motivation.

Palazzo Porto Breganze in Vicenza demonstrates a similar rivalry with the antique (plate 193). Not mentioned in the *Quattro Libri*, the palace stands as a two-bay hulk, dominating the Piazza Castello. Its building history is somewhat murky, but Palladio's younger rival Vincenzo Scamozzi stated that he himself finished the palace, although he didn't claim credit for it.[15] Scamozzi gave the owner of the property as Alessandro Porto, who apparently acquired the site and its fifteenth-century family palace after the death of his father in 1570. Porto's sister Isabella was married to Francesco Thiene, who was the patron of the palace on the opposite side of Piazza Castello, also begun by Palladio and finished with a more decisive intervention by Scamozzi. As in other Vicentine cases, family rivalry may have given a competitive edge to the creation of the two palaces.[16] Since the eighteenth century, the Palazzo Porto Breganze has been accepted as Palladio's, and indeed it would be difficult to imagine another architect wielding this style in Vicenza during the 1570s. Like his contemporary Loggia del Capitaniato, the Palazzo Porto Breganze is an exercise in the monumental, conceived to dominate the large open space of its piazza. Over-life-sized pedestals are surmounted by colossal engaged columns of a Composite order, with narrow window bays wedged between. The attic floor above is punctuated by the entablature, which is brought forward above each capital. So much effort went into the vertical thrust of the building, which towers over its surroundings, that it manages to fit into two bays as much space as the average palace would in five.

Palladio's design must have been persuasive to induce the enormous financial outlay demanded here, and perhaps because of the cost only a glorious fragment was achieved. In 1776 Bertotti Scamozzi published a reconstruction of the project with a seven-bay facade and a courtyard of two orders terminating in a hemicycle.[17] The introduction of a curve into the design of the courtyard may seem surprising at first glance, but the abruptly abandoned construction has left enough evidence to confirm almost every particular. In plan, the entrance wing would have consisted of a spacious rectangular atrium with columns to support a vaulted ceiling and presumably a *salone* of comparable proportions on the floor above. To either side of the atrium there would have been two rectangular and two square rooms of standard Palladian type. But the most arresting feature is the hemicyclical courtyard. Hemicycles feature in some of Palladio's villa projects, that of the Villa Sarego being close in time to the Palazzo Porto Bre-

ganze, but this is the only such example among Palladio's palaces. Proof of the accuracy of Bertotti's reconstruction can be found in the extant columns of the courtyard, where the last of these initiates the curve that would have described the hemicycle. It is a bold conception, and one can read into it an influence from Palladio's more grandiose villas on his urban projects during his last decade.

The Loggia del Capitaniato in Vicenza continued Palladio's exploitation of the giant order and indicates how the architect could modify his style according to the site (plates 194, 195). This was a project commissioned by the city council and planned as an addition to the official residence of the *capitanio*, the second Venetian official in command of the city.[18] A loggia had existed on this site since the late fourteenth century, which had been patched up in 1521 and again in 1541. The old building had a ground floor loggia of the kind found in most Italian cities, with a public room above. In 1565 the city council of Vicenza decided to purchase the houses between the old loggia and the contrà dei Giudei, the present-day contrà Cavour, in order to build a new loggia and a permanent chamber for the council. Facing the Basilica on the northern side of the piazza, the old structure must have looked increasingly shabby as the new Basilica arcades took shape across the main square. Any new loggia would inevitably have to equal its predecessor, and thus it was probably a foregone conclusion that Palladio would be called in as architect. He may have been sounded out as early as 1565, but it was only in April 1571 that money was

193. *(top)* Palazzo Porto Breganze, Vicenza.

194. *(left)* Lateral facade of the Loggia del Capitaniato.

195. *(opposite)* Loggia del Capitaniato, Vicenza.

found to rebuild the old loggia. Work followed swiftly, with Palladio recorded as having furnished moldings, probably those of the entablature, in March 1572, just as the ceiling of the chamber on the *piano nobile* was being painted by Gianantonio Fasolo that August.[19] Work continued into 1574, when the three-bay unit must have been essentially complete.

The main facade of the building contains an inscription by the city to the then-*capitanio*, Giovanni Battista Bernardo, who played an active role in embellishing the city. Writing in 1630, Silvestro Castellini, a local historian, praised him for widening the main square, removing wooden stalls near the house of the *podestà*, and restoring the port situated in the *Isola*, the open space in front of Palazzo Chiericati.[20] Castellini further credited Bernardo with being a chief instigator of the Loggia's rebuilding and as having sustained some of the expense himself. In this, however, Bernardo had the active support of the city council, which declared that the new Loggia "will be of such beauty that it will adorn our piazza to the marvel of everyone."[21] Though sometimes seen as a fragment of a larger design, Palladio's Loggia was constructed as a self-contained unit, something more easily appreciated in photographs taken before the demolition of the houses on its left. In these, the building's height does not appear out of proportion with its surroundings and has a proper size for its functions. Attempts to reconstruct it with a facade of five or even seven bays have only served to underscore the implausibility of a loggia on such a scale.[22]

The commission for the Loggia del Capitaniato gave Palladio the opportunity to return to urbanistic themes three decades after his first Basilica designs. It is unlikely that he ever intended to build a simple replica of the double loggia on the Basilica opposite, but rather employed the giant Composite semicolumns here in order to create a counterweight to the broad expanse of the Basilica. The four columns divide the principal facade into three bays with roundheaded arches on the ground floor and floor-length windows above. As with Palazzo Porto Breganze, the entablature breaks forward above the Composite capitals and is surmounted by a small attic story with a balustrade. Each column rests on a high base of the kind favored by Palladio for his church facades and for Palazzo Valmarana. Because the bases are such an important element at eye level, Palladio gives them elaborate récherché moldings copied from the Maison Carrée in Nîmes. The contrast between the stone bases and brick shafts is highly effective, suggesting that it is unlikely that the columns were ever intended to receive stuccoing.[23] The resulting bichromy is similar to that found on the Villa Malcontenta (plate 110). Dynamism is introduced into the facade not only by the colossal order and the varied coloration but through the tension between the windows and their surrounding field, their frames biting into the entablature while their balconies project forward in Michelangelesque brackets. The total impact is of an overpowering, monumental architecture that has more in common with Michelangelo's free use of classical motifs on the exterior of Saint Peter's and at the Palazzo Farnese than with the architectural milieu from which Palladio emerged.

A plethora of stucco borders the arches and windows, including river gods, cartouches, and military regalia, which serve as a link with the even more highly decorated lateral facade (plate

194). During construction Venetian naval forces won a victory against the Turks at Lepanto, in Greece, and though the victory proved less significant in the long term, it immediately became part of Venetian mythology.[24] Vicenza had equipped two warships and gave the substantial sum of twelve thousand ducats toward the military campaign, and the council decided to celebrate the victory by turning the second facade of the Loggia into a memorial, introducing a triumphal arch, allegorical figures, and ancillary decorations executed by Lorenzo Rubini.

The appearance of the lateral facade has been interpreted by some as an intrusion upon Palladio's design, as something forced upon the architect by his patrons.[25] While the change of scale does seem abrupt, the evident delight in stucco decoration remains a constant factor on both facades, and the poor reception of the Loggia as an ensemble may have more to do with changes in taste and a rather narrow range of expectations among Palladio's later critics than anything else. In this context it is worth noting that the great nineteenth-century historian Jacob Burckhardt actually preferred the lateral facade and believed it to be the architect's acknowledgment of the miscalculated use of a giant order on the main front.[26] Burckhardt's response was conditioned by his innate dislike of dramatic architectural gestures of the kind typified by the Loggia's main facade, but he must have been right to see the minor facade as a deliberate adjustment on the architect's part. Indeed, when one surveys the two facades together it is difficult to imagine how Palladio could have employed the same architectural language on both—there is simply not enough space on the second front for a set of giant semicolumns. Moreover, had Palladio wished to have a giant order on both sides of the building, he would have used the order to turn the corner rather than setting the columns back from the edge as he did. Thus a change in scale for the lateral front was probably intended when the major facade was being designed.

The objections leveled against the minor facade of the Loggia del Capitaniato illustrates a critical blind spot concerning the flexibility of Palladio's last works. Chiefly, critics tend to disregard the evidence of other projects like the Teatro Olimpico, the projected reconstruction of the public palace in Brescia, or the Doge's Palace in Venice (plates 201, 202), all of which show the same tendency toward a higher quotient of plastic decoration and a favoring of sequences of small orders rather than colossal ones. Evidently Palladio believed that buildings seen from some distance, like San Giorgio Maggiore, Palazzo Valmarana, or the principal facade of the Loggia, were right for a colossal order, while those seen from nearby required smaller-scale decorative work.

The abrupt change in the facade of Palazzo Barbaran must reflect a similar line of thought. Its facade reads like a résumé of earlier and contemporary Palladian buildings and gives the impression of many motifs jumbled together (plate 196). The ground floor shows layers of rustication and relief panels like Palazzo Valmarana while the upper floor displays an abundance of decoration that appears to have strayed from the Loggia del Capitaniato. Yet these elements have been overlaid with a grid of Ionic and Corinthian semicolumns, recalling early essays in palace design like Palazzo Iseppo da Porto (plate 38).[27] Palazzo Barbaran is unusual

among Palladio's works since its development is recorded on the pages of the *Quattro Libri* (plate 178). The initial facade project is something of a cross between Palazzo Valmarana, still novel in 1570 and also endowed with a giant order of pilasters, and the Loggia del Capitaniato with its crowning balustrade and attic story. In addition to this version of the earlier facade, Palladio reproduced the penultimate ground plan, explaining that the final version was not available because the recent acquisition of more land had caused a recasting of the plan, though too late for inclusion in the publication.[28] He did manage, however, to prepare a detail of the facade's corner elevation as built.

This publication of changes in the project is remarkable, and three preliminary studies for the palace also show the architect developing many elements found in the published plan.[29] The studies oscillate between a columned vestibule and small *cortile* to one with no *cortile* and an expanded vestibule. In the published version, the cross-vaulted hall, inspired by the vestibules of the Theater of Marcellus in Rome, is flanked by two square and rectangular rooms, much as in the unfinished Palazzo Porto Breganze. Beyond this the plan extends, via a narrow passageway

196. Palazzo Barbaran da Porto, Vicenza.

and service rooms, to a vestigial courtyard scarcely large enough for a two-columned loggia; to the right of the courtyard is a staircase reminiscent of that in the Villa Sarego, and stables.

While the *Quattro Libri* plan had the merit of creating an approximately symmetrical entrance block, Montano Barbaran's subsequent purchase of an adjacent lot to the left allowed him to introduce a proper loggia into his courtyard even as it presented more problems for his architect. The additional ground space required shifting the project's center of gravity to the left. This made for a longer facade but an irregularly shaped one, given the necessity of keeping the entrance where it had been. Consequently, Palladio may have then decided to discard the giant order for two reasons: the narrowness of the street may have encouraged a smaller scale and more highly decorated facade, as on the lateral facade of the Capitaniato; at the same time, the one-story units vary in width and minimize the rambling, asymmetrical frontage. Palladio reverted to the same expediency employed in the Basilica loggias two decades before and for much the same purpose. He was faced with an intractable problem here, not only because of the irregular plot but also because he had to use walls of the earlier palace on the site, which accounts for the varying thickness of walls and the unusual shapes of the rooms. Palladio did manage to salvage the splendid concept of the Roman atrium divided into three bays by two Serlian arches and supporting the cross-vaulting above (plate 197). Bertotti Scamozzi recorded that the proportions of the columns of the atrium were midway between those recommended by Palladio for the Doric and Ionic orders. This may explain why for the only time the architect employed capitals based on those of the Temple of Saturn in Rome, which he described as a mixture of Doric and Ionic in the *Quattro Libri*.[30] The atrium itself leads onto the courtyard, which has a two-story loggia only on the left. Palladio was probably prevented from achieving a balanced effect here by the need to conserve the fifteenth-century wing on the right, but the two-story loggia, the first he designed for a Vicentine palace since Palazzo Chiericati, adds a grandiloquent note to an otherwise utilitarian space.

Given the problems and inconsistencies that characterize the extant Palazzo Barbaran, it may be, as Bertotti Scamozzi stated, that Palladio was being less than candid in his reasons for not publishing the final plan.[31] Bertotti, too, seems to have felt uncomfortable with the final version, and he wrote of the discrepancies between the two ground plans as if out of painful necessity, scrupulously noting the lack of symmetry and absence of right angles anywhere in the building. As elsewhere in the *Quattro Libri,* Palladio felt here that he was responding to a higher truth by presenting designs that corresponded to his own system rather than the accidental state of an existing structure. But it is these alterations that throw light on Palladio's thinking and on his reasons for reconsidering the facade.

Palazzo Barbaran bears the hallmarks of its original patron, at once grand, lavish, and overly ambitious. Montano Barbaran came from an old family knighted in 1539, and one of his three wives was Dorotea, daughter of Palladio's early patron Marc'antonio Thiene.[32] As a young man he probably contemplated the splendid beginnings and abrupt conclusion to his father-in-law's

palace, virtually across the street from his own Gothic one, and resolved to vie with it. Beyond the traditional ingredient of family rivalry, Barbaran's contacts with Palladio would have been strengthened in 1561 when he changed his membership from one local humanist academy, the Accademia dei Costanti, to the Accademia Olimpica, in which the architect was an active member. Over the next decade Barbaran also served conspicuously as a deputy of the Vicentine council, which would have exposed him to the debate over the upper story of the Basilica and the first phases in the rebuilding of the Capitaniato. Around 1570 Barbaran acquired the property adjacent to his own from relatives, and on March 31 of that year he petitioned the council to close an alleyway behind his house in order to begin work on the new palace. Palladio was

197. Atrium of the Palazzo Barbaran.

frequently in Vicenza at that date for the Loggia del Capitaniato, and Barbaran wrote another of Palladio's patrons, Federigo Sarego of Verona, in July 1570, saying that he would send the architect "as soon as I have begun work on my facade, which cannot be done without the presence of Messer Andrea Palladio."[33] Palladio oversaw work on the palace through the rest of that year, and building continued through 1572, probably ceasing by 1575.

Barbaran enjoyed the reputation of a generous patron of the arts, and this same impulse was channeled into the decoration of the palace; indeed so much did he spend on it that his family was forced to sell it shortly after his death.[34] An inventory of 1592 speaks of damask and velvet hangings throughout the house and of a maiolica service, all now lost, but even as the interiors survive they are among the most sumptuous of Palladio's palaces, rivaling those of Palazzo Thiene. Barbaran assembled the best artists available for work on the large *salone* of the first floor (plate 198) and for other main rooms of the palace. The stucco decoration is by Lorenzo Rubini, who previously worked with Palladio on the Loggia del Capitaniato, and by Francesco Albanese, documented in the house in 1577; their emphatic figures and strapwork frame paintings by Andrea Vicentino and the Maganza family.

The combination of the dramatic and the decorated, so common in his later work, was obviously congenial to his patrons and probably to Palladio as well. It also corresponded to an emphasis upon imagination and the use of ornament among architects in general, themes that were recurrent in contemporary discussions of the discipline. Architecture was often judged to be midway between an art and a craft, a refuge for mediocre artists or for anyone "capable of drawing two lines," as the sculptor Vincenzo Danti sneered. Compared with the great architects of antiquity, modern architects were criticized for their lack of imagination and inventiveness. Anton Francesco Doni also saw architecture as less challenging than painting or sculpture, but he believed it could rise to the level of an art if it were of proper form and used infinite ornament.[35] The greater reliance on ornamentation in Palladio's later work may have been a counter to such jibes although it coincided with his preference for the most embellished of the orders, the Composite. Like Michelangelo, Palladio set great store by *fantasia* in architecture, whether in his own buildings or in his recreations of the antique (plate 206), and the imaginative element became more dominant as Palladio grew more secure in his convictions.

In what was yet another Vicentine initiative combining civic prestige and antiquarianism (plates 199, 201), the Teatro Olimpico incorporates these and other strands that comprise the late style of Palladio. The Accademia Olimpica, from which the theater derives its name, was one of many private academies that sprang up in Italy during the Renaissance.[36] The scope of such societies was partly social and partly dedicated to debates and what would now be called humanistic pursuits. Founded in 1555, the Olimpica was slightly atypical in not being restricted to aristocrats, counting Palladio and the sons of the artist Valerio Belli among its early members. This mixing of artists and aristocrats on neutral territory went back to Trissino's academy at Cricoli and to the circle that met around Alvise Cornaro in Padua. It had also been common in the

Rome of Pope Leo X where talent was recognized regardless of social background.[37] One of the main pastimes of the Olimpica was the production of plays, both classical and modern, for which Palladio collaborated with artists like Lorenzo Rubini and Giovanni Antonio Fasolo on the sets. The stages were temporary, generally built in the council chamber of the Basilica, and paintings of the first productions reveal a stage and auditorium not unlike the Olimpico itself.[38] The stage or *frons scenae* was conceived as a triumphal arch while the spectators sat in semi-elliptical tiers like the *cavea* of an ancient theater; these elements had already been featured in the architect's reconstruction of the ancient theater in Barbaro's Vitruvius (plate 168) and were the product of a long-meditated study of classical remains.

By 1579 the academy felt that its quarters were not suitable for theatrical productions or its own activities and petitioned the city council for a more permanent site. They were given a derelict building on the edge of town, a combination of prison and arsenal located diagonally opposite Palazzo Chiericati on a corner of the Piazza dell'Isola. Erecting the theater in this area, which included the port of Vicenza and the entrance to the city from Padua, was as much an element in upgrading this part of town as were Palladio's new palaces for the Chiericati and Piovene families.[39] Given his involvement in the academy, Palladio was inevitably drafted as the designer of the new theater. His initial project must have been ready by May 1580, when the academicians decided that the niches adorning the *frons scenae* should contain statues of themselves rather than allegorical figures, and plans were well advanced by the time of Palladio's death in August of that year.[40]

198. *Salone* on the *piano nobile* of the Palazzo Barbaran.

The new theater was finally inaugurated in 1585, and when the curtain rose the audience saw the same spectacle we witness today: a monumental, boxlike facade divided into three stories and punctuated by five doorways. The basic metaphor of the stage is a triumphal arch, loosely based upon the Arch of Constantine. The *frons scenae* is divided into a sequence of bays by two orders of Corinthian columns, freestanding on the ground floor and engaged above. Statues of academicians fill the aedicules between the columns and more stand above the projecting entablatures of both orders. The statues were principally executed by Agostino Rubini,

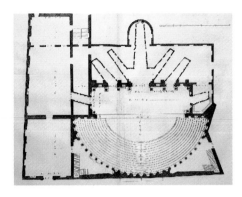

199. *Plan of the Teatro Olimpico,* from Ottavio Bertotti Scamozzi, *Le fabbriche e i disegni di Andrea Palladio,* 1796.

Ruggiero Bascapè, and Domenico Fontana; some were begun as female, presumably as allegorical figures, but Fontana and Bascapè contracted to turn female into male figures in order to supply the missing statues of academicians.[41] Across the top of the stage runs an attic story with reliefs of the labors of Hercules, patron of the Accademia Olimpica. The whole facade is effectively turned into a triumphal arch celebrating the victory of Hercules and virtue over vice.[42] Completing the illusion of an antique theater is the semielliptical *cavea* surmounted by a Corinthian colonnade reminiscent of the Roman theaters at Pola and Verona; the colonnade is especially effective in giving a greater sense of spaciousness to the cramped quarters of the building (plate 199).

Palladio's solution for the Teatro Olimpico was predicated upon his reading of Vitruvius and his extensive examination of Roman theaters. Vitruvius recommended that the key parts of a Roman theater could be defined by a circle within which were inscribed four equilateral triangles. The intersection of the lines of the triangles would indicate the ordering of the staircases,

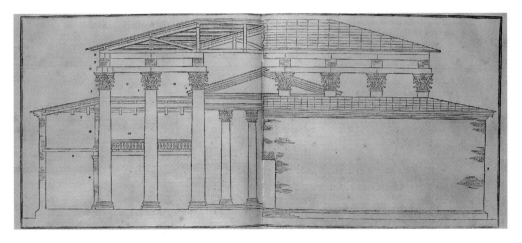

200. *Basilica at Fano* from Daniele Barbaro's *Vitruvius,* 1556.

the size of the orchestra, the depth of the stage, and the like,[43] all issues that were bound up with the question of acoustics. Yet Palladio did not have enough land to create a proper Roman theater, so instead he settled upon an oval plan that defined a narrower curve for the *cavea;* this gave the illusion of a semicircular terrace for the spectators while being more economical with space. Enough room remained for a shallow stage, which Palladio's design would have taken into account. After his death, however, several factors contributed to a decision to change the stage design. In 1581, the academy decided to perform a Greek tragedy rather than an Italian pastoral as their first production in the new theater. This meant that the perspective backdrop had to be more imposing than the kind of landscape scene normally reserved for a pastoral. The academy also realized it needed more land to create a proper theater as well as a center for its meetings; consequently it petitioned the Vicentine council, receiving an extension of the site in January 1582.[44] The additional land allowed for the construction of deep perspective scenes with palaces and temples, and Vincenzo Scamozzi was then brought into finish the theater.

Scamozzi designed the passageways that extend from the *frons scenae,* and to do this he enlarged the three principal openings of the stage and added two more in the wings (plate 201). This move was probably dictated by the choice of Sophocles' *Oedipus Rex* as the inaugural play, since the streets leading away from the stage could thus become the principal thoroughfares of Thebes leading to its seven gates.[45] While Scamozzi's intervention did not greatly alter the original conception, it was based upon a view of theatrical perspective at variance with Palladio's.[46] Both Barbaro and Palladio understood *periaktoi,* the mechanism for changing scenes in classical theaters, to be triangular pieces of scenery that could be rotated in order to change the backdrop. The scenery varied according to the type of play—satiric, comic, or tragic. Vitruvius glossed the appropriate backdrop for the tragic scene as columns and pediments while the comic scene displayed more modest buildings and the satiric employed landscape. In Renaissance theatrical conventions, these types of scenes became associated with the social hierarchy of buildings and were a standard feature of perspective backdrops for plays. However Palladio's reconstruction of the Roman theater placed more emphasis on the *frons scenae,* with its orders of columns and statues, and treated the perspective scenes as modest painted backdrops (plate 168). Given the limitations of the original site, Palladio's design would have included space for only a painted backdrop, but as the plans for the theater grew more ambitious, this would have seemed less satisfactory to the academicians and their new architect, Scamozzi. His steeply raked streets, with their ingeniously designed palaces and temples, create an illusion of vistas disappearing into the distance.

While the Teatro Olimpico is more imposing than any other early surviving theater, it did not really exercise much influence on the development of later theaters—indeed plays were rarely given on its stage before the twentieth century, and its chief attraction lay in seeing the spectacle offered by the illumination of the theater and the perspective streets, as was performed for Pius VI and Napoleon.[47] Still, the Teatro Olimpico remains a potent testimonial to its creator's imaginative recreation of the antique, even as it reveals motifs found in a number of Palladio's late unexecuted projects. The sequence of one-story orders, the gridlike division of the facade, the increased reliance on aedicules, statuary, and reliefs, all find parallels in works like Palladio's proposal for rebuilding the Doge's Palace in Venice (plate 202) or the new civic palace for Brescia or even some aspects of the facade designs for San Petronio in Bologna (plate 203).[48] Although most of these projects never evolved beyond the design phase, those for the Doge's Palace and San Petronio in Bologna were not only important in Palladio's eyes but also display his tendency to become the prisoner of his own imagination in his last years.

Palladio's involvement with the Doge's Palace began in 1555 when he submitted an unsuccessful design for the new ceremonial staircase, a project won by the older established architect Sansovino.[49] By 1570, however, Palladio had established himself in Venice as the heir to Sansovino and resided in the palace of his friend, the aristocrat and connoisseur Giacomo Contarini. From that time virtually any major Venetian project required an opinion from or collaboration with Palladio, as was definitely the case when the center of Venetian government, the Doge's Palace, was damaged by fires in 1574 and 1577. The fires were a magnification of a problem common to all buildings in Venice—a particularly fierce one had laid waste to the Rialto area in 1514.[50] When the fire of 1574 caused damage in some of the ceremonial rooms on the first *piano nobile* of the Doge's Palace, Palladio's role was limited to acting as consultant to the architect for the palace, Antonio da Ponte, in tandem with Giovanni Antonio Rusconi. The scope of this first intervention was limited to the restoration of a few rooms, but the second fire swept through much of the southern and western wings of the palace, devastating the oldest parts of the building. The disruption caused by the fire was enormous: the Great Council had to meet in the Tana or rope factory of the Arsenal, the only available space large enough to accommodate it, while the Senate and other governmental bodies met in improvised settings around the city.

Palladio's brief was to report on the stability of the old building, a task that he accomplished with several other architects and engineers. The group was charged with finding some means of saving the palace, but Palladio characteristically went beyond this and argued for something more. His report was long disregarded, even though Palladio's earliest biographer mentioned the episode along with Marc'antonio Barbaro's support for creating a new ducal palace. Until the recent rediscovery of a large drawing at Chatsworth, little attention was paid to this report, however the drawing clarifies Palladio's recommendation for a new palace (plate 202).[51]

Palladio's report began with a rather lukewarm account of the Doge's Palace, which makes it evident that he lacked sympathy with the late Gothic structure he was called upon to save. He noted that the walls sustained heavy damage in the latest fire and drew attention to an anomaly in the building's architecture: the ground and first floors of the Palace, he pointed out, were composed of arcades, but the diameter of the columns on the first floor was less than those of the ground floor and also less than the thickness of the walls above. This meant that the building lacked a stable foundation, even as the capitals of the columns of the first floor were

splitting from stress and the wall above had been seriously weakened by the intense heat of the fire. The structure of the Doge's Palace ran counter to what Palladio saw as the laws of nature whereby organisms with a fixed base like plants and trees become slenderer as they grow taller. But it also offended against the fundamental principles of good architecture as seen in ancient buildings like the Coliseum or Pantheon in Rome or the Arena in Verona. In Palladio's mind, nature and the antique were at one in their principles of construction, and it followed that no building could endure for centuries unless it subscribed to their tenets.[52]

Palladio's list of structural faults led him to the conclusion that the present structure was irretrievable and should be replaced by a modern one. As in his 1567 report on the proposed new cathedral in Brescia, Palladio's dictated recommendations began to recast the extant building in the light of his own architectural preferences.[53] Thus he urged that sturdy piers be introduced on the ground floor while the loggia on the upper floor be enclosed and the windows replaced; any ornamentation should be appropriate to the building as a whole. What Palladio had in mind can be appreciated in light of the Chatsworth drawing. Here we see that the new Doge's Palace would have had three floors, as before, but the whole would have been treated in a Roman manner—in fact very much like the Coliseum. Engaged Ionic columns would have framed the arches of the ground floor and a similar arrangement with a Corinthian order would have defined the window bays of the floor above. Palladio embellished the first floor further with

201. Teatro Olimpico, Vicenza.

aedicules modeled on the altars of the Pantheon, their columns having alternately straight and spiral fluting. The second floor would have had Composite pilasters instead of columns, simpler frames for the windows, and statues before the pilasters. At either end of the facade the orders were doubled, and the center contained a triple arch motif with statues and reliefs reminiscent of Sansovino's nearby Loggetta (plate 157) and crowned by a small pediment. A lion of Saint Mark occupied the tympanum of the pediment and the wealth of statuary would doubtless have celebrated the Venetian state in allegorical terms.

The Chatsworth drawing is not without its critics, but while it does not strictly correspond to Palladio's dictated comments it would be difficult to imagine another author or an alternative site.[54] As Burns argued, it may well represent an ideal solution not specifically tied to the dimensions of the old Doge's Palace. The drawing bears all the hallmarks of a Palladian production and reads like a cross between the scheme for the Teatro Olimpico and the courtyard of the Carità (plate 115). It may seem strange that Palladio rejected the giant order for such a large facade, but his decision was probably conditioned by the prescribed functions of the old palace, which a new one would have to replicate. He may also have felt that a new palace would have to harmonize with Sansovino's Library (plate 81), situated on the other side of the Piazzetta. The approach does reflect favorite classical motifs that recur in the *frons scenae* of the Teatro Olimpico, in the project for Brescia, and in the drawings for San Petronio, and in this regard the design embodies Palladio's late thoughts on public architecture. Although the proposal to sweep away the Doge's Palace seems as audacious to us as it did to his contemporaries, Palladio evidently believed it justifiable on aesthetic as well as practical grounds. He might have defended his project in terms of the new urbanistic concept of regularized classical facades then being introduced in other Italian cities. He also might have reminded listeners that Sansovino had pro-

202. *Elevation for a new Doge's Palace*, c. 1577. Devonshire Collection, Chatsworth, Derbyshire, England. Pen, ink, and wash over incised lines, 45.9 x 105.2 cm.

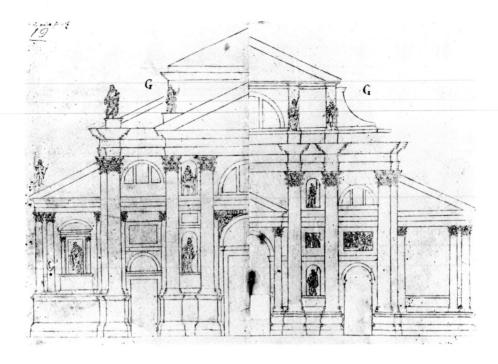

posed refacing the houses on the Piazza San Marco with identical facades based upon the Library, a proposal no less utopian than Palladio's equally impractical plans for a new palace.[55] Needless to say, Palladio's advice was rejected by the city's government, and the exterior of the Doge's Palace was restored as it had been.

Palladio's misreading of his audience here and his succumbing to his own aesthetic prejudices were not isolated incidents but find an uncanny parallel in his dealings with the church of San Petronio, which occupied him intermittently from 1572 until his death. The church was the great civic monument of Bologna and stood in relation to that city much as San Marco did to Venice. Like San Marco, San Petronio had a lay governing body composed of local aristocrats who were at loggerheads with each other over the completion of the church's facade.[56] Work on the vast frontage had begun as early as the 1390s and continued spasmodically under Jacopo della Quercia in the early fifteenth century, with a brief revival in the first years of the sixteenth century. By this date, however, the great age of Gothic architecture lay in the past and a faction within the governing body wanted to bring San Petronio up to date. From the 1520s onwards, eminent architects like Baldassare Peruzzi, Giulio Romano, and Giacomo Vignola were summoned to submit designs for a new facade. Although all attempted to blend contemporary architectural styles with the Gothic form of the building, the results were hardly inspired. Only Peruzzi produced an impressive Gothic pastiche, but even his projects were rejected as not conforming to the style of the

203. *Facade project "G-G" for San Petronio,* 1578–1579. San Petronio, Bologna. Pen and ink over incised lines, 52 x 75 cm.

building.[57] Deadlock prevailed until 1572 when Palladio's views were sought on all the drawings, including the most recent one by the acting architect of San Petronio, who enjoyed the inauspicious nickname of Terribilia. Palladio's opening line of argument was unusual—departing wholly from the prevailing point of view, he cautioned against completing the facade in the Gothic manner; such a style was costly, presumably because of its detailed carved ornamentation, and it would be cheaper to dismantle what had been begun, reusing the same stones in a more "correct" classicizing style. Of the drawings shown to him, Palladio pronounced Terribilia's "il meno cattivo"—the least bad. Undaunted by this cold shower, the governing body of San Petronio invited him to visit Bologna for a further consultation. This he did in June 1572 and followed his inspection with a report less radical in tone than his earlier comments.[58]

As with his remarks on the Doge's Palace, Palladio here offered unenthusiastic praise for San Petronio but accepted that the Gothic facing would be too costly to remove. He inclined toward Terribilia's design, which was less flamboyantly Gothic than a contemporary one by Domenico Tibaldi, but recommended toning down the wealth of ornamentation. He concluded by saying that he would provide his own designs irrespective of the existing structure if the committee were interested. Palladio's letter and his verbal comments to Terribilia led to a composite design, which broke with the compromises of earlier ones. This drawing pared down the Gothic component, effectively relegating it to the ground floor. Classical pilasters were introduced on this level as Peruzzi and Vignola had done, but the upper floors were exclusively conceived in terms of a Renaissance church facade with two stories of Corinthian and Composite orders. Obelisks supplanted crocketing, gables were turned into pediments, and the central Gothic window became a Serlian one.[59]

The novelty of this compromise project must have captivated a sufficient number of the committee at San Petronio because an emended version was adopted by them. Plans were drawn up, but objections emerged from within the committee on the eve of construction, centering on the long-standing problem of combining Gothic and classical elements in a single facade. Palladio's uncharacteristically vehement reply to his critics equated criticism with ignorance and brushed aside the objections as uninformed comment.[60] Despite this outburst, his reputation exerted an attraction for the committee, and he was eventually given leave to submit new designs. Two of these follow the three-story concept of Terribilia's project and include his Serlian windows, but all Gothic elements and even the obelisks were purged. Instead, there is an ascending sequence of orders and aedicules for statuary as in the contemporary project for the Doge's Palace. A third design (plate 203) broke away from Terribilia altogether and presented two alternatives more in the tradition of Palladio's own church facades. While the basic proportions of San Petronio are recognizable, the church appears to have been pushed in the direction of San Francesco della Vigna (plate 118) or even San Pietro di Castello. From here it was a short step to Palladio's final recommendation, a portico based on the Pantheon.[61] Two drawings survive for this alternative, and they simply show the portico taking over the major part of the facade in a manner more obsessive than inventive.

Such a facade ignores the character of the church and may have been an expression of his unstated preference for demolishing the old San Petronio and starting afresh. Alternatively, it could have been conceived as a false front for the Gothic church, but in either case Palladio's convictions appear to have led him further away from a realistic solution.

The debate over Palladio's designs and the question of a portico went up to the highest councils in Rome, and the proposal for a portico was finally rejected in 1580. The composite Terribilia-Palladio project of 1572 was then readopted on November 16 of that year, only to be revoked two days later. No agreement was ever reached at San Petronio, but the episode illustrates a pattern common to many of the projects from his last years. Palladio had the capacity to provide detailed comprehensive projects that drew upon his extensive experience of architecture and the antique. He had, moreover, arrived at a fully articulated approach to design, one in which there was some scope for variety although, as we saw with the *Quattro Libri*, only within carefully defined limits. Self-assurance and megalomania led him to assume positions that undermined his proposals and contributed to many of his late projects remaining on the drawing board. Many that were begun like the Villa Sarego or Palazzo Porto Breganze only attained partial realization, although what was built testifies to their creator's *fantasia*.

Still, Palladio was an extraordinary architect, one who amply fulfilled Vasari's prediction that great things would issue from his pen. So it is fitting to conclude with Palladio's most famous and influential building, the Rotonda (plates 204, 205, 207, 208). In many ways, the Rotonda draws together so many strands from Palladio's life that it can be seen as the great

204. The close relationship between the interior and exterior of the Villa Rotonda is evident in its central, domed hall where passageways lead to the four porticos.

205. Cupola of the Villa Rotonda.

summa of his achievement. Its novelty immediately recognized, the Rotonda became one of the most imitated buildings in the history of architecture.[62] The very name of the villa indicates its indebtedness to the great rotonda of antiquity, the Pantheon, and Palladio leaves many hints about the building's genesis in his account in the *Quattro Libri*.[63]

Created for a retired monsignor, the Rotonda stands on a hillock described by Palladio as of easy ascent and surrounded by other hills "that give the appearance of a grand theater." The hills were cultivated and there were excellent views in all directions—hence loggias were added to all four facades. The *Quattro Libri* text self-consciously echoes Pliny's account of his Tuscan villa on the slopes of the Apennines, a site the Latin writer termed an "immense amphitheater that only nature could create." Palladio also had in mind Alberti's account of the ideal suburban villa, located just outside of town and slightly elevated above the road so that it offered and commanded a splendid view.[64] From his account it seems clear that Palladio was reminded of ancient hillside complexes, especially the theater at Verona and the Temple of Fortune at Palestrina, both of which he had reconstructed (plate 206). In his studies of such complexes, the summit of the site was invariably crowned with a temple, pantheonic in plan and, in the case of Palestrina, with four porticos.[65] The evidence for such reconstructions was, of course, ambiguous, but Palladio evidently believed such sites lent themselves to compact, centrally planned temples with porticos for commanding views. The association led him to pay his finest tribute to the kind of Roman architecture he admired above all others.

Rising above the undulating countryside, the Rotonda still has the power to startle as well as delight (plate 208). Its impact is even more pronounced now that a sympathetic conservation has restored the exterior to an iridescent *marmorino* white that sets the building off from the surrounding greensward. The ascent to the Rotonda instills a note of Roman *gravitas*, a feeling further enhanced by the temple staircases, which slow the pace of those entering to a measured tread and amplify the classical associations of the building. From the stairs one passes through the Ionic porticos, modeled on Palladio's favorite Portico of Octavia in Rome, and enters the domed central *sala* by means of a short passageway. This room is the still point at the center of the building and was originally open to the elements above (plate 205); an antique faun mask in the floor still recalls its early function for catching rain. The room rises to the full height of the building and a handsome wooden balustrade encircles it, marking the division between the *piano nobile* and the upper floor.

In plan, the Rotonda combines two aesthetically satisfying forms, the circle and square, for the sequence of rooms surrounding the central *sala* describes a cube to enclose the Rotonda.[66] Since a large living space was not a high priority for the patron, only one chamber and an antechamber define each corner of the building (plate 207). Mezzanine rooms reminiscent of similar rooms in many of Palladio's villas occupy the space between the antechambers and the upper floor, which was initially undivided and used for storage although subsequently converted into more living space.[67] The decoration of the *piano nobile* is typical of Palladio's later works, with paintings by Anselmo Canera, Bernardino India, and Alessandro Maganza, and stuccowork by the same trio of sculptors who completed the figures at the Teatro Olimpico; unfortunately, neither painting nor sculpture lives up to the high quality of Palladio's design.[68] In many ways the simple brick vaults of the ground floor are more in keeping with modern tastes, and though functional they are impressive. Palladio designed the villa so that the services could be contained on this floor, and deflected attention from it by the external staircases.[69]

The origins of the Rotonda's design can be traced back to the earliest of his villa projects. In one of Palladio's first drawings (plate 59), the cubic block of the villa contains a central *sala* rising one and a half stories.[70] In a larger villa or palace design, this central space would have been defined by a courtyard, although in lieu of this Palladio gave the *salone* cross vaulting with thermal windows and a vestigial pediment on the exterior. Francesco di Giorgio's projects had previously shown the interchangeability of rooms and courtyards at the center of a house, and Raphael also took up this concept with the circular courtyard of the Villa Madama, a work of paramount importance for the young Palladio.[71] These ideas came together in Palladio's work as early as the late 1540s, when he sketched an anticipation of the Rotonda on a sheet of studies for Palazzo Iseppo da Porto.[72] Though scarcely more than a squiggle, the design is of great importance for what it tells us of the architect's thoughts. The basic plan appears to be a villa castle with corner bastions and suggestions of two freestanding porticos; the central space, on the other hand, shows at least four different proposals, varying from a simple square or a circular courtyard to a room with cross vaulting supported on four columns or possibly a domed *sala.* Thus Palladio articulated the essential features of the Rotonda almost two decades before its conception. He only had to wait until he found the right patron to carry out his plans.

The Rotonda was as much a happy conjunction of patron and architect as it was the fruition of Palladio's ideas. Paolo Almerico came of an aristocratic family, though not one of the grand Vicentine clans.[73] As was often the case with younger members of such families, he sought a career in the church, becoming a canon of Vicenza's cathedral at the age of fourteen. By all accounts Almerico's early years were troubled ones. After studies in Padua he passed two years imprisoned in Venice on a charge of homicide; upon release he fell into dispute with his fellow canons in Vicenza over his right to draw money from his benefice for the period when he was a student and in prison. The case was eventually settled in Almerico's favor, and he diplomatically applied the sum in question toward a new portal for the cathedral, a portal for which Palladio furnished the design.[74] The monsignor spent most of 1560–66 in Rome, years when Palladio refers to Almerico as having been a referendary at the papal courts of Pius IV and V. Both before and after his return from Rome, Almerico began acquiring an estate in a hamlet called Ponzano, the setting for the Rotonda. The first parcel of land there was acquired in 1550 and he added more in 1564. The actual date of construction for the new house is not known, but it probably began in the latter part of 1566. Almerico sold his family house in Vicenza the

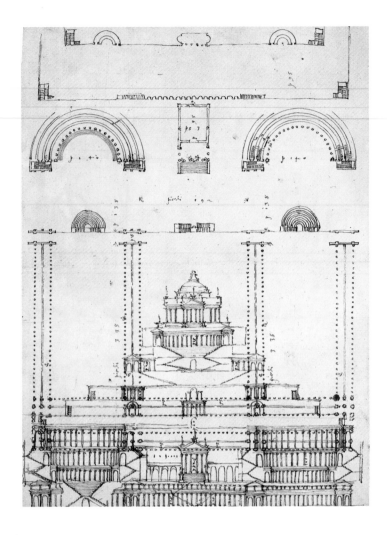

following year, presumably to gain ready money for construction, and must have moved into one of the existing houses on the estate at Ponzano. The Rotonda was habitable by June 1569, though work continued on it down to its first owner's death in 1589.

As a rich bachelor with antiquarian interests, Almerico could indulge his own and Palladio's fancy in building and decorating the Rotonda. Although he had an illegitimate son, he apparently did not maintain a large household, and his surrounding farms absolved the Rotonda from the clutter of barns or stables. These factors allowed Palladio to design a new kind of house, one that was not exactly a suburban villa nor yet a palace; indeed, Palladio confessed his uncertainty about the status of the Rotonda by placing it among the palaces in the *Quattro Libri*.[75] At the same time he had in Almerico a cosmopolitan, well traveled patron whose years in Rome exposed him to the building activity of Cardinal Ippolito d'Este and Pope Pius IV as well as the

206. *Ideal reconstruction of the Temple of Fortune, Palestrina*, 1560s. (RIBA IX/7.) Pen and ink, 39.5 x29 cm.

work of their architect, Pirro Ligorio. Ligorio had been the cardinal's architect when Palladio was last in Rome, and he had been responsible for the fountains and for Rometta, the miniature recreation of Rome complete with centralized temples at the Villa d'Este at Tivoli.[76] During the early 1560s Ligorio was at work on the Casino of Pius IV in the Vatican where, like Palladio, he strove for his own distinctive vision of classical architecture. The archaeological nature of his work set Ligorio apart from the majority of contemporary architects, although there is a curious similarity between the preciosity and inventiveness of the Casino and that of its near contemporary, the Rotonda. Both were conceived as statements of the patron's erudite, antiquarian interests and are consecrated to humanistic pursuits; with the Rotonda, these functions overlaid those of a private house, but the residence took second place to the representational functions of the domed *sala* and its surrounding suites.[77]

207. Vault in one of the lateral rooms at the Villa Rotonda.

It was the inclusion of a dome in the Rotonda that has fascinated later generations, for it embodied one of Palladio's most audacious gestures. Lotz characterized the Rotonda as a secular version of the Renaissance centrally planned church, and Palladio's use of the dome here "transferred the concept of the building as a monument from sacred to secular architecture." In one of the first printed descriptions of the Rotonda, the English traveler John Raymond explained that the name derived "from the Cupola at the top, or likeness it hath with the Pantheon at Rome."[78] Thus the novelty of its dome and its associations with the Pantheon were current in the early seventeenth century and doubtless went back to Palladio's day. As we have seen, the dome was determined by the site and its associations as well as by the four porticos and circular *sala*. These elements were conjured up by the architect in his studies of classical temples, but Palladio also believed that houses and temples in the ancient world were to some degree interchangeable— hence the adaptation of the temple portico.[79] If Palladio could "borrow" the portico for a house, then it follows that the cupola could also be adapted for domestic architecture.

Mention of the dome raises the vexed question: what kind of dome did Palladio want? The discrepancy between the low, stepped profile of the dome as built and the cupola proposed in the *Quattro Libri* has given rise to wide-ranging explanations, from an intervention by Palladio's nemesis, Vincenzo Scamozzi, to the proposal that Palladio wanted two domes, a stepped dome inside a higher cupola.[80] As for the Scamozzi theory, the schedule of construction would not seem to have allowed for significant modification. In a poem dedicated to Almerico, Palladio's friend, the painter Maganza, spoke of the Rotonda as having been built quickly, and certainly work must have reached a fairly advanced stage by 1570 if Palladio could mention the statues by Lorenzo Rubini adorning the staircase.[81] Although the Rotonda was described as somewhat incomplete at the time of its sale to the Capra family in 1591, eleven years after Palladio's death, it would seem strange if the cupola, the focal point of the structure, had not been constructed by then, nor should one imagine that the actual dome was not wanted by Palladio. The suggestion that two domes were intended strains credulity, for the open oculus would have made no sense encased in a hemispheric cupola. The divergences between the executed dome and the published alternative may reflect a difference of opinion between architect and patron centering on cost or aesthetic judgments. The cupola in the woodcut makes Lotz's point about the deconsecration of the dome more emphatically than the stepped one does, but it would have had an overpowering effect on the rather diminutive proportions of the Rotonda, as is the case with imitations like Colen Campbell's Mereworth or Julian Bicknell's Henbury Hall.[82]

Palladio's pride in his creation is evident, not only by his reuse of the idea in a grander, unexecuted project for Francesco and Ludovico Trissino at Meledo, but also in his commentary on the Rotonda.[83] His hesitation over what to term it—palace or villa—is an indirect acknowledgment that he had created a new type of building, one both secular but with distinctive overtones of the sacred. Posterity has paid the architect the compliment of elevating the Rotonda into the realm of a cult object like the Pantheon or the *Mona Lisa*, a confirmation, one could say, of its status as a classic. Above all, the Rotonda embodied a lifelong pursuit of an ideal, a vision of antiquity not so much rediscovered in the ruins of Rome as re-created in Palladio's mind.

Andrea Palladio died on August 19, 1580, a few months short of his seventy-second birthday. The place of death is not known, but his body was buried shortly afterward in a family vault purchased by his surviving son, Silla, in the Vicentine church of Santa Corona, not far from the funerary chapel designed by Palladio for the Valmarana family a few years earlier.[84] Though he had not lived in Vicenza for over a decade, his family kept a house there and he must have considered it an adopted home. Tradition has it that the funeral was small, but some fellow members of the Accademia Olimpica appear to have attended. There may have been an oration or poems recited by the architect's old friend Giambattista Maganza. In any case, the academy subsequently decided to publish a volume of poems and prose written on the occasion of Palladio's death and even deliberated on erecting a statue of their architect to fill one of the niches on the top order of the stage of the Teatro Olimpico; like many a good intention, neither resolution was executed.[85]

Vicenza made it up to Palladio in the nineteenth century when the architect's body was disinterred and reburied in a prominent tomb in the new civic cemetery. A statue of Palladio was also raised in the center of town and now stares pensively at the Basilica. But these pious gestures merely confirmed the centuries-long debt the city owed its most distinguished architect. Palladio transformed the image of Vicenza just as clearly as he changed the concept of the villa. He lavished his genius on Vicenza's public and private architecture and created a style of building that was imitated at first in Vicenza and then throughout the world. For this reason travelers began to make Vicenza an obligatory stage in their tours of Italy—indeed the study of Palladio's architecture arose as much from the curiosity of eighteenth-century tourists, especially the English, as from a purely Vicentine zeal to proselytize.[86] Palladio even lent his name to a loosely defined architectural movement, which has helped to keep his name alive from London to Pavlovsk and beyond. Still, most of the buildings dubbed "Palladian" have only the vaguest connection with Palladio's own work; columns and symmetry alone were never a passport to immortality.[87] No, one still must return to the source, to Vicenza, the Veneto, and Venice, to see Palladio's works first hand, to experience their attraction and wonder at their perfection. In 1786 the great German writer Goethe visited Vicenza for a few days en route to Rome, primarily to study Palladio's buildings. He already knew of Palladio from the pages of the *Quattro Libri*, but his first and only encounter with the architect's work made a deep impression on him. In a few sentences of his journal, Goethe best encapsulated the enduring appeal of Palladio's architecture and touched the nub of his artistic personality: "There is something divine about his talent, something comparable to the power of a great poet who, out of the worlds of truth and falsehood, creates a third whose borrowed existence enchants us."[88]

208. *(overleaf)* Villa Rotonda, Vicenza.

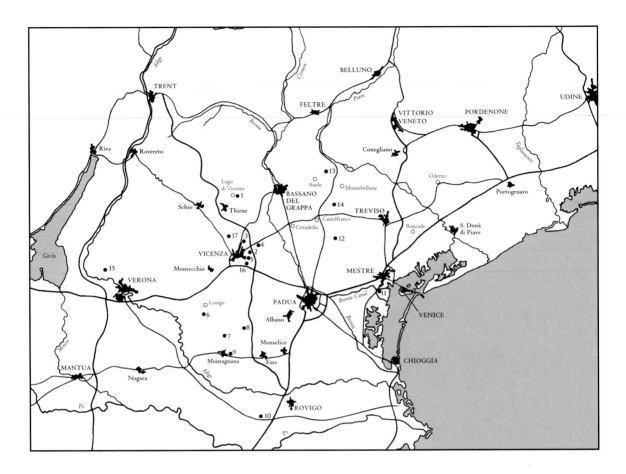

VENETO

1. Villa Godi, Lugo di Vicenza

2. Villa Gazzotti Marcello Curti, Bertesina

3. Villa Valmarana, Vigardolo

4. Villa Thiene, Quinto

5. Villa Chiericati, Vancimuglio di Grumolo

6. Villa Pisani, Bagnolo

7. Villa Poiana, Poiana Maggiore

8. Villa Saraceno, Finale

9. Villa Pisani, Montagnana

10. Villa Badoer, Fratta Polesine

11. Villa Malcontenta (Foscari), Gambarare di Mira

12. Villa Cornaro, Piombino Dese

13. Villa Barbaro, Maser

14. Villa Emo, Fanzolo

15. Villa Sarego, Santa Sofia

16. Villa Rotonda, Vicenza

17. Villa Caldogno, Caldogno

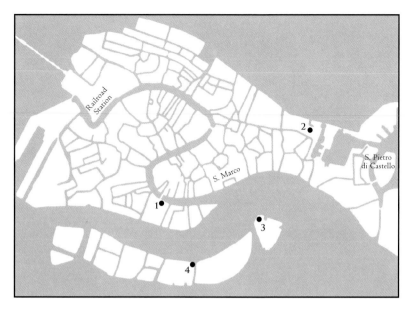

VENICE

1. S. Maria della Carità
2. S. Francesco della Vigna
3. S. Giorgio Maggiore
4. Redentore

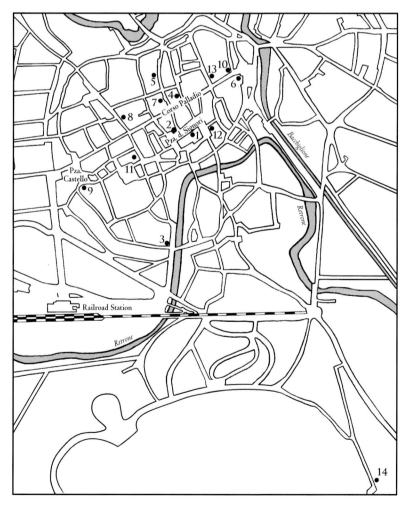

VICENZA

1. Basilica
2. Loggia del Capitaniato
3. Casa Civena
4. Palazzo Thiene
5. Palazzo Porto
6. Palazzo Chiericati
7. Palazzo Barbaran da Porto
8. Palazzo Valmarana
9. Palazzo Porto Breganze
10. Teatro Olimpico
11. Cathedral
12. S. Maria dei Servi
13. S. Corona
14. Villa Rotonda

CHRONOLOGY

1508 Palladio is born in Padua on November 30

1509–16 War of the League of Cambrai

1521 Apprenticeship to Bartolomeo Cavazza

1523 Family moves to Vicenza; apprenticeship broken

1524 Palladio enrolls in Vicentine guild of stonemasons

1524 Giulio Romano enters service of the marquis of Mantua

1527 Sack of Rome; Jacopo Sansovino and Sebastiano Serlio arrive in Venice

1528 Michele Sanmicheli enters service of Venetian state

1529 Treaty of Cambrai

1532–37 Giangiorgio Trissino rebuilds his villa at Cricoli

1534 Palladio marries Allegradonna, daughter of a carpenter named Marc'antonio, in April

1534–36 Pedemuro bottega executes high altar of Vicenza's cathedral

1535 Giovanni Maria Falconetto dies

1536 Portal of Domus Comestabilis executed

1536 Sansovino in Vicenza for Basilica consultation

1537 Serlio publishes Book IV of *Regole generali* in Venice

1537 Villa Godi begun; last mention of Palladio in Pedemuro bottega

1538–41 Palladio with Trissino in Padua and Venice [?]

1539 Serlio constructs theater in garden of Palazzo Colleoni Porto in Vicenza

1540 Serlio publishes Book III of *Regole generali* and enters service of Francis I of France

1540–42 Casa Civena under construction

1541 Palladio's first trip to Rome with Trissino in summer

1541 Sanmicheli in Vicenza for Basilica consultation in November

1541 Villa Valmarana at Vigardolo begun

1541–42 Villa Gazzotti begun

1542/46–58 Palazzo Thiene under construction

1542 Giulio Romano in Vicenza for Basilica consultation in December

1542–45 Villa Pisani at Bagnolo under construction

1543 Palladio designs temporary architecture for entry of Cardinal Ridolfi into Vicenza

1543[?]–52 Palazzo da Porto Festa under construction

1545 Second trip to Rome with Trissino in September

1545–46 Villa Thiene at Quinto begun

1546 Basilica project submitted with Giovanni da Porlezza in February

1546 Third trip to Rome in March

1546 Giulio Romano dies

1547 Palladio returns from Rome in July

1548 Palladio recorded in Venice in September

1548–49 Villa Saraceno in Finale di Agugliaro and Villa Poiana in Poiana Maggiore begun

1549 Construction of Basilica arcades begun in May

1549 Contract for completion of facade of Palazzo da Porto Festa in December

1549 Fourth trip to Rome in December[?]

1550 Trissino dies

1550–52 Bridge on the Cismon River near Bassano del Grappa built

1551–54 Palazzo Chiericati begun

1551 Palazzo della Torre in Verona begun

1552 Villa Pisani at Montagnana begun

1552–54 Villa Cornaro at Piombino Dese under construction

1554 Palladio competes unsuccessfully for office of chief architect to the Salt Magistracy in Venice in January

1554 *Le antichità di Roma* and *Descrizione delle chiese di Roma* published

1554 First Rialto Bridge project

1554 Last visit to Rome

1554[?] Villa Mocenigo at Dolo on the Brenta Canal begun

1554–74 Villa Chiericati at Vancimuglio under construction

1555 Unsuccessful design submitted for new staircase in Doge's Palace, Venice

1555 Villa Badoer in Fratta Polesina begun

1556 Daniele Barbaro's *Vitruvius* with illustrations by Palladio published in Venice

1556 Accademia Olimpica founded in Vicenza

1556 Palazzo Antonini in Udine begun

1556–58 Villa Barbaro in Maser begun

1556 Villa Repeta in Campiglia begun

1558–61 Villa Foscari, La Malcontenta, under construction

1560 Palladio briefly suspended from his role as architect of the Basilica from May to July

1560–65 Villa Emo in Fanzolo under construction

1560–63 Refectory of San Giorgio Maggiore in Venice under construction

1561 Payment for model of convent of Santa Maria della Carità in Venice in March

1561–62 Classical wooden theater constructed inside the Basilica at Vicenza

1562[?] Design of San Francesco della Vigna in Venice approved

1564 Design submitted for Ionic order of Basilica in March

1565[?] Second Rialto Bridge project designed

1565 Commission for the rebuilding of Santa Lucia in Venice

1565 Church of San Giorgio Maggiore in Venice planned

1565–69 Villa Sarego at Santa Sofia under construction

1565 Contract for Palazzo Valmarana in Vicenza in December

1566 Construction of San Giorgio Maggiore begins in March

1566 Palladio visits Turin as the guest of Emanuele Filiberto of Savoy

1567 Consultation on the proposed model for a new cathedral in Brescia

1566–69 Villa Rotonda in Vicenza under construction

1570–75 Palazzo Barbaran in Vicenza under construction

1570 Daniele Barbaro and Jacopo Sansovino die

1570 *Quattro Libri* published in Venice

1571–74 Loggia del Capitaniato in Vicenza under construction

1571[?] Palazzo Porto Breganze in Vicenza begun

1571 Battle of Lepanto won by the Venetian fleet in October

1572 Palladio's sons Leonida and Orazio die

1572 Consultation and first design for the facade of San Petronio, Bologna

1574 Temporary triumphal arch and loggia for the reception of Henry III of France on the Lido in July

1574 Consultation on the restoration of the Senate and College in the Doge's Palace in Venice

1575 Main fabric of San Giorgio Maggiore finished

1575–77 Severe plague in Venice

1576 Decision to build Il Redentore (church of the Redeemer) taken by Venetian Senate in September

1577 Foundation stone laid for Redentore in May

1577 Consultation on Doge's Palace after fire in December

1578–79 Further projects for the facade of San Petronio submitted

1580–85 Construction of Teatro Olimpico in Vicenza

1580–89 Choir of San Giorgio Maggiore under construction

1580 Palladio dies on August 19

1592 Redentore consecrated

1599–1610 Facade of San Giorgio Maggiore completed

GLOSSARY

Aedicule
The architectural frame of an opening, usually consisting of two columns or pilasters supporting an entablature and pediment.

Araeostyle
See **Intercolumniation**

Architrave
The beam that spans from column to column, resting directly upon their capitals, comprising the lowest of the three primary divisions of the entablature. Also used to describe any molding around a window or door.

Atrium
Originally the central inner hall in an ancient Roman domestic building or the open colonnaded forecourt of a church; in Italian Renaissance architecture, an entrance hall.

Barrel vault
A continuous vault of semicircular section.

Base molding
Contours given to projecting members on the foot of a column or bottom of a wall.

Bay
The vertical division of the exterior or interior of a building marked by fenestration, units of vaulting, an order, or roof compartments.

Bucrania [Bukrania]
Carved relief ornament representing the head or skull of an ox, often used as a decorative motif on friezes, found in the metopes of a Doric frieze (from Greek *boukranion*, "oxhead").

Cella (Latin)
The central structure of a Classical temple, excluding the portico and colonnade, where the Cult statue was located.

Chamfered
The surface created by cutting or beveling the edge of a block at an angle, usually at forty-five degrees to adjacent faces.

Colossal order
An order spanning more than one story.

Column
A freestanding, vertical body, consisting of a base, shaft, and capital, that functions as a support for some part of a building.

Console
Decorative bracket in the form of an S-shaped scroll, with one end broader than the other, projecting from a wall to support a cornice, door, window, or piece of sculpture.

Cornice
The top or crowning portion of an entablature; also applied to any crowning ornamental molding.

Course
A horizontal layer of masonry units.

Coved ceiling
A ceiling with a concave or canted interior corner or molding where it meets the wall.

Diastyle
See **Intercolumniation**

Domical vault
An arched ceiling in the form of a dome rising directly from a square or polygonal base, the curved surfaces separated by groins.

Engaged order
Column attached to, or apparently partially built into, a wall.

Entablature
The horizontal area of an order above the columns, composed, from top to bottom, of a cornice, frieze, and architrave.

Eustyle
See **Intercolumniation**

Exedra [Exhedra] (Latin)
A semicircular or apsidal end of a room or exterior wall recess.

Fascia
A plain, flat, horizontal band projecting slightly from the surface of a wall.

Frieze
The middle section of an entablature, often decorated.

Giant order
See **Colossal order**

Hemicycle
A semicircular structure or apselike recess, sometimes used on facades or courtyards.

Herm
Rectangular stone column or post that tapers downward, surmounted by a bust of Hermes, another divinity, or a human head.

Impost
A square or carved molded bracket or projection on a pier or wall from which an arch springs.

Intercolumniation
The distance between the centers of the bases of adjacent columns measured in multiples of the column diameters. As given by Vitruvius, they are:

pycnostyle	1½ diameters
systyle	2 diameters
eustyle	2¼ diameters
diastyle	3 diameters
araeostyle	4 diameters

Mascaron
A human or partly human head, often grotesque, viewed frontally, employed as an architectural ornament.

Membering
Any part of an edifice, or any molding in a collection of moldings, as those in a cornice, capital, or base.

Narthex (Greek)
A single-story enclosed porch or vestibule, often arcaded, at the entrance to a church.

Octastyle
Columned facade or portico with eight frontal columns, before the entrance to a building.

Oculus (*pl.* oculi)
A small circular panel or window; also an opening at the apex of a dome.

Ogive
A pointed arch or a diagonal rib in a vault.

Order
In Classical and Renaissance architecture, a column with a base (normally), shaft, capital, and entablature designed according to one of the recognized modes: Tuscan, Doric, Ionic, Corinthian, or Composite.

Pavilion vault
An arched ceiling reminiscent of a pavilion, sloping equally on all sides.

Piano nobile
Principal floor in an Italian palazzo, formal residence, or Renaissance domestic building, containing the reception rooms, usually raised one story above ground level and of greater height than the floors above.

Pulvinated
Term usually applied to a frieze and signifying a cushion-shaped or convex profile.

Putto (Italian, "boy"; *pl.* putti)
Representation of a chubby, usually naked, infant.

Quadrant
A quarter-round molding.

Quatrefoil (Anglo-French, "four-leaf")
A four-lobed decorative motif divided by cusps.

Quoin
The dressed stones at the corners of buildings, usually laid so that their faces alternate large and small.

Rustication
Masonry, or its simulation in materials such as stucco or other compositions, in which the joints between the stones are deliberately emphasized by chamfered or beveled edges or in which the stones are left roughly hewn to create a striking visual effect.

Salone (Italian)
Reception room or large hall.

Serlian arch [*Serliana*]
A tripartite archway or window casement with a larger and arched central opening and lateral openings that support a flat entablature; so called after its publication by Sebastiano Serlio.

Socle
A low, plain pedestal or plinth base.

Soffit
The visible undersurface of any architectural component, in particular an overhead structure, i.e., an arch, beam, cornice, lintel, vault, or architrave where it does not rest on columns.

Spandrel
The space between two arches in an arcade.

Stanza
A small or medium-size room, usually one of a suite.

Stoa (Greek)
A detached colonnade, comparable to a portico, providing a shaded promenade or public meeting place.

String course
A horizontal band of masonry on the exterior of a

building that is generally narrower than other courses, usually molded and serving to separate one story from another.

Stylobate
The steps under a portico or colonnade; a continuous base, plinth, or pedestal upon which a row of columns stand.

Systyle
See **Intercolumniation**

Tabernacle
A decorative niche or receptacle, sometimes housing a statue or framing a window.

Tetrastyle
A portico with four frontal columns.

Thermal window [Diocletian window]
A semicircular window divided into three lights by two vertical mullions, sometimes called a Diocletian window because of its use in the Roman baths (Thermae) of the emperor Diocletian.

Triangulation
An assembly of beams in a continuous network of triangles in order to achieve a balance of forces, used in the creation of roof and bridge trusses.

Tympanum (Latin, "drum")
Triangular or segmental space enclosed by the moldings of a pediment, a corbeled arch, or above a window; the area between the lintel of a door and the arch above.

Volute
Spiral scroll-shaped architectural ornament on Ionic and Composite capitals and, in a smaller form, on Corinthian capitals.

Voussoir (French)
Wedge-shaped masonry block forming part of a series constituting an arch or vault.

NOTES

Chapter I. Palladio's Formation as an Architect

1. Plutarch, *Life of Pericles*, xiii, 3. The translation quoted here is by B. Perrin in the Loeb edition of Plutarch's *Lives*, III, London, 1916, p. 41. For orientation in the vast bibliography surrounding Palladio, see Howard (1980); and Ackerman (1990-II). For a general introduction, Ackerman (1966) remains incomparable.

2. Palladianism lies beyond the scope of this volume, but see the panorama in *Palladio: la sua eredità nel mondo* (1980). For Palladianism in the Anglo-American world, see Köster (1990); and Tavernor (1991).

3. Burns (1975), pp. 72–73, no. 135, with further references.

4. Rigoni (1970), pp. 319–24; see also the recent analyses by Bellinati and Battilotti in Puppi (1980-I), pp. 164–73, 338–41.

5. On the Grandi, see Cessi (1967); and Rigoni (1970), pp. 223–29.

6. On the historical background to Cambrai, see especially Gilbert (1973).

7. On Cornaro, see Fiocco (1965); Puppi (1980-I); and Holberton (1990), pp. 81–89.

8. Goldthwaite (1980), p. 85. On the concept of magnificence, see especially Fraser Jenkins (1970) and the observations of Burckhardt (1985), p. 9.

9. Vasari, V, pp. 318–25. See also Schweikhart (1968); as well as Bresciani Alvarez and Schweikhart in Puppi (1980-I), pp. 36–57, 64–71.

10. The Arco dei Gavi was mistakenly believed to be by the Vitruvius of the Latin treatise, which gave the arch an added cachet. See Tosi and Burns in Marini (1980), pp. 34–49, 103–17.

11. Keller (1971); Berger (1978), pp. 16–20; Puppi (1980-I), p. 53; and Günther (1981), pp. 50–54.

12. Serlio (1619), VII, pp. 218–22; and Günther (1981), pp. 52–53.

13. Forssman (1966); Burns in Marini (1980), p. 108; and here, chapter six.

14. Zorzi (1949), pp. 147–48, no. vii; and Rigoni (1970), pp. 167–68, 301–2. Puppi (1973), p. 8, has a higher estimation of Cavazza's architecture. See also Bellinati in Puppi (1980-I), pp. 166–67.

15. Zorzi (1949), p. 148, no. viii.

16. Zorzi (1937), pp. 83, 88, and (1959), pp. 2–3; Barbieri (1967); Puppi (1973), pp. 8–10; Berger (1978), pp. 3–8; Cevese (1980); and Zaupa (1990), pp. 39–73.

17. On the temporary decorations for Ridolfi's entry, see Zorzi (1965), pp. 167–69; Puppi (1973), p. 257; and Burns (1975), p. 73, no. 137. On the Basilica project, see chapter four.

18. "Vicenza Città non molto grande di circuito, ma piena di nobilissimi intelletti, & di richezze assai abbondante." Palladio (1570), I, proem, p. 5.

19. For the political background, see Ventura (1964), pp. 118–25; Burns (1975), pp. 9i–12; Grubb (1988); and Zamperetti (1989).

20. Puppi (1973), p. 237.

21. See chapter three; also Battilotti (1980), pp. 217–18 n. 180, for the correct dating of the Godi chapel in San Michele.

22. Barbieri (1967), pp. 26–27; Puppi (1973), pp. 237–38; and Cevese (1980), p. 160.

23. Zorzi (1916); and Burns (1975), p. 69.

24. Cevese in Burns (1975), p. 19, no. 13; also Cevese (1980), pp. 161–62. Cevese compared the door with a design in Serlio (1619), VII, p. 77, fig. a, and with the main door of the Villa Todescato at Caldogno, datable to around 1534 and reproduced in Cevese (1971), II, pp. 364–65.

25. On Trissino, see the fundamental study by Morsolin (1878). For more recent literature, see Wittkower (1962), pp. 57–64; Burns (1975), pp. 77–82; Barbieri (1980); Dionisotti (1980); Daniele (1989), pp. 41–45, with further references; and Holberton (1990), pp. 73–80. Zaupa (1990), pp. 42–43, argues that another Vicentine noble, Antenore Pagello, was an important patron of Palladio before Trissino, but the evidence is far from convincing.

26. The name *Palladio* derives from Pallas, one of the names of the Greek goddess of wisdom. It was also the name of a Roman writer on agriculture, and was employed by Trissino for Belisarius's guardian angel in the *Italia liberata*. See Wittkower (1962), p. 58; and Burns (1975), pp. 81–82, nos. 150–51.

27. For his fragmentary writings, see Morsolin (1878), pp. 224–26; and Puppi (1973-II), pp. 79–86.

28. Cevese (1971), I, pp. 72–79, with an extensive bibliography. See also the description in Morsolin (1878), pp. 226–31; Puppi (1971); and Burns (1975), pp. 78–80, no. 148.

29. Günther (1981), pp. 47–50, emphasizes the differences between the facade of Cricoli and Serlio's woodcut; this theme has also been adopted by Frommel (1990), p. 146.

30. The idea was first proposed by Temanza (1778), p. 288; and accepted by Milizia (1785), II, p. 34. Bertotti Scamozzi (1796), II, pp. 61–62, expressed doubts about Palladio's authorship of the design, but the idea has periodically returned. See the account in Cevese (1971), I, p. 74 n. 6.

31. Zorzi (1959-II) published Gualdo's text of 1616 and established its basic probity.

32. Zorzi (1959), pp. 3–5, 17–18.

33. Morsolin (1878), pp. 232–40; Puppi (1971); and Niccolini (1989), pp. 89–94, on the intellectual context of Trissino's academy.

34. See chapter nine.

35. See especially Burns in Marini (1980), pp. 83–84, 103–21.

36. Palladio (1570), I, xxviii, p. 61: "magnifico signor Luigi Cornaro, Gentil'huomo di eccellente giuditio, come si conosce dalla bellissima loggia, & dalle ornatissime stanze fabricate da lui per sua abitatione in Padova." For Cornaro's writings on architecture, see Fiocco (1965); and Carpeggiani in Puppi (1980-I), pp. 28–35. See also chapter eight.

37. Battilotti (1982), pp. 175–76, with further references. On Gualtiero dall'Arzere at the Villa Godi, see chapter three, p. 83.

38. Cornaro's son-in-law was a member of the Accademia degli Infiammati, which included notable figures like Barbaro, Benedetto Varchi, Sperone Speroni, Maganza, Ruzzante, and Francesco Sansovino. During Trissino's period in Padua, he and Palladio would have taken part in the academy's activities. See Maylender (1926–30), III, pp. 266–70. For a survey of Barbaro's life, see Alberigo (1964), with further references. See also the new edition of Palladio's guide to the churches of Rome by Howe (1991).

39. Ferrari (1976), pp. 480–81, 484–85; Puppi (1988), pp. 3–36.

40. Morsolin (1878), p. 321; see also Burns (1975), pp. 74–75, nos. 139–40. On Maganza as poet, see especially Bandini (1989), pp. 16–17.

41. Palladio (1570), I, p. 5; Puppi (1973), p. 14. See also the general observations in Ackerman (1966), pp. 171–77.

42. Serlio (1619), III, p. 69v; de l'Orme is quoted by Burns (1975), pp. 84–85. See also Burns in Marini (1980), p. 83. Compare Montaigne's initial reaction to the ruins of Rome in Montaigne (1942), pp. 94–95.

43. On this topic, see especially Spielmann (1966); Burns (1966) and (1973-I); Lewis (1981), especially pp. 28–70; and Nesselrath (1986).

44. "The difference between the drawings of the painter and those of the architect is this: the former takes pains to emphasize the relief of objects in paintings with shading and diminishing lines and angles; the architect rejects shading but takes his projections from the ground plan and, without altering the lines and by maintaining the true angles, reveals the extent and shape of each elevation and side." Alberti (1988), p. 34 (*De re* II, i). See the classic studies by Lotz (1956) and (1962), reprinted in (1977), pp. 1–65, 181–90.

45. See Burns (1973-II), pp. 183–86 and (1975), pp. 247–48; Gioseffi (1973); and Fagiolo (1978). See also chapters six and nine.

46. Puppi (1988), p. 11, and (1989), p. 31.

47. "Me ne porge una gran luce Vitruuio, ma non tanto che basti"; Golzio (1936), p. 30. See also the essays by Burns and Nesselrath in Frommel et al. (1984), pp. 381–99. According to Cellini, Peruzzi expressed a similar criticism of Vitruvius's selective account of classical architecture; see Lotz (1963).

48. Spielmann (1966), pp. 144, 169–70, nos. 45, 207, 211, 215; Burns (1973-I), pp. 151–52, 153–54; Puppi (1989), pp. 104–6, 109, nos. 19, 23, 27, 40.

49. For the terraces above the Roman theater at Verona, see Franzoni in Marini (1980), pp. 54–62; and Lewis (1981), pp. 31–32, nos. 10–11. Burns (1975), p. 111, no. 209, thought Palladio's drawings

of the terraces were after Sanmicheli, which seems plausible. On the Portico of Octavia, see Burns (1975), p. 254; and Puppi (1989), p. 103, no. 16.

50. These points are discussed in chapter eight.

51. On the temples at Nîmes, see Burns (1975), pp. 253, 259, no. 482; also Magagnato and Marini (1980), pp. xxi–xxii, with further references.

52. See Zorzi (1959), p. 18 n. 29, on Marco Thiene's letter. On Palestrina, see especially Fancelli (1974); Burroughs (1988); and here chapter nine.

53. Serlio (1619), III, p. 95r, quoted by Burns (1973-I), p. 137; see also Lewis (1981), pp. 130–40.

54. See chapter six; on Adam's criticism of the "Palladian" style, see Summerson (1989), p. 428.

55. See Burns (1975), pp. 94–96; Boucher (1979); and Holberton (1990), pp. 90–100. See also chapter eight.

56. Vasari, IV, p. 146: "Se pure i Greci furono inventori della architettura, e i Romani imitatori, Bramante non solo imitandogli con invenzion nuova ci insegnò." On the House of Raphael, see Frommel (1973), II, 80–87; and Bruschi (1977), pp. 173–75. On the drawing of the House of Raphael, wrongly attributed to Palladio but certainly in his collection, see Burns (1975), p. 231, no. 407.

57. Vitruvius, II, iii, and VII, ii–vi, refers to covering brick with stucco and returns to the subject in his discussion of vault and wall decorations. See also Vasari, I, pp. 139–40, 165–66.

58. For Palazzo Branconio, see Pagliara in Frommel et al. (1984), pp. 197–204. On Giulio Romano's Roman works, see Tafuri et al. (1989), pp. 97–133, 289–305.

59. See the general account of St. Peter's in Bruschi (1977), pp. 145–62. With special reference to Palladio, see Timofiewitsch (1968); and Frommel (1977).

60. On the literary and architectural sources for the Belvedere, see Ackerman (1954) and Coffin (1979), with further references.

61. Shearman (1968); Burns (1975), pp. 88–89 and 264–66, nos. 163 and 401; Frommel et al. (1984), pp. 311–22, 390.

62. Vasari, V, p. 324.

63. Palladio (1570), I, proem, p. 5: "Il più ricco, & ornato edificio, che forse sia stato da gli Antichi in

qua." On Sansovino, see Tafuri (1972); Howard (1975); and Boucher (1991).

64. On Sanmicheli, see the catalog entries in Gazzola (1960); Puppi (1986); and also the important articles by Davies and Hemsoll (1991 and 1995). Palazzo Canossa has recently been seen as an original design by Giulio Romano, finished by Sanmicheli after Giulio's death; see Burns in Tafuri et al. (1989), p. 510.

65. Vasari, VI, p. 350.

66. Burns (1975), pp. 30–31, no. 34; and Burns in Marini (1980), pp. 118–20. Section V, no. 5.

67. See chapter four, p. 115.

68. See especially Magagnato (1968); Schweikhart (1971); and the discussion in chapters two and five.

69. See the essays by Burns and Gombrich in Chambers and Martineau (1981); and the copious documentation in Tafuri et al. (1989).

70. Vasari, V, pp. 547–48.

71. Serlio (1537), p. 133v; see also Shearman (1967); Forster and Tuttle (1971); and Verheyen (1977).

72. See especially Forster and Tuttle (1973); also Burns in Tafuri et al. (1989), pp. 502–4; and here chapter two.

CHAPTER II. VICENZA AND PALLADIO'S FIRST PALACES

1. Sanudo (1847), pp. 108–10; see also Franzina (1980), pp. 140–41.

2. Montaigne (1942), p. 70.

3. Summerson (1991), pp. 63–98, on the "Prodigy Houses" of the Elizabethan and Jacobean periods; on Weser Renaissance architecture see Hitchcock (1981), pp. 171–200.

4. Mantese (1964), pp. 611–14, 630–35.

5. Barbieri (1973); and Battilotti (1980), pp. 13–82, especially p. 16.

6. Ibid., pp. 124, 126, 136, 139, 145–46.

7. Grubb (1988).

8. See the useful survey by Barbieri (1981).

9. Mantese (1964), p. 890.

10. See chapter one; Trincanato (1948); and Goy (1989), especially pp. 123–71.

11. Barbieri (1981), pp. 92–98.

12. Ibid., pp. 27–29, 43–46.

13. Burns (1975), p. 13; and Barbieri (1981), p. 12.

14. Palladio (1570), II, iii, p. 4: "Quella invechiata usanza di fabricare senza gratia, e senza bellezza alcuna."

15. Cf. Barbieri, Cevese, Magagnato (1956), p. 230.

16. See chapter one, pp. 17–23.

17. On the changes to Casa Civena, see Barbieri (1972), p. 29 n. 11; for a résumé of its earlier history and critical opinion, Puppi (1973), pp. 242–45, and Barbieri (1987), pp. 65–66.

18. Bertotti Scamozzi (1796), I, pp. 105–6. The reference to the name "Palladio" comes in his payments for work on the Villa Godi; see here chapter three, pp. 80–81.

19. See Puppi (1973), pp. 237–38. The documents are reprinted in Zorzi (1965), p. 187, nos. 1–2.

20. See especially Berger (1978), pp. 43–56, and 199–203. She includes RIBA XIII/10 as an alternative facade design for Casa Civena, but the proportions do not match those of the executed facade nor those of RIBA XVII/14; cf. Cevese (1964), p. 344; and Burns (1973-I), p. 146.

21. Lewis (1981), p. 54, no. 29, plausibly dates the study of San Biagio to Palladio's first Roman visit; see also Bruschi (1977), pp. 111–13, figs. 118–19, and 169, figs. 179–80.

22. This same feature can be found in a later work like the Villa Malcontenta (figs. 154, 156) or in an early villa study like RIBA XVII/15, on which see Burns (1973-I), p. 149; and Berger (1978), p. 69, fig. 6.

23. See Burns (1975), p. 35, no. 46; Berger (1978), pp. 53–54.

24. On Sanmicheli's Porta Nuova, see Puppi (1986), pp. 50–55; for the Palazzo Caffarelli Vidoni, which was built by Lorenzetto, see Frommel (1973), II, pp. 53–61, and III, pls. 25–27.

25. Berger (1978), p. 199.

26. Serlio (1619), III, p. 74v; cf. Palladio (1570), I, xx, p. 52: "Ma quello, che a mio parere importa molto, e l'abuso del fare i frontespici delle porte, delle finestre, e delle loggie spezzati nel mezo: con-ciosiache essendo essi fatti per dimostrare, & accusare il piovere delle fabriche."

27. See, for example, RIBA XVII/1r, 2r, and 15r, discussed here in chapter three, pp. 85, 88–89. The thickness of the piers of the Casa Civena also resemble those adopted by Palladio in his early drawings for the Basilica; see chapter four, pp. 113–15.

28. Zorzi (1965), pp. 24, 30–32; Berger (1978), pp. 57–61; and Morresi (1988), pp. 48–54. These drawings and RIBA XVII/11 have been associated with the Vicentine Palazzo Da Monte at Santa Corona, but the palace bears the date of 1581 on its facade, which was apparently executed after 1563 by Domenico Groppino, a local mason and follower of Palladio. See Morresi (1990).

29. See the discussion in Frommel et al. (1984), pp. 157–64.

30. For earlier discussions of the palace, see especially Puppi (1973), pp. 251–53; Burns (1975), pp. 36–37, no. 47; Berger (1978), pp. 137–61, 218–28; and Barbieri (1987), pp. 42–43, 66–68.

31. Battilotti (1980), p. 49, observes that Ottavio Thiene, son and heir of Marc'antonio, was by far the richest person in Vicenza, and his holdings on the block in which Palazzo Thiene stands had the highest property valuation in the *estimo* of 1563–64.

32. See especially Cevese (1952), pp. 13–36; and Magagnato (1966), pp. 11–16.

33. Cevese (1952), p. 43 n. 2, argued that the palace designed by Lorenzo da Bologna was L-shaped, citing the similarity of the cornices on the internal facade and that facing the stradella. In addition, he pointed to the two vaulted rooms on the ground floor of the north wing, then recently covered but now once again revealed, as stylistically at one with Lorenzo's work. This is the case, and there is also no break in the brickwork on the stradella facade until it reaches the three bays built under Palladio. Zorzi (1965), p. 205 n. 6, published a notarial reference to Giangaleazzo's unidentified project, which involved ordering several thousand bricks, tiles, and a quantity of lime.

34. Cevese (1952), pp. 39–50, and (1973), p. 95, argued that Palladio's design for the palace as it appears in the *Quattro Libri* must date from 1542, but this has only been seconded by Forssman (1973), pp. 13–14. Cogent arguments against such an early intervention have been put forth by Berger (1978), pp. 219–22.

35. Ackerman (1966), pp. 94–98, first proposed that Palazzo Thiene was built after designs by Giulio

Romano; see also Lewis (1981), p. 90, no. 50, with reference to earlier literature. On Scamozzi, see Barbieri (1952); for Jones's marginalia, see Newman (1980).

36. In the courtyard, the northeast corner pier is of brick rendered to look like stone, but the remaining piers are of sandstone, up to the imposts of the arches.

37. On Palazzo Maccarani, see especially Frommel in Tafuri et al. (1989), pp. 117–26.

38. Puppi (1973), p. 254, proposed that Giangaleazzo Thiene may have obtained a project for a new palace from Giulio shortly after the latter's arrival in Mantua; the project lapsed and would have been revived by Marc'antonio Thiene in 1542. This seems less plausible than the alternative theory that the Thiene approached Giulio around 1542. Burns (1973-II), pp. 189–90 n. 25, suggested that the Thiene could have been instrumental in having Giulio invited to Vicenza for the Basilica loggias as a result of his involvement with their palace; these ideas are further developed by Burns in Tafuri et al. (1989), pp. 502–4. Forster and Tuttle (1973) follow a similar line of argument, stressing that only an architect conversant with Roman palace typologies could have planned Palazzo Thiene.

39. Two such examples are the designs for the frescoes of Verona Cathedral and the project for Landshut; see the observations by Oberhuber and Forster in Tafuri et al. (1989), pp. 135–41, and 512–15.

40. See chapters three, pp. 96–97, and five, pp. 149–56.

41. See chapter four, p. 113; and Forster and Tuttle (1973), pp. 108–18.

42. On Thiene's reconfirmed knighthood, see Zorzi (1965), p. 206.

43. See Forster and Tuttle (1973), p. 111; and Burns (1975), pp. 230–31, nos. 404–5.

44. See Burns in Tafuri et al. (1989), p. 502, who calculates that the palace would have occupied around 54 by 62 meters. The Vicentine foot equalled 35.7 cm or slightly more than one English foot; see Martini (1883), p. 823.

45. See Burns (1973-II), p. 181 and (1975), p. 38, no. 51; also Berger (1978), pp. 223–26. RIBA XVII/12 r-v contained early studies for Palazzo Porto, which must now be dated to the middle of the 1540s in view of the new documentary evidence produced by Battilotti (1981); see here pp. 59–60.

46. Zorzi (1965), pp. 209–10. Zorzi's assertion that Vittoria was also responsible for the earlier ceiling in Casa Civena is more debatable; see also Magagnato (1966), pp. 43–44; and Wolters (1968-I), pp. 32–34, 46–49.

47. See especially Wolters (1968-I), pp. 49–51, and (1968-II); Magagnato (1968); Marinelli in Marini (1980), pp. 187–202; and Boucher (1994).

48. "And once he [the visitor] has entered, let him be unsure whether it would be more pleasurable to stay where he is or to venture further, enticed by its gaiety and splendor. Let him pass from quadrangular *areae* [i.e., spaces] to round ones, and from round ones back to quadrangular ones, and then on to those that are neither completely round nor rectilinear" (*De re*, IX, ii); see Alberti (1988), p. 296; Palladio (1570), I, xxiii–xxiv, pp. 53–54; and the notes in the edition by Magagnato and Marini (1980), pp. 434–36, with further references to Alberti.

49. See Wolters (1968-I), pp. 46–47. Adriano Thiene died in France and Ottavio, the son of Marc'antonio, served Henry II as a soldier during the 1550s; a cousin named Ludovico had previously served as a *condottiere* for Francis I. On these connections see Marzari (1591), pp. 178, 195–96.

50. See Rumor (1912), pp. 16, 31.

51. See especially Cevese (1973), pp. 96–99.

52. See Battilotti (1980), pp. 47–49. The bird's-eye view of Vicenza of 1581 errs in showing too many properties between the courtyard of Palazzo Thiene and the corso.

53. In the *estimo* of 1563–64, the palace earned an unusually glowing account as "La più bella et adornata che sia in la magnifica città de Vicenza"; cf. Battilotti (1980), p. 49 n. 41–42.

54. See da Schio, *ad vocem*; also Zorzi (1965), p. 190; and Puppi (1973), pp. 277–81.

55. See especially Morresi (1988).

56. Magrini (1845), p. 295; and Battilotti (1981), pp. 41–43.

57. The phrase reads: "in modo et forma è la fazada facta al presente"; cf. Battilotti (1981), p. 44.

58. Some notable examples of churches without facades are Santi Giovanni e Paolo in Venice and San Lorenzo in Florence. With San Giorgio Maggiore and the Redentore, the facades were built last, just as

occurred with Palazzo da Schio in Vicenza, for which Palladio provided a facade sometime before May 1561 but after the house had been rebuilt; see Battilotti (1977), pp. 232–33.

59. Burns (1973-I), pp. 147–48; and Berger (1978), pp. 177–80. RIBA XVII/9v is not reproduced here but is so by Berger (1984), p. 21, fig. 1. Cevese (1973), p. 103, has expressed some reserve on the connection between the drawings and the palace. Lewis (1981), pp. 110–12, no. 64, has proposed that RIBA XV/1 is an alternative project for Palazzo Porto, but the area does not correspond with that of the palace and has been rejected by Battilotti (1981), p. 43 n. 22, and Barbieri (1987), p. 73.

60. See Berger (1978), p. 180, and (1984), pp. 22–24; also Puppi (1988), p. 90.

61. Forssman (1973-I), pp. 23–33; Puppi (1973), pp. 280–81; Burns (1975), pp. 232–34, nos. 413–16; Berger (1978), pp. 174–76; and Lewis (1981), pp. 112–16, nos. 65–66.

62. Vitruvius, III, v, 3.

63. Forssman (1973-I), pp. 36–38.

64. Following the measurements in the *Quattro Libri* woodcuts, the height of the ground floor of Palazzo Thiene is 24½ Vicentine feet and the *piano nobile* is 24 feet; the respective measurements for Palazzo Porto are 23½ versus 19¼. In other palaces, the heights of the two main floors tend to be more balanced. See also Cevese (1973), p. 102.

65. On the tetrastyle atrium, see Vitruvius, VI, iii, 8. See also Palladio (1570), II, viii, p. 36; and Prinz (1969). For more recent discussion, see Burns (1975), p. 231, no. 406; and Magagnato and Marini (1980), pp. 464–65.

66. Forssman (1973-I), pp. 39–40; also Barbieri (1987), pp. 73–74.

67. Zorzi (1965), p. 190 n. 7. Pignatti (1976), I, pp. 106–7, nos. 20–21, dates both paintings around 1551; see also Rearick (1990). Puppi (1990) wants to see Veronese's work in Palazzo Porto as dating from the late 1540s, shortly after the completion of the palace. It has largely disappeared; see Forssman (1973), pp. 40, 61–67.

68. Zorzi (1965), pp. 190–91 and (1969), p. 230; see also Puppi (1973), p. 400.

69. Zorzi (1965), p. 203, no. 2. See the useful discussions in Magrini (1855); Cevese (1973), pp. 100–2; Puppi (1973), pp. 281–86; Burns (1975),

pp. 38–39, nos. 53–54, and 216–17, no. 384; and Barbieri (1987), pp. 74–76.

70. Battilotti (1980), p. 24; and Magrini (1855), pp. 57–58. Lewis (1981), pp. 158–59, no. 91, has argued that the projects for Palazzo Chiericati should date from the division of property in 1546, but this is probably too early by a couple of years. The palace's design is generally assigned to 1550, which may be slightly later than was the case. See, however, Ackerman (1984), p. 213 n. 2.

71. The surviving documents have been published by Zorzi (1965), pp. 203–4. See also Burns (1991), pp. 211–13.

72. Ackerman (1984), pp. 214–15, sees the petition of 1551 as establishing a chronological break between drawings like the Worcester College HT 93 and Burlington-Devonshire VIII/11, on the one hand, and RIBA XVII/5 and 8, on the other. It would seem more likely that no great gap separated the production of all the drawings, which the petition of 1551 suggests were already prepared. Moreover, Chiericati's contracts with the masons actually predate the petition to the council by one month, which would imply that permission to build was largely a formality.

73. See Burns (1975), p. 40, nos. 56–58; Berger (1978), pp. 170–74; Lewis (1981), pp. 158–62, nos. 91–93; and Ackerman (1984).

74. On Palazzo Piovene, see Puppi (1973), pp. 388–89; for the Teatro Olimpico, see chapter nine.

75. See the excellent analysis in Ackerman (1966), pp. 164–66.

76. See chapter five, pp. 139–41; and Burns (1975), p. 195, no. 349.

77. Franco (1958), pp. 232–33; Spielmann (1966), pp. 91–92; and Puppi (1973), p. 286. On the similarities between Palazzo Chiericati and the Villa Rotonda, see Pée (1941), pp. 56–57 n. 40.

78. Bruschi (1977), p. 116; and Heydenreich and Lotz (1974), pp. 292–93.

79. Barbieri (1987), especially pp. 74–75.

80. Zorzi (1965), pp. 198–200; Wolters (1968-I), pp. 49–50; Conforti Calcagni in Marini (1980), pp. 180–81.

81. Bertotti Scamozzi (1761), p. 83. Vicenza's deceptively grand appearance was also commented upon by Bertotti Scamozzi's contemporary, Charles de Brosses; see Franzina (1980), pp. 132, 151–52.

CHAPTER III. EARLY VILLAS AND VILLEGGIATURA

1. Priuli (1938), pp. 29–45; for recent discussions of this celebrated passage, see Ventura (1969), pp. 65–66; Gilbert (1973), pp. 274–77; and Ackerman (1982), pp. 45–46, and (1990-I), pp. 92–93.

2. Priuli (1938), pp. 49–51.

3. Stella (1958); Beltrami (1961); Villani (1966); Woolf (1968); and Corazzol (1979).

4. Quoted by Stella (1958), pp. 51, 70–71; on Cornaro, see also Fiocco (1965) and Puppi et al. (1980).

5. Woolf (1968), p. 182.

6. For Villani, see Ackerman (1990-I), p. 64. For the observation of Marco Foscari, Venetian ambassador in Florence in 1527, see Segarizzi (1912–16), III-1, p. 19: "Che vanno per il mondo e, avendo guadagnato ducati 20,000, ne spendono 10,000 in un palazzo di fuori della città; e l'uno in questo va seguendo l'orma dell'altro." I owe my knowledge of this comment to the good offices of Kate Lowe.

7. For the parallel investment of Genoese in Naples, see Villani (1966), pp. 473–76. On the phenomenon of land investment on a Mediterranean scale, see Braudel (1972), I, pp. 418–27. Roberto di Spilimbergo is quoted by Ventura (1969), p. 66 n. 4.

8. Vespasiano (1963), pp. 224–25. On Lorenzo de' Medici's interest in agriculture, see Foster (1978), I, pp. 1–34.

9. Vasari (1878–85), II, pp. 442–43. Lillie (1987), pp. 404–5 n. 124, cites an inventory of 1492 that refers to room in the basement of the villa for the storage of agricultural implements; as she argues, this implies some agricultural activity at Fiesole. The view that the villa at Fiesole was built without any agricultural purpose has recently been restated by Ackerman (1990-I), p. 78. On Paolo Morosini's visit to Fiesole in 1475, see Foster (1978), I, p. 31.

10. See especially Rupprecht (1966); Heydenreich (1969); Ackerman (1990-I), pp. 108–33; and Holberton (1990), pp. 103–78.

11. Rupprecht (1966), p. 232; Morresi (1988), p. 7.

12. Hale (1961), p. 139.

13. Sereni (1961), pp. 199, 230.

14. This theory was first expounded by Swoboda (1924), pp. 77–132; and developed notably by Ackerman (1963) and (1967). It was met with skepticism by Rosci (1968) and (1969); Biermann (1969), pp. 36–37; and Forster (1974). The case against it has been elegantly summarized by Schulz (1982), p. 294: "The facade system of the Venetian buildings is usually considered unique to that city and is always traced to late-antique and Byzantine sources, a theory comforted by the byzantinism of their details. This is not the place to enter into the difficulties of the proposed filiation (late-antique or Byzantine buildings quite like the Venetian ones have not been found, and the avenues by which their putative influence reached Venice remain unexplained). But the Podestà's Residence of Parma shows that the system was more widely known." Ackerman has modified his original argument in (1982), pp. 67–68 n. 22, and (1990-I).

15. Rupprecht (1964) and Kubelik (1977). The recent tendency to see villas as exclusively indebted to vernacular architecture or the creative powers of great architects misses the point that the two are not mutually exclusive: both contributed to the development of the villa as a special architectural genre.

16. On the *barco* of Caterina Cornaro, see Kubelik (1977), pp. 41, 51–52. For the Villa Giustinian and Villa Porto Colleoni, see Kolb Lewis (1977) and Morresi (1988) respectively.

17. For recent surveys of Roman villas, see McKay (1975), especially pp. 100–35; Mielsch (1987); and Ackerman (1990-I), pp. 35–61.

18. The context of Palladio's remarks is a discussion of architectural decorum, but the interchangeability of his ideas on town and country houses is evident in the plans and elevations in the *Quattro Libri*. See Palladio (1570), II, cap. xiii, p. 46. See also Ventura (1969), p. 68; and Burns (1975), p. 180.

19. See especially Dalla Pozza (1943–63), pp. 120–24; Burns (1975), p. 166; and Cosgrove (1989).

20. Dalla Pozza (1943–63), pp. 121, 124; also Cevese (1965), pp. 307–8; and Ackerman (1967), p. 52.

21. For the portal of Santa Maria dei Servi, see Puppi (1973), p. 237; on the portal of the Domus Comestabilis, see Burns (1975), p. 19, no. 13. The Godi brothers again turned to the Pedemuro workshop for the construction of their father's mortuary chapel in the church of San Michele between 1546 and 1550; see Battilotti (1980), pp. 217–18 n. 180.

22. Bertotti Scamozzi (1796), II, p. 29 n. c. See also Zorzi (1969), p. 24. For a résumé of earlier literature on the villa, see Puppi (1973), pp. 238–40.

23. Palladio (1570), II, cap. xv, p. 65. See also Barbieri (1970), pp. 64–66; and Berger (1978), pp. 194–99.

24. Serlio (1619), III, p. 81r. Bertotti Scamozzi (1796), II, p. 31, first drew attention to the citation from Serlio.

25. See especially Cevese (1971), pp. 83–85.

26. Fiocco (1965), p. 167. On Gualtiero, see Sartori (1976), pp. 78–79; for his collaboration with Sustris at the Villa dei Vescovi, see Ballarin (1968). The frescoes have also been the subject of an analysis by Cosgrove (1989).

27. Bertotti Scamozzi (1796), II, p. 30 n. e. Restoration work in the early 1960s uncovered traces of a thermal window in the garden facade which was sacrificed for Zelotti's ambitious programme of frescoes; see Cevese (1965).

28. For the wellhead, see Burns (1979), p. 21, figs. 17, 21.

29. Bertotti Scamozzi (1796), II, p. 30: "Non si può negare che questa Fabbrica, il di cui merito maggiore e la robustezza, abbia del grandioso."

30. Dalla Pozza (1964–65), p. 233: "Item ho a Vigardolo una casa da lavoratori coperta de copo cum tegola una teza de dodici cassi de paia et uno principio di altra casa." The villa is now generally accepted as Palladio's, although Cevese (1971), II, pp. 506–7, and (1973), pp. 51–53, demurred; see, however, Puppi (1973), pp. 245–47; Burns (1975), p. 182, nos. 320–21; Lewis (1981), pp. 78–80, no. 44; and Holberton (1990), pp. 212–14.

31. On the Serlian arch in Palladio's work, see Wilinski (1968).

32. Dalla Pozza (1964–65), pp. 233–34. The date of 1562 is inscribed over the rear entrance.

33. Shearman (1968), p. 400; and Pagliara in Frommel et al. (1984), p. 417.

34. The early history of the villa has been reconstructed by Dalla Pozza (1943–63), pp. 106–18; see also Puppi (1973), pp. 250–51; and Burns (1975), pp. 182–85, nos. 323–25.

35. Zaupa (1990), pp. 21–22, has discovered new documents that show the acquisition of land at Bertesina between 1533 and 1534. He found, too, that Palladio was present as a witness to an act in Gazzotti's Vicentine house in December 1534 and again as a witness to a notarial in 1547. Zaupa suggests that the construction of the villa could date

from 1534 although in view of the preexisting buildings on the site such an early date still seems less likely than the conventional dating of the early 1540s.

36. Berger (1978), pp. 66–68, surprisingly rejects the connection; but see Lewis (1981), p. 76, no. 42.

37. See Pane (1961), pp. 108–9; Ackerman (1966), p. 43; Burns (1975), p. 182, no. 322; Berger (1978), pp. 79–84; Lewis (1981), pp. 77–78, no. 43 (as for Vigardolo). On these drawings in general, see Forssman (1969); and Barbieri (1970).

38. Puppi (1973), pp. 254–57; Burns (1975), pp. 185–88, nos. 327–32; Berger (1978), pp. 94–102; and Lewis (1981), pp. 81–87, nos. 45–48. Cevese (1973), p. 56, reserved judgment on the relationship of the drawings to the villa.

39. For the earlier villa, see Kubelik in Burns (1975), p. 187, no. 328.

40. For the Temple of the Sibyl at Tivoli, see Palladio (1570), IV, cap. xxiii, p. 94.

41. See especially Dalla Pozza (1964–65), pp. 203–16.

42. Ibid., p. 206.

43. See Magrini (1845), p. 79, for a lost inscription of 1544 inside the villa. See also Dalla Pozza (1964–65), p. 210; Pereswet Soltan (1978); and Lewis (1981), pp. 86–87.

44. See Burns (1975), pp. 30–31, no. 34; and here chapter one, p. 34, and chapter four.

45. Palladio (1570), I, xxiii, pp. 53–54. In modern times, the significance of Palladio's approach to proportion was given an influential elaboration by Wittkower (1962), pp. 129–32; see also the note in Magagnato and Marini (1980), pp. 434–35, and the discussion here in chapter eight.

46. The arcade was noted by Vasari, VII, p. 528; see also Puppi (1973), pp. 341–42, with further references.

47. For a résumé of earlier opinions on the villa's dating, see Magagnato and Marini (1980), p. 485 n. 32–34. See also the exhaustive stylistic analysis in Berger (1978), pp. 116–36; and, more recently, Holberton (1990), pp. 41–43. The start of construction is generally dated to 1545–46, prior to Adriano Thiene's departure for France around 1547; on Adriano Thiene's dabbling in heresy, see Puppi (1973), p. 262.

48. Harris (1971); Burns (1975), p. 191, no. 338; and Lewis (1981), pp. 94–96, no. 54.

49. See the recent archival study of the property made by Cavaggioni and Del Zoppo (1989–90); also Holberton (1990), p. 54; and Carunchio (1990). On its appearance after restoration, see Haslam (1994).

50. On the various datings of these villas see Cevese (1971), I, pp. 133–47; Puppi (1973), pp. 247–48, 259–61, 373–75; Burns (1975), pp. 190–91 and 202–3, nos. 336–37 and 361. Burns makes a plausible case for a late dating of the Villa Forni, which is generally held to be an early work; see, however, Ackerman (1967), pp. 59–60; and Lewis (1981), p. 105, no. 60.

51. The lines of rustication were illustrated by Bertotti Scamozzi (1796), II, p. 45 and pl. xxiv, but its authenticity was questioned by Zorzi (1969), p. 73. Despite Zorzi's reservations, rustication must have been intended by Palladio, as Cevese (1965) argued.

52. See Dalla Pozza (1965), p. 56; and Puppi (1973), pp. 274–77. For the fifteenth-century villa, see Cevese (1971), II, p. 535.

53. See Burns (1975), p. 193, no. 343; and Berger (1978), pp. 183–84. RIBA XVI/3 was formally associated with the Villa Poiana but was shown to be a project for Bartolomeo Pagliarino at Lanzi; see Burns (1979), p. 16; and Lewis (1981), pp. 102–3, no. 58.

54. Reproduced in Lewis (1981), p. 77, fig. 19.

55. See the fine appreciation of the interior by Cevese (1971), I, pp. 112–13.

56. Burns (1975), p. 52; Holberton (1990), pp. 56–57.

57. In 1886, Giuseppe Pasqualigo referred to the dispersal of statuary from the palace and garden of the villa and to the destruction of "il brolo e la pescheria e il giardino"; see Zorzi (1969), p. 87 n. 26. On Pozzoserrato's painting, see Burns (1975), p. 203, no. 363. On gardens in Palladian villas, see especially Holberton (1990), pp. 143–55.

58. As Battilotti (1980), p. 75, points out, the reference is to the "tezza . . . fata alla palladia," meaning the roof with a temple pediment. The villa in question is called Tornieri dal Lago and generally given to a follower of Palladio; see Cevese (1971), II, pp. 668–69.

Chapter IV. The Basilica

1. The most comprehensive treatment of the Basilica is that by Barbieri (1968). Among earlier contributions, those by Dalla Pozza (1943), pp. 95–142; and Zorzi (1965), pp. 43–75, 303–46, are especially noteworthy. See also the useful résumé in Puppi (1973), pp. 266–71; and Burns (1975), pp. 27–31, nos. 30–37. For a discussion of the similar urbanistic developments in Brescia, see Hemsoll (1992–93).

2. Barbieri (1968), p. 13.

3. On the communes, see especially Waley (1978).

4. Barbieri (1968), p. 12.

5. Ibid., p. 24.

6. Ibid., pp. 24–25.

7. Mantese (1964), p. 487.

8. For the late fifteenth-century appearance of the building, see Barbieri (1968), pp. 28–29.

9. Ibid., pp. 37–38.

10. Ibid., pp. 39–40.

11. See especially Burns (1975), pp. 29–30, no. 33; also Forster and Tuttle (1973).

12. Tafuri et al. (1989), pp. 538–47.

13. Lotz (1977), pp. 74–116.

14. See chapter one, pp. 23–27.

15. Burns (1975), p. 31, nos. 35–36; and Lewis (1981), pp. 106–9, nos. 61–62. Zorzi (1965), p. 46, interpreted RIBA XIII/9 as the design submitted in 1546, but the sheet bears the characteristics of a drawing of the early 1540s and must predate the final solution; cf. Burns in Marini (1980), p. 118. Barbieri (1968), p. 59, suggested that RIBA X/15 was a preliminary study, but it is actually connected with the loggias of Brescia; see Burns (1973-I), p. 145.

16. Burns (1975), p. 31; Lewis (1981), pp. 107, 109. On the Palazzo Roncali in Rovigo, see Puppi (1986), pp. 160–61.

17. Serlio (1619), IV, p. 154r.

18. See Lotz (1977), p. 146. Palladio's praise of the Library as "il più ricco, et ornamentato edificio, che fosse stato fatto da gli Antichi in qua" is well known; see Palladio (1570), I, p. 5.

19. See Zorzi (1949), figs. 28, 39, 60–72. On the Arco dei Gavi, see Tosi in Marini (1980), pp.

34–48. For the Arch of the Sergii, see Spielmann (1966), pp. 47, 90, 174–75. On the influence of the Arch of the Sergii in Venetian Renaissance architecture, see Lieberman (1982), p. 11 and pl. 70.

20. Palladio (1570), III, xx, p. 42.

21. Burns (1975), pp. 27–28, no. 30; see also Zorzi (1965), pp. 46–47, on Palladio's supporters.

22. Zorzi (1965), pp. 308, 313.

23. See chapters two and nine; also Burns (1991), pp. 191–208.

24. Barbieri (1968), pp. 76–77.

25. See especially Dalla Pozza (1943), pp. 125–26.

26. Ibid., pp. 129–30; and Barbieri (1968), p. 77.

27. Zorzi (1965), p. 58, doc. 11.

28. Ibid., pp. 309–12.

29. Ibid., p. 310.

30. Howard (1975), pp. 20–21; and Boucher (1991), I, pp. 43–44.

31. Zorzi (1965), pp. 310–11.

32. Ibid., p. 303.

33. Monza (1888), p. 10.

34. Dalla Pozza (1943), p. 137.

35. Barbieri (1968), p. 80; Burns (1975), p. 31; and Lewis (1981), p. 110.

36. Dalla Pozza (1943), pp. 137–38 n. 3.

37. Ibid., p. 139; Pane (1961), p. 30; and Barbieri (1968), p. 81. Both Dalla Pozza and Pane give twelve thousand ducats as the sum disbursed by Vicenza while Barbieri has it as thirty-six thousand.

38. Zorzi (1965), p. 64, doc. 30.

39. Ibid., pp. 64–65, doc. 31.

40. Ibid., pp. 68–70, docs. 42–43.

41. Barbieri (1968), pp. 104–10, ascribes the majority to the Albanese, a local family of sculptors, and six, less plausibly, to Camillo Mariani.

42. Zorzi (1965), pp. 71–72, docs. 47, 49. The reference to inflationary pressures on costs will have a familiar ring to modern ears: "Et perché per la varietà di tempi et per esser cresciute le spese così della robbe come delle condutture et altro" (p. 71, doc. 47).

43. Barbieri (1968), pp. 81–82.

44. Palladio (1570), III, xx, p. 42.

45. Barbieri (1968), p. 82.

CHAPTER V. MATURE VILLAS

1. Doni (1555), p. 155; and Barbaro (1556), p. 179. See also the recent observations of Puppi (1988), pp. 59–69.

2. Zorzi (1965), p. 137.

3. Fiocco (1965); Rupprecht (1966), especially p. 241; Bentmann and Müller (1981); Muraro (1987); and Huse and Wolters (1990), pp. 115–28.

4. Rupprecht (1966), pp. 225–30, 235–41; and Ackerman (1990), pp. 108–33.

5. Bellocchi (1969); and Barocchi (1977), III, pp. 3,321–3,357. Doni began work on his essay in Rome in 1545 but revised it in the 1550s or 1560s. See also Holberton (1990), pp. 170–72.

6. "Et son fatte tanto belle, ricche, et comode, la fuori, che non v' è differenza, da Palagi e luoghi di dentro"; cf. Bellocchi (1969), p. 26. See also Rupprecht (1966), p. 240; and Wolters (1969), p. 84.

7. Palladio (1570), II, i, xii–xiii, pp. 3, 45–46.

8. See chapter two, pp. 65–71.

9. Zorzi (1965), pp. 218–24, placed it among Palladio's palaces. See, however, Puppi (1973), pp. 288–89; Burns (1975), p. 193, no. 345; and Kolb (1984).

10. Zorzi (1965), pp. 222–23; Boucher (1979), p. 279 n. 9; and Puppi (1988), pp. 109–11, 121–22.

11. See chapter three, pp. 100–105.

12. It is commonly referred to as "giallo della soprintendenza" in Italy.

13. Chapter two, pp. 59–65, and here p. 139.

14. Chapter two, pp. 55–56.

15. Palladio (1570), II, viii, pp. 36–37.

16. See chapter two; also Shearman (1968).

17. Palladio (1570), I, xxiii, pp. 53–54.

18. See Bassi (1978); and Mielke (1980).

19. Ackerman (1967), p. 58; Burns (1975), p. 193; and Magagnato and Marini (1980), pp. 476–77, nos. 28, 30 for a résumé of opinions.

20. Chapter three, pp. 89–90; also chapter eight.

21. Lewis (1972); Puppi (1973), pp. 292–95; and Burns (1975) p. 194.

22. Kolb (1977) attributes the villa to Tullio Lombardo; see also Huse and Wolters (1990), pp. 115–18.

23. Palladio also made the Doric order of the *salone* of the Villa Pisani at Montagnana one-fifth thinner than the Doric columns of the facade; see Burns (1975), p. 193, no. 345. In both cases, it was a visual adjustment, and in the Villa Cornaro, it was analogous to Vitruvius's recommendation that the upper order of the loggia on a forum should be one-quarter shorter than that below (V, i, 3). Vitruvius draws a comparison with trees, which taper as they grow, an analogy employed by Serlio (1619), IV, p. 104; and also by Palladio. See Burns (1975), pp. 206–7; and Puppi (1988), pp. 153–59, especially 158.

24. For a résumé of documents, see Lewis (1972).

25. Leithe-Jasper (1975); see also Rigoni (1970), p. 307 n. 6.

26. See chapter six.

27. "I Venetiani si dilettano molto ne le sue fabriche d'opera Corinthia"; cf. Serlio (1619), IV, p. 55ᵛ. See Forssman (1961), p. 34; and Burns (1975), p. 227.

28. The eustyle has 2¼ diameters between the columns, 3 diameters between the central ones; it is particularly praised by Vitruvius (III, iii, 1–6). See Burns (1975), p. 227; and here chapter eight.

29. "I capitelli che sono negli angoli del portico. . . fanno fronte da due parti, il che non so d'aver veduto altrove e, perche me è paruta bella e graziosa invenzione, io me ne son servito in molte fabriche." Palladio (1570), IV, xiii, p. 48; and chapter eight, p. 257.

30. This treatment of the ceiling beams corresponds to the "Aggionta del Palladio;" see Burns (1975), pp. 108–10; and Puppi (1988), pp. 68, 101.

31. Executed by Camillo Mariani between 1587 and 1597, they represent Caterina Cornaro, her husband James II Lusignan, Doge Marco Cornaro, Giorgio Cornaro, Girolamo Cornaro, and Cardinal Andrea Cornaro. See Zorzi (1969), pp. 194–95.

32. Palladio (1570), II, xiii, p. 46. On the fluidity of Palladio's building types, see Zorzi (1969), pp. 182–201; Cevese (1973), p. 69; and Burns (1975), p. 180.

33. Zorzi (1965), pp. 224–27; Venditti (1971); Cevese (1973), pp. 106–7; Puppi (1973), pp. 306–7; and Burns (1975), p. 235, no. 417.

34. Zorzi (1965), pp. 81–82; and Burns (1975), pp. 246–47, no. 436.

35. Muttoni (1740), I, pp. 6–7, believed the single wing to be an error in the woodcut though a similar wing appears in preliminary designs for the Villa Pisani at Bagnolo; cf. chapter three, p. 89, note 38.

36. Rizzi (1967), p. 95, pls. 5, 6.

37. Howard (1975), pp. 38–47.

38. Palladio (1570), II, xvii, p. 77; cf. also Puppi (1973), pp. 349–50.

39. Puppi (1973), pp. 296–97; and Burns (1975), p. 195, nos. 349–50.

40. Puppi (1972), pp. 13–25, figures iv, v.

41. Palladio (1570), II, xiv, p. 48. See also Forssman (1965), pp. 66–69; and Burns (1975), pp. 237–38.

42. In this case, the arms are those of the Mocenigo, who subsequently owned the villa. A Badoer coat of arms is frescoed on the entrance wall under the portico.

43. See especially Ackerman (1983), pp. 20–22.

44. Palladio (1570), I, xiv, pp. 16–19; and here, chapter eight.

45. Bellocchi (1969), pp. 34–35. In one manuscript, Doni recommends Palladio as architect of the *villa civile.*

46. This is the central theme of the stimulating if partial account by Bentmann and Mueller (1981).

47. See Burns in Frommel et al. (1984), pp. 393–94. Palladio employed the same device in his early palace designs; see chapter two, pp. 61–62.

48. Giallo Fiorentino, not to be confused with the miniaturist Jacopo del Giallo, also collaborated with another member of Palladio's circle, Giuseppe Salviati, on the facade frescoes of Palazzo Loredan in Campo Santo Stefano in Venice; cf. Puppi (1972), pp. 68–86.

49. Palladio (1570), II, xvi, p. 69. Both Leoni and Ware translate *frontespizio* as frontispiece, which obscures the sense of Palladio's argument. For the context and his reference to Vitruvius (III, v, 12), it is clear that he had pediments in mind.

50. Vitruvius, II, i. See also Polacco (1965), p. 67 n. 36; Magagnato and Marini (1980), pp. 488–89,

nos. 10–11; Alberti (1988), pp. 298–301 (*De re* IX, iv); and Forssman (1965), pp. 52–53.

51. Barbaro (1556), p. 170; see also Forssman (1962), pp. 36–37. Palladio's argument has been criticized most forcefully by Wittkower (1962), p. 74: "His conclusion was founded on two fallacies, an erroneous theory of the development of society, and an erroneous theory of the genesis of architecture." See also Ackerman (1966), pp. 61–65.

52. Swoboda (1924), pp. 145–46, 194–99.

53. RIBA IX/13ᵛ, and X, 16. See Spielmann (1966), pp. 53–53; and Burns (1975), pp. 89–90, nos. 164–65.

54. Ackerman (1990), pp. 78–86; and Huse and Wolters (1990), pp. 115–18.

55. Alberti (1988), pp. 155–57 (*De re* VI, ii); cf. Wittkower (1962), p. 33.

56. Puppi (1973), pp. 318–20; Burns (1975), pp. 83–84; and Muraro (1980).

57. On Repeta's heretical leanings and his controversial life, see Fogolari (1935); Zorzi (1969), pp. 119–29; and Tafuri (1969), pp. 128–29.

58. Palladio (1570), II, xv, p. 61.

59. Palladio mentioned particular rooms dedicated to continence and justice while in his book Agostino Gallo praised continence and temperance as the most important virtues of villa life; cf. Rupprecht (1966), p. 238.

60. Palladio (1570), II, xiv, p. 51. See Ackerman (1967), p. 58; Cevese (1973), p. 78; and Puppi (1973), pp. 314–18. The villa is generally dated in the late 1550s though Lewis has proposed an earlier dating on the basis of a sketch by Palladio, which he assigned to the late 1540s. As Huse observed, the sketch bears only a superficial resemblance to Maser and appears to have been planned for a level site, not an inclined slope as at Maser. See, however, Lewis (1973), fig. 193; and Huse (1974), p. 119 n. 6.

61. See especially Huse (1974). Among other recent assessments of the Villa Barbaro, see also Forssman (1965), p. 79; Ackerman (1966), p. 40 and (1967), pp. 1–3; Burns (1975), p. 196; and Bentmann and Mueller (1981), p. 36.

62. See the reservations expressed by Huse (1974); and also Burns (1975), p. 196.

63. See chapter two, pp. 50–54.

64. Palladio's role in the lateral facade of the Loggia del Capitaniato has been questioned by Wolters (1968-I), pp. 83–86, (1968-II), pp. 264–66.

65. Vasari, VII, p. 530.

66. On these buildings, see Coffin (1979), pp. 202–14, 267–79, and 311–40, with further references.

67. In the recent literature, see especially Forssman (1967); Ackerman (1967), p. 58; Wolters (1968-II), pp. 262–63; Cevese (1973), p. 81; Huse (1974), pp. 110–11; Magagnato and Marini (1980), p. lx; and Lewis (1981).

68. Burger (1909), p. 108. Doni has the courtyard of the *podere di spasso* decorated with landscapes; cf. Bellocchi (1969), p. 46. Lomazzo recommends for garden walls: "Prospettive diverse, le quali facciano allungare i portici e le pareti del giardino, et oltre alle colonne ne gli intervalli, paesi cosi accompagnati che paiano seguire il naturale" (*Trattato della pittura*, VI, cap. xxvi); cf. Ciardi (1973–74), II, p. 301. See also Huse (1974), pp. 116–118.

69. Wolters (1968-II), pp. 262–64; Zorzi (1969), p. 174; Puppi (1973), p. 316; Boucher (1979), p. 280 n. 18; Magagnato and Marini (1980), p. lx.

70. Serlio (1619), IV, fol. 191ᵛ; cf. Wolters (1968-II), pp. 255, 266; and Boucher (1994).

71. Fiocco (1965), p. 167.

72. Palladio (1570), I, xxii, p. 53.

73. Their biographical sketches appear after the life of Sanmicheli in Vasari, VI, pp. 366–75. See also the important study by Magagnato (1968); and Schweikhart (1971); see also chapter two, pp. 55–58, 65.

74. Zorzi (1965), pp. 194–95, 198–99 and 208–10.

75. Wolters (1968-I), pp. 35, 49; and Boucher (1991), I, pp. 153–55.

76. See chapter three, p. 105.

77. A more active role in the decoration of his villas has been assigned to Palladio by Forssman (1967); Puppi (1972), pp. 89–90; Magagnato (1980), pp. lviii–lxi; and Lewis (1981).

78. Ackerman (1967), pp. 44–46; Bordignon Favero (1970); Puppi (1973), pp. 352–53; Burns (1975), p. 197, no. 355; and Tessarolo (1991).

79. Puppi (1988), p. 94.

80. See especially Ackerman (1967), pp. 44–46.

81. Cevese (1973), pp. 81–82.

82. The proportions of the column are 1:8, which falls within Palladio's norm for the Doric, but the intercolumniation is close to the eustyle, which Palladio reserved for the Ionic order; cf. Forssman (1978), p. 81.

83. These doors are now closed.

84. See Summerson (1966), p. 43.

85. The frescoes are generally dated c. 1565; see Bordignon Favero (1970), pp. 35–51.

86. The name "Malcontenta" may have originated with the banishment of a woman of the Foscari family to the villa in the seventeenth century, but the name could equally well have arisen from the malarial nature of the site. On the villa, see Ackerman (1967), pp. 53–55; Puppi (1973), pp. 328–30; Forssman (1973); Cevese (1973), pp. 73–74; and Burns (1975), p. 197.

87. Zorzi (1969), p. 151.

88. This is recorded in the draft manuscript of the second book of the *Quattro Libri*; cf. Puppi (1988), p. 93.

89. RIBA XVI/20; cf. Burns (1975), p. 195, no. 350; and Lewis (1981), p. 152, no. 88.

90. See chapter three, pp. 88–89.

91. See chapter two, pp. 45–46; see also Zorzi (1965), pp. 183–85, figs. 145, 147–48; and Burns (1975), p. 185, no. 326 (RIBA XVII/15).

92. Zorzi (1969), p. 155. See also Spielmann (1966), pp. 45–46; and Burns (1973-I), p. 153; and Puppi (1989), p. 102, no. 12.

93. The Sansovinesque balustrades found on the staircase are a later addition out of keeping with Palladio's style and the lines of the staircases.

94. As Palladio notes, the rooms on the floor above the *piano nobile* form a mezzanine; cf. Palladio (1570), II, xiv, p. 50.

95. Cevese (1965), p. 305. This was rejected by Zorzi (1969), p. 155. Forssman (1973), p. 32, tended to agree with Cevese. See also Foscari (1978).

96. On the Carità, see chapter six pp. 172–76; for the Loggia del Capitaniato, see chapter nine, pp. 273–76.

97. Forssman (1973), p. 34, provides a series of measurements of various parts of the villa.

98. De Nolhac and Solerti (1890), p. 159.

99. See chapter nine, pp. 270–71, 290–98; on the Villa Trissino at Meledo, see Puppi (1973), pp. 385–88; and Burns (1975), pp. 251–52, no. 453.

CHAPTER VI. RELIGIOUS ARCHITECTURE

1. The contract is published in Zorzi (1966), pp. 28–30; for critical opinion in favor of and against, see Puppi (1973), pp. 321–23. Cogent arguments in favor of the facade's authenticity have been advanced by Timofiewitsch (1980); see also Huse and Wolters (1990), pp. 95–96.

2. See chapters five and eight.

3. See the detailed account by Bassi (1971).

4. Bassi (1971), pp. 23–24, figs. xvii–xix, reproduces a project from the 1550s, which she believed to be by Palladio. Her conclusions were accepted by Cevese (1973), p. 85. The drawing is not, however, in Palladio's hand and only vaguely anticipates his project; see Puppi (1973), p. 335.

5. Palladio (1570), II, vi, p. 29: "Ho cercato di assimigliar questa casa a quelle degli antichi, e però vi ho fatto l'atrio corinthio." See Vitruvius, VI, iii and vii; and Barbaro (1556), pp. 171–72.

6. See Biermann (1970); Burns (1974); and Bruschi (1977), pp. 59–69, 87–113.

7. Vasari, VII, p. 529.

8. Palladio (1570), I, xxviii, pp. 61–62. See also Bassi (1978); and Mielke (1980).

9. Huse and Wolters (1990), p. 95. On neoclassical criticism of this combination, see Bassi (1971), pp. 54–56.

10. Howard (1975), pp. 64–74, and (1977); also Foscari and Tafuri (1983).

11. Howard (1977), p. 54; and Ackerman (1980), 295–98.

12. See especially Foscari and Tafuri (1983), pp. 131–38. A drawing in Vicenza (D17) has been convincingly connected with the Grimani monument; see McTavish in Burns (1975), pp. 135–36, no. 245; and Puppi (1989), pp. 112–13, no. 50.

13. Boucher (1979); and Tafuri (1985), pp. 185–212.

14. Vasari, VII, pp. 529–30. Although there is no documented date of commencement, the year 1562 is generally accepted; see Puppi (1973), pp. 345–47.

15. Wittkower (1962), pp. 89–94; see also Vitruvius, V, i, 10. Wittkower's theory has been championed by Barbieri (1966); Puppi (1973), p. 347; Foscari and Tafuri (1983), p. 151; and Tavernor (1991), pp. 64–65. This interpretation has been challenged by Pane (1956); Timofiewitsch (1968), pp. 52–53; Gioseffi (1973); and Burns (1975), pp. 142–45. Wittkower (1969), p. 9, reaffirmed his theory in reply to Timofiewitsch. Ackerman (1966), pp. 138–48, and Cevese (1973), pp. 87–88, interpreted the facades more as spatial metaphors. Lewis (1981), p. 185, leaves the question open.

16. See Wittkower (1962), pl. 32b, for Cesariano's reconstruction. On this point, Barbaro's translation of Vitruvius does not refer to gables or pediments but rather to "un continuato colmo della basilica, & un'altro dal mezzo sopra l'Antitempio, & così la doppia dispositione delle volte, & de i colmi, l'una di fuori del tetto, et l'altra della Testuggine porge una veduta, che ha del buono"; Barbaro (1556), p. 134.

17. Barbieri (1966), p. 340, proposed the connection with San Francesco; this was endorsed by Gioseffi (1973); and Puppi (1973), p. 347. Burns (1975), p. 135, no. 244, argued that the formula was similar, but the incised scale on the sheet "excludes the possibility that this drawing is directly connected with either San Francesco della Vigna or San Giorgio"; see, however, the counterarguments put by Lewis (1981), pp. 184–85, no. 110. On San Petronio, see chapter nine.

18. See especially Burns (1973-I); Gioseffi (1973); and Fagiolo (1978). On Palladio's reconstruction of the Temple of Minerva in the Forum of Nerva, see Burns (1975), p. 248, no. 439; and Puppi (1989), pp. 100–110, no. 8.

19. Bertotti Scamozzi (1796), IV, pp. 27–28; Gallo (1955); and Puppi (1973), pp. 361–62.

20. Puppi (1973), pp. 358–61; also Burns (1975), p. 223, nos. 392–93.

21. On the Corinthian room, see Palladio (1570), II, ix, p. 38. Palladio mentions the use of wooden arches and cane vaulting at the Carità to reduce weight; see Burns (1975), p. 212, no. 377. On Codussi's San Giovanni Crisostomo, see Lieberman (1982), pp. 14–21, pls. 37–38; on the Roman influence on Palladio's churches, see Timofiewitsch (1968), 77–78.

22. Damerini (1956); Zorzi (1966), pp. 36–77, with documents; and Cooper (1990-I).

23. Damerini (1956), pp. 58–64. The plan in fig. 174 (Misc. Mappe 744) was discovered by Timofiewitsch (1963). His attribution to Tullio Lombardo was challenged by Isermeyer (1968), p. 57 n. 32, who ascribed it to Leopardi; this was accepted by Ackerman (1980), p. 301. The presence of the Buora as site architects may point to them as the authors.

24. Zorzi (1966), pp. 36–42; and Puppi (1973), pp. 338–39.

25. Burns in Marini (1980), pp. 109, 112; Puppi (1986), p. 76.

26. Vasari (1878–85), VII, p. 193.

27. Burns (1979), pp. 21–22, figs. 17–21.

28. Damerini (1956), pp. 59–60; Zorzi (1966), pp. 42–43, fig. 56.

29. Burns (1975), p. 142, no. 253; Ackerman (1980), pp. 298–302.

30. Zorzi (1966), p. 89; Puppi (1988), p. 124.

31. Zorzi (1966), p. 64, no. 19; and Burns (1975), p. 140, no. 252. Sansovino (1581), p. 81v, mentions that Palladio had to "rifar la chiesa su la forma fatto altre volte." The phrase is obscure although it may refer to the 1521–22 project and subsequent work about which we are not informed. See, however, Isermeyer (1968), p. 47; and Cooper (1990-I), p. 63.

32. Zorzi (1966), pp. 75–76, nos. 46–47.

33. Palladio (1570), IV, vi, p. 11. Spielmann (1966), pp. 30–31, observed that Palladio's reconstruction erred in giving the basilica twin apses where there was only one apse and a lateral entrance; see also chapter eight, p. 257. Frommel (1977), pp. 107–8, made a comparison with Peruzzi's plan for the cathedral of Carpi.

34. See the description of these ceremonies in Stringa (1604), pp. 341v–342r; also Cooper (1990-I).

35. Wittkower (1962), p. 98 n. 1; and Huse and Wolters (1990), p. 97.

36. Isermeyer (1972), p. 112, and (1980), pp. 263–64, sees the present choir as a late modification to the model of 1565, but his arguments are tendentious. Palladio (1570), IV, ii, pp. 6–7, lists the elements of a cruciform church, like San Giorgio, as nave, high altar, and choir; see also Cooper (1990-I), pp. 63, 107.

37. Cooper (1990-II) provides a sensible analysis of the debates surrounding the drawing and plans connected with the facade. Frommel (1977) attempts to reconstruct the early stages in the project and the portico facade, but his conclusions do not strike me as very plausible.

38. On Sant'Andrea, see Wittkower (1962), pp. 53–55; and Burns in Chambers and Martineau (1981), pp. 126–27, no. 36. On Palladio's report to Brescia, see Zorzi (1966), pp. 84–89; and Puppi (1988), pp. 123–25. Its general implications are discussed by Isermeyer (1972), pp. 114–16.

39. Forssman (1966), p. 60. On the Temple of Minerva at Assisi, see chapter eight, pp. 257–59.

40. The most comprehensive account of plague in Venice is in Mason Rinaldi and Zitelli (1979). On the historical background to the Redentore, see Timofiewitsch (1969), pp. 13–19.

41. Doge Alvise Mocenigo compared Venice with the Israelites suffering under the plague in his speech announcing the decision to erect a votive church; see Timofiewitsch (1969), pp. 65–66, no. 2. See also Niero in Mason Rinaldi and Zitelli (1979), p. 289.

42. Timofiewitsch (1969), p. 65, no. 1; Burns (1975), p. 143, no. 256.

43. Zorzi (1966), p. 125, 133, no. 7; and Timofiewitsch (1969), p. 17. See also the profile of Barbaro by Ventura (1964).

44. Palladio (1570), IV, ii, pp. 6–7; and Witt-kower (1962), pp. 3–32. The connection between these drawings and the first stage of the Redentore was definitely established by Burns (1975), pp. 146–47, no. 258. Lewis (1981), pp. 192–98, nos. 114–17, interprets fig. RIBA XIV/16 as for the church of the Zitelle although it was obviously designed for the same site as RIBA XIV/13.

45. Ackerman (1966), pp. 128–32; Timofiewitsch (1968), p. 108; and Burns (1975), p. 145, no. 256. On the Gesù and Cardinal Farnese, see Robertson (1992), pp. 187–88.

46. Burns (1975), p. 145, no. 256; on Genga's church, see Groblewski (1976). On the influence of Raphael's plan for Saint Peter's, see Timofiewitsch (1968), pp. 78–79.

47. Ackerman (1966), pp. 128–29; Timofiewitsch (1968), p. 78. Earlier examples of this type include the Badia at Fiesole, Sant'Andrea in Mantua, and Santa Maria di Monserrato in Rome.

48. On the Roman influence, see Timofiewitsch (1968), p. 77. Both Bramante's and Sanmicheli's churches derive from early Christian buildings like San Lorenzo in Milan, on which see Krautheimer (1975), pp. 82–86. For Santa Maria delle Grazie, see Bruschi (1977), pp. 52–57; for the Madonna di Campagna, see Puppi (1986), pp. 182–87.

49. Palladio (1570), IV, xxix, p. 118, singled out the base moldings of the temple for special praise.

50. See especially Basso (1968), pp. 107–14; also Lotz (1977) and Lewis (1981), pp. 193–94, no. 115.

51. Palladio (1570), IV, i, p. 5: "Se si fabricheranno Tempii fuori della città, all'hora le fronti loro si faranno, che guardino sopra le strade publiche, ò sopra i fiumi, se appresso quelli si fabricherà: acciochè i passaggieri possano vederli, e fare le lor salutationi, e riverenze dinanzi la fronte del Tempio." This follows Vitruvius IV, v, 2; see Lotz (1977-II), pp. 127–28.

52. On the Cappella Pellegrini, see Puppi (1986), pp. 33–37; on Sant'Andrea in via Flaminia, see Lewine (1973).

53. See Temanza (1778), p. 381; and Bertotti Scamozzi (1796), IV, pp. 20–24. On Almerico and the Villa Rotonda, see Mantese (1988), p. 40.

54. Puppi (1973), p. 435; and Burns (1975), pp. 244–45, no. 432.

55. The marble statues of the Redeemer, the Virgin, and Saint John the Baptist were added in the nineteenth century; see Basso (1968), p. 116; and Lotz (1977-II), p. 131.

56. Timofiewitsch (1968), pp. 92–93; and Boucher (1979), p. 279 n. 12. In a lengthy aside in his edition of Vitruvius, Barbaro attacks the practice of erecting private monuments in churches rather than in the piazza; see Barbaro (1556), p. 125.

57. Palladio may have furnished a model for the church, but construction only began in 1581; see especially Lunardon (1982).

CHAPTER VII. BRIDGES

1. See in particular the excellent catalog on this subject edited by Rigon (1980), as well as the more detailed account in Zorzi (1966).

2. On bridge technology, see Hamilton in Singer (1954–84), III, pp. 432–33; and Mainstone (1975), p. 154. On Leonardo's bridge designs, see Firpo (1963), pp. 78–80; and Pedretti (1979), pp. 170–71.

3. Zorzi (1966), pp. 189–91; and Puppi (1973), pp. 257–58. See also chapter five.

4. Zorzi (1966), pp. 204, 214.

5. Cf. Alberti (1988), pp. 107–13 (*De re* IV, vi); also Magagnato and Marini (1980), pp. 498–99 (III, iv–v).

6. *De bello gallico*, IV, 17; see also Masini in Rigon (1980), pp. 14–16.

7. Palladio (1575); see also the discussions in Hale (1977) and Puppi (1988), pp. 173–85.

8. On Fra Giocondo's edition of Caesar, see Fontana (1988), pp. 74–76. For the pre-Palladian reconstructions, see especially Masini in Rigon (1980), pp. 14–15.

9. Magagnato and Marini (1980), p. 499 n. 6.

10. Zorzi (1966), pp. 202–7; and Puppi (1973), pp. 327–28. Martino Dezin and Battista Marchesi executed the bridge after a design by Palladio.

11. Palladio (1570), III, vii–viii, pp. 15–18. See also Zorzi (1966), pp. 212–17; Puppi (1973), pp. 286–87; and Azzi Visentini in Rigon (1980), pp. 7–9.

12. Palladio (1570), II, xv, p. 63; cf. Puppi (1973), pp. 271–73.

13. See Gauthey (1809–16), II, pp. 53–54; and Mainstone (1975), pp. 56, 149–54. I am particularly grateful to Roland Mainstone for discussing structural aspects of Palladio's timber bridges with me and for his extensive comments on an earlier draft of this chapter.

14. See Zorzi (1966), p. 214; Zocconi (1972), pp. 280–81; and Mainstone (1975), especially pp. 150–51. Mainstone refers to the specific early Christian example of the basilica of Saint Catherine on Mount Sinai. David Hemsoll drew my attention to the Diribitorium of ancient Rome, which Palladio would probably have known by report. This structure stood on the Campus Martius and had larch tie beams one hundred feet long; they were the longest such roof posts known in antiquity, and Pliny the Elder reported that an unused larch beam from the Diribitorium was kept as a curiosity in the Saepta. After the great fire of 80 A.D., the Diribitorium stood unroofed; see Platner and Ashby (1929), p. 151.

15. Pane (1961), pp. 305–6.

16. Palladio (1570), III, viii, p. 16; and Magagnato and Marini (1980), p. 500 n. 2.

17. Zorzi (1966), p. 216, believed this design was an armature for a stone bridge, but that is not mentioned by Palladio in his account. Obviously, the resemblance suggests a derivation from timber centering.

18. Scamozzi (1615) II, viii, cap. xxiii, p. 347; see also Zorzi (1966), pp. 204, 214; and Puppi (1973), p. 286.

19. Magrini (1845), p. 130, indicates that the bridge lasted approximately fifty years. Temanza (1778), pp. 339–40, records having seen the stone piers of the Cismon bridge.

20. See especially Azzi Visentini in Rigon (1980), pp. 21–24, with reference to earlier literature.

21. A useful photographic survey of Alpine covered bridges is given by Horn (1980).

22. Zorzi (1966), p. 218; see also Rigon (1980), p. 25.

23. Zorzi (1966), pp. 204, 218–19; and Puppi (1973), p. 389.

24. Palladio (1570), III, ix, pp. 19–20; and especially Rigon (1980), pp. 25–28.

25. Palladio (1570), I, xiv, p. 16. Scamozzi (1615), II, pp. 54–55, mentions that the Tuscan order was especially suitable for bridges. See also Forssman (1961), pp. 51–52, 72–74; and Ackerman (1983).

26. Zorzi (1966), pp. 270–75.

27. Palladio (1570), III, xiv, pp. 28–29. The idea goes back to Temanza (1778), p. 331, and has been persuasively argued by Rigon (1980), pp. 27–28. Those who believe the plate to be for the Torri di Quartesolo bridge, rebuilt after the flood of 1559, include Puppi (1973), pp. 326–27; Burns (1975), pp. 214–15, no. 383; and Magagnato and Marini (1980), p. 505 n. 1. Zorzi (1966), p. 191, saw a similarity between the two projects and suggested that the Torri di Quartesolo project must have resembled that published in the *Quattro Libri*, although he noted that the measurements corresponded with the project for the Brenta at Bassano.

28. Palladio (1570), II, x–xi, pp. 20–23. See also Alberti (1988), p. 107 (*De re* IV, vi); and Azzi Visentini in Rigon (1980), pp. 10–13.

29. See especially Burns (1975), pp. 206–7, and here chapter eight, pp. 257–59.

30. Palladio was probably thinking of medieval bridges or even of more recent ones like the Ponte Alidosi at Castel del Rio near Imola, constructed by Andrea Furrieri in 1499. With a span of some eighty meters, the semicircular arch made the crossing almost a vertical ascent; cf. Pedretti (1979), p. 170. Palladio's reference to the strength and stability of the roundheaded arch may echo similar remarks in Raphael's letter to Leo X: see Golzio (1936), pp. 86–87.

31. Temanza (1778), p. 345, notes that the spurs were actually oblique to the former flow of the current, and Palladio may not have been able to see this.

32. Palladio (1570), III, xii and xv, pp. 24, 30. Both were destroyed at the end of the last century; see Magagnato and Marini (1980), pp. 503–4, 505, respectively.

33. The most recent and detailed account of Rialto comes in the excellent book by Calabi and Morachiello (1987); see also Cessi and Albert (1934); and Zorzi (1966), pp. 223–63.

34. See Calabi and Morachiello (1987), pp. 173–85.

35. Ibid., pp. 184–85.

36. Cicogna (1824–53), VI, p. 712; see also Calabi and Morachiello (1987), pp. 188–91.

37. Calabi and Morachiello (1987), pp. 190–91; and Fontana (1988), p. 52.

38. Calabi and Morachiello (1987), pp. 194–95.

39. Ibid., pp. 41–49.

40. Vasari, V, pp. 269–72; Puppi (1973), p. 299; Burns (1975), p. 125, no. 221; Calabi and Morachiello (1987), pp. 53–54; and Fontana (1988), pp. 77–80.

41. Lotz (1977), pp. 117–39; and Bruschi (1977), pp. 169–73. Fontana (1988), p. 79, noted that Filarete had earlier advised putting a church in the center of a rectangular forum, and Palladio's contemporary, Pietro Cattaneo, also proposed placing a church in honor of Saint Matthew in the center of a square reserved for commerce. See also Calabi and Morachiello (1987), p. 65.

42. Calabi and Morachiello (1987), pp. 57–65; also Calabi (1992–93).

43. Ibid., pp. 197–206.

44. Ibid., pp. 215–18.

45. Howard (1975), pp. 8–37; and Calabi and Morachiello (1987), pp. 142–59.

46. On the dating, see Zorzi (1966), p. 224. On the drawing, see Burns (1975), pp. 124–25, no. 221; Lewis (1981), p. 122, no. 70; Calabi and Morachiello (1987), pp. 221–22; and Puppi (1989), pp. 110–11, nos. 44–45.

47. See Puppi (1973), p. 303, with further references.

48. On the dimensions, see Burns (1975), pp. 124–25, no. 221; Morachiello (1983); and Calabi and Morachiello (1987), pp. 223–24 n. 22.

49. Cf. Magagnato and Marini (1980), p. 504 n. 4 (book III, chapter xiii).

50. On the Temple of Clitumnus, see here chapter five, and also the discussion in Puppi (1989), p. 102, no. 12.

51. For an accessible survey of the "myth of Venice" and Venetian ceremonial, see Muir (1981); for Sansovino's Loggetta, see Boucher (1991), I, pp. 73–88.

52. See especially Morachiello's analysis of the effect of Palladio's design on both sides of the bridge in Calabi and Morachiello (1987), pp. 226–27, figs. 79–80.

53. Morachiello remarks: "A Rialto o altrove Palladio non ignora il dato: semplicemente lo giudica e lo corregge. Lo giudica perché architetto in pieno possesso dei principi, infallibili perché fondati sull'universale empirico tratto dalla natura"; see Calabi and Morachiello (1987), p. 231. On the other projects mentioned, see chapter nine.

54. Palladio (1570), III, xiii, pp. 25–27. See Zorzi (1966), pp. 225–26; Puppi (1973), pp. 301–2; Burns (1975), pp. 125–26, no. 222; and Calabi and Morachiello (1987), pp. 229–32.

55. For San Giorgio, see chapter six. On the Mocenigo villa, see Puppi (1973), pp. 358–61; and also Lewis (1981), pp. 98–100 and 126–28, nos. 56–57 and 73, respectively.

56. See Burns (1975), p. 126, no. 223, and (1979), pp. 119–20 (D19 and 20). Burns's observations were followed by Lewis (1981), pp. 121–22, no. 70. See also Morachiello in Puppi and Romanelli (1985), pp. 62–64, nos. 25–26; and Puppi (1989), pp. 111–12, nos. 46–47. Burns did not indicate a date for either drawing, but Lewis wanted to place D19 to 1554 although seeing its greater affinity with the *Quattro Libri* woodcuts. Morachiello and Puppi have followed with reservation, but it seems clear that

such a structure as found on D19 could not be accommodated on the bridge drawn on D25v.

57. Burns (1975), p. 126. See also Calabi and Morachiello (1987), p. 227 n. 34.

58. On Scamozzi's drawing, see Burns (1975), pp. 126–28, no. 224; see also Lewis (1981), pp. 208–9, no. 123. On the bridge as executed, see Calabi and Morachiello (1987), pp. 235–300.

59. See Gauthey (1809–16) and also Ruddock (1979), pp. 28–35.

60. Harris (1970), p. 203, no. 22; on the bridge at Wörlitz, see Alex (1988).

61. Summerson (1989), p. 362.

62. Constable and Links (1976), II, pp. 435–38, nos. 457–58.

63. Algarotti (1792), VIII, p. 90: "Ella saprà, non avere il ponte di Rialto con tutta la sua fama altro pregio, che quello di essere una gran massa di pietre conformate in uno arcone, che ha cento piedi di corda, e porta in sulla schiena due mani di botteghe della più tozza e pesante architettura che forse immaginare si possa . . . In luogo adunque del ponte di Rialto quale ora si vede . . . si è posto il ponte disegnato già dal Palladio per quel luogo, il quale è bene il più bello ed ornato edifizio che vedere si possa." Algarotti was writing to Prospero Pesci of Bologna in 1759. See also Links (1977), pp. 83–84; and Puppi and Romanelli (1985), pp. 76–77, nos. 2.12–15.

CHAPTER VIII. THE *QUATTRO LIBRI*

1. For a comprehensive introduction to the *Quattro Libri*, see Magagnato and Marini (1980). See also Forssman (1965), pp. 142–76; Burns (1975), pp. 101–4, no. 193; and Ferrari (1980), pp. 233–58, no. 58. A reliable English translation does not exist, but see the reprint of Ware (1738).

2. Alberti (1988), p. 154 (*De re* VI, i): "[Vitruvius's] very text is evidence that he wrote neither Latin nor Greek, so that as far as we are concerned he might just as well not have written at all, rather than write something that we cannot understand." On Alberti and Vitruvius, see the important essay by Krautheimer (1969-I). See also Pagliara (1986).

3. Schlosser Magnino (1964), p. 121.

4. On Filarete and his treatise, see Spencer (1965). For his architectural theory, see also Saalman (1959).

5. See the critical edition of the *Trattati* by Maltese (1967) and the article by Scaglia in Guillaume (1988), pp. 91–97.

6. See de la Croix (1960), p. 269; and Maltese (1967), II, p. 422, where Francesco di Giorgio refutes the notion that the ancients invented artillery.

7. See the survey in Kruft (1986), especially pp. 72–76. On the Italian editions of Alberti, see Orlandi and Portoghesi (1966), I, pp. xlvii–xlviii. Magagnato has demonstrated that Palladio used Lauro's edition of Alberti; see Magagnato and Marini (1980), p. lv.

8. An excellent introduction to Serlio can be found in Dinsmoor (1942), especially pp. 55–64; see also Rosenfeld (1978). On Serlio's relationship with Peruzzi, see the articles by Burns and Günther in Guillaume (1988), pp. 207–45. For a different interpretation, see Onians (1988), pp. 263–86.

9. Serlio (1537), p. iii: "Messer Aluigi Cornarno non solamente architetto da se grande, ma fautor grandissimo di tuuti gli architetti, la bella loggia del quale da inditio di quello c'ha da reuscir la sua casa in Padoa con moltissimo ornamento & gloria di tutta la Città." On Serlio and Cornaro, see Wolters (1969); Carpeggiani in Puppi (1980-I), pp. 28–35; and Günther (1981), pp. 50–54. Palladio's contacts with Cornaro's circle have recently been examined by Battilotti in Puppi (1980-I), pp. 168–73; and by Holberton (1990), pp. 81–89.

10. Berger (1978), pp. 62–86.

11. Palladio (1570), I, p. 3. On de l'Orme, see Blunt (1958), pp. 108–35.

12. Doni (1555), p. 155; see also Magagnato and Marini (1980), pp. xi–xii.

13. Barbaro (1556), p. 179. On the preparatory stages and manuscript fragments of the *Quattro Libri*, see Zorzi (1959), pp. 147–93; and Puppi (1988), pp. 59–101.

14. On Cornaro's treatises, see Fiocco (1965), pp. 156–67; and Carpeggiani in Puppi (1980), pp. 28–35. For Trissino's draft, see Puppi (1973), pp. 79–86.

15. Puppi (1988), pp. 59–60.

16. Palladio (1570), I, pp. 5–6; see Magagnato and Marini (1980), p. 415 nn. 26, 27.

17. Palladio (1570), I, xxiii, pp. 53–54. See Zorzi (1959), pp. 155, 174–76; and Puppi (1988), pp. 81–83, for the manuscript text. Palladio deletes a lengthy definition of proportion from the final text for the *Quattro Libri* and only mentions vaulting in his descriptions of Palazzo Porto and the Villas Zeno, Foscari, Pisani at Montagnana, and Cornaro. See also Magagnato and Marini (1980), p. 434 n. 1.

18. Wittkower (1962), pp. 126–42; Ackerman (1966), pp. 160–70; Rowe (1976), pp. 8–16; Magagnato and Marini (1980), pp. xxxiii–xxxvi; and also Mitrović (1990). See also the questions raised by this approach in Battisti (1973); Burns (1975), pp. 224–25; and Howard and Longair (1982), especially pp. 136–37. More recently, the measured surveys of Palladian villas by Elwin Robison have shown that interlocking proportions were not strictly observed by Palladio in his buildings, where room dimensions were adjusted in order to accommodate the building's structure.

19. "Le proporzioni delle voci sono armonia delle orecchie, così quelle delle misure sono armonia degli occhi nostri, la quale secondo il suo costume sommamente diletta senza sapersi il perché fuori che da quelli che studiano di sapere la ragioni delle cose." The context was Palladio's opinion on a model for a new cathedral for Brescia in 1567, printed in Zorzi (1966), p. 88; see also Puppi (1988), p. 123, and here chapter six. Palladio may be unconsciously echoing a passage in Barbaro's Vitruvius where the same metaphor of voices was employed. See Barbaro (1556), p. 57.

20. On this topic, see the studies by Forssman (1961) and (1978); also Onians (1988); Pauwels (1989); Günther (1990); and Guillaume (1992).

21. Palladio (1570), I, xiii, p. 15; see also Burns (1975), p. 207, no. 370; and Magagnato and Marini (1980), p. 423 nn. 1–4.

22. Palladio (1570), I, xii, p. 15. Compare the pronouncement of Serlio in a discussion of the Theatre of Marcellus: "Mentre la ragione non ci persuade altrimenti, habbiamo da tenere la dottrina di Vitruvio come guida et regola infallabile" (1619, III, p. 69v).

23. Thoenes (1983).

24. Spielmann (1966), pp. 27–29; and Günther (1990). See also Scamozzi (1615), II, vi, cap. xxiv, pp. 102–5, especially p. 104. Scamozzi's arguments were later endorsed by Fréart de Chambray (1650), pp. 97–99.

25. Vitruvius III, iii, 1; and Palladio (1570), I, xiii, pp. 15–16, and IV, iv, pp. 8–9. Palladio based his conclusions concerning the appropriateness of the sistyle and pycnostyle for the Corinthian and Composite orders on his measurements of classical porticos.

26. On du Cerceau's *Livre*, see Thomson (1984), pp. 12–27.

27. Palladio (1570), I, xx, p. 51, and II, i–ii, pp. 3–4. On Palladio's appeal to nature, see also Burns (1975), pp. 206–7.

28. Palladio (1570), II, vi, pp. 29–32; see also chapter six.

29. See chapters three and nine.

30. Palladio (1570), II, xvii, pp. 71–72. Huse (1979) has plausibly connected the two Venetian palaces with Palazzo Cornarno at San Maurizio and Palazzo Grimani at San Luca; see also Foscari (1979).

31. Palladio (1570), II, iii, pp. 4–5; see here chapter five.

32. Muttoni (1740), pp. 6–7.

33. On this unfinished project, see Zorzi (1965), p. 213; Puppi (1973), p. 287; and especially Marini (1980), pp. 232–34.

34. Girolamo and Marco Cornaro, sons of the original patron Giorgio, declared that the house was not finished in 1582, but it appears as completed in a plan of the site in 1613; see Puppi (1973), pp. 293–94. A similar case occurred with the building of the Villa Poiana; see Cevese (1973), pp. 64–65.

35. Bertotti Scamozzi (1796), I, pp. 12–13: "Notabilissime sono le differenze che si ritrovano fra i disegni pubblicati . . . e le Fabbriche eseguite prima della loro pubblicazione." In more recent times, Pane (1948), pp. 32–34, and Zorzi (1961) mistook the preparatory drawings for the *Quattro Libri* plates as original projects for buildings like Palazzo Porto and Palazzo Thiene. A comparison of the plates with the buildings themselves led Barbieri (1972) to condemn the former as unreliable, and he was followed, to an extent, by Puppi (1974) and Lewis (1981), pp. 5–6. More balanced and convincing assessments of the role of the *Quattro Libri* and its illustrations can be found in Gioseffi (1978); Rupprecht (1980); Kubelik (1981); and Berger (1984), to which my own observations are indebted.

36. See Burns (1973-I), p. 138, no. 52; and Berger (1984), p. 24.

37. See chapter four.

38. Berger (1984), pp. 22–24, fig. 1. Palladio's original manuscript entry for the Palazzo da Porto reads: "Nella parte di dietro vi si truova come un'altra casa, cioè cucine et appartamento da donne"; see Puppi (1988), p. 90. This would correspond to the less ambitious scope of the second wing in the early

drawings as opposed to that found in the *Quattro Libri* plate.

39. Gioseffi (1978), p. 42.

40. Zorzi (1959), p. 151; Puppi (1988), p. 59.

41. Magagnato and Marini (1980), 1980, pp. xiv–xvii.

42. Alberti (1988), pp. 107–13 (*De re* IV, 6); see here chapter seven.

43. Magagnato and Marini (1980), pp. 505–6 n. 1.

44. Zorzi (1959), pp. 116–17, 124–25; and here chapter nine.

45. Zorzi (1959), p. 191; and Puppi (1988), p. 97.

46. Hale (1977).

47. Alberti (1988), pp. 194–96 (*De re* VII, 3–4). On Alberti's influence on later writers, see especially Wittkower (1962), pp. 3–32.

48. Palladio (1570), IV, ii, pp. 6–7; and here chapter six.

49. Vitruvius I, ii, 5; see also Alberti (1988), p. 195 (*De re* VII, 3): "What has been said, that temples dedicated to Venus, Diana, the Muses, Nymphs, and other more delicate goddesses must take on the slenderness of a virgin and the flowery tenderness of youth, is very pertinent; buildings to Hercules, Mars, and other great gods must impose authority by their solemnity, rather than charm [the worshipper] by their grace." See also the similar thoughts in Serlio (1619), IV, p. 126r–v.

50. Palladio (1570), IV, i, p. 5: "E molto brutta, & biasimevol cosa, che noi, i quali il vero culto habbiamo; siamo superati in ciò da coloro, che nessun lume haveano della verità." Compare Palladio's lukewarm remarks about San Petronio in Bologna, reprinted here in chapter nine, p. 288.

51. On this subject, see especially Spielmann (1966), pp. 26–50. Palladio's reconstructions were particularly guided by Vitruvius, I, III, and IV. Compare also Serlio's explanation for not investigating the Mausoleum of Romulus on the Via Appia: "Circa alle altezze, per esser moltoripieno, & anco perché ci era bestiame dentro, io non le [i.e., the base of the structure] misurai, & anco per non ci esser belezza di architettura, non tenni conto del dritto" (1619, III, p. 69r). Serlio gives similar explanation for not publishing detailed measurements of the Baths of Diocletian and for publishing a fragmentary colonnade of unknown purpose; see Serlio (1619), III, pp.95r, 97v.

52. Palladio (1570), II, xi and xvi, pp. 43–44, 69–71, respectively; see also Spielmann (1966), pp. 97–100.

53. Palladio (1570), I, xx, p. 52: "E benché il variare & le cose nuove à tutti debbano piacere, non si deve però far ciò contra i precetti dell'arte, e contra quello, che la ragione ci dimostra: onde si vede che anco gli antichi variarono: nè però si partirono mai da alcune regole universali & necessarie dell'arte."

54. See especially Spielmann (1966), pp. 30–31.

55. Palladio (1570), IV, xxvi, pp. 103–6; also Vitruvius, III, i. See also Antolini (1803), and Spielmann (1966), pp. 46–47.

56. Palladio (1570), IV, viii, pp. 23–29. Nash (1961–62), I, p. 433, fig. 530, reproduces a Du Perac engraving of the Forum of Nerva and Temple of Minerva in 1575; see also Spielmann (1966), pp. 32–33.

57. Palladio (1570), IV, xvii, pp. 64–66; Serlio (1619), III, pp. 67r–68v. Palladio's proportional alterations were first noted by Spielmann (1966), pp. 42–43. See also Burns (1973-I), pp. 151, 153; and Puppi (1989), pp. 109–10, no. 42, for the preliminary drawing.

58. Shearman (1972), p. 125, saw the round Doric temple in *Saint Paul Preaching in Athens* not so much as a variation on Bramante's Tempietto as "an informed criticism of the circular temples of Francesco di Giorgio and Bramante." See also Burns in Frommel et al. (1984), p. 387.

59. Palladio (1570), IV, xvi, pp. 61–63. Palladio's reconstruction appears to follow an earlier drawing by Peruzzi; see Spielmann (1966), pp. 41–42, figs. 35, 36.

60. See, for example, his proposals for rebuilding the Doge's Palace and San Petronio, discussed here in chapter nine.

61. Palladio (1570), IV, xxii, pp. 88–89; Serlio (1619), III, p. 69r. See also Spielmann (1966), pp. 43–44; Burns (1973-I), p. 142, and (1975), p. 104, no. 194; and Rasch (1984).

62. On the Pantheon in this period, see especially Buddensieg (1971); on the differences between Serlio and Palladio in their presentation of the Pantheon, see Burns (1975), pp. 106–7, no. 262.

63. Palladio (1570), I, p. 6; see also I, xix, p. 51, for a reference to a book of arches. Spielmann (1966), pp. 51–96, sets out the literary remains of the pro-

jected volumes. On Palladio's study of Roman baths, see the recent article by La Follette (1993).

64. See Zorzi (1959-II). Silla's petition to the Accademia was first mentioned by Magrini (1845), p. 99; see also Magagnato and Marini (1980), p. xvii.

CHAPTER IX. PALLADIO'S LATE STYLE

1. Vasari (1878–85), VII, p. 531; see also Davis et al. (1981), pp. 295–96.

2. Franzina (1980), p. 453. The scarcity of housing may explain the high valuation of the Casa Civena in 1563–64; see Battilotti (1980), p. 46.

3. Palladio (1570), II, iii, pp. 20–21. On Palazzo Capra, see especially Zorzi (1965), pp. 260–63. On Montano Barbaran, see Mantese (1980).

4. The most celebrated example of this is the Casa Cogollo, incorrectly known as Palladio's house. See Burns (1975), pp. 40–41, no. 59; and Cevese (1990).

5. On Giovanni Alvise Valmarana, see Zorzi (1965), pp. 247–48; for the palace, see Burns (1975), pp. 235–36, nos. 418–20.

6. On these churches, see chapter six.

7. Palladio could have seen the beginnings of work on the Palazzo del Senatore and the exterior of the southern hemicycle of Saint Peter's during his last trip to Rome in 1554; see Ackerman (1986), pp. 159, 202–8, respectively. On the Villa Madama, see chapter one, and Frommel et al. (1984), pp. 311–56. Palladio may have known that Raphael intended to use a giant order on the facade of his own palace in the Via Giulia; see Frommel (1973), II, pp. 268–69.

8. On the Greek house, see Vitruvius, VI, vii, 1–7; and Palladio (1570), II, xi, pp. 43–44. The connection was noted by Pée (1941), pp. 102–11; see also Forssman (1965), pp. 102–5; and Puppi (1973), pp. 369–71.

9. Zorzi (1965), p. 192, saw the design of the courtyard of Palazzo Porto as dating from the 1540s, but this was rejected by Forssman (1973), p. 32; Burns (1973-I), p. 148; Lewis (1981), pp. 116–17, no. 67; and Berger (1984), pp. 22–24. Cevese (1973), pp. 102–3, inclines toward an early dating of the whole project.

10. Vitruvius, V, i, 6. See also Barbaro (1556), pp. 135–37. The importance of Palladio's reconstruction was underscored by Zorzi (1959), pp. 116–17.

See also Magagnato and Marini (1980), p. 450 n. 30.

11. See Forssman (1973), figs. 40–44; and also Cevese (1976), pp. 21–31.

12. Cevese (1973), pp. 57–62, preferred dating the villa to the 1540s on stylistic grounds, but the documents published by Marini (1980), pp. 247–50, show fairly conclusively that the construction took place in the second half of the 1560s.

13. If the final columns were part of an interrupted arcade, one would expect their capitals to face the same direction as the adjacent ones rather than turning forty-five degrees.

14. Alberti (1988), p. 294 (*De re* IX, 2): "There is a further difference between a town house and a villa: the ornament to a town house ought to be far more sober in character, whereas in a villa the allures of license and delight are allowed."

15. Scamozzi (1615), I, iii, cap. xi, p. 266. See also Puppi (1973), pp. 395–96; and Jaroszewski (1975).

16. Battilotti (1980), pp. 69–70, sees the date of construction as 1580 or after because nothing appears on the Angelica plan of that year, but this does not rule out planning from the early 1570s. See also Ackerman (1967-II), pp. 59–60. On Palazzo Thiene Bonin, see the résumé in Puppi (1973), pp. 401–3.

17. Muttoni's earlier reconstruction of the courtyard with a rectangular plan is reproduced in Zorzi (1965), fig. 358. See also Bertotti Scamozzi (1796), I, pp. 100–5, pls. xxxii–xxxiv.

18. For the history of the Loggia, see Zorzi (1965), pp. 109–24; also Venditti (1969); Puppi (1973), pp. 376–79; and Burns (1975), pp. 31–32, no. 38.

19. Fasolo died while painting the ceiling of the upper chamber in August 1572.

20. Castellini (1783–1822), XIV, pp. 105–6: "[Giovanni Battista Bernardo, capitanio in 1572] dilettandosi molto di fabbricare e di abbellire la Città fece alargare nel corso del suo reggimento la Piazza Grande, atterando alcune botteghe di legname, ch'erano vicine al palazzo del Podestà. Il simile fece di un magazzino dei Barcajuoli, che stava in mezzo all'Isola, ed in ultimo della beccaria situata nell'Isoletta in capo al Ponte degli Angeli. Fece altresi ristaurare il Porto dell'Isola, ch'era molto rovinata. . . . Altro simile monumento fu a lui eretto dalla Città per essere egli stato cagione che si ristaurasse la loggia vecchia. L'iscrizione è posta nella facciata del

Palazz, ed è questa: Io: Baptistae Bernardo Praef. Civ. dicavit."

21. Quoted by Burns (1975), p. 32, no. 38.

22. Bertotti Scamozzi (1796), I, pp. 66–67, pl. xiv; Venditti (1969), fig. V, reproduces Muttoni's earlier five-bay proposal.

23. For the Maison Carrée, see Palladio (1570), IV, xxviii, pp. 111–17. On the absence of stuccoing on the columns of the Capitaniato and the Malcontenta, see Cevese (1965), and here, chapter five.

24. On Lepanto, see Lane (1973), pp. 369–74; on its iconography, see Gombrich (1967).

25. See, for example, Wittkower (1962), pp. 86–89: "It seems justifiable to conclude that Palladio sacrificed an originally uniform plan to the exigencies of the victory" (p. 88). See also Wolters (1968), pp. 83–86. Pée (1941), p. 151, saw the stuccowork as intrinsic to the visual impact of the Loggia; see also the positive response of Pane (1961), p. 357 n. 12.

26. Burckhardt (1964), p. 339.

27. Unusually for a Palladian palace, the facade of Palazzo Barbaran is stone up to the sills of the ground-floor windows; see the discussion of its current restoration by Boschi (1990). Zorzi (1965), p. 257, observed that the stucco panels above the ground-floor windows were added only in the eighteenth century; this does not exclude the possibility that they may have been intended as a late addition by Barbaran and Palladio after the publication of the *Quattro Libri* plate.

28. Palladio (1570), II, iii, pp. 22–23.

29. The drawings are found on RIBA XVI/14. See Burns (1975), p. 220, no. 387. They are illustrated by Lewis (1981), pp. 164–68, no. 99, but he proposes a dating from the late 1540s by analogy with a similar ground plan, which he believed to be for Palazzo Iseppo da Porto and therefore around that date. However the drawing in question (RIBA XVI/10; Lewis no. 64) shows a site at variance with that of Palazzo Porto and appears to date from the 1560s or 1570s; consequently, there seems to be no reason for dating Palazzo Barbaran much before 1570.

30. Palladio (1570), IV, xxx, pp. 124–27. Palladio refers to it as the Temple of Concord rather than its actual name of Saturn. Although he describes the capitals as a mixture of Doric and Ionic, their proportions are 1:9, which is standard for Palladio's Ionic order.

31. Bertotti Scamozzi (1796), I, pp. 71–77, pls. xvii–xix.

32. On Barbaran, see especially Zorzi (1965), pp. 255–57; and Mantese (1980).

33. Zorzi (1965), p. 257; see also Magagnato and Marini (1980), pp. 458–79 n. 65. Montano Barbaran petitioned the town council to repair the pavement in front of his house in October 1575, which suggests that the main phase of building on the front had finished; see Battilotti (1980), pp. 67–69.

34. Cevese (1973), p. 110. Francesco Albanese's presence in the palace is reported by Battilotti (1980), p. 67; see also Mantese (1980).

35. See the discussion of the attitudes of Michelangelo and his circle in Summers (1972) and (1981), pp. 274–78. Danti's treatise is reprinted by Barocchi (1960–62), I, pp. 209–69; see especially p. 237: "Oggi, che sotto tante regole, ordini e misure [l'architettura] è stata ridotta, le quali la rendono facilissima nelle sue esecuzioni. Quegli antichi primi ritrovatori di tanti begli ordini, con tanti begli ornamenti e comodità, furono quelli i quali si può dire che fussero in ciò di grandissimo ingegno e giudizio, e che allora essa architettura per i suoi esecutori fusse nobilissima e molto artifiziosa. Ma
. . . in questi tempi quasi ognuno che sappia tirare due linee può fare l'architettore." See also Doni (1549), fols. 13v–14r.

36. On the history of the academy and its theater, see Zorzi (1969), pp. 257–63, 282–327, with further references; and Puppi (1973), pp. 435–39. See also the excellent short account by Beyer (1987).

37. Pastor (1958–64), IV-I, pp. 351–56. A rival Vicentine academy, the Accademia dei Costanti, was founded only for members of the nobility, but it ceased to function in 1568. Members of the Costanti included Palladio's early supporter, Giovanni Alvise Valmarana, and Daniele Barbaro; see Zorzi (1969), pp. 252–55.

38. Zorzi (1969), pp. 260, 266–72, figs. 463–65, 511. The grisaille paintings are found in the Antiodeo, one of the series of rooms added to the theater by Scamozzi. They date from the 1590s but correspond to eyewitness accounts of the first productions by the Accademia Olimpica.

39. On Palazzo Piovene, see especially Puppi (1973), pp. 288–89; and Battilotti (1980), p. 67.

40. Beyer (1987), pp. 40–42, points out that RIBA XIII/5 must predate the decision of May 1580 because the aedicules contain allegorical figures much

as in Palladio's earlier reconstruction of the Roman stage for Barbaro.

41. The specific passage from the contract of 1584 reads: "Di far le figure tuttora mancanti al prezzo di scudi sette d'oro l'una, e di racconciar tutte quelle che sono difettose, vestir le nude, mutar le teste a quelle che le hanno da donna"; see Mantese (1988), p. 41.

42. Magagnato (1951), p. 215 n. 3.

43. Vitruvius V, vi. On Palladio's studies of ancient theaters, see Spielmann (1966), pp. 60–66; and Burns (1975), pp. 44–45, nos. 66–71.

44. Zorzi (1969), pp. 289–90. On the development of the theater, see the seminal article by Magagnato (1951).

45. See especially Beyer (1987), pp. 47–50. Already in 1583, the theater designer Angelo Ingegneri recommended that the appearance of the stage should suggest the city of Thebes; see Zorzi (1969), p. 297 n. 22.

46. Krautheimer (1969-II), pp. 345–59, discusses the development of the Renaissance perspectival scene. See also Barbaro (1556), p. 155, 157–58. Zorzi (1969), pp. 293–303, argued that the perspectival streets of the Olimpico were by Palladio, but there is no question that the extant drawings are from Scamozzi. See Burns (1975), pp. 46–47, no. 76; and Lewis (1981), pp. 211–12, no. 125.

47. On the recent cleaning of the theater, see Avagnina (1990). The history of the theater between 1585 and 1970 is given by Nogara (1972).

48. On Palladio's proposal for rebuilding the civic palace of Brescia, see especially Burns (1975), pp. 239–41, nos. 426–27.

49. Puppi (1973), p. 303.

50. See chapter seven, pp. 219–21.

51. The drawing was first identified as related to Palladio by Harris (1971) and was subsequently connected with Palladio's proposal for rebuilding the Doge's Palace in a detailed analysis by Burns (1975), pp. 158–60, no. 279. The identification has been seconded by Olivato in Puppi (1980-II), p. 102; and Lewis (1981), pp. 204–5, no. 121. The project is mentioned in the earliest biography of Palladio, which was written by the Vicentine Paolo Gualdo, in 1615; see Zorzi (1959-II), p. 94.

52. The two versions of Palladio's report are published by Puppi (1988), pp. 151–59, especially pp.

157–58. On Palladio's dealings with the Doge's Palace in the 1570s, see Zorzi (1965), pp. 137–67. Palladio's concept of nature has been discussed by Burns (1975), pp. 206–7; many of the same comparisons made in the report on the Doge's Palace can be found in the famous chapter on the misuses of architecture; see Palladio (1570), I, xx, pp. 51–52.

53. See Zorzi (1966), pp. 84–89; and here chapter six, pp. 192–93.

54. Tafuri (1985), pp. 272–78, and (1990) presents the most detailed case against the connection of the drawing with Palladio and the Doge's Palace, but his attempts to ascribe the sheet to Scamozzi or Cristoforo Sorte are less compelling than an attribution to Palladio or at the least his workshop. Among others who have expressed reservations are Huse (1979), pp. 98–99 n. 154; and Puppi (1988), p. 146 n. 31.

55. On Sansovino's plans for the Piazza San Marco, see Lotz (1977), pp. 83–84; and Hirthe (1986).

56. The relationship of San Petronio and the city of Bologna is discussed in an article by Fanti (1983), especially p. 26.

57. On the debates over the facade and the subsequent vaulting of the church, see Wittkower (1974), pp. 65–78; and the more recent survey by Belluzzi (1984). On Peruzzi's projects, see also Burns (1975), p. 241, no. 428.

58. Palladio's remarks and his report are published by Zorzi (1966), pp. 105–7, nos. 1, 7. The report is also available in Puppi (1988), pp. 129–30.

59. The drawing is reproduced by Zorzi (1966), fig. 117; see also Timofiewitsch (1962-II). For Terribilia's and Tibaldi's projects and the Terribilia–Palladio compromise, see Wittkower (1974), p. 75 and figs. 102, 105, 106.

60. Zorzi (1966), pp. 109–10, no. 14; and Puppi (1988), pp. 131–33.

61. Burns (1975), p. 243–44, no. 431; Lewis (1981), pp. 198–99, no. 118.

62. For a critical survey of the Rotonda, see especially Cevese (1971), I, pp. 150–55; and Puppi (1973), pp. 380–83. On its chronology, see especially Isermeyer (1967); and Battilotti (1977). The Rotonda's influence on seventeenth- and eighteenth-century architecture is discussed by Jaroszewski (1967) and Sicca (1988).

63. Palladio (1570), II, iii, p. 18.

64. G. Plinius Secundus Minor, *Epistularum libri novem,* V, vi; see also Ackerman (1990), pp. 54–57. For the *villa suburbana,* see Alberti (1988), p. 295 (*De re* IX, ii); and also Forssman (1965), pp. 50–51.

65. Burns (1975), pp. 110–11, no. 208, and pp. 250–51, no. 451. On Palestrina, see especially Fancelli (1974); Burroughs (1988); and Hemsoll and Caplin (1989).

66. On the symbolism of circle and square in the Rotonda, see Prinz (1980), pp. 69–81. One of the earliest published accounts of the Rotonda refers to it as Palladio's "Masterpiece; for tis so contriv'd, that it containes Geometrically a Rond, a Crosse, and a Square"; see Raymond (1648), p. 225; and Sicca (1988), p. 174.

67. This floor was divided into more rooms in the eighteenth century by Muttoni for the Capra family. Cevese believes it was the area referred to as the "luogo da passeggiare" in Palladio's account of the Rotonda; see Cevese (1971), p. 152.

68. See especially Mariacher (1988); and Rossi (1988).

69. Scamozzi opened a passageway in the external stairways leading directly to the ground floor. This was restored to Palladio's published design by Bertotti Scamozzi between 1761 and 1778; see Bertotti Scamozzi (1796), II, pp. 12–13 n. g; and Isermeyer (1967), p. 216.

70. See chapter three, pp. 88–89. Burns (1975), p. 182, no. 322, draws attention to the derivation from the Odeo Cornaro in Padua. Lewis (1981), pp. 77–78, no. 43, reproduces the similar early villa study, RIBA XVI/19b, which also anticipates the Rotonda.

71. An influence of Francesco di Giorgio's studies of rotondas on Palladio was first suggested by Rosenthal (1962). For the Villa Madama, see chapter one, pp. 30–31.

72. This was first published by Burns (1975), p. 200, no. 357.

73. The most comprehensive study on Almerico is that by Mantese (1988).

74. Puppi (1973), p. 351; and Mantese (1988), pp. 34–38. Mantese points out that the workmen involved in the Rotonda were among Palladio's close collaborators on other Vicentine projects of the period.

75. "La quale [i.e., the Rotonda] non mi è parso mettere tra le fabbriche di Villa per la vicinanza ch'ella ha con la Città, onde si può dire che sia nella Città istessa"; Palladio (1570), II, iii, p. 18.

76. On Ligorio and the Villa d'Este, see Coffin (1960) and (1979), pp. 311–40; and Lazzaro (1990), pp. 215–42.

77. For the Casino of Pius IV, see Smith (1977); and Coffin (1979), pp. 267–79.

78. Lotz (1977-I), p. 192; and Raymond (1648), p. 225. On Raymond, see Sicca (1988), p. 174. Raymond's comments are much more incisive than the earliest published account by Thomas Coryate in 1611; see, however, Strachan (1962), pp. 58–59. Forster (1980) downplayed the significance of the temple overtones in the Rotonda, but Raymond's connection of the Rotonda with the Pantheon show that these associations were well known, even a few decades after Palladio's death.

79. See chapter five, pp. 145–48.

80. See the discussions in Isermeyer (1967), pp. 210–14; and Ackerman (1967), pp. 68–72. The proposal of a double dome was first made by Muttoni (1740), I, p. 12; it has been argued by Cevese (1976), pp. 80–83. The theory that the present dome was built by Scamozzi has been reproposed in a recent article, but on the basis of rather eccentric results of thermoluminescence testing of bricks from the Rotonda; see, however, Goedicke, Slusallek, and Kubelik (1986), p. 402.

81. Isermeyer (1967), p. 210, argues cogently that the essential nature of the Rotonda had been decided in Palladio's lifetime and probably before the publication of the *Quattro Libri.*

82. See Sicca (1988). When he published his designs for Mereworth, Campbell went out of his way to distinguish it from the Rotonda; see Tavernor (1991), pp. 161–62.

83. Palladio (1570), II, xv, p. 60. On this problematic project, see Puppi (1973), pp. 386–88; Burns (1975), pp. 251–52, nos. 453–55; and Gioseffi (1978).

84. The scant information on Palladio's death has been summarized by Puppi (1982). On the Valmarana chapel, see Puppi (1973), pp. 417–18.

85. Olivato and Puppi (1980), p. 179.

86. Bertotti Scamozzi explained that his survey of Palladio's buildings arose from the visits of so many foreigners to Vicenza in order to study them. The engravings in his early guide to Vicenza contain mea-

surements in Vicentine and English feet; see Bertotti Scamozzi (1761), pp. 7–10.

87. Palladianism lies beyond the scope of this book, but see the useful surveys of Palladianism in the English-speaking world by Summerson (1989), pp.

295–353; Köster (1990); Tavernor (1991); and Harris (1994). For its European context, see the articles in *Palladio* (1980).

88. Goethe (1962), p. 47. See also von Einem (1982).

BIBLIOGRAPHY

The following abbreviations have been used:

Bollettino C.I.S.A.=Bollettino del Centro Internazionale di Studi di Architettura "Andrea Palladio"

RIBA=Royal Institute of British Architects, London

Ackerman, J. S. 1954. *The Cortile del Belvedere (Studi e documenti per la storia del Palazzo Apostolico Vaticano, III).* Rome.

———. 1963. "Sources of the Renaissance Villa." In *Renaissance and Mannerism: Studies in Western Art,* Acts of the XX International Congress of History of Art, vol. 2, pp. 6–18. Princeton, N.J.

———. 1966. *Palladio.* Rev. ed. 1977. Harmondsworth, England.

———. 1967. *Palladio's Villas.* Locust Valley, N.Y.

———. 1980. "Observations on Renaissance Church Planning in Venice and Florence, 1470–1570." In *Florence and Venice: Comparisons and Relations,* vol. 2, *Cinquecento,* edited by S. Bertelli and N. Rubinstein, pp. 287–307. Florence.

———. 1982. "The Geopolitics of Venetian Architecture in the Time of Titian." In *Titian: His World and His Legacy,* edited by D. Rosand, pp. 41–72. New York.

———. 1983. "The Tuscan/Rustic Order: A Study in the Metaphorical Language of Archaeology." *Journal of the Society of Architectural Historians* 42:15–34.

———. 1986. *The Architecture of Michelangelo.* 2d ed. London.

———. 1990-I. *The Villa: Form and Ideology of Country Houses.* Princeton, N.J.

———. 1990-II. "Gli studi palladiani degli ultimi trent'anni." In *Andrea Palladio: Nuovi contributi,* edited by A. Chastel and R. Cevese, pp. 122–26. Milan.

———. 1994. "Palladio: in che senso classico?" *Annali di architettura* 6:11–22.

Alberigo, G. 1964. "Daniele Barbaro." In *Dizionario biografico degli italiani,* vol. 4, pp. 89–95. Rome.

Alberti, L. B. 1988. *On the Art of Building.* Translated by J. Rykwert and R. Tavernor. Cambridge, Mass.

Alex, R. 1988. *Schlößer und Gärten um Wörlitz.* Leipzig, Germany.

Algarotti, F. 1791–94. *Opere.* 17 vols. Venice.

Antolini, G. 1803. *Il tempio di Minerva in Assisi confrontato colle tavole di Andrea Palladio.* Milan.

Avagnina, M. E. 1990. "Marmorini e stucchi: il restauro delle superficie architettoniche e plastiche del Teatro Olimpico di Vicenza." In *Andrea Palladio: Nuovi contributi,* edited by A. Chastel and R. Cevese, pp. 226–35. Milan.

Ballarin, A. 1968. "La decorazione ad affresco della villa Veneta nel quinto decennio del cinquecento: La villa di Luvigliano." *Bollettino C.I.S.A.* 10:115–26.

Bandini, F. 1989. "La letteratura in dialetto dal cinquecento al settecento." *Storia di Vicenza.* Edited by F. Barbieri and P. Preto, vol. 3, pp. 15–26. Vicenza, Italy.

Barbaro, D. 1556. *I dieci libri dell'architettura.* Venice.

Barbieri, F. 1952. *Vincenzo Scamozzi.* Vicenza, Italy.

———. 1966. "*Le chiese e i ponti di Andrea Palladio* di G. Zorzi." *Bollettino C.I.S.A.* 8:337–55.

———. 1967. "Il primo Palladio." *Bollettino C.I.S.A.* 11:24–36.

———. 1968. *La Basilica palladiana.* Corpus Palladianum, vol. 2. Vicenza, Italy.

———. 1970. "Palladio in villa negli anni quaranta: Da Lonedo a Bagnolo." *Arte Veneta* 24:63–80.

———. 1972-I. *Illuministi e neoclassici a Vicenza.* Vicenza, Italy.

———. 1972-II. "Il valore dei *Quattro Libri.*" *Bollettino C.I.S.A.* 14:63–79.

———. 1973. *La pianta prospettica di Vicenza del 1580.* Vicenza, Italy.

———. 1980. "Giangiorgio Trissino e Andrea Palladio." In *Convegno di studi su Giangiorgio Trissino,* pp. 191–211. Vicenza, Italy.

———. 1981. *Vicenza gotica: Il privato.* Vicenza, Italy.

———. 1987. *Vicenza: Città di palazzi.* Milan.

Barbieri, F., R. Cevese, and L. Magagnato. 1956. *Guida di Vicenza.* Vicenza, Italy.

Barrocchi, P., ed. 1960–62. *Trattati d'arte del Cinquecento.* 3 vols. Bari, Italy.

———. 1977. "A. F. Doni: *Le Ville.*" In *Scritti d'arte del'500,* vol. 3, pp. 3,321–57. Milan.

Bassi, E. 1971. *Il convento della Carità.* Corpus Palladianum, vol. 6. Vicenza, Italy.

———. 1978. "La scala ovata del Palladio nei suoi precedenti e nei suoi conseguenti." *Bollettino C.I.S.A.* 20:89–111.

Basso, U. 1968. *Cronaca di Maser, delle sue chiese e della villa palladiana dei Barbaro.* Montebelluna, Italy.

Battilotti, D. 1977. "Nuovi documenti per Palladio." *Arte Veneta* 31:232–36.

———. 1980. *Vicenza al tempo di Andrea Palladio attraverso i libri d'estimo del 1563–1564.* Vicenza, Italy.

———. 1981. "Per il palazzo di Iseppo da Porto del Palladio: Un documento inedito e una nota." *Antichità viva* 20:40–44.

———. 1982. "Palladio a Venezia: Registri per un itinerario." In *Palladio e Venezia,* edited by L. Puppi, pp. 175–212. Florence.

Battisti, E. 1973. "Un tentativo di analisi strutturale del Palladio tramite le teorie musicali del cinquecento e l'impiego di figure rettoriche." *Bollettino C.I.S.A.* 15:211–32.

Bellocchi, U., ed. 1969. *Le Ville di Anton Francesco Doni.* Modena, Italy.

Belluzzi, A. 1983–84. "La facciata: I progetti cinquecenteschi." In *La Basilica di San Petronio,* vol. 2, pp. 7–28. Bologna, Italy.

Beltrami, D. 1961. *La penetrazione economica dei Veneziani in terraferma.* Venice and Rome.

Bentmann, R., and M. Mueller. 1981. *Die Villa als Herrschaftsarchitektur: eine kunst- und sozialgeschichtliche Analyse.* Frankfurt (rev. ed.).

Berger, U. 1978. *Palladios Frühwerk: Bauten und Zeichnungen.* Vienna and Cologne, Germany.

———. 1984. "Palladio publizierte seine eigenen Bauten: Zur Problematik des 'Secondo Libro.'" *Architectura* 14:22–40.

Bertotti Scamozzi, O. 1761. *Il forestiere istruito. . . .* Vicenza, Italy.

———. 1796. *Le fabbriche e i disegni di Andrea Palladio raccolti ed illustrati.* 4 vols. Reprint, 1968. Vicenza, Italy.

Beyer, A. 1987. *Andrea Palladio: Teatro Olimpico.* Frankfurt.

Biermann, H. 1969. "Lo sviluppo della villa toscana." *Bollettino C.I.S.A.* 11:36–46.

———. 1970. "Das Palastmodel Giuliano da Sangallos für Ferdinand I. König von Neapel." *Wiener Jahrbuch für Kunstgeschichte* 23:154–95.

Blunt, A. 1958. *Philibert de l'Orme.* London.

Bordignon Favero, G.P. 1970. *La Villa Emo di Fanzolo.* Corpus Palladianum, vol. 5. Vicenza, Italy.

Boschi, R. 1990. "I restauri a Palazzo Barbaran da Porto." In *Andrea Palladio: Nuovi contributi,* edited by A. Chastel and R. Cevese, pp. 220–25. Milan.

Boucher, B. 1979. "The Last Will of Daniele Barbaro." *Journal of the Warburg and Courtauld Institutes* 42:277–82.

———. 1991. *The Sculpture of Jacopo Sansovino.* 2 vols. New Haven, Conn., and London.

———. 1994. "Decorating Balancing Act: The Frescoes of Palladio's Villas," *Country Life* 188: 80–83.

Braudel, F. 1972–73. *The Mediterranean and the Mediterranean World in the Age of Philip II.* 2 vols. London.

Bruschi, A. 1977. *Bramante.* London.

Buddensieg, T. 1971. "Criticism and Praise of the Pantheon in the Middle Ages and the Renaissance." In *Classical Influences on European Culture, A.D. 500–1500,* edited by R. R. Bolgar, pp. 259–67. Cambridge, England.

Burckhardt, J. 1964. *Der Cicerone.* Stuttgart, Germany.

———. 1985. *The Architecture of the Italian Renaissance.* Translated by J. Palmes and edited by P. Murray. London.

Burger, F. 1909. *Die Villen des Andrea Palladio.* Leipzig, Germany.

Burns, H. 1966. "A Peruzzi Drawing in Ferrara." *Mitteilungen des Kunsthistorischen Institutes in Florenz* 12:245–70.

———. 1973-I. "I disegni." In *Palladio,* pp. 133–54. Vicenza, Italy.

———. 1973-II. "I disegni del Palladio." *Bollettino C.I.S.A.* 15:169–91.

———. 1974. "Progetti di Francesco di Giorgio per i conventi di San Bernardino e Santa Chiara di Urbino." In *Studi bramanteschi: Atti del Congresso internazionale,* pp. 293–311. Milan.

———. 1979-I. "Le opere minori del Palladio." *Bollettino C.I.S.A.* 21:9–34.

———. 1979-II. "Suggerimenti per l'identificazione di alcuni progetti e schizzi palladiani." *Bollettino C.I.S.A.* 21:113–40.

———. 1991. "Building and Construction in Palladio's Vicenza." In *Les chantiers de la Renaissance*, edited by J. Guillaume, pp. 191–226. Paris

Burns, H., L. Fairbairn, and B. Boucher. 1975. *Andrea Palladio, 1508–1580.* London.

Burroughs, C. 1988. "Palladio and Praeneste: Notes on the Sources and Meaning of the Villa Rotonda." *Architectura* 18:59–91.

Calabi, D. 1992–93. "Le due piazze di San Marco e di Rialto . . ." *Annali di architettura* 4–5:190–201.

———, and P. Morachiello. 1987. *Rialto: le fabbriche e il ponte.* Turin, Italy.

Carunchio, T. 1974. *Origini della villa rinascimentale: La ricerca di una tipologia.* Studi storici dell'arte, vol. 4. Rome.

———. 1990. "La villa Saraceno a Finale di Augugliaro." In *Andrea Palladio: Nuovi contributi*, edited by A. Chastel and R. Cevese, pp. 198–207. Milan.

Castellini, S. 1783–1822. *Storia della città di Vicenza . . . sino all'anno 1630.* 14 vols. Vicenza, Italy.

Cavallari Murat, A. 1972. "Palladio ingegnere." *Bollettino C.I.S.A.* 14:253–70.

Cavaggioni, I., and C. del Zoppo. 1989–90. "Villa Saraceno a Finale di Augliaro attraverso i documenti e la cartografia." *Arte Veneta* 43:142–51.

Cessi, F. 1967. *Vincenzo e Giangirolamo Grandi.* Trent, Italy.

Cessi, R., and A. Alberti. 1934. *Rialto: L'isola, il ponte, il mercato.* Bologna, Italy.

Cevese, R. 1952. *I palazzi dei Thiene.* Vicenza, Italy.

———. 1964. *"Le opere pubbliche e i palazzi privati . . .* di G. G. Zorzi." *Bollettino C.I.S.A.* 6:334–59.

———. 1965. "Appunti palladiani." *Bollettino C.I.S.A.* 7:305–15.

———. 1971. *Ville della provincia di Vicenza.* 2 vols. Milan.

———. 1973. "L'opera del Palladio." In *Palladio*, pp. 45–130. Venice.

———. 1976. *I modelli della Mostra del Palladio.* Milan.

———. 1980. "Andrea Palladio architetto nella bottega di Pedemuro." *Bollettino C.I.S.A.* 20:159–66.

———. 1990. "La casa del notaio Pietro Cogollo, detta volgamenta 'casa del Palladio.'" In *Andrea Palladio: Nuovi contributi*, edited by A. Chastel and R. Cevese, pp. 73–82. Milan.

Chambers, D., and J. Martineau, eds. 1981. *Splendours of the Gonzaga.* London.

Ciardi, R. P., ed. 1973–74. *Gian Paolo Lomazzo: Scritti sulle arti.* 2 vols. Florence.

Cicogna, E. A. 1824–53. *Delle iscrizioni veneziane.* 6 vols. Venice.

Coffin, D. 1960. *The Villa d'Este at Tivoli.* Princeton, N.J.

———. 1979. *The Villa in the Life of Renaissance Rome.* Princeton, N.J.

Constable, W. G., and J. G. Links. 1976. *Canaletto: Giovanni Antonio Canaletto, 1697–1768.* 2 vols. Oxford.

Cooper, T. E. 1990-I. "The History and Decoration of the Church of San Giorgio Maggiore in Venice." Ph.D. diss., Princeton University.

———. 1990-II. "La facciata commemorativa di S. Giorgio Maggiore." In *Andrea Palladio: Nuovi contributi*, edited by A. Chastel and R. Cevese, pp. 136–45. Milan.

Corazzol, G. 1979. *Fitti e livelli a grano: Un aspetto del credito rurale nel Veneto del '500.* Milan.

Cosgrove, D. 1989. "Power and Place in the Venetian Territories." In *The Power of Place: Bringing Together Geographical and Sociological Imaginations*, edited by J. Agnew and J. Duncan, Boston.

de la Croix, H. 1960. "Military Archaeology and the Radial City Plan in Sixteenth-Century Italy." *Art Bulletin* 42:263–90.

Dalla Pozza, A. M. 1943. *Andrea Palladio.* Vicenza, Italy.

———. 1943–63. "Palladiana, VIII–IX." In *Odeo Olimpico:* 99–131.

———. 1964–65. "Palladiana, X–XII." In *Odeo Olimpico:* 203–38.

Damerini, G. 1956. *L'isola e il cenobio di San Giorgio Maggiore.* Venice.

Da Mosto, A. 1960. *I dogi di Venezia nella vita pubblica e privata.* Milan.

Daniele, A. 1989. "Attività letteraria." In *Storia di Vicenza*, vol. 3, pt. 2. edited by F. Barbieri and P. Preto, pp. 39–68. Vicenza, Italy.

Davis, C., et al. 1981. *Giorgio Vasari: Principi, letterati e artisti nelle carte di Giorgio Vasari.* Florence.

Davies, P., and D. Hemsoll. 1991. "Palazzo Bevilacqua e la tipologia del palazzo veronese." *Annali di architettura* 3:58–69.

———. 1995. "Sanmicheli's Palazzo Pompei: Site, Date and Design." *Annali di architettura* 7:95–110.

Dinsmoor, W. R. 1942. "The Literary Remains of Sebastiano Serlio." *Art Bulletin* 24:55–91, 115–54.

Dionisotti, C. 1980. "L'Italia del Trissino." In *Convegno di studi su Giangiorgio Trissino*, pp. 11–22. Vicenza, Italy.

Doni, A. F. 1549. *Disegno del Doni*. Venice.

———. 1555. *La seconda libreria*. Venice.

v. Einem, H. 1982. "Palladio und Goethe." In *Vierhundert Jahre Andrea Palladio, 1580–1980*, pp. 131–41. (Conference in Wuppertal, 1980.) Heidelberg, Germany.

Fagiolo, M. 1978. "Le facciate palladiane: La progettazione come proiezione sul piano di spazi dietro spazi." *Bollettino C.I.S.A.* 20:47–70.

Fancelli, P. 1974. *Palladio e Preneste: Archeologia, modelli, progettazione*. Rome.

Fanti, M. 1983–84. "La Basilica di San Petronio nella storia religiosa e civile della città." In *La Basilica di San Petronio*, vol. 1, pp. 9–40. Bologna.

Ferrari, G. E. 1976. "La raccolta palladiana e collaterale di Guglielmo Cappelletti al C.I.S.A. di Vicenza, Italy." *Bollettino C.I.S.A.* 18:333–550.

———. 1980. "La raccolta palladiana e collaterale di Guglielmo Cappelletti al C.I.S.A. di Vicenza." *Bollettino C.I.S.A.* 22:227–412.

Fiocco, G. 1965. *Alvise Cornaro: Il suo tempo e le sue opere*. Vicenza, Italy.

Firpo, L., ed. 1963. *Leonardo architetto e urbanista*. Turin, Italy.

Fogolari, G. 1935. "Il processo dell'inquisizione a Paolo Veronese." *Archivio Veneto*, 5th ser. 17:352–86.

Fontana, V. 1988. *Fra Giovanni Giocondo*. Vicenza, Italy.

Forssman, E. 1961. *Dorisch, Ionisch, Korinthisch*. Stockholm.

———. 1965. *Palladios Lehrgebäude*. Stockholm.

———. 1966. "Falconetto e Palladio." *Bollettino C.I.S.A.* 8:52–67.

———. 1973-I. *Il Palazzo da Porto Festa di Vicenza*. Corpus Palladianum, vol. 8. Vicenza, Italy.

———. 1973-II. *Visible Harmony: Palladio's Villa Foscari at Malcontenta*. Stockholm.

———. 1978. "Palladio e le colonne." *Bollettino C.I.S.A.* 20:71–87.

Forster, K. 1974. "Back to the Farm." *Architectura* 1:1–12.

———. 1980. "Is Palladio's Villa Rotonda an Architectural Novelty?" In *Palladio: Ein Symposium*, edited by K. Forster and M. Kubelik, pp. 27–34. Einsiedeln, Germany.

Forster, K., and R. Tuttle. 1971. "The Palazzo del Te." *Journal of the Society of Architectural Historians* 30:267–93.

———. 1973. "Giulio Romano e le opere vicentine del Palladio." *Bollettino C.I.S.A.* 15:107–19.

Foscari, A. 1978. "Malcontenta: Il restauro delle facciate." *Bollettino C.I.S.A.* 20:273–82.

———. 1979. "L'invenzione di Palladio per un 'sito Piramidale' in Venezia." *Arte Veneta* 33:136–41.

Foscari, A., and M. Tafuri. 1983. *L'armonia e i conflitti*. Turin, Italy.

Foster, P. 1978. *A Study of Lorenzo de Medici's Villa at Poggio a Caiano*. 2 vols. Outstanding Dissertations in the Fine Arts. New York.

Franco, F. 1958. "I Disegni delle antichità del Palladio." *Arte Veneta* 12:230–33.

Franzina, E. 1980. *Vicenza: Storia di una città*. Vicenza, Italy.

Fraser Jenkins, A. 1970. "Cosimo de' Medici's Patronage of Architecture and the Theory of Magnificence." *Journal of the Warburg and Courtauld Institutes*. 33:162–70.

Fréart de Chambray, R. 1650. *Parallèle de l'architecture antique et de la moderne*. Paris.

Frommel, C. L. 1973. *Der römische Palastbau des Hochrenaissance*. 3 vols. Tübingen, Germany.

———. 1977. "Palladio e la chiesa di San Pietro a Roma." *Bollettino C.I.S.A.* 19:111–24.

———. 1990. "Roma e la formazione architettonica del Palladio." In *Andrea Palladio: Nuovi contributi*, edited by A. Chastel and R. Cevese, pp. 146–65. Milan.

Frommel, C., et al. 1984. *Raffaello architetto*. Milan.

Gallo, R. 1955. "Andrea Palladio e Venezia. . . ," *Rivista di Venezia*, n.s. 1:23–48.

Gauthey, E. M. 1809–16. *Traité de la construction des ponts*, 3 vols. Paris.

Gazzola, P. 1960. *Michele Sanmicheli*. Verona.

Gilbert, F. 1973. "Venice in the Crisis of the League of Cambrai." In *Renaissance Venice*, edited by J. R. Hale, pp. 274–92. London.

Gioseffi, D. 1972. "Il disegno come fase progettuale dell'attività palladiana." *Bollettino C.I.S.A.* 14:45–62.

————. 1973. "Palladio e l'antico." *Bollettino C.I.S.A.* 15:43–66.

————. 1978. "Dal progetto al trattato: Incontro e scontro con la realtà." *Bollettino C.I.S.A.* 20:27–45.

Goedicke, C., K. Slusallek, and M. Kubelik. 1986. "Thermoluminescence Dating in Architectural History: The Chronology of Palladio's Villa Rotonda." *Journal of the Society of Architectural Historians* 45:396–407.

Goethe, J. W. 1962. *Italian Journey, 1786–1788*. Translated by W. H. Auden and E. Mayer. London.

Goldthwaite, R. A. 1980. *The Building of Renaissance Florence*. Baltimore.

Golzio, V. 1936. *Raffaello nei documenti*. Vatican City.

Gombrich, E. H. 1967. "Celebrations in Venice of the Victory of Lepanto." In *Studies . . . Presented to Anthony Blunt*, pp. 62–68. London.

Goy, R. J. 1989. *Venetian Vernacular Architecture*. Cambridge, England.

Groblewski, M. 1976. *Die Kirche San Giovanni Battista in Pesaro von Girolamo Genga*. Regensburg, Germany.

Grubb, J. S., 1988. *Firstborn of Venice: Vicenza in the Early Renaissance State*. Baltimore and London.

Guillaume, J., ed. 1988. *Les Traités d'Architecture de la Renaissance*. Paris.

————. 1992. *L'emploi des ordres dans l'architecture de la Renaissance*. Paris.

Günther, H. 1981. "Studien zum venezianischen Aufenthalt des Sebastiano Serlio." *Münchner Jahrbuch der bildenden Kunst*, 3rd ser., 32:42–94.

————. 1990. "Palladio e gli ordini di colonne." In *Andrea Palladio: Nuovi contributi*, edited by A. Chastel and R. Cevese, pp. 182–97. Milan.

Hale, J. R. 1977. "Andrea Palladio, Polybius and Julius Caesar." *Journal of the Warburg and Courtauld Institutes* 40:240–55.

Hamilton, S. B. 1954–84. "Bridges." In *A History of Technology*, edited by C. J. Singer et al., vol. 3, pp. 417–37. Oxford, England.

Harris, J. 1970. *Sir William Chambers*. London.

————. 1971. "Three Unrecorded Palladio Designs from Inigo Jones' Collection." *Burlington Magazine* 113:34–37.

————. 1994. *The Palladian Revival: Lord Burlington, His Villa and Garden at Chiswick*. New Haven and London.

Haslam, R. 1994. "Villa Saraceno . . ." *Country Life* 188:44–49.

Hemsoll, D. 1992–93. "Le piazze di Brescia nel medioevo e nel rinascimento . . ." *Annali di architettura* 4–5:168–77.

Hemsoll, D., and E. Caplin. 1989. *The Temple of Fortune as an Inspiration to Architects*. London.

Heydenreich, L. H. 1969. "La Villa: Genesi e sviluppi fino al Palladio." *Bollettino C.I.S.A.* 11:11–22.

Hirthe, T. 1986. "Il foro all'antica di Venezia: La trasformazione di Piazza San Marco nel cinquecento." *Centro Tedesco di Studi Veneziani:Quaderni*, no. 35.

Hitchcock, H. R. 1981. *German Renaissance Architecture*. Princeton, N.J.

Holberton, P. 1990. *Palladio's Villas: Life in the Renaissance Countryside*. London.

Horn, T. 1980. *Gedeckte Holzbrücken: Zeugen alter Holzbaukunst*. Klagenfurt, Austria.

Howard, D. 1975. *Jacopo Sansovino: Architecture and Patronage in Renaissance Venice*. New Haven, Conn., and London.

————. 1977. "Le chiese di Jacopo Sansovino a Venezia." *Bollettino C.I.S.A.* 19:49–67.

————. 1980. "Four Centuries of Literature on Palladio." *Journal of the Society of Architectural Historians* 39:224–41.

Howard, D., and M. Longair. 1982. "Harmonic Proportion in Palladio's *Quattro Libri*." *Journal of the Society of Architectural Historians* 41:116–43.

Howe, E. D. 1991. *Andrea Palladio: The Churches of Rome*. Binghampton, N.Y.

Huse, N. 1974. "Palladio und die Villa Barbaro in Maser: Bemerkungen zum Problem der Autorschaft." *Arte Veneta* 28:106–22.

————. 1979. "Palladio am Canal Grande." *Städel Jahrbuch*, (new series), VII, 1979, 61–99.

Huse, N., and W. Wolters. 1990. *The Art of Renaissance Venice*. Chicago.

Isermeyer, C. A. 1967. "Die Villa Rotonda von Palladio: Bemerkungen zu Baubeginn und Baugeschichte." *Zeitschrift für Kunstgeschichte* 30:207–21.

————. 1968. "Le chiese del Palladio in rapporto al culto." *Bollettino C.I.S.A.* 10:42–58.

————. 1972. "La concezione degli edifici sacri palladiani." *Bollettino C.I.S.A.* 14:105–35.

————. 1980. "Il primo progetto del Palladio per San Giorgio secondo il modello del 1565." *Bollettino C.I.S.A.* 22:259–68.

Jaroszewski, T. 1967. "Alcuni tentativi di imitare la Rotonda compiuti nel secolo XVII." *Bollettino C.I.S.A..* 9:417–24.

————. 1975. "Il palazzo Da Porto Breganze e gli influssi serliani." *Bollettino C.I.S.A.* 17:397–400.

Keller, F. E. 1971. "Alvise Cornaro zitierte die Villa des Marcus Terrentius Varro in Cassino." *L'Arte*, n.s. 14:29–53.

Köster, B. 1990. *Palladio in Amerika: Die Kontinuität klassizistischen Bauens in den USA.* Munich.

Kolb Lewis, C. 1977. *The Villa Giustinian at Roncade.* Outstanding Dissertations in the Fine Arts. New York.

Krautheimer, R. 1969-I. "Alberti and Vitruvius." In *Studies in Early Christian, Medieval and Renaissance Art*, pp. 323–32. New York.

————. 1969-II. "The Tragic and Comic Scene of the Renaissance." In *Studies in Early Christian, Medieval and Renaissance Art*, pp. 345–59. New York.

————. 1975. *Early Christian and Byzantine Architecture.* Harmondsworth, England (rev. ed.).

Kruft, H.-W. 1986. *Geschichte der Architektur Theorie.* Munich, Germany.

Kubelik, M. 1977. *Die Villa im Veneto: Zur typologischen Entwicklung im Quattrocento.* Munich, Germany.

————. 1981. "Palladios Werk im Spannungsfeld zwischen Bau-Realisation und Bau-Publikation." *Bauforum* 14:13–22.

La Follette, L. 1993. "A Contribution of Andrea Palladio to the Study of Roman Thermae." *Journal of the Society of Arhchitectural Historians* 52:189–98.

Lane, F. C. 1973. *Venice, a Maritime Republic.* Baltimore.

Lazzaro, C. 1990. *The Italian Renaissance Garden.* New Haven, Conn., and London.

Leithe-Jasper, M. 1975. "Beiträge zum Werk des Agostino Zoppo." *Jahrbuch des Stiftes Klosterneuburg.* 9:109–38.

Lemerle, F., and Y. Pauwels. 1991. "L'ionique: enquête de base." *Annali di architettura* 3:7–13.

Lewine, M. J. 1973. "Vignola e Palladio: Sant' Andrea in via Flamina e la chiesa di Maser." *Bollettino C.I.S.A.* 15:121–30.

Lewis, D. 1981. *The Drawings of Andrea Palladio.* Washington, D.C.

Lieberman, R. 1982. *Renaissance Architecture in Venice 1450–1540.* New York.

Lillie, A. 1987. "Florentine Villas in the Fifteenth Century: A Study of the Strozzi and Sassetti Country Properties." Ph.D. diss., University of London.

Links, J. G. 1977. *Canaletto and his Patrons.* London.

Lotz, W. 1956. "Das Raumbild in der Architekturzeichnung der italienischen Renaissance." *Mitteilungen des Kunsthistorischen Institutes in Florenz* 7:193–226.

————. 1962. "Osservazioni intorno ai disegni palladiani." *Bollettino C.I.S.A.* 4:61–68.

————. 1963. "Mannerism in Architecture: Changing Aspects." In *Studies in Western Art*, vol. 2, *The Renaissance and Mannerism*, pp. 239–46. Acts of the Twentieth International Congress of the History of Art. Princeton, N.J.

————. 1977-I. *Studies in Italian Renaissance Architecture.* Cambridge, Mass.

————. 1977-II. "Il Tempietto di Maser: Note e riflessioni." *Bollettino C.I.S.A.* 19:125–34.

Lunardon, S. 1982. "Interventi di Palladio sui luoghi pii: Le Zitelle." In *Palladio e Venezia*, edited by L. Puppi, pp. 103–20. Florence.

Machiavelli, Niccolò. 1961. *The Literary Works of Machiavelli.* Translated by J. R. Hale. Oxford.

Magagnato, L. 1951. "The Genesis of the *Teatro Olimpico*." *Journal of the Warburg and Courtauld Institutes* 14:209–20.

————. 1966. *Palazzo Thiene.* Vicenza, Italy.

————. 1968. "I collaboratori veronesi di Andrea Palladio." *Bollettino C.I.S.A.* 10:170–87.

Magagnato, L., and P. Marini, eds. 1980. *Andrea Palladio: I Quattro Libri dell'architettura.* Milan.

Magrini, A. 1845. *Memorie intorno la vita e le opere di Andrea Palladio.* Padua, Italy.

————. 1855. *Il Palazzo del Museo Civico in Vicenza.* Vicenza, Italy.

Mainstone, R. 1975. *Developments in Structural Form.* London.

Maltese, C. 1967. *F. di Giorgio Martini: Trattati di architettura, ingegneria, e arte militare.* 2 vols. Milan.

Mantese, G. 1964. *Memorie storiche della chiesa vicentina,* vol. 3, pt. 2. Vicenza, Italy.

———. 1980. "Montano IV Barbarano committente del palladiano Palazzo Barbarano da Porto." *Bollettino C.I.S.A.* 22:147–57.

———. 1988. "Paolo Almerigo, committente della Rotonda." In *La Rotonda,* Novum Corpus Palladianum, vol. I, pp. 33–46. Milan.

Marder, T. 1981. "La dedica e funzione del Tempietto di Palladio a Maser." *Bollettino C.I.S.A.* 23:241–46.

Mariacher, G. 1988. "Le sculture e gli stucchi." In *La Rotonda,* Novum Corpus Palladianum, vol. I, pp. 123–41. Milan.

Marini, P., ed. 1980. *Palladio e Verona.* Verona, Italy.

Martini, A. 1883. *Manuale di metrologia. . . .* Reprint, 1976. Turin, Italy.

Marzari, G. 1591. *La historia di Vicenza.* Vicenza, Italy.

Mason Rinaldi, S., and A. Zitelli, eds. 1979. *Venezia e la peste, 1348–1797.* Venice.

Maylender, M. 1926–30. *Storia delle accademie d'Italia.* 5 vols. Bologna, Italy.

McKay, A. G. 1975. *Houses, Villas and Palaces in the Roman World.* London.

Mielke, F. 1980. "Die Treppen im Werk Andrea Palladios." *Bollettino C.I.S.A.* 22:167–86.

Mielsch, H. 1987. *Die römische Villa: Architektur und Lebensform.* Munich, Germany.

Milizia, F. 1785. *Memorie degli architetti antichi e moderni.* 2 vols. Bassano, Italy.

Mitrović, B. 1990. "Palladio's Theory of Proportions and the Second Book of the *Quattro Libri dell'Architettura.*" *Journal of the Society of Architectural Historians.* 49:279–92.

Montaigne, M. de. 1942. *Journal de voyage en Italie par la Suisse et l'Allemagne en 1580 et 1581. . . .* Edited by M. Rat. Paris.

Monza, F. 1888. *Cronaca.* Edited by D. Bortolan. Vicenza, Italy.

Morresi, M. 1988. *Villa Porto Colleoni a Thiene.* Milan.

———. 1990. "Un apocrifo palladiano: Palazzo da Monte Migliorini a Vicenza." In *Andrea Palladio: Nuovi contributi,* edited by A. Chastel and R. Cevese, pp. 112–21. Milan.

Morsolin, B. 1878. *Giangiorgio Trissino.* Vicenza, Italy.

Muir, E. 1981. *Civil Ritual in Renaissance Venice.* Princeton, N.J.

Muraro, M. 1980. *La villa palladiana dei Repeta a Campiglia dei Berici.* Campiglia dei Berici, Italy.

———. 1987. *Venetian Villas.* New York.

Muttoni, F. 1740. *Architettura di Andrea Palladio vicentino: Con le osservazioni dell'architetto N. N.* Venice.

Nash, E. 1961–62. *Pictorial Dictionary of Ancient Rome.* 2 vols. London.

Nesselrath, A. 1986. "I libri di disegni di antichità: Tentativo di una tipologia." In *Memoria dell'antico nell'arte italiana,* vol. 3, *Dalla tradizione all'archeologia,* edited by S. Settis, pp. 89–147. Turin, Italy.

Newman, J. 1980. "Inigo Jones e la sua copia de 'I Quattro Libri' di Palladio." *Bollettino C.I.S.A.* 22:41–62.

Niccolini, E. 1989. "Le Accademie." In *Storia di Vicenza,* vol. 3, pt. 2, pp. 89–108. Vicenza, Italy.

de Nolhac, P., and A. Solerti. 1890. *Il viaggio in Italia di Enrico III. . . .* Turin, Italy.

Nogara, G. 1972. *Cronache degli spettacoli nel Teatro Olimpico di Vicenza dal 1585 al 1970.* Vicenza, Italy.

Olivato, L., and L. Puppi. 1980. "Andrea Palladio, accademico Olimpico." In *Andrea Palladio: Il testo, l'imagine, la città,* edited by L. Puppi, pp. 166–200. Milan.

Onians, M. 1988. *Bearers of Meaning: The Classical Orders in Antiquity, the Middle Ages and the Renaissance.* Princeton, N.J.

Orlandi, G., and P. Portoghesi, eds. 1966. *Leon Battista Alberti: L'Architettura (De re aedificatoria).* 2 vols. Milan.

Pagliara, P. N. 1986. "Vitruvio da testo a canone." In *Memoria dell'antico nell'arte italiana,* vol. 3, *Dalla tradizione all'archeologia,* edited by S. Settis, pp. 5–85. Turin, Italy.

Palladio, A. 1570. *I quattro libri dell'architettura.* Reprint, 1960. Venice.

Palladio, Andrea. 1738. *The Four Books of Andrea Palladio's Architecture.* Translated by I. Ware. Reprint, 1965. London.

Palladio: La sua eredità nel mondo. 1980. Milan.

Pane, R. 1956. "Andrea Palladio e la interpretazione dell'architettura rinascimentale." In *Venezia e l'Europa,* Atti del XVIII Congresso Internazionale di storia dell'arte, pp. 408–12. Venice.

———. 1961. *Andrea Palladio*. Turin, Italy.

Pastor, L. v. 1958–64. *Storia dei papi*. 17 vols. Rome.

Pauwels, Y. 1989. "Les origines de l'ordre composite." *Annali di architettura* 1:29–46.

Pedretti, C. 1979. *Leonardo architetto*. Milan.

Pée, H. 1941. *Die Palastbauten des Andrea Palladio*. 2d ed. Würzburg.

Pereswet Soltan, A. 1978. "Il restauro della Villa Pisani, ora Ferri, a Bagnolo." *Bollettino C.I.S.A.* 20:283–96.

Platner, S. B., and T. Ashby. 1929. *A Topographical Dictionary of Ancient Rome*. London.

Polacco, L. 1965. "La posizione di Palladio di fronte all'antichità." *Bollettino C.I.S.A.* 7:59–76.

Prinz, W. 1969. "La 'sala di quattro colonne' nell'opera di Palladio." *Bollettino C.I.S.A.* 11:370–86.

———. 1980. *Schloss Chambord und die Villa Rotonda in Vicenza: Studien zur Ikonologie*. Berlin.

Priuli, G. 1938. *I. Diarii*. Vol. 4. Rerum Italicarum Scriptores, vol. 24, part 3, edited by R. Cessi. Bologna, Italy.

Puppi, L. 1972. *La Villa Badoer di Fratta Polesine*. Corpus Palladianum, vol. 8. Vicenza, Italy.

———. 1973-I. *Andrea Palladio*. 2 vols. Milan.

———. 1973-II. *Scrittori vicentini d'architettura del secolo XVI*. Vicenza, Italy.

———. 1974. "Dubbi e certezzi per Palladio construttore in villa." *Arte Veneta* 28:93–105.

———. 1980-I. *Alvise Cornaro e il suo tempo*. Padua, Italy.

———. 1980-II. *Architettura e utopia nella Venezia del 500*. Milan.

———. 1982. "La morte e i funerali di Andrea Palladio." In *Palladio e Venezia*, pp. 155–72. Florence.

———. 1986. *Michele Sanmichele architetto: L'opere completa*. Rome.

———. 1988. *Andrea Palladio: Scritti sull'architettura, 1554–1579*. Vicenza, Italy.

———. 1989. *Palladio: Corpus dei disegni al Museo Civico di Vicenza*. Milan.

———. 1990. "La committenza vicentina di Paolo Veronese." In *Nuovi studi su Paolo Veronese*, edited by M. Gemin, pp. 340–46. Venice.

Puppi, L., and C. D. Romanelli, eds. 1985. *Le Venezie possibili*. Venice.

Rasch, J. J. 1984. *Das Maxentius-Mausoleum an der Via Appia in Rom*. Mainz am Rhein, Germany.

Raymond, J. 1648. *An Itinerary Contayning a Voyage Made Through Italy*. London.

Rearick, W. R. 1990. "The Early Portraits of Veronese." In *Nuovi studi su Paolo Veronese*, edited by M. Gemin, pp. 347–58. Venice.

Rigon, F., ed. 1980. *I Ponti di Palladio*. Milan.

Rigoni, E. 1970. *L'arte rinascimentale a Padova: studi e documenti*. Padua, Italy.

Robertson, C. 1992. *"Il gran cardinale": Alessandro Farnese, Patron of Arts*. New Haven, Conn., and London.

Rosci, M. 1968. "Forme e funzioni delle ville venete pre-palladiane." *L'Arte*, n.s. 2:27–54.

———. 1969. "Ville Rustiche del Quattrocento Veneto." *Bollettino C.I.S.A.* 11:78–82.

Rosenfeld, M., ed. 1978. *Sebastiano Serlio on Domestic Architecture*. Cambridge, Mass.

Rosenthal, E. 1962. "The House of Andrea Mantegna in Mantua." *Gazette des Beaux-Arts* (6th ser.) 60:327–48.

Rossi, P. 1988. "Gli affreschi." In *La Rotonda*, Novum Corpus Palladianum, vol. 1, pp. 143–67. Milan.

Rowe, C. 1976. *The Mathematics of the Ideal Villa and Other Essays*. Cambridge, Mass.

Ruddock, T. 1979. *Architectural Bridges and Their Builders, 1735–1835*. Cambridge, England.

Rumor, S. 1912. *Il Palazzo della Banca Popolare già dei conti di Thieni di Vicenza*. Vicenza, Italy.

Rupprecht, B. 1966. "Villa: Zur Geschichte eines Ideals." In *Probleme der Kunstwissenschaft*, vol. 2, *Wandlungen des Paradieischen und Utopischen*, pp. 210–50. Berlin.

———. 1969. "Ville venete del' 400 e del primo '500." *Bollettino C.I.S.A.* 7:239–50.

———. 1982. "Prinzipien der Architektur-Darstellungen in Palladios *I Quattro Libri dell'Architettura*." In *Vierhunderte Jahre Andrea Palladios, 1580–1980*, pp. 11–43. Heidelberg, Germany.

Saalman, H. 1959. "Filarete's Theory of Architecture." *Art Bulletin*, 41:89–106.

Sanudo, M. 1847. *Itinerario . . . per la Terraferma Veneziana nell'anno MCCCCLXXXV*. Padua, Italy.

Sansovino, F. 1581. *Venetia città nobilissima et singolare*. Venice.

Sartori, A. 1976. *Documenti per la storia dell'arte a Padova*. Edited by C. Fillarini. Vicenza, Italy.

Scamozzi, V. 1615. *L'idea dell'architettura universale*. Venice.

da Schio, G. *Persone memorabili in Vicenza*. Biblioteca Bertoliana, Vicenza, MSS. Bertoliana, G. 5.9.5–16 / G. 6.10.1–11.

Schlosser Magnino, J. 1964. *La letteratura artistica*. Edited by O. Kurz. Florence.

Schulz, M. 1982. "The Communal Buildings of Parma." *Mitteilungen des Kunsthistorischen Institutes in Florenz* 26:279–324.

Schweikhart, G. 1968. "Studien zum Werke des Giovanni Maria Falconetto." *Bollettino dei Musei Civici di Padova* 57:17–67.

———. 1971. "Paolo Veronese in der Villa Soranza. . . ." *Mitteilungen des Kunsthistorischen Institutes in Florenz* 15:187–206.

Segarizzi, A. 1912–16. *Relazioni degli Ambasciatori veneti al Senato*. 3 vols. Bari, Italy.

Serlio, S. 1537. *Regole generali di architettura*. Venice.

———. 1619. *Tutte le opere d'architettura*. Venice.

Semenzato, C. 1988. "L'architettura della Rotonda." In *La Rotonda*, Novum Corpus Palladianum, vol. I, pp. 55–121. Milan.

Sereni, E. 1961. *Storia del paesaggio agrario italiano*. Bari, Italy.

Shearman, J. 1967. "Giulio Romano: Tradizione licenze, artifici." *Bollettino C.I.S.A.* 9:354–68.

———. 1968. "Raphael as Architect." *Journal of the Royal Society of Arts* 116:388–409.

———. 1972. *Raphael's Cartoons in the Collection of H.M. The Queen and the Tapestries for the Sistine Chapel*. London.

Sicca, C. M. 1988. "La fortuna della Rotonda." In *La Rotonda*, Novum Corpus Palladianum, vol. I, pp. 169–204. Milan.

Singer, C. M., et al. 1954–84. *A History of Technology*. 8 vols. Oxford.

Smith, G. 1977. *The Casino of Pius IV*. Princeton, N.J.

Spencer, J. 1965. *Filarete's Treatise on Architecture*. 2 vols. New Haven, Conn.

Spielmann, H. 1966. *Andrea Palladio und die Antike*. Munich, Germany and Berlin.

Stella, A. 1958. "La proprietà ecclesiastica nella Repubblica di Venezia dal secolo XV al XVII." *Nuova rivista storica* 42:50–77.

Strachan, M. 1962. *The Life and Adventures of Thomas Coryate*. London.

Stringa, G. 1604. *Venetia città nobilissima et singo-lare. . . .* Venice.

Summers, D. 1972. "Michelangelo on Architecture." *Art Bulletin* 54:147–57.

———. 1981. *Michelangelo and the Language of Art*. Princeton, N.J.

Summerson, J. 1966. *Inigo Jones*. Harmondsworth, England.

———. 1989. *Architecture in Britain, 1530–1830*. Rev. ed. London.

Swoboda, K. 1924. *Römische und romanische Paläste*. Vienna.

Tafuri, M. 1972. *Jacopo Sansovino e l'architettura del '500 a Venezia*. Rev. ed. Padua, Italy.

———. 1985. *Venezia e il Rinascimento: Religione, scienza, architettura*. Turin, Italy.

———. 1990. "Il disegno di Chatsworth (per il palazzo Ducale di Venezia?) e un progetto perduto di Jacopo Sansovino." In *Andrea Palladio: Nuovi contributi*, edited by A. Chastel and R. Cevese, pp. 100–11. Milan.

Tafuri, M., et al. 1989. *Giulio Romano*. Milan.

Tavernor, R. 1991. *Palladio and Palladianism*. London.

Temanza, T. 1778. *Vite dei più celebri architetti*. Venice. Reprint. Milan, 1966.

Tessarolo, A. 1991. "Per la cronologia di villa Emo a Fanzolo." *Annali di architettura* 3:90–97.

Thoenes, C. 1983. "Vignolas *Regola delli cinque ordini*." *Römisches Jahrbuch für Kunstgeschichte* 20:345–76.

Thomson, D. 1984. *Renaissance Paris*. London.

Timofiewitsch, W. 1962-I. "Eine Zeichnung Andrea Palladios für die Klosteranlage von San Giorgio Maggiore." *Arte Veneta* 16:160–63.

———. 1962-II. "Fassadenetwürfe Andrea Palladios für S. Petronio in Bologna." *Arte Veneta* 16:82–97.

———. 1963. "Ein neuer Beitrag zu der Baugeschichte von S. Giorgio Maggiore." *Bollettino C.I.S.A.* 5:330–39.

———. 1968. *Die sakrale Architektur Palladios*. Munich, Germany.

———. 1969. *La Chiesa del Redentore*. Corpus Palladianum, vol. 3. Vicenza, Italy.

———. 1980. "Alcune osservazioni in rapporto alle facciate delle chiese palladiane." *Bollettino C.I.S.A.* 22:237–46.

Trincanato, E. 1948. *Venezia minore*. Milan.

Vasari, G. 1878–85. *Le vite de' più eccellenti pittori, scultori e architettori.* 9 vols. Edited by G. Milanesi. Florence.

Venditti, A. 1969. *La Loggia del Capitaniato.* Corpus Palladianum, vol. 4. Vicenza, Italy.

———. 1971. "Un'opera di Palladio nel Friuli: Il Palazzo Antonini a Udine." *Aachner Kunstblätter* 41:75–89.

Ventura, A. 1964. *Nobiltà e popolo nella società veneta del '400 e '500.* Bari, Italy.

———. 1969. "Aspetti storico-economici della villa veneta." *Bollettino C.I.S.A.* 11:65–77.

Ventura, M. 1964. "Marc'antonio Barbaro." *Dizionario biografico degli italiani* 6:110–13.

Verheyen, E. 1977. *The Palazzo del Te in Mantua. . . .* Baltimore.

Vespasiano da Bisticci. 1963. *Renaissance Princes, Popes and Prelates: The Vespasiano Memoirs.* Translated by W. George and E. Walters. New York.

Villani, P. 1966. "Il capitalismo agrario in Italia (secoli XVII–XIX)." *Studi storici* 7:471–513.

Waley, D. 1978. *The Italian City-Republics.* Rev. ed. London.

Ware, I. See Palladio (1738).

Wilinski, S. 1968. "La serliana di Villa Poiana Maggiore." *Bollettino C.I.S.A.* 10:79–84.

Wittkower, R. 1962. *Architectural Principles in the Age of Humanism.* Rev. ed. London.

———. 1963. "L'influenza del Palladio sullo sviluppo dell'architettura religiosa veneziana nel sei e settecento." *Bollettino C.I.S.A.* 5:61–72.

———. 1969. *Grundlagen der Architektur im Zeitalter des Humanismus.* Munich, Germany.

———. 1974. *Gothic versus Classic: Architectural Projects in Seventeenth Century Italy.* London.

Wolters, W. 1968. *Plastische Deckendekorationen des Cinquecento in Venedig und im Veneto.* Berlin.

———. 1968-II. "Andrea Palladio e la decorazione dei suoi edifici." *Bollettino C.I.S.A.* 10:255–67.

———. 1969. "Sebastiano Serlio e il suo contributo alla villa veneziana prima del Palladio." *Bollettino C.I.S.A.* 11:83–94.

Woolf, S. J. 1968. "Venice and the Terra Ferma: Problems of the Change from Commercial to Landed Activities." In *Crisis and Change in the Venetian Economy,* edited by B. Pullan, pp. 175–203. London.

Zamperetti, S. 1989. "Poteri locali e governo centrale in una città suddita d'antico regime dal dopo Cambrai al primo seicento." In *Storia di Vicenza,* vol. 3, pt. I, edited by F. Barbieri and P. Preto, pp. 67–113. Vicenza, Italy.

Zanazzo, G. B. 1964–65. Bravi e signorotti in Vicenzi e nel Vicentino nei secoli XVI e XVII." *Odeo Olimpico* 5:97–138.

———. 1966–67. "Bravi e signorotti in Vicenza. . . ." *Odeo Olimpico* 6:259–72.

———. 1969–70. "Bravi e signorotti in Vicenza. . . ." *Odeo Olimpico* 8:187–225.

Zaupa, J. 1990. *Andrea Palladio e la sua committenza: Denaro e architettura nella Vicenza del Cinquecento.* Rome.

Zocconi, M. 1972. "Techniche construttive nell'architettura palladiana." *Bollettino C.I.S.A.,* 14:271–89.

Zorzi, G. G. 1916. "Il matrimonio di Andrea Palladio." *Nuovo Archivio Veneto* 32:172–86.

———. 1937. *Contributo alla storia dell'arte vicentina dei secoli xv e xvi: Il preclassicismo e i prepalladiani.* Venice.

———. 1949. "Ancora della vera origine e della giovinezza di Andrea Palladio secondo nuovi documenti." *Arte Veneta* 3:140–42.

———. 1959-I. *I disegni delle antichità di Andrea Palladio.* Venice.

———. 1959-II. "Paolo Gualdo: Vita di Andrea Palladio." *Saggi e Memorie di Storia dell'Arte* 2:93–104.

———. 1961. "I disegni delle opere palladiane pubblicate ne *I Quattro Libri dell'Architettura* di Andrea Palladio." *Bollettino C.I.S.A.* 3:12–17.

———. 1965. *Le opere pubbliche e i palazzi privati di Andrea Palladio.* Venice.

———. 1966. *Le chiese e i ponti di Andrea Palladio.* Venice.

———. 1969. *Le ville e i teatri di Andrea Palladio.* Venice.

INDEX

Page numbers in *italic* refer to illustrations.

Abbondi, Antonio (called Scarpagnino), 194–95
Accademia Olimpica, 17, 233, 248, 249–50, 265;
    theater at, 17, 56, 184, 236, 245, 249, 250–53,
    251, 254, 255, 261, 265
Ackerman, James, 56
Acropolis, Athens, 9
Albanese, Francesco, 249
Alberti, Leon Battista, 22, 47, 128, 129, 193, 240,
    260; architectural drawing and, 20; architectural
    treatise by, 11, 205–6, 210, 211, 212, 214, 215,
    222, 223, 225; bridge design and, 182, 190,
    223; religious architecture of, *170, 175*
Algarotti, Francesco, 203
Almerico, Paolo, 178–79, 261–63, 264
Alternative facade solutions for the Palazzo Porto, 49–51, *50*
Alternative plan for the Palazzo Porto, 49
Alternative project for a stone bridge at Bassano, 190, *191*
ancestor worship, 120
Angaran, Giacomo, 183, 187, 188, 207, 210
Antichità di Roma, L', 19, 20
Antonini, Floriano, 121, 217
Architecturae Libri XXV (Filarete), 206, *208, 209*
architectural drawing, 20; orthogonal elevations and,
    20, 105, 157–59, 225, 232
Architettura, L' (*Le Regole generali dell'architettura*) (Serlio),
    17, 68, 75, 99, 112, 206–7, *207,* 210, 212–13,
    214, 215, 224, 227, 229, 231, *232*
Arch of Constantine, Rome, 51, 251
Arch of the Gavi, Verona, 11, *12,* 100
Arch of the Sergii, Pula, 100
Arch of Titus, Rome, 100; entablature from, *15,* 21
Aristotle, 206
Arzere, Gualtiero dall', 18, 69; works by, *10, 70*
Augustus: Rimini bridge of, 190–91, *191,* 198, 223
Averlino, Antonio (called Filarete), 206, 212; works
    by, *208, 209*

Bacchiglione River: bridge over, 182, 191
Badoer, Francesco, 123, 124
Baldelli, Francesco, 182

Barbaran, Montano, 236, 247–49
Barbari, Jacopo de', 192
Barbaro, Daniele, 18, 29, 113, 121, 131, 134, 136,
    179, 214, 252; old London Bridge studied by,
    181; Palladio's religious architecture and,
    151–52, 156; portrait of, *212;* Vitruvius edition
    by, 20, 22, 111, 128, 134, 151, 152–53, 157,
    182–83, 209, 211, *213,* 223, 237, 250, *251*
Barbaro, Marc'antonio, 131, 136, 151–52, 153,
    172, 195, 253; Tempietto and, 176, 179
Bartoli, Cosimo, 182, 206
Bascapè, Ruggiero, 251
Basilica, Fano, 223, 237–39, 241, *251*
Basilica, Vicenza, 38, 52–53, 57, 93–109, 111,
    182, 203, 221, 247, 248, 250, 265; aerial view
    of, *93;* assessment of, 108–9; configuration of
    bays in, 95; construction of, 101–8;
    consultations on renovation of, 29, 42, 43,
    97–98; corners of, 95, 98, 100, 101, 102, *103,*
    104; Doric arcades of, 101–4, *102;* history of,
    93–98; interior view of ground-floor arcade of,
    99; Ionic order on upper floor of, 105–8, *106,*
    107, 120; Loggia del Capitaniato and, 242, 244;
    Palladio's commission for, 84, 93, 98, 101, 236;
    Palladio's final solution for, 99–100; Palladio's
    preliminary design for, 13, 27, 78, *98,* 98–99,
    100; Palladio's stipend for, 101, 104–5; plan of,
    95, *97,* 98; portal of Domus Comestabilis in,
    15–16, *16,* 65; private commissions resulting
    from, 101; in *Quattro Libri,* 108–9, 222, 223,
    224; stone for, 101
Basilica at Fano, 237–39, 241, *251*
Basilica of Maxentius, Rome, 23, 165, 226–27
Bassano del Grappa: bridge at, 108, *180,* 187–90,
    188, 189, 191, 198, 222
baths. *See* Roman baths
Baths of Agrippa, Rome, 21; elevation of, *231;*
    finished plan of, *230;* sketches of, *175*
Baths of Caracalla, Rome, 21, 44
Baths of Diocletian, Rome, 21
Battisti, G. A.: work by, *12*
Belli family, 210, 249
Bellini, Giovanni, 95
Belluno: wooden bridge at, 189–90

Beretta, Lodovico, 170

Berger, Ursel, 221

Bernardo, Giovanni Battista, 244

bichromy, 148–49, 244

Bicknell, Julian, 264

Bird's-eye view of Vicenza (Pittoni), 31, *32*

Bisticci, Vespasiano da, 60

Borromini, Francesco, 149, 176

Bortolo, Giulio di, 164

Bortoloni, Mattia, 120; work by, *120*

Bracciolini, Poggio, 205

Bramante, Donato, 9, 11, 22–23, 24, 25, 29, 36, 37, 57, 71, 72, 73, 75, 153, 161, 175, 193–94, 226–27; Tempietto of, 229–30; work by, *23*

Brescia: Palladio's critique of model for new cathedral in, 170; public palace of, 95, *96*, 100, 105, 223, 245, 253, 255

Bridge at Bassano del Grappa, 188

Bridge of Augustus at Rimini, 190–91, *191*

Bridge over the Cismon River, *183*, 185

bridges, 181–203; antique, 181, 182–83, *183*, 190–91, *191*, 198, 223; at Bassano del Grappa, 108, *180*, 187–90, *188*, *189*, *191*, 198, 222; building techniques for, 181, 182; Cismon River projects, *183*, 183–87, *186*, 188; legacy of Palladio's designs for, 200–203; *Quattro Libri* and, 182–83, *183*, 185–87, *186*, *188*, 190–91, *191*, *192*, 197, 198, 199, 200, 201, 222–23; Rialto, 190, 191–200, *192*, *194*, *196*, *197*, *199*, *200*, *202*, 202–3, 223; stone, 181, 187, 190–91, *191*, *192*, 192–200, 202, 223; triangulation in, 184–85; wooden, *180*, 181–90, *183*, *186*, *188*, *189*, 191–93, 195, 201–2, 223

Brunelleschi, Filippo, 166

Brusasorzi, Domenico, 52, 57, 138

bugnato graffito, 114

Buora, Andrea, 162

Buora, Giovanni, 162, 163

Burckhardt, Jacob, 245

Burger, Fritz, 135

Burns, Howard, 134, 175, 199, 200, 255

Cabianca, Bartolomeo, 120

Caesar, Julius, 182–83, 223

Campagna, Girolamo, 164

Campbell, Colen, 264

Canaletto, Antonio, 160, 203; work by, *202*

Canera, Anselmo, 45, 90, 138, 261

Canossa, Ludovico, 25

Capello, Antonio, 195

Capra, Gabriele, 53, 101

Caprice with Palladian Bridge at the Rialto (Canaletto), *202*, 203

Carità. *See* Santa Maria della Carità

Carpaccio, Vittore, 192

Casa Civena, Vicenza, 35–38, 53, 73, 75, 121, 123; facades of, *35*, *36*, 37–38; plan of, *36*, 36–37, *37*; vestibule of, *37*, 52

Casa Pigafetta, Vicenza, 31, 34–35

Casino of Pius IV, Vatican Gardens, 134, 263

Castellini, Silvestro, 244

Cathedral, Vicenza, 32, 34; high altar of, *14*, 15

Cato, 61

Cavazza, Bartolomeo, 10, 12–13

Cesariano, Cesare, 157, 206, 214

Cevese, Renato, 148–49

Chambers, Sir William, 201–2

Chiericati, Giovanni, 56, 122, 123

Chiericati, Girolamo, 53, 57, 71, 101

Cismon River: designs for bridge over, *183*, 183–87, *186*, 188

Civena family, 36–37

Codevigo (Padua): Falconetti's parish church at, 12, 170, *171*

Codussi, Mauro, 156, 161, 166

Coliseum, Rome, 68, 153, 254

Commentaries (Caesar), 182–83, 223

Composite order, 153, *204*, 212, 213–14, 215, 230

Composite order with capital and entablature, *204*

Contarini, Giacomo, 253

Corinthian Hall, 90, 161, *216*

Corinthian order, 212, 213–14, 215, 225; Venetian fondness for, 119

Cornaro, Alvise, 10–12, 18, 19, 60, 207, 249; architectural treatise by, 18, 84–85, 138, 209–10, 211; on decoration of villa interiors, 68, 69, 138; Loggia and, 11, 12, 16, 49; Odeo Cornaro and, 11, 12, 16, 44, 45, 47, 49, 71, 74, 76

Cornaro, Giorgio, 118

Cornaro, Giovanni, 18

Cornaro, Girolamo, 91, 118

Cortile del Belvedere, Rome, 23, 29, 71, 74, 75

Coryat, Thomas, 31

Council of One Hundred (Vicenza), 93, 100–101, 102–5, 108

Courtyard of the Palazzo Thiene, Vicenza, 220–21, *221*

Crescenzi, Pier de', 61, 112

Dall'Acqua, Aurelio, 15, 36

Dalla Pozza, Antonio, 72

Daniele Barbaro (Veronese), *212*

Danti, Vincenzo, 249

de Jongh, Claude: work by, *184*

De re aedificatoria (Alberti), 11, 205–6, 210, 211, 212, 214, 215, 222, 223, 225

Detail of plan for the Palazzo Porto, 49

Details of Pantheon (Palladio), *229*

Dezin, Martino, 182, 187

Diedo, Vicenzo, 151

Doge's Palace, Venice, 95, 97, 138, 145, 151, 195, 245; design for new ceremonial staircase at, 195, 253; Palladio's proposal for rebuilding of, 198, 253–56, *255, 257*

Domenico da Venezia, 94–95, 100

Domus Comestabilis, Basilica, Vicenza: portal of, 15–16, *16*, 65

Doni, Anton Francesco, 111, 112, 126, 145, 207–9, 249

Doric entablature (Giocondo), *207*

Doric order, 213–14, 215, 225

Dragoncino, Giovan Battista, 35

du Cerceau, Jacques Androuet, 215

Early project for the Rialto, 195–98, *196, 197*

Elevation and Plan of the Odeo Cornaro (Battisti), *12*

Elevation for a new Doge's Palace, 254–55, *255*

Elevation of the Baths of Agrippa, 231

Elevation of the facade and courtyard of the Palazzo da Porto Festa, 237, *238*

Elevation of the facade and courtyard of the Palazzo Valmarana, 237, *238*

Elevation of the Temple of Minerva in the Forum of Nerva, 160

Elevation of the upper story of the Basilica, 105–6, *106*

Emanuele Filiberto, duke of Savoy, 210, 222

Entablature from the Arch of Titus, 15, 21

entasis, 204, 211–12

Este, Cardinal Ippolito d', 134, 262–63

Etheridge, William, 201; work by, *202*

Facade of the Palazzo Branconio dell'Aquila, Rome (Raphael), *40*

Facade project for unidentified palace, 38, *39*

Facade project "G-G" for San Petronio, 256, *257*

Falconetto, Giovanni Maria, 11–12, 17, 18, 19, 20, 24, 27, 37, 38; religious architecture of, 170, *171*; works by, *10, 11, 171*

Fano, Basilica at, 237–39, 241, *251*

Farnese, Cardinal Alessandro, 172

Fasolo, Gianantonio, 244

Fasolo, Giovanni Antonio, 138, 250

Feramosca, Girolamo, 104, 105

Ficino, Marsilio, 61

Filarete (Antonio Averlino), 206, 212; works by, *208, 209*

Final variation on the Cismon River design, 185, *186,* 187

Finished plan of the Baths of Agrippa, 230

Fiorentino, Giallo, 127, 135, 138

Five Orders, The (Serlio), *214*

five orders, The (Vignola), *214*

Fogolino, Marcello, 95

Fontana, Domenico, 251

Forbicini, Eliodoro, 45, 57, 138; work by, *87*

Formenton, Tommaso, 95, 97, 98, 101, 106

Forum, Rome, *19,* 22

Forum of Nerva, Rome, 196, 225, 228–29; Temple of Minerva in, 156, 157–59, *160,* 196, 229

forums: in *Quattro Libri,* 222, *223. See also specific forums*

Foscari, Alvise, 145, 146, 149

Foscari, Francesco, 145

Foscari, Nicolò, 145, 146, 149

Francesco di Giorgio Martini, 153, 206, 212, 215, 219, 261

Franco, Battista, 138, 145, 149; works by, *147*

Garzadore, Giovanni Battista, 122

Gauthey, E. M., 201

Gazzotti, Tadeo, 72–73

Genga, Girolamo, 174–75; work by, *175*

Gesù, Rome, 173, 175

Giocondo, Fra Giovanni: architectural treatise by, 206, *207*; Caesar's *Commentaries* edition by, 182; Rialto project and, 193–94, *194,* 195–96, 198, 200; Vitruvius edition by, 206, *207*

Giovanni da Porlezza, 13, 182

Giovanni da Udine, 127; work by, *26*

Godi, Francesco, 13

Godi, Girolamo, 63, 64

Godi family, 63–65

Goethe, Johann Wolfgang von, 265

Gonzaga, Federico, 24, 28

Gonzaga, Ferrante, 57

Gothic architecture, 95; Renaissance elements combined with, *34,* 34–35; Vicentine, *32,* 33–35

Grandi, Vincenzo, 11, 12

Grazioli, Giovanni Antonio, 108

Grimani, Antonio, 156, 157

Grimani, Giovanni, 156

Grimani, Vettor, 156, 195
Gritti, Andrea, 154–55
Groppino, Domenico, 123
Gualdo, Paolo, 17, 233
Guardi, Francesco, 203
Guberni, Pietro di, 195

harmonic proportions, 211
Heemskerck, Marten van, 19; work by, 19
hemicycles: in Palladio's late projects, 241–42
Henry III, king of France, 149, 164
Hercules, 182, 251
House of Raphael (Palazzo Caprini), Rome, 22, 23, 25, 37, 38, 52, 73
Huse, Norbert, 134, 135

Ideal reconstruction of the Temple of Fortune, Palestrina, 21, 260, 262
India, Bernardino, 45, 90, 138, 261
intercolumniation, 214–15
Ionic capital with canted volute at the Temple of Fortuna Virilis, 226
Ionic order, 212, 213–15, 216, 225, 226

Jacopo della Quercia, 256
Jones, Inigo, 31, 41, 82, 143
Julius II, Pope, 97

Labacco, Antonio, 207
Lafrery, Antonio: work by, 23
Lateran Baptistry, Rome, 226, 230
Laurentian Library, Florence, 126, 163
Lauro, Pietro, 206
Leo X, Pope, 16, 43, 212, 250
Leonardo da Vinci, 181
Leopardi, Alessandro, 164
Lepanto, Greece, Battle of (1571), 245
Library of San Marco, Venice, 24, 99, 100, 102, 104–5, 109, 171, 255–56
Ligorio, Pirro, 134, 148, 263
Livre d'architecture (du Cerceau), 215
Loggetta in Piazza San Marco, Venice, 197, 199, 255
Loggia, Padua, 11, 12, 16, 49
Loggia del Capitaniato, Vicenza, 53, 106–8, 134, 149, 241, 242–45, 243, 246, 248, 249; lateral facades of, 242, 244–45, 247

Lombardo, Pietro, 97, 162
Lombardo, Tullio, 15; work by, 62
London Bridge, 181, 184
Longitudinal sketch of Santa Lucia, Venice (Visentini), 161
Lorenzo da Bologna, 40
Lotz, Wolfgang, 264

Machiavelli, Niccolò, 61
Madonna di Campagna, near Verona, 174
Maganza, Alessandro, 261, 265
Maganza, Giambattista, 19, 131, 249, 264
Magistrato sopra i Beni Inculti, 111
Maison Carrée, Nîmes, 244
Marchesi, Battista, 108, 188
Marchesi, Guglielmo, 182
Marriage at Cana (Veronese), 162
Marzari, Giuseppe, 65
Mathematical Bridge, Queens' College, Cambridge, England, 201, 202
Mausoleum of Romulus, Via Appia, 231
Medici, Cosimo de', 60
Medici, Giovanni de', 60
Medici, Lorenzo de', 60, 61
Merlino, Giacomo di, 48
Michelangelo, 9, 71, 126, 134, 153, 163, 195, 235, 237, 244, 249
Minio, Tiziano, 18, 69
Mio, Giovanni de, 83
Mocenigo, Leonardo, 159–60, 199
Montaigne, Michel de, 31, 57
Monza, Fabio, 105
Moro, Battista dal, 45, 69, 138
Moro, Cristoforo, 192
Morosini, Paolo, 61
Morris, Roger, 202
Muttoni, Francesco, 217

Natural History (Pliny), 212
Nogarola, Isabella, 236
Nogarola family, 76–77

Odeo Cornaro, Padua, 10, 11, 12, 16, 44, 45, 47, 49, 71, 74, 76
Old London Bridge (de Jongh), 184
Opus ruralium commodorum (de Crescenzi), 61, 112
orders: adapted to Christian church facades, 156; codification of, 212–13; deities associated with, 225; earlier writings on, 212–13, 214;

orders *(continued)*: *entasis* and, 211–12; giant, introduced into domestic architecture, 236–37; intercolumniation and, 214–15; Palladio's intuitive sense of, 120; Palladio's writings on, 124, 211–15; proportional system for, 213–14; proportions of, in Palladio's early work, 50. *See also specific orders*

Origins of building (Filarete), 209

Orme, Philibert de l', 19, 207

Orsini, Fulvio, 225

orthogonal elevations, 20, 105, 157–59, 225, 232

Pagello, Bernardino, 61

palaces: distinction between villas and, 121, 219; increased use of ornament in, 249; Palladio's early designs for, 35–57; Palladio's late style in, 235–39, 341–42, 245–49, 258–65; in *Quattro Libri*, 38–40, *41, 42, 43, 44, 47, 49*, 54, 121, 122, 216–22, *218, 219, 221, 222*, 237, *238*, 246–47, 262

Palazzo Antonini, Udine, 86, 114, 120, 121–22, 217, *218*, 219, 220

Palazzo Antonini in Udine, 218

Palazzo Barbaran da Porto, Vicenza, *222*, 245–49; atrium of, 247, *248*; facades of, 245–46, *246*, 247; interior decoration of, 138, 249, *250*; plan of, 246–47

Palazzo Barbaran da Porto, Vicenza, 222

Palazzo Bevilacqua, Verona, 25

Palazzo Bissari, Vicenza, 93

Palazzo Branconio dell'Aquila, Rome, 22, 38, 40, 50, 72

Palazzo Braschi Brunello, Vicenza, *34*

Palazzo Brescia, Rome, 38

Palazzo Caffarelli Vidoni, Rome, 37

Palazzo Canossa, Verona, *24*, 25, 45, 57, 138

Palazzo Capra, Vicenza, 236, 237

Palazzo Caprini, Rome. *See* House of Raphael, Rome

Palazzo Chiericati, Vicenza, *30*, 44, 48, 50, 53–57, 101, 117, 121, 123, 127, 143, 145, 203, 219, 236, 244, 250; drawings for, 54, *56*; facades of, 53, *54*, 54–56, 57, 112, 118; interior decoration of, *55*, 57, 138; plan of, *56*; site of, 53, 56; villa design and, 112, 113, 121

Palazzo Colleoni Porto, Vicenza, *32, 33*, 48

Palazzo da Porto Festa, Vicenza. *See* Palazzo Porto, Vicenza

Palazzo della Ragione, Padua, 95, 118, 223

Palazzo della Torre, Verona, *219*

Palazzo della Torre in Verona, 219

Palazzo delle Trombe, Finale (Vicenza), *83, 84*

Palazzo del Te, Mantua, 27, *28*, 28–29, 42, 43, 44, 47, 57, 72, 82, 111

Palazzo Farnese, Rome, 44, 99, 153, 244

Palazzo Iseppo da Porto, Vicenza. *See* Palazzo Porto, Vicenza

Palazzo Piovene all'Isola, Vicenza, 56, 236, 250

Palazzo Porto, Vicenza, *32*, 37, 48–53, 113, 117, 121, 138, 217, 261; atrium of, 44, 52; drawings for, *49*, 49–51, *50*; facades of, 48–52, *50, 51*, 57, 237, 245; proposed courtyard of, 49, 237–39, *238, 239*, 241; in *Quattro Libri, 49*, 220, 221–22, 237, *238*

Palazzo Porto Breganze, Vicenza, 33–34, 49, 236, 241–42, *242*, 244, 258; plan of, *33*, 241, 246

Palazzo Pubblico, Brescia, 95, *96*, 100, 105, 223, 245, 253, 255

Palazzo Sangiovanni, Vicenza, 35

Palazzo Thiene, Vicenza, 29, 33, 38–48, 52, 71, 82, 134; atrium of, 42, *43*, 44, 52; courtyard of, 220–21, *221*; dating and authorship of, 41, 42–44, 47; facades of, 159, 38, *41, 42*, 44; halting of construction at, 47, 247–48; interior decoration of, 45–47, *46*, 52, 91, 114, 138, 249; plan and section of, *41*, 44, 47; in *Quattro Libri*, 38–40, *41, 42, 43*, 44, 47, 220–21, *221*

Palazzo Thiene Bonin, Vicenza, 236

Palazzo Valmarana, Vicenza, 101, 138, 220, 222, 236–37, 244; facades of, *234*, 236–37, *238*, 245, 246

palestra, 222, 223

"Palladian bridge," 201–2

"Palladianism," 9, 265

Palladio (Andrea di Pietro dalla Gondola): artists associated with, 45–47, 138; bridges designed by, 181–203; death of, 179, 233, 265; draftsmanship of, 105, 157–59; early career of, 13–16, 17; early palaces of, 35–57; early villas of, 59–91; family background of, 10; influences on, 10–29, 36–37, 38, 42–44, 45, 73, 75, 204–6; later projects of, 235–65; marriage of, 15; mature villas of, 111–49; name taken by, 16, 36; portrait of, *8*, 9; religious architecture of, 151–79; Roman architecture studied by, *15*, 19–22, 36, 71, 72, 84, 98, 100–101, 207; training of, 9, 12–13; treatise on architecture written by, 205–33. *See also Quattro Libri dell'Architettura; specific buildings*

Palladio (Zucchi), *8*

Palladio, Allegradonna, 15, 85, 104

Palladio, Marc'antonio (nephew), 78, 102

Palladio, Marc'antonio (son), 15

Palladio, Silla, 15, 233, 265

Palladius, Rutilius Taurus Aemilianus, 61

Pampuro, Andrea, 164

Pane, Roberto, 185

Pantheon, Rome, 23, 73, 145, 173, 178–79, *232*, 254, 255, 257; in *Quattro Libri*, 224, 226, *229*, 231–32; Villa Rotonda and, 260, 264

Pasqualino da Venezia, 106

patron-architect relationship, 104–5

Pedemuro bottega, 13–16, 17, 20, 27, 35, 36, 63, 65, 84, 101

Pembroke, Henry Herbert, 9th Earl of, 202

Penultimate plan and elevation of the Villa Pisani, 76

Peruzzi, Baldassare, 19, 21, 153, 206–7, 232, 256–57

Piazza dei Signori (formerly Piazza Peronio), Vicenza, 32, *92*, *93*, *95*, 98, 100, 102, 104, 106

Piazza San Marco, Venice: Loggetta in, 197, *199*, 255

Picheroni, Alessandro, 185

Pietro da Nanto, 236

Pighius, Stephanus, 225

Piovene family, 64–65

Piovene quarries, 101, 105

Pisani, Francesco, 91, 113

Pisani family, 77–78, 113

Pittoni, Battista: work by, *32*

Pittoni, Girolamo, 13

Pius IV, Pope, 261, 262–63; Casino of, 134, 263

plague, 171

Plan and elevation of the Basilica, 223, 224

Plan and elevation of the Carità, 152

Plan and elevation of the Villa Godi, 65

Plan and elevation of the Villa Repeta, 130, 131

Plan and section of the Palazzo Thiene, 41, 44, 47

Plan of San Giorgio Maggiore, 164

Plan of San Giovanni Battista, Pesaro (Genga), 175

Plan of Santa Lucia, 161

Plan of the Basilica, 97

Plan of the Casa Civena, 37

Plan of the Palazzo Chiericati, 56

Plan of the Palazzo Porto Breganze, 33

Plan of the Redentore, 173

Plan of the Teatro Olimpico, 251

Plan of the Tempietto, 178, 179

Plan of the Temple of Hercules, Tivoli, 129, 130

Plan of the Villa Emo, 139

Plan of the Villa Poiana, 86

Plan of the Villa Saraceno, 85

Plan of the Villa Trissino at Cricoli, 17

Plan of Villa Trissino, 64

Plato, 206

Pliny, 63, 135, 212, 260

Plutarch, 9

Poiana, Bonifazio, 85

Pons Sublicius, Rome, 182

Ponte, Antonio da, 200, 253; work by, *200*

Ponte della Pietra, Verona, 192

Ponte Sant'Angelo (Pons Aelius), Rome, 197

Ponte Scaligiero, Verona, 181, *184*

Pont Nôtre-Dame, Paris, 193

Porta Maggiore, Rome, 27

Porta Nuova, Verona, *25*, 25–27, 37, 78

Porta San Giovanni, Padua, 11, 27

Porta Savonarola, Padua, *11*, 27

Portico of Octavia, 20

Portico of Octavia, Rome, *20*, 21, 57, 260

Porto, Alessandro, 241

Porto, Alvise da, 33

Porto, Iseppo da, 44, 48, 49, 51, 52, 57

Porto family, 32, 48, 52

Pozzoserrato (Lodewyck Toeput), 91

Preliminary design for the Basilica, 98, 98–99

Preliminary study for the Villa Gazzotti, 73

Priuli, Girolamo, 59, 60, 61, 72

Project for entrance to the Rialto Bridge, 199, 199–200

Project for piano nobile of the Palazzo Chiericati, 54, 56

Project for San Francesco della Vigna, 157, 159

Project for the Casa Civena, 36

Project for the Rialto (Giocondo), 193–94, 194

Project for the Villa Thiene, 82

quadrant notion, 124

Quattro Libri dell'Architettura, 13, 35, 38, 111, 205–33, 235, 258, 265; Basilica in, 108–9, 222, 223, *224*; Book I of, 211–15; Book II of, 211, 215–22; Book III of, 222–23; Book IV of, 215, 223–32; bridges in, 182–83, *183*, 185–87, *186*, *188*, 190–91, *191*, *192*, 197, *198*, *199*, *200*, *201*, 222–23; dedications in, 207, 210, 222; harmonic proportions in, 211; incomplete nature of, 233; integration of words and pictures in, 212; intended readership of, 211; interior decoration described in, 138; orders described in, 124, *204*, 210, 211–15; organization of volumes in, 80, 210, 222; palaces in, 38–40, *41*, *42*, *43*, *44*, *47*, *49*, *54*, 121, 122, 216–22, *218*, *219*, *221*, *222*, *237*, *238*, 246–47, 262; Palladio's notion of domestic architecture in, 215–16; Palladio's working procedure for, 209;

Quattro Libri dell'Architettura (continued): predecessors of, 18, 205–7, 209–10, 210, 213–15, *214*; presentation of Palladio's own buildings in, 215; purpose of, 210–11; quality of plates in, 215; reconstructions of antiquities in, 19, 22, 117, 120, 207, *216*, 216–17, 223–32, *226–31*, 239; reliability of plates in, 220–22, *223*; religious architecture in, *152*, 153, 172, 217, 223; style of, 211; temple pediment described in, 128; testimonial to Vicentine patrons in, 216; unexecuted projects included in, 217; villas in, 64, *65*, 72, 75, *76*, 80, 82, *85*, *86*, 112, 117, 118, 122, *124*, *131*, 134, 135–36, *139*, 216–22, *220*, 239–40, 260, 262, 264

Rabelais, François, 206
Raphael, 16, 21, 22, 24, 57, 71, 76, 174, 212, 230; architectural drawing and, 20; designs reflecting Palladio's study of, 38, *39*, 50; Giulio's training with, 28–29; Palazzo Branconio dell'Aquila and, 22, 38, *40*, 50, 72; Villa Madama and, 16–17, *17*, 23, *26*, 28–29, 47, 50, 60, 73, 80, 111, 127, 237, 261
Raymond, John, 264
Reconstruction of Caesar's Bridge, 183
Redentore, Venice, 151, 152, 161, 165, 170–76, 179; crossing of, 175, *176*; facades of, *172*, 173; interior of, *174*, 174–76; lateral facades of, 175, *176*; plague and, 171; plan of, *173*, 174
Regola degli cinque ordini (Vignola), 213–14, *214*, 215
Regoli generali dell'architettura, Le. See *Architettura, L'*
Repeta, Mario, 130, 131
Rhine: Caesar's bridge over, 182–83, *183*
Rialto Bridge, Venice, 190, 191–200, *192*, *202*, 202–3, 223; Giocondo's project for, 193–94, *194*, 195–96, 198, 200; history of, 191–95; Palladio's first proposal for, 195–98, *196*, *197*, 200; Palladio's second proposal for, 198–200, *199*; da Ponte's design for, *200*
Rialto Bridge project, 192
Ridolfi, Bartolomeo, 27–28, 45, 52, 57, 90, 138; work by, *55*
Ridolfi, Cardinal, 13, 236
Rimini: Augustus's bridge at, 190–91, *191*, 198, 223
Rizzo, Antonio, 97, 100
Roberti, Roberto: work by, *189*
Roccatagliata, Niccolò, 164
Roman baths: Palladio's domestic architecture and, 44, 72, 80, 152, 239; Palladio's reconstructions of, 21, 129, *130*, *175*, 230, *231*; Palladio's

religious architecture and, 152, 162, 166, 174, 175, 176
Romano, Giulio (Giulio Pippi), 22, 24, 28–29, 72, 127, 256; Basilica of Vicenza and, 29, 42, 43, 97–98, 100; Palazzo del Te and, *27*, *28*, 28–29, 42, 43, 44, 47, 57, 72, 82; Palazzo Thiene and, 41, 42–44, 45, 47, 82; Villa Thiene and, 82, 221; works by, *26–28*
Rome: Palladio's visits to, 18, 19–23, 29, 36, 71, 72, 84, 98, 100–101, 207. *See also specific buildings*
Round Temple at Tivoli (Serlio), 207
Rubini, Agostino, 250
Rubini, Lorenzo, 245, 249, 251, 264
Rucellai, Giovanni, 10
Rusconi, Giovanni Antonio, 182, 253
rustication, 22; in Palladio's late work, 240–41

Saint Peter's, Rome, 20, 23, 76, 134, 165, 174, 237, 244
San Francesco della Vigna, Venice, 151, 152, 154–59, 164, 166, 259; facades of, 156–57, *158*, 173, 237; preliminary project for, 157, *159*
Sangallo, Giuliano da, 71, 99, 129, 153
San Giorgio Maggiore, Venice, 21, 151, 159, 161–70, 173, 174, 176, 179, 199, 222; aerial view of, *163*; construction of, 164; crossing of, 165, *168–69*; cupola of, 165, *166*; facades of, *12*, 164, 166–70, *167*, 173, 237, 245; history of, 161–62; interior decoration of, 136, 164; nave of, *150*, 165; orchestration of scales and spaces in, 165–66; plan of, *164*, 165, 225; project for renewal of, 163–64; refectory and vestibule of, *162*, 162–63
San Giovanni Battista, Pesaro, 174–75, *175*
Sanmicheli, Michele, 13, 24–28, 29, 37, 38, 45, 57, 65, 68, 73, 78–79, 97, 98, 99, 163; artists associated with, 27–28, 71, 138; religious architecture of, 174, 178; works by, *24*, *25*
San Petronio, Bologna: Palladio's plans for rebuilding of, 157, 198, 253, 255, *256*, 256–58
San Pietro di Castello, Venice, 151–52, 156, 257
Sansovino, Jacopo, 13, 17, 18, 24, 29, 122, 138, 145, 195, 210, 235, 253; Basilica of Vicenza and, 97, 98, 99; Library of San Marco and, 24, 99, 100, *102*, 104–5, 109, 171, 255–56; Loggetta in Piazza San Marco and, 197, *199*, 255; San Francesco della Vigna and, 154, 155, 156; Villa Garzoni and, *68*
Santa Costanza, 226, 230
Santa Croce (Vicenza): bridge at, 182, 183, 188

Santa Giustina, Padua, 164

Santa Lucia, Venice, 159–61, *161*, 164

Santa Maria dei Servi, Vicenza, 13

Santa Maria della Carità, Venice, 21, 152–54, 164, 179, 198, 222, 235, 237, 255; atrium of, 153, 217; cloister of, 149, 152, 153, *154*; plan of, *152*, 153; sacristy of, 152, 153, *155*

Santa Maria delle Grazie, Milan, 175

Santa Maria Mater Domini, Venice, 155

Sant'Andrea, Mantua, *170*, 175

Sant'Apollinare Nuovo, Ravenna: mosaic of Theodoric's palace in, 129

Sanudo, Marin, 31, 34, 193

Saraceno family, 83–84

Sarego, Federigo, 249

Sarego, Marc'antonio, 239, 240, 241

Sbari, Alvise, 101, 106

Scamozzi, Gian Domenico, 105

Scamozzi, Ottavio Bertotti, 36, 52, 57, 71, 160, 187, 220, 241, 242, 247; plates from, *17, 37, 56, 161, 164, 251*

Scamozzi, Vincenzo, 105, 200, 241; architectural treatise by, 214; Palazzo Thiene and, 41, 43; Teatro Olimpico and, 252; Villa Rotonda and, 264

Scarpagnino (Antonio Abbondi), 194–95

Senate, Venetian, 164, 171, 173, 210

Serlio, Sebastiano, 12, 15, 16, 19, 20, 21, 28, 38, 48, 74, 119, 145; architectural treatise by, *17*, 68, 75, 99, 112, 206–7, *207*, 210, 212–13, *214*, 215, 224, 237, 229, 231, *232*; Basilica of Vicenza and, 97, 99–100; on decoration of villa interiors, 138

Sixtus V, Pope, 176

Sketches of the Baths of Agrippa, 175

Smeraldi, Francesco, 152

Smith, Joseph, 203

Spavento, Giorgio, 97, 193

Spilimbergo, Roberto di, 60

stuccowork, 22

Study for the Villa Valmarana, 71, 71–72

Study of villa, 74, 75, 80, 145, *261*

Study of villa with pediment, 44, 74, 75

Teatro Olimpico, Vicenza, 17, 56, 184, 236, 245, 249, 250–53, *254*, 255, 261, 265; plan of, *251*; Scamozzi's intervention in, 252

Tempietto at the Villa Barbaro, Maser, 118, 176–79, *177, 178*

Temple of Antoninus and Faustina, Rome, 226

Temple of Clitumnus, near Spoleto, 147–48, 197, 225

Temple of Diana, Nîmes, 176

Temple of Fortuna Virilis, Rome, 21, 120, *226*

Temple of Fortune, Palestrina, 23; ideal reconstruction of, 21, 260, *262*

Temple of Hercules, Tivoli, 129, *130*

Temple of Mars Ultor, Rome, 226

Temple of Minerva, Assisi, 21, 170, *227*, 227–28, *228*

Temple of Minerva at Assisi, 228

Temple of Minerva in the Forum of Nerva, Rome, 156, 157–59, 196, 229; elevation of, *160*

Temple of Saturn, Rome, 247

Temple of the Sibyl, Tivoli, 76

Temple of Vesta, Tivoli, 153

temple pediment: first appearance of, 73; Palladio's approach to, 128–29; in Palladio's early drawings, 38, *39*, 54

temples: reconstructed in *Quattro Libri*, 224–32, *226–29*. See also *specific temples*

Ten Books on Architecture (Vitruvius), 205

Terribilia, 257, 258

Tesina River: stone bridge over, 181–82, 190, 191

Theater of Marcellus, Rome, 19, 49, 153, 246

Theodoric's Palace: mosaic in Sant'Apollinare Nuovo of, 129

Thiene, Adriano, 40, 42–43, 44, 47–48, 80, *82–83*, 210

Thiene, Francesco, 241

Thiene, Marc'antonio, 40, 42–43, 44, 45, 47–48, 53, 57, 80, 82, 104, 210, 247–48

Thiene, Marco, 21, 82

Thiene family, 29, 32, 40–41, 47–48, 52

Tibaldi, Domenico, 257

Tintoretto, 164

Toeput, Lodewyck (called Pozzoserrato), 91

Torbido, Francesco, 45

Torri di Quartesolo: bridge at, 181–82, 190, 191

Trajan's Forum, Rome, 22, 124

triangulation, 184–85

Trissino, Francesco, 264

Trissino, Giangiorgio, 11, 12, 16–18, 19, 21, 22, 25, 29, 36, 182, 210, 223; academy conducted by, 17–18, 249; architectural treatise by, 209–10; Basilica of Vicenza and, 98, 100–101; Cricoli villa of, 16–17, *17, 18*, 35, 48; Palladio taken to Rome by, 18, 19–23, 98, 100–101; work by, *18*

Trissino, Ludovico, 264

Tuscan order, 124–25, *125*, 212, 213–14, 215

Two variations on the Cismon River design, 185–87, 186

urbanism: Palladio's comments on, 222, 223

Valmarana, Giovanni Alvise, 53, 101, 236
Varro, Marcus Terentius, 12, 61
Vasari, Giorgio, 11, 22, 24, 25, 28, 60, 134, 153, 156, 163, 193, 239, 258; Palladio's meeting with, 235
Vatican: Casino of Pius IV at, 134, 263; Palace at, 57
Veneto: land investment in, 59–60, 61, 72–73; villa tradition lacking in, 61–63. See also Vicenza; specific buildings
Verona: Roman theater at, 254, 260
Veronese, Paolo, 27–28, 45, 52, 113, 135, 136, 138, 143, 145, 162; works by, 137, 212
Via Ostiensis, 222–23
Vicentino, Andrea, 249
Vicenza, 31–35, 236; bird's-eye view of, 31, 32; commitment to building manifested in, 109; earliest signs of Renaissance style in, 34–35; Gothic architecture in, 32, 33–35, 34, 95; history of, 33, 94; overlapping of public and private patronage in, 57; Palladio's early palaces in, 35–57; prior to Palladio's arrival, 32–35; public palace of (see Basilica, Vicenza); Roman and medieval bridges in, 181–82, 191; visitors' impressions of, 31. See also specific buildings
View of Bassano (Roberti), 189
View of Roman Forum in 1535 (Heemskerck), 19
Vignola, Giacomo Barozzi da, 178, 195, 213–14, 215, 256, 257; work by, 214
Villa Agostini, Arcade, 131
Villa Badoer, Fratta Polesine, 85, 86, 123–28, 139; aerial view of, 123; facades of, 127, 128, 148; interior decoration of, 127, 135, 138, 143; medieval ruins on site of, 126, 127; plan of, 124, 127; plate in Quattro Libri of, 124; portico of, 126, 127, 143; staircase of, 126–27; temple pediment of, 127, 128–29; Tuscan arcades for farm buildings at, 124–25, 125, 129
Villa Barbaro, Maser (Treviso), 43, 128, 130, 131–36, 139, 151–52; eccentricities of, 131–34; facades of, 131–34, 132–33; interior decoration of, 135–36, 136, 137, 138; nyphaeum at, 131, 134, 135; salone of, 134, 135, 137; site of, 131, 134; Tempietto at, 118, 176–79, 177, 178
Villa Caldogno, Caldogno (Vicenza), 85, 138, 143
Villa Capra Filippi, Carrè (Vicenza), 62
Villa Chiericati, Vancimuglio di Grumolo (Vicenza), 56, 122, 122–23, 127, 145

Villa Cornaro, Piombino Dese, 57, 86, 111, 112, 117–21, 149, 217; Corinthian capitals in, 118–19, 119; decorative program at, 91, 120; facades of, 54, 56, 110, 118, 121, 122, 148; in Quattro Libri, 117, 118, 219; salone of, 116, 117–18, 120; staircases of, 120–21
Villa Cornaro at Piombino Dese, 117
Villa d'Este, Tivoli, 263
Villa Emo, Fanzolo (Treviso), 131, 134, 139–45, 149; facades of, 139, 140–41; interior decoration of, 142, 143, 143–45; plan of, 139, 139–43
Villa Farnesina, Rome, 28–29
Villa Forni, 85
Villa Foscari. See Villa Malcontenta, Gambarare di Mira, Venice
Villa Garzoni, Pontecasale (Padua), 68
Villa Gazzotti Marcello Curti, Bertesina (Vicenza), 15, 72–73, 73, 74, 123
Villa Giulia, Rome, 134
Villa Giustinian, Roncade (Treviso), 62, 118, 129
Villa Godi, Lonedo di Lugo (Vicenza), 13, 18, 63–71, 66–67, 143, 220; facades of, 65–66; garden hemicycle and wellhead of, 69–71; interior decoration of, 68–69, 70, 135, 138, 145; kitchen at, 68, 69; plan and elevation of, 65, 68
Villa Imperiale, near Pesaro, 111
Villa Madama, Rome, 16–17, 17, 23, 26, 28–29, 47, 50, 60, 73, 80, 111, 127, 237, 261
Villa Malcontenta (Villa Foscari), Gambarare di Mira, Venice, 111, 128, 145–59; bichromy in, 148–49, 244; facades of, 121, 144, 145, 146, 147, 147–49; ground floor of, 146–47; interior decoration of, 120, 138, 145, 147, 149; plan of, 145–46; salone of, 74, 80, 134, 145–46, 147, 148, 149; site of, 146, 147; staircase on main facades of, 145, 146, 147–48; surface treatment of, 148–49
Villa Medici, Poggio a Caiano, 60–61, 129
Villa Mocenigo, on Brenta River, 199
Villani, Giovanni, 60
Villa Piovene, Brendola (Vicenza), 62, 63
Villa Pisani, Bagnolo (Vicenza), 27, 59, 75–80, 82, 85, 91, 111, 117, 123, 134, 145, 198, 217; aerial view of, 77, 79; facades of, 38, 78, 78–79, 85, 99, 220, 240; history of, 76–77; interior of, 45, 79, 79–80, 80; preliminary studies for, 75–76, 76, 78, 86
Villa Pisani, Montagnana, 37, 44, 57, 86, 112–17, 121, 217; facades of, 54, 56, 113, 113–14, 114,

118, 122, 128; interior decoration of, 91, 114–17, *115*, 120, 138; plan of, 114; in *Quattro Libri*, 117, 118, 219; *salone* of, 114–17, *115*, 120, 138; staircases at, 117, 120

Villa Poiana, Poiana Maggiore, 57, 72, 83, 85–91, 113, 118; facades of, 86–87, *88–89, 91,* 145; interior of, *87,* 87–91, *90,* 138, 143, *217;* plan of, *86,* 124

Villa Repeta, Campiglia, 130–31, *131*

Villa Rotonda, Vicenza, 57, 74, 145, 149, 178, 219, *220,* 258–65; classical prototypes for, 21, 260; dome and cupola of, *259,* 260, 261, 264; entrance to, 260; facades of, *266–67;* interior of, *258,* 260–61, *263;* origin of design of, 261; patron of, 261–63; plan of, 260, 261

Villa Rotonda, 220

villas: agricultural functions of, 60–61, 111–12; as architectural form, 111–12; distinction between palaces and, 121, 219; drawings exploring problems in, 74–76, *75;* efficacy of Tuscan order in farm buildings of, 124–25; importance of staircases for, 126–27; interior decoration of, 127, 135–39; life-style of, 61, 112; motifs from sacred architecture in, 128–29; Palladio's early designs for, 59–91; Palladio's late style in, 258–65; Palladio's mature style in, 111–49; Palladio's supervision of, 130; quadrant concept and, 124; in *Quattro Libri,* 64, 65, 72, 75, 76, 80, 82, *85, 86,* 112, 117, 118, 122, *124, 131,* 134, 135–36, *139,* 216–22, *220,* 239–40, 260, 262, 264; regional prototypes and, 61–63; shift in Palladio's approach to, 111, 112; use of word, 63; vertical distribution of functions in, 79. *See also specific villas*

Villa Saraceno, Finale (Vicenza), 83–85, *84, 85,* 86, 91

Villa Sarego, Santa Sofia (Verona), 149, 217, 220, 239–41, *240,* 246, 258

Villa Simonetta, Milan, 57

Villa Thiene at Quinto (Vicenza), *80,* 80–83, *82,* 117, 198, 217, 220

Villa Trissino, Cricoli (Vicenza), 16–17, *17, 18,* 35, 48, 68, 72; academy at, 17–18

Villa Trissino, Meledo, 149, 220, 264

Villa Trissino, Paninsacco (Vicenza), *64,* 65

Villa Valmarana, Vigardolo (Monticello Conte Otto, Vicenza), *71,* 71–72, 73, 85, 91

Villa Zeno, 85

Ville, Le (Doni), 112

villeggiatura (villa life), 61, 112

Visentini, Antonio, 160; work by, *161*

Vitruvius (Marcus Vitruvius Pollio), 11, 17, 18, 20, 52, 100, 128, 153, 161, 190, 193, 205–6, 210, 211, 225, 226, 227–28, 237, 239; Alberti's approach to, 205–6; Barbaro's edition of, 20, 22, 111, 128, 134, 151, 152–53, 157, 182–83, 209, 211, *213,* 223, 237, 250, *251;* basilica and temple built at Fano by, 157, 223, 237–39; Francesco di Giorgio's writings and, 206; Giocondo's edition of, 206, *207;* orders described by, 212, 213, 214–15; theater design and, 251–52

Vitruvius (Barbaro), 20, 22, 111, 128, 134, 151, 152–53, 157, 182–83, 209, 211, *213, 223,* 237, 250, *251*

Vitruvius (Giocondo), 206, *207*

Vittoria, Alessandro, 15, 45, 47, 114, 138; work by, *46, 115*

War of the League of Cambrai, 10, 16, 59, 77, 124, 187, 195

Wittkower, Rudolf: church facades analyzed by, *157;* on harmonic proportions in Palladian buildings, 211

Woodcut of the Villa Pisani, 76

Wren, Christopher, 130

Zelotti, Giambattista, 45, 57, 71, 90, 135, 138, 143–45, 149; works by, *55, 142, 143, 147*

Zitelle, Venice, 179

Zoppo, Agostino, 118

Zorzi, Alvise, 236

Zorzi, Francesco, 155

Zucchi, Francesco: work by, *8*

PHOTOGRAPHY CREDITS

The photographers and sources of photographic material other than those indicated in the captions are as follows (numbers refer to plates):

Jörg P. Anders, Staatliche Museen Preußicher Kulturbesitz, Berlin: 11; After A. Boethius and J. B. Ward-Perkins, *Pelican History of Art: Etruscan and Roman Art*, Harmondsworth, England, 1970: 99; Osvaldo Böhm/Archivio Fotografico del Museo Correr, Venice: 4; Archivio Museo di Bassano del Grappa, Italy: 143, 144, 147–51, 153; Courtesy Bruce Boucher, London: 16, 164; Alan Buchanan, Oxford, England: 41, 67; Geremy Butler Photography/ The British Architectural Library, The Royal Institute of British Architects, London: 25, 28, 29, 37, 55, 58–60, 98, 119, 121, 122, 135, 182, 185, 186, 188, 189, 206 ; Centro Internazionale di Studi di Architettura "Andrea Palladio," Vicenza, Italy: 5, 8, 9, 22, 26, 27, 32, 36, 42, 48, 61, 62, 70, 71, 78, 94, 100, 105, 114, 126, 141, 162, 163, 168–71, 173–75, 177–80, 183, 199, 200, 203; After Cevese, *Le Ville di Vicenza:* 47; Courtesy of the Conway Library, Courtauld Institute of Art, London: 20, 30, 35, 56, 79, 83, 133; Photographic Survey of Private Collections, Courtauld Institute of Art, London: 202; English Heritage Photographic Library, London: 146; Foto Toso, Venice: 165, 166; Fototecnica, Venice: 6, 12, 76, 155, 156, 158; Giovetti Fotografia & Comunicazioni Visive, Mantua, Italy: 18; After Groblewski: 136; Copyright © 1993 Howling Moon Graphics, Medford, Oreg.; After R. Wittkower, *Architectural Principles in the Age of Humanism:* 117; G. Paolo Marton, Treviso, Italy: frontispiece, 150, 154, 204; The Metropolitan Museum of Art, New York; Harris Brisbane Dick Fund, 1941: 13; The Royal Collection, Windsor, Berkshire/Copyright © 1993 Her Majesty Queen Elizabeth II: 161; Bernardino Sperandio—Azienda di Promozione Turistica, Assisi, Italy: 181; Julian Thomas, Cambridge, England: 160.